Menace to Society

DATE DUE

Menace to Society

Political-Criminal Collaboration Around the World

Roy Godson
editor

Transaction Publishers
New Brunswick (U.S.A.) and London (U.K.)

This book is printed on acid-free paper that meets the American National Standard for Permanence of Paper for Printed Library Materials.

Library of Congress Catalog Number: 2002032444
ISBN: 0-7658-0502-2
Printed in the United States of America

Library of Congress Cataloging-in-Publication Data

Menace to society : political-criminal collaboration around the world / Roy Godson, editor.
       p. cm.
   Includes bibliographical references and index.
   ISBN 0-7658-0502-2 (pbk.: alk. paper)
      1. Organized crime—Political aspects. 2. Political corruption.
   I. Godson, Roy, 1942-

HV6441.M46 2003
364.1'06—dc21

                                   2002032444

Contents

1

The Political-Criminal Nexus and Global Security

Roy Godson

One of the more dangerous threats to the quality of life in the contemporary world is at once both old and new. It is the collaboration of the political establishment with the criminal underworld—the political-criminal nexus (PCN). This active partnership increasingly undermines the rule of law, human rights, and economic development in many parts of the world. States in transition are especially at risk. The insidious effects of the PCN, and even its very existence, are often obscured, not only deliberately by the players themselves, but also by the tendency of security specialists to underestimate groups outside the formal political structures.

In some areas, the problem of the PCN is chronic—for example in Mexico, Nigeria, Turkey, and Taiwan. In such cases, only the forms and balance of power among the players change. In other countries and regions—Colombia, Afghanistan, Sierra Leone, the Balkans and the Caucuses—the problem is more acute, violent, and kaleidoscopic, and often it dominates political, economic, and social life.

As local problems become global, and global problems have local effects, its appears that the complex and murky relations between criminals and political elites in many parts of the world explain much not only about local politics, but regional and global trends in world politics as well. These increasingly complicated dynamics have also created a different kind of security challenge, the contours of which are only gradually coming into focus.

Part I of this chapter highlights the significance of this problem, and explains why it has now become of major importance in regional and global trends. Part II seeks to diagnose contemporary factors or causes that create the problem—the "drivers" or "linchpins." Some will be skeptical that valid causal generalizations are possible—especially about clandestine relationships. Indeed, such generalizations—and well-grounded theory and data—are not easy to come by. However, as the chapters in the book illustrate there have been studies of diverse cases—some well documented—so that patterns, generalizations, and hypotheses can be put forward to facilitate further study, and draw implications for policy.

In addition, and significantly, governmental leaders from the global level—the UN, the G8, and the World Bank—to the regional—the EU and OAS—to national and subnational elites have begun to grapple with aspects of the problem. They are beginning to prescribe solutions, pass international conventions, and authorize expenditures for the use of force and other techniques of statecraft to manage the malady. Having reached conclusions about the cause of the problem, they are developing and implementing policy aimed at its management.

Part III of the chapter summarizes the main elements of governmental diagnosis and prescriptions. It then seeks to address causal factors that appear to have been under- or over-estimated (for intellectual and bureaucratic reasons) and suggests directions for future research and policy planning to strengthen analysis and prescriptions that ultimately will help to prevent and ameliorate this global security challenge.

Part I. The Political-Criminal Nexus:
A Major Security Problem or a Nuisance?

Definitions of Key Terms

Definitions are necessary to avoid the confusion that accompanies the many different types of political and criminal actors. Nonetheless, some definitions now in use are extremely broad.

Some define regimes or governments as "criminal" because they systematically violate international conventions, such as the UN's 1948 Universal Declaration of Human Rights. While not disputing the criminal nature of some of these regimes, this definition is too broad for analytical purposes. It would include most if not all authoritarian regimes from the Nazis and Communist regimes to Panama under Noriega, and would erase the distinctional problems created by the collaboration of two sets of actors, the political and the professional criminal.

Other definitions focus on individual political leaders and define their governments as criminal because the leaders themselves, or the political systems they manage, regularly violate the criminal statutes in their own societies. This would include what have come to be known as "kleptocracies," very corrupt leaders who use their political authority to enrich themselves, their families and their political allies. Mobutu (The Congo), Abacha (Nigeria), and Estrada (Philippines) would appear to fall into this category.

The focus here is on the collaboration between two sets of groups and institutions, the political establishment and the criminal underworld. The involvement is sustained, although it may take different forms. Sometimes it is easy to distinguish between the two sets of players, as in the case of the American Cosa Nostra, and the U.S. political establishment. When political establishment knowingly and regularly does business with gang leaders, or when professional criminals are actually elected to power, as has happened in Sicily and Taiwan, the distinction is less straightforward. The lines between the two sets of players become less distinctive; and sometimes the political and the criminal merge.

The Criminals (Underworld). The criminals, whose activities are substantially shielded from public view in the underworld, have a number of characteristics:[1] They are professionals, usually, but not always. They make their livelihood primarily from crime. Some also engage in legal as well as illegal professional activities. The principal motive is profit making, but this is not the exclusive driver. The most important criminals are part of an organization, i.e., part of an ongoing relationship with other criminals. The organization can be a hierarchical, vertical structure, such as the U.S. or Sicilian Cosa Nostra, or a more horizontal, egalitarian network, such as those found in organized crime in and around China and the Chinese diasporas scattered throughout the world. Geographic location can be local, regional, or transstate. The criminals purposefully violate national and often international conventions, (e.g., most importantly, the anti-drug trafficking regime).

The Political Establishment (Upper World). The political establishment on the other hand, must conduct at least some of its business in public. It is important to note the major distinction between the legal-governmental establishment, and the non-legal, terrorist/separatist, revolutionary groups, such as al-Qae'da, Colombia's FARC, the Irish IRA, and Kosovo's KLA. The focus here is on the legal, governmental, and political establishment. Within this establishment, there are diverse players and levels.

The first are *office holders* in the executive, legislative, and judicial branches of government. They include those in security bureaucracies, the military, paramilitary, intelligence and security services, diverse police and law enforcement, prosecutors and judges. Usually, these are both national and local, but they interact with transstate criminals who operate both inside and outside their territory. At the top are the president, prime minister, and various other ministers. These operate usually at the national level, but sometimes they also interact with transstate criminals.[2]

A second group are *front men* who work for or support official office holders. They include political party officials, public relations firms, businesses, legal advisers, accountants, and NGOs supportive of parties. They usually are based nationally, but they often operate across state borders.[3]

The third group is the *legal opposition* that rotates in and out of official positions; they and their front men and organizations are usually nationally based, but often with transstate links to both legal and criminal actors.[4]

The PCN consists of relationships of varying degrees of cooperation among these political and criminal participants at the local, national, and transstate levels. These patterns fluctuate between various combinations of collaboration and conflict.[5] An initially stable pattern may, over time, become unbalanced until a new more stable equilibrium is reached. It sometimes evolves into open war between the partners, and the PCN is seriously weakened if not destroyed. For example, after decades of mostly collaboration both the criminals and the politicians were seriously damaged in Sicily in the 1980s and 1990s.[6] However, in most cases where a crime group has endured and prospered—whether in a democracy or an authoritarian regime—the criminals have reached some type of accommodation with political authorities at the local, national, or transstate level.

Criminal organizations that exist over a period of time are advantaged by collaboration, at least in their home state or region. Typically, where one sees a long history of organized crime, there is a PCN, for example, in southern Italy and the U.S.-Mexican border.[7]

However, it should be noted that not all political actors that engage in criminal/corrupt activities require a PCN. Political actors can behave in a criminal fashion—for example, become corrupt—without collaborating with the underworld, yet often they believe that such alliances are advantageous.

Why the PCN is a Transstate Security Threat

Why is the PCN a transstate security threat and not simply a local law enforcement or policy problem? Security threats interfere dramatically with the functioning of society. Conditions that threaten the political, economic, social infrastructure of a system cannot be considered ordinary crime problems. Normally, the infrastructure or framework provides the means for the reconciliation of differences within the system. For example, street crime and public health problems are not generally a security problem in the United States. The infrastructure can handle such problems and they generally do not threaten the functioning of the legal or health systems. On the other hand, contemporary organized crime in Mexico and the spread of AIDS in much of Southern Africa threaten the legal, economic, and social infrastructure of those societies. Even the perception that they threaten the infrastructure creates a security problem by diminishing confidence in central authority, or creating alternative structures of power.

Especially in the world's many weak states and small states, the PCN is a major threat to the infrastructure of governability and the rule of law. The PCN may not *become* the government. There may be major foreign policy or economic decisions that the top political leaders undertake without consultation or major participation by criminal groups. However, the PCN in these societies plays a role in determining major aspects of the infrastructure. For example, in elections or the appointments of key executives or judicial figures, or in key public investment decisions, tax policy, trade policy, coalitions on diverse issues will be formed between political and criminal leaders. This will result in political appointments in the security area, prosecution policies, border controls, etc. In the courts, it will extend to who is prosecuted, who is convicted, what prison conditions or sanctions prevail. The PCN involves much more than a few corrupt officials. It can and sometimes does substantially control the politics of a country and how it normally works. It affects the functioning of much of the system, and threatens the security of the rule of law.

However, the balance within the PCN may at times go back and forth. Sometimes the politicians will dominate, sometimes the criminals. The specifics of how the PCN dominates a state vary. Regardless of who is dominant, the politicians or the criminals, the coalition of forces that is created influences many aspects of government, and the reconciliation of differences inside the country.

A key factor in the ability of the PCN to maintain power is the fact that it can resort to violence and intimidation. In addition to the use of violence by criminals, the PCN can mobilize the forces of the state when necessary to attain its goals. Once the public comes to fear those who should be their protectors—the police, intelligence, and security forces—and loses confidence in the electoral and the judicial systems, they will seek alternatives, creating different patrons and loyalties, and further weaken the national infrastructure.

Particularly in a globalizing world, all areas are of concern. This is because the PCN can operate on a local, national, regional or transstate level. Their activities in one country or region undermine democratic governabililty, the rule of law, economic development, human rights, and the environment in that region. But a local or regional PCN also can, and often does, take advantage of zones of impunity, or sanctuary in other regions to operate more effectively in its home state as well as in other regions. For example, a PCN in one state will use safe havens in other regions for production of illegal products, such as drugs and counterfeit goods; they use transit zones in other regions for illegal activities, such as smuggling and access to markets; and they use services in still other regions for money laundering, safe meetings, false documents, particularly passports (including diplomatic passports). The fact that the central governments of such states often have difficulty maintaining control over all their territory, make the possibility of an effective governmental response less likely.

This influence now often reaches beyond domestic activities. The PCN in one country or region also is in a position to influence regional and global security concerns. It can affect state-to-state relationships, making normal relations all but impossible. For example, political decisions in the Balkans, on the U.S.-Mexican border, in central and SW Asia, the Golden Triangle and Central Africa are affected by the PCN in other countries. Smuggling routes for drugs, arms, resources, and people from SW Asia are controlled by PCNs in the former CIS, the Balkans, and southern Italy. The reverse is also true. The Colombia PCN has played a major role in the evolution of politics and security in Mexico and the Caribbean. Decisions by the Colombian cartels to use the Mexican and Caribbean smuggling routes to the United States have resulted in the massive national PCNs in these regions. Prior to these developments, they were local organizations, affecting local crime and corruption. This transformation changed the nature of politics and security in Central and South America, Mexico, the Caribbean, and the U.S. border area during the 1990s.

Of 192 states in the world today, approximately 35 have characteristics that maintain strong governability and rule of law—and weak PCNs. On the other hand, approximately 120 states can be classified as medium to weak to failed states (zones with very weak to nonexistent infrastructures).[8] They have medium to strong PCNs. In these states, PCNs threaten the security of their own people as well as the security of people in other regions.

For example, the United States is affected by the activities of the PCNs in Eurasia, Mexico and the Caribbean. Their involvement in drugs, illegal migration, violation of intellectual property rights, and the dissemination of weapons of mass destruction, has a direct impact within the U.S. even though the U.S. itself appears to be relatively free of a domestic regional or national PCN.

To take another example, the People's Republic of China (PRC) faces current and future threats from the PCN, both from inside the country and from PCNs abroad. Inside the PRC, organized crime appears to be growing, and the PCN is also expanding. In some regions there is considerable Chinese public acknowledgement of these developments.[9] In others, the sources are murkier. However, it appears that inside Mainland China, the PCN gives power to particular coalitions who can use money and violence to maneuver against other groupings and undermine decisions about the infrastructure of society.

The activities of the PCNs on the borders of China can also affect the infrastructure inside the PRC. For example, drug trafficking from SE Asia appears to be contributing to the spread of AIDS inside China as well as increased addiction levels. These internal effects may be strengthening political-criminal coalitions inside major areas of the PRC. More powerful PCNs in China facilitate PCNs in other parts of the world through its involvement in intellectual property violations, piracy in the South China Sea, and the manufacture of precursor chemicals. All of the foregoing are becoming problems. China has lengthy borders, which are difficult to control, and its economy is now developing at a rapid rate, offering attractive opportunities for exploitation, both legitimate and illegitimate.

The activities of PCNs become particularly important in certain circumstances. For example, in regions that possess weapons of mass destruction (WMD) PCNs can facilitate the export of WMD or their components and also facilitate the import of components of WMD into their own or other states. This could be a threat in Russia and perhaps the PRC.[10]

Those regions and sectors that are important to the global economy such as the economic, financial sectors, or mass production are vulnerable to PCNs. China, S. Asia, and Mexico, for example, are involved in massive counterfeiting of goods and violations of intellectual property rights damaging to the U.S. and other economies. The PCNs may also assist criminals to gain control of key sectors of the economic security infrastructure, such as telecommunications or financial services. PCNs affect regional cooperation, color relations with other states, and contribute to local instability in geostrategic regions of concern.

Increasing Recognition of the PCN by Global and Other Organizations

Many governments and international institutions now maintain that "organized crime," "transstate crime," and "corruption" are security threats. There also has been increasing recognition that there is a linkage between the upper and underworlds, although few have explicitly recognized the PCN as a security threat.

The United States, for example, first spelled out the security threat from organized crime in a comprehensive manner in 1995, and has been incorporating it into policy and planning ever since. The Clinton Administration's Presidential Decision Directive (PDD) 42 states unequivocally that organized crime is a threat to national security. The same year, President Clinton's address to the UN 50th Anniversary Assembly, drew attention to organized crime as a global threat. Three years later the *U.S. International Crime Control Strategy*, the first attempt to devise a national strategy, was published. It recognizes the threat of international crime to the integrity of government. By 2000, there was specific recognition of the PCN. A U.S. Interagency Working Group published the first *International Crime Threat Assessment*, recognizing the PCN as a security threat.[11]

At its 1998 Summit in Birmingham, UK, the G8 began to focus on organized crime as a security threat, and established a senior experts group, known as the "Lyon Group." Not all members of the G8 specifically endorsed the perception of the PCN as a security problem, but some, especially Germany, regard the PCN as a significant security threat.

The United Nations, and especially its Office of Drug Control and Crime Prevention in Vienna, has been increasingly concerned with transstate crime, particularly drugs, trafficking in people, and corruption in recent years. Budgets and contributions for countering high-level crime and corruption have been increased, but as yet there has been little explicit recognition by the UN of the PCN as a significant threat.[12]

Part II. Causes and Conditions That Give Rise to and Sustain PCNs

The generalizations in this chapter have been made possible in large part by case studies that are included in this book. The chapters were written by regional specialists who were asked to address a common set of questions. Beginning in 1997, the specialists were asked to identify various stages in the development of political-criminal relationships, and based on their diagnosis to highlight techniques that have proved effective or show promise in combating them. This framework included questions about the singular conditions in their region that have led to alliances between the upper and underworlds, how the relationships were established and maintained, what is the currency of these relationships—what does each party want from the other, and what inferences can be drawn from their analysis that would be useful to practitioners in and outside government, to prevent such relationships developing in future, and weakening those that already exist.

In 1998, drafts were exchanged and discussed by commentators with particular knowledge of the subject matter at a colloquium at Georgetown University.[13] The papers then were revised.[14] The editor of this volume subsequently developed generalizations based on the conclusions and discussion of the papers. He also has benefited from repeated travel to most of the regions discussed in the papers where it was possible to interview local law enforcement practitioners, researchers, and civil society leaders responsible for neutralizing PCNs, and sometimes even with actual former participants in regional PCNs.

Motives of the Actors/Agents

Criminals are insecure. Their lives and well-being are at risk. There is no individual or group to protect them and their (real) families from their own governments, foreign political actors, or rivals inside or outside their own circles. Criminals need protection, impunity, security—and assistance in facilitating their activities. Collaboration with the upper world can bring protection against law enforcement, and also some protection from rival criminals, both inside and outside their own organization. As further protection, through their PCN connections, they can obtain information from the police, intelligence and military to help neutralize their opponents.[15]

The criminals also want economic information from government sources that can be exploited for profit. For example, advance information on government economic policy and regulatory activity enables them to take advantage of privatization plans, bids for public contracts, sales of licenses, and other opportunities. For states in transition, such as the countries of the former Soviet Union, this has been a particular problem.[16]

Successful criminal elites often want to be accepted by the upper world and seek social mobility for themselves and their families. They often want to mix with celebrities, be seen in fashionable places, and have their families blessed by senior religious authorities. They want respect from the best and most powerful in their societies. Often, they surround themselves with symbols of wealth and power, large houses, even private zoos.[17] After they are rich and powerful in the underworld, what else is there to do with their money and power?

The political elites who collaborate with the powerful underworld are driven by a variety or mix of motives. A principal motive is surely money for personal or political purposes—to finance lavish lifestyles, to win elections, and maintain their leadership roles. Criminal connections can also facilitate services for corrupt business or money laundering for the politicians.[18]

Fear—physical threats to family and position have influenced some. The offer of "Silver or Lead," either accepting their money or being killed is the usual threat. If the political person had collaborated with criminals at an early stage in his career and later become successful, he will not be allowed to walk away from the relationship, or may well continue them out of physical or psychological pressure.[19]

Criminals often are in a position to perform other services and favors such as providing intelligence on rivals at home and abroad, disrupting or even eliminating political rivals (e.g., Taiwan in the 1970s), secure votes in particular regions (e.g., Sicily and Taiwan in the 1980s.)[20]

There are also areas where strong cultural and familial connections, and long traditions of association and collaboration, bring politicians and criminals together. For example, in Southern Italy, and the island of Sicily.[21]

Specific Structural Conditions

It appears to be possible to identify political, social, and economic factors that (a) facilitate or catalyze the formation and (b) evolution of a PCN.

Political Factors. Where the state is too unitary or noncompetitive, and/or where the state and its bureaucracies are too strong relative to civil society, PCNs tend to develop. Examples of the former were Mexico's one-party system, Russia's one-party legacy, and Colombia's clientelistic system in which state assets and services are viewed as bounty. The lack of checks and balances, either from civil society or opposition political parties helps explain this tendency. Even in the United States, there are particular regions where this condition appears to be present. One example was New York City. In spite of a generally vibrant civil society, contractors for decades worked with the U.S. Cosa Nostra and local officials in order to meet construction schedules and to prevent becoming bogged down in red tape or labor strife. The PCN was used to bypass bureaucratic inefficiencies. A policy implication of this finding is that the promotion of democracy, checks and balances, the development of civil society, and particularly various types of watchdog groups help to weaken the PCN.[22]

Regimes and bureaucracies that are weak relative to society or other political actors, tend to develop PCNs. In this circumstance, inefficient premodern institutions, personalistic and/or patronage systems, and governmental inability to compel citizens or officials to obey the laws appears to explain the tendency. Examples include Colombia's inability in the 1980s to stamp out prolonged narco-violence or to resolve conflicts in the private sector. Similarly, the Nigerian government's inability to police itself and Mexico's antiquated law enforcement agencies as it began to engage in a democratic transition in the 1980s and 1990s also illustrate this condition.

In his case study of Mexico, Stan Pimentel concluded that PCN there fits the "elite-exploitative" model in which politicians and government officials treat organized crime as useful or necessary evils, as "cash cows to be exploited." During almost seventy years in power, the Partido Revolucionario Institucional (PRI) according to Pimentel used its military, police, and internal security agencies to control, tax, and export from criminal groups. The politicians and the establishment provided immunity from prosecution, while gaining access to funds for party political campaigns, as well as personal enrichment.[23]

The PCN in Mexico has its origins in the complex patronage system rooted in Mexico's colonial heritage. A hierarchical and interdependent series of relationships among the stakeholders kept organized crime in check. As PRI's political dominance began to wane, however, the equation with the crime groups changed. The PRI was no longer able to exert control over the organized crime elements that had gained more autonomy and become more aggressive and violent in their dealings, not only with the state but also with society in general.

By implication, where this condition is present, efforts should be made to strengthen the state's weak institutions. For example, foreign aid programs to professionalize law enforcement agencies and strengthen conflict resolution mechanisms could ameliorate this condition. U.S. law enforcement assistance to Italy in the 1980s and 1990s appears to have played a role in dramatically weakening the PCN in Sicily. Aid to Colombia in the 1980s, contributed to the near total destruction of the Medellin and Cali PCNs.[24]

The particular focus in the American case study by Robert Kelly, in contrast to the other contributions, is on the local urban political-criminal nexus. Even in the national crisis of the Prohibition era, the fragmented nature of enforcement and authority at the local level prevented the formation of a national-level PCN, according to Kelly. While the existence of organized crime groups in the United States has long been known, and their links to political figures and law enforcement officials have been exposed on many occasions, there appears to be little evidence of national PCN. Kelly points to several reasons for this, not least the lack of a central police force. Law enforcement efforts to counter crime and corruption have therefore been directed mostly against local targets, producing numerous commissions and cases in major U.S. cities over the past 100 years.[25]

Contemporary political systems in transition appear to be particularly susceptible to the development of PCNs. Russia, Ukraine, Mexico, Georgia, Taiwan, and maybe China illustrate this propensity. (Portugal and perhaps Spain, possibly because their transitions transpired during the Cold War, appear to be exceptions to this general pattern.) This seems to be true for most if not all former communist/totalitarian states and authoritarian regimes, in the post-Cold War era. Economic and political transitions create uncertainty regarding what norms of behavior are acceptable, and provide an extremely favorable environment for former and current state officials to work with criminal opportunists. Moreover, the transition of institutions (e.g., law enforcement) appears to be accompanied by a period where control is secured neither by the old, authoritarian or premodern institutions, nor by the new, more modern, democratic successor institutions. This condition may over time be amenable to change by policy actions, e.g., transfer of institutional expertise and experience from other states. The policy implication is that in giving aid to transition states, one should be mindful of this problem and focus on developing efficient institutions, even perhaps before the framework of the old ones are discarded. This finding bears directly on current policymaking towards, for example, Cuba and the PRC.

Louise Shelley maintains that the PCN that emerged in Russia and Ukraine during the 1990s represents the evolution or transformation of the PCN that existed in the Soviet period. Power that was formerly rooted in the managerial apparatus of the Soviet state and the consumer economy was transformed into control of very large shares of the domestic economy, and one with international dimensions. The successor states, according to Shelley, are characterized by symbiotic relationships between government officials and criminals that have their origins in the Soviet era. Both Russia and Ukraine are societies in transition. During this period, the PCN has expanded. Ukraine needed immediately to create laws and the bureaucracy capable of governing the population of over 40 million in the midst of an economic crisis. Russia was somewhat better off. However, the former nomenklatura, the party elite, along with their criminal associates with whom they were allied long before the breakup of the former Soviet Union, have appropriated much of the state property. The transformation Shelley describes has been facilitated to some extent by the West, which viewed privatization as a route to democracy. However, in both states, an unofficial economy that arose to satisfy the unmet needs of the population has flourished parallel to the state economy these many years. The shadow economy could not have existed without the complicity of government officials at many levels. This laid the basis for illicit relationships between those officials and criminals. When the USSR collapsed, these unofficial relationships did not.[26]

A criminal organization's capacity to mediate between the state and individuals tends to focus loyalties away from the state and towards the criminal organization, thereby increasing the strength of the criminal organization and increasing points of political-criminal collaboration. This occurred in Sicily, where for many decades the Mafia interfaced between the state and local communities.[27] The degree to which state institutions can prevent penetration and exploitation by cohesive subnational groups is another factor. For example, Nigeria's PCN has been entrenched by ethnic groups and probably also secret societies that penetrated and occupied state institutions.[28]

Cultural Factors. Cultural factors also play a role in facilitating the PCN. Certain subcultural traits or characteristics have been identified as significant variables. Patron-client systems, for example in Mexico or southern Italy, tend to make politics personalistic. Individuals, criminal and noncriminal, accept that solutions to economic and personal needs, and to conflicts, reside with given leaders who have the capacity to solve problems with their personal clout and ability to threaten or provide physical security.

In his case study of Nigeria, Obie Ebbe maintains that the highly developed and complex PCN there has its roots in Nigeria's colonial past and in its culture. Ebbe contends that intense inter-ethnic struggles have contributed to the strength of the PCN today. These began immediately after Independence, with politicians leading the way, closely followed by civil servants. Each ethnic group vied for the "National Cake," as Ebbe terms it, which as a result was divided into precise, often ethnically based slices, with each corrupt tier of the Criminal partnership taking its cut. These intricate relationships helped perpetuate the PCN because the participants were so interdependent. Strong family and cultural traditions reinforce these patterns. The "Cake" is still a target, but the strategies of the contemporary political and criminal partners have moved far beyond that.[29]

A history and prevalence of secret societies has existed in China and in ethnic Chinese societies in many parts of the Pacific Rim.[30] Similarly, secret societies in Nigeria appear to have been significant. Also, the Italian Mafia-Freemasonry connection in the 1970s and 1980s helped create conditions of covertness that facilitated PCNs.[31]

A widespread public perception that corruption is "normal" has been the case in much of twentieth-century Nigeria, Mexico, and in Hong Kong. This facilitated a PCN by, for example, de-professionalizing government service.

This included views on government (accountability, trustworthiness, and efficiency), criminality (defining which behaviors are considered criminal, determining the level of social stigmatization attached to graft and official corruption), and wealth (respect for wealth regardless of its source).[32]

In some societies, public perception of criminals as cultural heroes bestows an aura of legitimacy on illegal activities.[33] When, for example, Mexican drug barons are idolized by young people for their power and money such as in the popular music along the U.S.-Mexican border, the "narco-corridas," or by the church for their charitable work, the stigma attached to criminal conduct and violence is diminished.[34]

In the case of southern Italy, Letizia Paoli emphasizes the social and cultural factors surrounding the PCN. Since their beginnings in the mid-nineteenth century, organized crime groups there have had longstanding relationships with the political establishment in southern Italy, where major organized crime groups are still based. Indeed, according to Paoli, much of their enduring power and freedom of action was a direct result of these relationships that she traces through the last 150 years. The relationships have evolved along with organized crime structures and the development of the Italian state. The weakness of the state, and its inability to maintain law and order fostered an alternative form based on "code of honor, " and a willingness to use violence. The criminal association thus filled much of the void left by weak state institutions particularly in Sicily. For its part, the state tolerated the Mafia as a means to control public order. As the relationships evolved, the Mafia sought more influence in politics, to distribute its spoils and increase its own power.[35]

These factors contribute to the social context that facilitates or retards political-criminal relationships. Changes in culture can facilitate a breakup of a PCN, as evidenced by the apparently effective efforts in Sicily and Hong Kong. Wing Lo contends that there are two distinct phases in the PCN's existence in Hong Kong. The vast refugee population that streamed across the border from China after 1949 was disinterested in politics and wary of government, and made no attempt to challenge the existing elite. This changed in the late 1960s as the children of the refugees came of age and watched the Cultural Revolution in China. Rioting threatened both the power of the elite and the economy on which it was based. Wing Lo argues that these developments catapulted ethnic considerations to the fore, and that the gulf between the haves and the have-nots and the latter's desire for political power forced the government to make hard choices. Other case studies have documented that PCN often deprives ordinary citizens of everyday services by illegally diverting resources away from their operations. In Hong Kong, the colonial government responded to the unrest by pouring money into social services, housing, and education, and bypassing new legislation aimed at improving the lives of ordinary people. Wing Lo argues that the motivating force was the need for a satisfied and pliable workforce that would assure continued economic prosperity.[36]

In Sicily, over the last twenty years, policymakers and law enforcement officials developed allies from many parts of society—religion, arts, entertainment, and education—in order to change cultural acceptance of patron-client relationships and the Mafia, and weaken the PCN.[37] Similarly, in Hong Kong since the mid-1970s law enforcement has been combined with extensive education and prevention campaigns. A central component of this effort is a strong community outreach program, including publicity campaigns (radio, television, and posters), business ethics programs, and moral education for primary and secondary school students. This approach in Sicily and Hong Kong appears to have been successful in weakening the traditional culture of corruption prevalent in these societies and strengthening a culture of lawfulness that has played a major role in weakening PCNs.[38]

Economic Factors. Not surprisingly, markets and economics bear on the PCN issue. For example, the sheer scale of money that needed to be laundered in Colombia made the establishment of national-level PCNs a major goal of the criminals. Another factor is the level of efficiency and service provided to legitimate economic actors by criminal organizations and their political collaborators. For example, when domestic currency is devalued and unstable, entrepreneurs' access to foreign currencies may be obtainable only through criminal organizations. Similarly, criminal bankers often provide speed, simplicity, and confidentiality that surpass the services offered by legitimate banks, even for legitimate activities, let alone tax evasion and money laundering. Specific national-level economic policies also can facilitate the creation of a climate conducive to criminal and political-criminal activities. For example, Colombia's tax-amnesty schemes tended to encourage development of links between illicit money and the formal economy.[39]

Concrete economic factors at the local level also play a role, for example in both Mexico and Sicily. Local criminal groups had the capacity to direct local government contracts and exercise control over local job opportunities.[40] Paoli also relates the Sicilian Mafia's rise to economic power. In the 1960s and 1970s, the subculture of "honor" began to fade and wealth became the basis of reputation and respect. This led to their "entrepreneurial transformation" fueling illicit—and licit—economic activities. In Palermo they established influence over four basic sectors of the economy, the credit market, the wholesale market, the construction sector and the labor market. Their leverage in the public works market was enhanced by their political connections at a time when public spending was growing by leaps and bounds. These endeavors were often financed with favorable loans obtained through their political friends. However, in the 1960s, the Mafia groups also entered the world drug trade with great success. This situation was tolerated by a populace, some of whom benefited to some extent from it.[41]

The supply and demand dynamics of illegal goods and services facilitate the PCN. The demand for illegal goods and services and the effort to supply the demand can contribute in a significant way to the creation of organized crime, and hence facilitates the creation of PCNs. But this general concern is often so broad and amorphous as to be unhelpful when formulating concrete diagnoses and policy prescriptions. The policy implications of economic factors will vary according to the specific economic factor in question. However, attentiveness to the kinds of economic situations that promote PCNs can help analysts detect and minimize them.

For example, drawing on interviews with past and recent Colombian politicians, Rensselaer Lee and Francisco Thoumi emphasize that the enormous size and financial resources of the cocaine cartels have driven the PCN there, and this has provided the resources for corrupt purposes. Because the money generated by drugs dominates the Colombian economy, the cartels can influence government officials and others to maintain their power. This influence may be exercised in more or less subtle ways. Lee and Thoumi argue that in addition the Colombian PCN has been defined by a number of other factors, some reaching deeply into Colombian society and history, and others that are products of the characteristics of the "cartels." [42]

Although difficult to use from a rigorous scientific perspective, it is important to recognize the role of contingent, accidental, or coincidental factors in the development of PCNs. Among the contingent factors that have been identified so far are (1) specific individuals; and (2) specific political circumstances.

PCNs often develop opportunistically, as when a specific person occupying a particular government or criminal position at a particular time may have a singular impact. Where in one instance a PCN blossoms or is destabilized, it might not in similar circumstances involving different personalities. An example of individuals who were critical to PCNs were Pablo Escobar and the Rodriguez-Orejuela brothers of the Colombian Medellin and Cali cartels, respectively, or Amado Carillo Fuentes in Mexico. In the 1970s and 1980s, these leaders brought the Colombian and Mexican drug producing and smuggling organizations into global prominence, in the process developing entrenched PCNs in Colombia, Mexico, and elsewhere. [43]

According to Lee and Thoumi, a number of deeper factors that led to Colombian dominance particularly of the cocaine industry in the 1970s and 1980s also contributed to growth of the PCN. The weakness of the government, and its inability to protect property or solve disputes during times of profound socioeconomic change diminished the government's legitimacy. At the same time, citizens were willing to avert the laws for economic or political gain. Weak nationalism, strong local parties, and lack of physical integration all contributed to a political system dominated by local clientelism. Local parties viewed the national government as a bounty for local distribution. An already weak civil society underwent further strain as more and more of the rural population migrated to the large cities, uprooting local ties and traditional values, and clearing the way for what has been termed a "savage capitalism." Rural violence has surfaced time and again in Colombia throughout the twentieth century. It has continued pushing people further into unsettled territory, where coca cultivation is argued to be one, if not the only, means of survival; and violence, as a tool in general, increasingly found its place in the modus operandi of the drug cartels. Finally, a period of economic recession led to a series of so-called tax reforms and amnesties that in fact further facilitated the growth of illicit drug business in Colombia.[44]

In certain cases one can identify particular political circumstances that led to the emergence of a PCN. For example, in Italy in 1948 the Christian Democratic (CD) party's need for political support in Sicily in order to compete with the only other national political party—the Communists—led the CD closer to the reviving Mafia.[45] This electoral reliance on the Mafia was a particular contingent condition. When this condition changed, as it did in the late 1980s with the end of the Cold War, the CD-Sicilian Mafia relationship was no longer so important to the CD and Italian politics. This change in conditions helped lead to the demise (but not the elimination) of the Sicilian Mafia.[46] There are clear policy implications for contingent factors. For example, where individuals appear to be the keys to a PCN, these people can be identified and targeted for law enforcement or other disruptive actions. In the 1980s, U.S. law enforcement came to the aid of specific parts of the Colombian and Mexican governments by helping to target the key figures of these cartels. This contributed to the incarceration, death, or removal of key members of the cartels' leadership, the splintering of the criminal organizations, and the weakening of the PCNs. [47]

Different types of criminal activity and diverse concentrations of criminal actors lead to different types of PCNs. Local smugglers and criminal organizations need to develop relationships with local law enforcement authorities, but they may have few relationships with state or national officials. In this case, the PCN would be narrow, focused, and would likely have only limited impact on the larger society. By contrast a criminal organization with a broader and deeper local or regional base, such as the Sicilian Mafia, with diverse profit-making activities, may seek numerous and varied relationships with political actors of all types, from the national level to local law enforcement. A PCN of this type would have more serious implications for the host society. Understanding these differences could inform policy by allowing the more dangerous types of PCN to be prioritized and targeted. As resources are limited, devising criteria for differentiating among PCNs is significant.

PCN relationships, like others, are dynamic. For example, at the beginning of a relationship one partner (either the political actor or the criminal) will be dominant. However, over time, as conditions change, the initially inferior partner may become dominant. In Sicily from the 1950s to the 1970s, the criminals were the dominant partners. When they felt their power waning in the 1980s, they went to war, that is, used terrorism against the political class and the state, including some of their former partners. Combined with other conditions, this led to the weakening and perhaps near destruction of the PCN as other political forces and civil society mobilized against the Mafia and their former political allies.

In Mexico, PCNs for decades tended to be dominated by political actors; however, this changed as political and economic transition began taking place in the 1980s.[48] During the 1980s, an increased concern for democracy and law enforcement consistent with human rights left government weaker and law enforcement less effective. Increasing resources from the cocaine trade and other activities enabled criminals to become more assertive and violent. It is unclear which element now dominates, as is demonstrated by the large-scale violence among political and criminal actors in that country.

In the twentieth century, PCNs have tended to arise, evolve, and sometimes disappear. In the United States the creation of oversight bodies for state contracting, programs to increase competency of government officials and administrators, the use of special prosecutors and task forces, and witness protection programs substantially diminished PCNs in various regions, particularly the demise of the American Cosa Nostra and its political connections.[49]

As this diagnosis has shown, PCNs have a variety of causes, both motivational and structural, and these appear in many complex combinations. Monocausal explanations are incomplete and insufficient. Money is not the only sine qua non. Criminals often pursue money, but they have other motives. Political actors frequently desire money, but they have other interests and insecurities. Remedies aimed solely at one type of motivation or one type of structural factor are not as likely to be successful as those that are more comprehensive, and tailored to the specific factors that seem to be in play. Some elements are generalizable, others are not.

States in transition, for example, in their fluid and complex conditions likely have few structures in place. These may need to be addressed differently from those with well-established institutions.

Many diagnoses tend toward political explanations and the financial motivations of criminals. Their policy implications emphasize professionalization of law enforcement, for example. Because they also tend to subscribe to the theory that money is the principal motivation of criminals, policy is focused on the effort to cut off the money and seize the assets. Those who employ economic explanations also seek to use market forces to affect outcomes by controlling the supply of drugs. However, the economic and law enforcement/regulatory approach, with its focus on financial motivation would appear to be inadequate. It fails to address the many other contributory factors.

Part III. What Needs to Be Done

In recent years, governments and global and regional bodies have focused primarily on ameliorating the causes and conditions that facilitate organized and transstate crime. Increasingly, some have addressed corruption and protecting the integrity of the political establishment. The PCN itself, however, has rarely been the focus, and when it has, governmental policy has addressed the political and institutional factors that facilitate organized crime, rather than the motivations of the establishment. Usually the focus on criminals has been on improving the effectiveness of law enforcement and regulatory systems in weak or transitional states, as well as on regional and global law enforcement cooperation. Hence, the focus has been on interdicting local and transstate criminals, with a little attention, sometimes, focused on criminal efforts to corrupt government officials, particularly at the lower levels of officialdom.

There also have been efforts to affect the supply of some illegal goods and services. Most efforts have been devoted to influencing the producers of opium and coca, particularly the farmers, providing opportunities for alternative development.[50] There have also been other financial incentives, and sanctions for establishment figures involved in laundering the illegally obtained funds, both of the criminals and the political establishment generally.[51]

So far, however, there have been only a few efforts to address the global challenge of the PCN. Perhaps others have not yet come to public attention. Moreover, in the main the problem has been viewed by governments and nongovernmental specialists from a criminal, law enforcement perspective, with supplementary assistance requested from diplomats and intelligence practitioners, and specialists in alternative development.

There also has been little effort to develop strategic approaches to managing the problem. Such an approach would involve (a) detailed assessments of the problem, (b) the prioritization of objectives, the sustained mobilization, calibration of resources, and means to achieve priority objectives, and (c) evaluations of performance.

Assessments are needed to identify the specific threats and their causes, as well as opportunities to prevent or break the linkages between the upper and underworlds. What factors or conditions are leading to the PCN, and which are amenable to change over what period of time? What practices have been effective in preventing or breaking such linkages, and are they replicable?

Second, what are the key priorities? Presumably some PCNs are more important than others. Many in the G8 have come to be particularly concerned with "Russian organized crime" and its recognized political linkages in Russia. What should the other priorities be? Should the PCN in China also be of regional and global concern? What efforts are being made to establish a global coalition to identify and build consensus on the priorities?

Third, there is a need for a realistic appraisal of the long-term means and resources that will be needed to address, manage, and minimize the priority PCNs. The relatively meager resources and means (in comparison to the magnitude of the problem) that have been mobilized to fight and prevent even transstate organized crime in the last decade have been insufficient. No doubt the problem would have been worse had governments not taken the steps they have. But even the United States, the United Kingdom, and the Federal Republic of Germany, among the most mobilized and capable governments, have not been able to reverse the general growth of transnational organized crime and PCNs, although there have been some successes.[52]

Also, it appears that more than governments will be needed to manage the problem of the PCNs. There is almost certainly a necessary and important role for civil society and private sectors in the mix—particularly to manage cultural factors. In recent years, there has been growing recognition (in some governments and international institutions) that cultural and educational resources (fostering a "culture of lawfulness") are necessary to complement law enforcement, intelligence, etc. in managing and preventing major crime and corruption.

The term "culture of lawfulness" means that the dominant or mainstream culture, ethos, and thought in a society are sympathetic to the rule of law. Such a culture would be characterized as one in which the average person believes that legal norms either are a fundamental part of justice or provide a gateway to attain justice, and that such a system enhances the quality of life of individuals and society as a whole. To achieve such a culture, various sectors of society and their institutions must be mobilized. Among the most important sectors that have contributed to building such a culture in such diverse areas as Western Sicily and Hong Kong, for example, are schools (formal school-based education for all youngsters), centers of moral authority (religious institutions and NGOs), and the mass media.[53]

Moreover, these "cultural" means are very inexpensive in comparison to the material costs of paramilitary activities, intelligence, and law enforcement. For a medium-sized state, it is estimated that as little as $1 million per year, for 5-10 years, would be needed to design and implement a basic program for the creation of a culture supportive of the rule of law.

In promoting this culture of lawfulness, some of those resources also could be devoted to intensifying the sense of insecurity among criminals and in deterring some from entering a life of crime in the first place. Projecting the criminal lifestyle as one of permanent anxiety, albeit under a thin camouflage of glamour, is one part. In addition, security can be offered to those willing to give up criminal lifestyles, and even witness protection programs to key figures that need it. Exposure and publicity in the media are powerful tools that can be used to shatter the links between criminals and their political allies. However, there has been almost no planning or implementation, on the regional or global level, to synchronize what have been called "two wheels of the cart"—law enforcement and culture; hence at this time little progress can be expected from exclusively political and economic "solutions."

Finally, there will be a need for a periodic review and evaluation of performance outputs. It is relatively easy to measure inputs such as how much money is spent. It is much more difficult intellectually and politically to measure outputs. Such measurements are needed to guide strategic planning to manage this very complex and murky problem of the collaboration between the political establishment and the underworlds.

However, evaluation, recalibration, and reevaluation are usually the weak points in strategy. While the U.S. International Crime Control Strategy was an important first step, almost no evaluation was built into the process to determine whether the means were achieving the intended goals. Nor were the goals prioritized in the Strategy and there is confusion between ends and means. (Only the U.S. Office of Drug Control Policy has proposed to engage in systematic evaluations of U.S. efforts.)[54]

Developing and refining the strategies are both the work of governments and nongovernmental specialists, both within and across state boundaries. One impediment in this case, however, is that many governmental leaders are uncomfortable with investigating their senior foreign political, intelligence, and law enforcement counterparts. It makes it very difficult to conduct official business, especially countering crime and corruption with officials or bureaucracies known to be corrupt. Moreover, some bureaucracies also are not comfortable with the dangerous work of probing the linkages of criminals with the political establishment around the world.[55]

While some of this work can be undertaken by academics and other nongovernmental specialists, the global security requirement of the early twenty-first century requires a partnership between the governmental and nongovernmental sectors. Democratic governments have the primary resources and capabilities to assess the clandestine linkages of the PCN. On the other hand, nongovernmental specialists have the independent analytical capabilities that can be helpful to governments in such assessments, as well as in studying effective practices, and evaluating performance.

Although there has been some teaching, research, and training on the security threat of nonstate actors in the U.S., U.K., and some other countries (for example, about terrorism and ethnic conflict) systematic work on these problems is only just beginning.

Conclusion

Collaboration between governments and gangsters, in ways that significantly affect security, is much more than the stuff of fiction. While it is not new, the magnitude of the problem now is unprecedented. Some regions are affected more than others, but in an era of increasing globalization the problem reaches into most corners of the world.

The causes, however, do not lend themselves to straightforward solutions. These causes can be viewed from the perspectives of economic, political, and cultural structures that give rise to the incentives for the collaboration of political and criminal elites. Or, they can be ascertained from examining the motivations of the respective elites, given the condition of contemporary world politics and the specific conditions in their environment.

As this overview has sought to demonstrate, however, contemporary evidence suggests that PCNs have a variety of causes and they appear in complex combinations. Monocausal explanations, particularly economic or financial explanations are inadequate. Moreover, some elements are generalizable; others are not. And prescriptions based on weak or faulty diagnosis are unlikely to lead to effective solutions.

Many governmental players—both at the national and the international level—and some civil society or "third sector" actors have begun to recognize the severity of the problem. On the whole, however, their prescriptions are not based on multi-causality, or on a strategic approach to the problem. Usually, the search for solutions has focused on criminals, and not on the dynamic relationships between the political and criminal players. Moreover, the basic explanation is that in the current era of multiple transitions to democracy, the problem is primarily one of weak governments and states, and the absence of strong rule of law institutions. While these appear to be major contributing factors, they are not the sole determinants.

Finally, few governmental players in the U.S. and elsewhere appear to have taken a strategic approach to the global challenge of the PCN. Very little exists by way of detailed assessments and studies. There has been little prioritization of objectives, too few calculations of the required resources, and the requirements for the mobilization and calibration of means both in government and the private sector that are needed over the short as well as the medium term. Nor has there been a systematic attempt to evaluate and recalibrate performance.

As a result, although it is not easy to measure with precision the wins and losses and what caused them, the results and outlook for the near to medium-term are not particularly encouraging. Since the 1980s, there have been some successes, for example in Sicily and the United States. The PCNs involving the Sicilian and the U.S. Cosa Nostra and the political establishments in their respective regions have declined dramatically. In other regions the problem probably would have been worse if governments and third sector organizations had not made some efforts to prevent or to break PCNs. On balance, however, it is hard to find reasons for optimism.

Governments and civil society were moving in the right direction prior to September 11, 2001. Since then, attention has shifted away from transnational crime and its connections to the political establishment, to focus on terrorism and its connections to strong and weak states. It is possible that the shift in priorities will have a positive effect in helping to combat and prevent PCNs. Terrorist-political linkages, particularly in regions that have weak governments are now viewed as important. Moreover, there are overlaps between terrorists and criminals. For example, both need money, arms, money laundering, false documents, secret methods of communication, safe havens, and are advantaged by political connections. As governments and civil society in various regions mobilize and collaborate to prevent and manage terrorist groups and their political linkages, they may find it useful to develop a strategic approach, which also will be helpful in preventing and curtailing PCNs.

Notes

1.   There have been many attempts to define organized crime and transstate organized crime, and definitions vary among countries, organizations, and agencies. In this chapter, *Crime* refers to illegal activities conducted either by organized groups/networks or individuals acting independently. *Organized crime* refers to individuals and groups who have ongoing working relationships, and who make their living primarily through profit-making activities that one or more states deem illegal and criminal. Organized crime can take a variety of institutional or organizational forms. This includes tight vertical hierarchies with lifelong commitments, as well as looser, more ephemeral, ongoing, non-hierarchical relationships. *Transstate crime* refers to organized criminal activities and enterprises that operate across state boundaries. *Disorganized crime*, in contrast, is crime committed by individuals or small groups acting in isolation.

     For another recent approach to definition, see United Nations Convention Against Transnational Organized Crime: "'Organized criminal group' shall mean a structured group of three or more persons, existing for a period of time and acting in concert with the aim of committing one or more serious crimes or offences established in accordance with this Convention, in order to obtain, directly or indirectly, a financial or other material benefit," G.A. res. 55/25, annex I, 55 U.N. GAOR Supp. (No. 49) at 44, U.N. Doc. A/45/49 (Vol. I) (2001). A total of 124 countries, including the U.S., signed the United Nations Convention against Transnational Organized Crime during the Palermo conference from 12-15 December 2000; Howard Abadinsky, *Organized Crime*, 6th ed. (Stamford, CT: Thomson Learning, 2000); on the problem of defining organized crime, see Michael D. Maltz, "Defining Organized Crime" in Robert J. Kelly et al., *Handbook of Organized Crime in the United States* (Westport, CT: Greenwood Publishing Group, 1994), pp. 21-37; Mark Findlay, *The Globalization of Crime: Understanding Transitional Relationships in Context,* (Cambridge: Cambridge University Press, 1999). Klaus von Lampe has compiled a useful compendium of definitions by organized crime specialists from various countries. It can be accessed at his website http://people.freenet.de/kvlampe/OCDEF1.htm. Criminologists in mainland China have also sought to differentiate between various types or levels of organized crime according to their levels of sophistication and organizational needs, namely, ordinary and relatively disorganized groups and gangs, "underground groups of a criminal nature," and the highest level, almost certainly involving significant political collaboration, "underground criminal organizations." See especially the work of Professor He Bingsong of the China University of Law and Political Science.

2. On the Salinas-Citibank connection, see United States General Accounting Office, "Private Banking: Raul Salinas, Citibank, and Alleged Money Laundering," Report to the Ranking Minority Member, Permanent Subcommittee on Investigations, Committee on Governmental Affairs, U.S. Senate, October 1998, GAO/OSI-99-1. John Bailey and Roy Godson, eds., *Organized Crime and Democratic Governability: Mexico and the US-Mexican Borderlands* (Pittsburgh, PA: University of Pittsburgh Press, 2001), Spanish Edition (Mexico, DF: Editorial Grijalbo, 2000), especially p. 21. Eduardo Varela-Cid, *Hidden Fortunes: Drug Money, Cartels and the Elite Banks,* translated by Michael C. Berman (New York: Hudson Street Press, 1999).

3. See also June T. Dreyer, "The Emerging Political-Criminal Nexus in the People's Republic of China." Draft paper prepared for joint meeting of the U.S. and Chinese Working Groups on Political-Criminal Collaboration in the PRC, National Strategy Information Center, December 2001.

4. See, for example, Ko-lin Chin, "Black Gold Politics: Organized Crime, Business, and Politics in Taiwan." Draft paper prepared for joint meeting of the U.S. and Chinese Working Groups on Political-Criminal Collaboration in the PRC, National Strategy Information Center, December 2001. Paul Klebnikov, *Godfather of the Kremlin: Boris Berezovsky and the Looting of Russia*, (New York: Harcourt, 2000).

5. For a description of a typology of PCNs within one country, see John Bailey and Roy Godson, eds., *Organized Crime and Democratic Governability,* especially the Introduction.

6. For the recollections of key leaders in the anti-Mafia movement, see Leoluca Orlando, *Fighting the Mafia and Renewing Sicilian Culture* (San Francisco, CA: Encounter Books, 2001). Among the best analysis in English and Italian is Letizia Paoli, "The Pledge to Secrecy: Culture, Structure and Action of Mafia Associations," Ph.D. diss., European University Institute, Florence, 1997.

7. Bailey and Godson, *Organized Crime and Democratic Governability,* especially chapter 2, Stanley A. Pimentel, "The Nexus of Organized Crime and Politics in Mexico;" chapter 3, Luis Astorga, "Organized Crime and the Organization of Crime;" and chapter 7, Louis R. Sadler, "The Historical Dynamics of Smuggling in the U.S.-Mexican Border Region, 1550-1998."

8. This calculation is based on several data sources, originally brought to my attention by Matthew M. Taylor, a Ph.D. candidate at Georgetown University. The major data sources are listed below. The combination of these sources suggests that most of the states in the world can be categorized as having medium to weak to failing governmental systems. This writer then deduced further that in many, if not all, of these states, the PCN tends to be medium to strong. As far as is known, there is no published survey of the strength and weakness of the PCN in states characterized as having weak or strong governments. See United Nations membership list, accessed at http://www. un.org/Overview/unmember.html; WorldAudit.org, site accessed at http://www.worldaudit.org/polrights.html; The World Bank, "Governance Matters" by Daniel Kaufman, Aart Kraay, and Pablo Zoido-Lobaton, May 1999, accessed at http:// www.imf.org/external/pubs/ft/fandd/2000/06/kauf.html; Freedom House, Annual Survey of Freedom Country Scores 1972-73 to 1999-00, accessed at http://216.119.117.183/ratings/index.html.

9. Dreyer, "The Emerging Political-Criminal Nexus in the People's Republic of China."

10. Former Senate Majority Leader, Howard Baker, and former counsel to the president, Lloyd Cutler, chaired a U.S. Department of Energy bipartisan task force in 2000-01 that concluded "The most urgent unmet national security threat to the United States today is the danger that weapons of mass destruction or weapons-usable material in Russia could be stolen and sold to terrorists or hostile nation states and used against American troops abroad or citizens at home." "A Report Card on the Department of Energy's Nonproliferation Programs, with Russia," Howard Baker and Lloyd Cutler, Co-Chairs, Russia Task Force, The Secretary of Energy Advisory Board, U.S. Department of Energy, Washington, DC, 10 January 2001. The report can be accessed at http://www.hr.doe.gov/seab/.

11. *International Crime Threat Assessment*, The White House, Washington, DC, 2000, especially pp. 10-13. See also President Clinton's National Security Adviser, Anthony Lake, *Six Nightmares: Real Threats in a Dangerous World and How America Can Meet Them,* (New York: Little Brown, and Co., 2000).

12. United Nations Convention Against Transnational Organized Crime, G.A. res. 55/25, annex I, 55 U.N. GAOR Supp. (No. 49) at 44, U.N. Doc. A/45/49 (Vol. I) (2001). United Nations Convention against Transnational Organized Crime Palermo conference from 12-15 December 2000: http://www.undcp.org/palermo/convmain.html. For estimates of prevalence and costs of transnational crime according to the UN's 18 categories of transnational crime, see Gerhard O. W. Mueller's "Transnational Crime: Definitions and Concepts" in Phil Williams and Dimitri Vlassis, eds., *Combating Transnational Crime: Concepts, Activities and Responses* (Portland, OR: Frank Cass, 2001).

13. Commentators at the Colloquium were Dr. Annelise Anderson, then undersecretary of the UN, Professor Pino Arlaachi, David Beall, Dr. J. Bowyer Bell, Douglas Farah, R. Penn Kemble, Dr. William Olson, Dr. Marin Strmecki, Professor Phil Williams, and Jonathan Winer.

14. The chapter on Taiwan by Ko-lin Chin was an exception. Professor Chin was able to undertake his research after the first drafts of most of the papers had been reviewed. His essay was completed in 2001.

15. See, for example, former senior FBI official Stanley A. Pimentel, "The Nexus of Organized Crime and Politics in Mexico," in Bailey and Godson, *Organized Crime and Democratic Governability.*

16. Louise I. Shelley, "Russia and Ukraine: Transition or Tragedy," chapter 7. "International Crime Threat Assessment," U.S. Government Interagency Working Group, Washington, DC, 2000. Richard Palmer, in collaboration with Vladimir Brovkin, "The New Russian Oligarchy: The Nomenklatura, the KGB, and the Mafiya" (unpublished manuscript).

17. Robert J. Nieves, *Colombian Cocaine Cartels: Lessons from the Front* (Washington, DC: National Strategy Information Center, 1997).

18. See Pimentel, "The Nexus of Organized Crime and Politics in Mexico."

19. Nieves, *Colombian Cocaine Cartels.* Roberto E. Blum, "Corruption and Complicity: Mortar of Mexico's Political System?" *Trends in Organized Crime*, Vol. 3. No. 1, Fall 1997.

20. David E. Kaplan, *Fires of the Dragon: Politics, Murder, and the Kuomintang* (New York: Atheneum, 1992). Leoluca Orlando, *Fighting the Mafia.*

21. Enzo Lodato, "The Palermo Renaissance," *Trends in Organized Crime*, Vol. 5. No. 3, Spring 2000.

22. Robert J. Kelly, "An American Way of Crime and Corruption," chapter 4.

23. Pimentel, "Mexico's Legacy of Corruption," chapter 6.

24. Nieves, *Colombian Cocaine Cartels.*

25. Kelly, "An American Way of Crime and Corruption."
26. Shelley, "Russia and Ukraine."
27. Paoli, "The Pledge to Secrecy."
28. Obei N. I. Ebbe, "Slicing Nigeria's 'National Cake'," chapter 5.
29. Ibid.
30. W. P. Morgan, *Triad Societies in Hong Kong* (Hong Kong: Government Press, 1960). *Triad Societies*, General Briefing Paper, Royal Hong Kong Police, 1996. Jean Chesneaux ed. *Popular Movements and Secret Societies in China 1840-1950* (Stanford, CA: Stanford University Press, 1972). Frederic Wakeman, Jr., *Policing Shanghai, 1927-1937* (Berkeley: University of California Press, 1995.) Benjamin T. M. Liu, Hong Kong Triad Societies Before and After the 1997 Change-Over (Hong Kong, SAR; Net e-Publishing, 2001).
31. Paoli, "The Pledge to Secrecy." See also Pino Arlacchi, *Addio Cosa Nostra. La vita di Tommaso Buscetta* (Milano: Rizzoli, 1994); Obe N. I. Ebbe, "Slicing Nigeria's 'National Cake.'"
32. T. Wing Lo, "Pioneer of Moral Education: Independent Commission Against Corruption (ICAC)," *Trends in Organized Crime*, Vol. 4. No. 2, Winter 1998.
33. Paoli, "The Pledge to Secrecy."
34. Terrence E. Poppa, *Drug Lord: The Life and Death of a Mexican Kingpin, A True Story,* 2nd ed. (Seattle, WA: Demand Publications, 1998).
35. Letizia Paoli, " Broken Bonds: Mafia and Politics in Sicily," chapter 2.
36. Wing Lo, "Minimizing Crime and Corruption in Hong Kong," chapter 8.
37. Leoluca Orlando, *Fighting the Mafia.*
38. T. Wing Lo, "Pioneer of Moral Education." Alan Lai, "A Quiet Revolution: The Hong Kong Experience," *Trends in Organized Crime*, Volume 5, No. 3, Spring 2000. Richard C. LaMagna, *Changing a Culture of Corruption: How Hong Kong's Independent Commission Against Corruption Succeeded in Furthering a Culture of Lawfulness* (Washington, DC: National Strategy Information Center, 1999).
39. Rensselaer W. Lee, III and Francisco E. Thuomi, "Drugs and Democracy in Colombia," chapter 3.
40. Orlando, *Fighting the Mafia.*
41. Paoli, "Broken Bonds."
42. Lee and Thuomi, "Drugs and Democracy."
43. See Pimentel, "The Nexus of Organized Crime and Politics in Mexico."
44. Lee and Thoumi, "Drugs and Democracy."
45. Salvatore Lupo, "The Allies and the Mafia," *Journal of Modern Italian Studies*, Volume 2, No. 1, Spring 1997.
46. Jane C. Schneider and Peter T. Schneider, *Reversible Destiny: Mafia, Antimafia and the Struggle for Palermo* (Berkeley: University of California Press, forthcoming).
47. Nieves, *Colombian Cocaine Cartels.*
48. Bailey and Godson, *Organized Crime and Democratic Governability.*
49. James B. Jacobs, *Gotham Unbound* (New York: New York University Press, 1999); James B. Jacobs, Christopher Panarella, and Jay Worthington, *Busting the Mob: The United States vs. Cosa Nostra* (New York: New York University Press, 1996).
50. *UN Action Plan on International Cooperation on the Eradication of Illicit Drugs and on Alternative Development,* 1998, accessed at the website of the UN Office for Drug Control and Crime Prevention at http://www.undcp.org/resolution_1998-09-08_3.html#E.

51. See, for example, The United Nations, *Declaration Against Corruption and Bribery in International Commercial Transactions*, December 1996. Organization for Economic Cooperation and Development (OECD) *Convention on Combating Bribery of Foreign Officials in International Business Transactions*, December 1997. *Guiding Principles for Fighting Corruption and Safeguarding Integrity Among Justice and Security Officials*, A Global Forum on Fighting Corruption: Safeguarding Integrity Among Justice and Security Officials, Washington, DC, 24-26 February 1999.

52. For one critique of the U.S. International Crime Control Strategy and the responses of some U.S. officials, see the U.S. General Accounting Office Report, "International Crime Control: Sustained Executive Level Coordination of Federal Response Needed," GAO-01-629, August 2001, Washington, DC.

53. See for example, the autobiography of Leoluca Orlando, *Fighting the Mafia.* See also the Special Issue of *Trends in Organized Crime*, Spring 2000, Vol. 5. No. 3, which is devoted to the concept of a "culture of lawfulness" as an indispensable ingredient in buttressing the rule of law and countering crime and corruption.

54. The Office of National Drug Control Policy, The White House, *Performance Measures of Effectiveness, Report for 2001*, Washington, DC, 2001. For a discussion of measuring outputs, see David H. Bayley, *Police for the Future* (New York: Oxford University Press, 1994).

55. There is also the matter of conflicting governmental priorities. It may be judged to be more important to secure the support of a foreign government or element of a foreign government to achieve overarching foreign policy objectives than to deal with the PCN relationships in that country. Many believe that this explains the U.S. government's apparent failure to confront, for example, the Italian and Mexican governments about their PCNs during much of the Cold War.

2

Broken Bonds: Mafia and Politics in Sicily

Letizia Paoli

On 27 March 1993, Palermo prosecutors asked Parliament for authorization to proceed against Giulio Andreotti, the seven-time prime minister and one of the most important characters of the Italian political scene throughout the postwar period, on the charge that from the early 1970s, he was the main political referent of the largest Sicilian mafia association, Cosa Nostra.[1] The authorization was granted, and from September 1995 to October 1999, Andreotti was on trial in Palermo.[2] At the same time he was also accused by the Perugia prosecutor's office of having asked Sicilian *mafiosi* to murder Mino Pecorelli, a journalist who blackmailed him. In autumn 1999, Andreotti was finally acquitted on both charges on grounds of insufficient evidence,[3] but the court decisions could not dispel all doubts about his political career.

Notwithstanding the verdicts of acquittal, no other case better illustrates the pervasiveness of the political-criminal nexus in Italian society and the efforts that have been made for the first time in the 1990s to denounce and to eradicate it. Furthermore, Andreotti's inquiry is far from being the only one. Many less important politicians and state officials are currently facing similar charges (see *infra*).

The investigations in the 1990s by several prosecutors' offices in the *Mezzogiorno* (southern Italy) confirm the denunciations repeatedly made by small minorities of "enlightened" (mostly left-wing) observers since the late nineteenth century. Despite the great variation of subjects and situations, both past denunciations and current judicial inquiries point to the same fact: collusive agreements with state representatives have been a key element of the success and, truly, the very survival of southern Italian mafia groups. Not by chance, the most durable and powerful Italian mafia associations—the Sicilian Cosa Nostra and the Calabrian 'Ndrangheta, upon which our attention will be largely focused—are those that have been able to infiltrate state institutions most deeply.

Long doubted by most scholars,[4] the existence of Cosa Nostra and the 'Ndrangheta has from the mid-1980s been confirmed thanks to information disclosed by hundreds of former mafia members who have cooperated with the judiciary, the so-called *pentiti* (literally "those who have repented"). Due to these inside sources and to the personal commitment of some prosecutors, judges and police officials, knowledge about mafia groups' internal organization, culture, and actions has also grown tremendously in the last fifteen years, today reaching a once inconceivable level. We now know that both Cosa Nostra and the 'Ndrangheta are consortia, each made up by about ninety mafia families. The 'Ndrangheta *cosche* (i.e., mafia families) are located predominantly in the Reggio Calabria province and its environs, but entire mafia groups are also settled in northern Italy and abroad, most notably in Australia and Canada. More than six thousand people are suspected of belonging to the 'Ndrangheta. Most of the ninety families associated with Cosa Nostra are based in western Sicily (the provinces of Palermo, Trapani, Agrigento, and Caltanissetta), though Cosa Nostra groups also exist in the eastern part of the island and there are branches in northern Italy and in several North and South American countries. Today there are at least three thousand men ritually affiliated with Cosa Nostra families.[5]

Since the rise of the earliest antecedents of these criminal coalitions around the mid-nineteenth century, there have been contacts and exchanges between their members and state representatives and politicians. Indeed, from the 1880s onwards, the relationship between mafia and politics has been so deep and intense that numerous scholars believed the mafia phenomenon to consist of the interaction between criminal structures and political circuits.[6] Given the information disclosed by former mafia members about the existence of formal mafia associations, this view appears simplistic, but it is nonetheless true that mafia groups owe much of their enduring power and freedom of action to their relationships with politicians.

To reconstruct this century-old relationship, this first section focuses on the social and political context that saw the rise of mafia associations in southern Italy and the spread of a subculture that may be defined loosely as a mafia type. This subculture, it will be argued, has been a fertile "culture medium" for both the consolidation of mafia associations' power and the political-criminal nexus. The following sections reconstruct the evolution of the political criminal nexus, by focusing on three distinct historical phases. The second section is devoted to the Liberal Age (1860-1922), and the third to the fascist regime and the Second World War (1922-1945). The Republican period (1946-today) is analyzed in the last three sections of the chapter: the fourth one is concerned with the first two postwar decades, the fifth covers the 1970s and the 1980s. The sixth and final section focuses on the situation today, highlighting the growing vulnerabilities of the political-criminal nexus and, at the same time, the factors that may favor its perpetuation in the near future.

The Rise of Mafia Groups and the Sociopolitical
Context in the Nineteenth Century

There is one factor that is pointed out by most scholars to explain the development of the mafia phenomenon, considered as both an attitude and an organization, in nineteenth-century southern Italy: the inability of both the Bourbon and (for a long time) even the Italian governments to monopolize physical force in large parts of the Mezzogiorno and to gain legitimacy from the local population.[7] As such, the mafia is not the residue of a lawless past: "it is an outgrowth of the particular form that the process of state formation took in Italy."[8] The mafia developed because national systems of power expanded without fully subordinating the local systems of power and indeed had to rely on them—landlords of feudal ambitions and *mafiosi*—if they wanted to govern at all these areas. A vicious circle was consequently set in motion: "the chronic weakness of the state resulted in the emergence of self-help institutions and the exclusive power positions of informal groups made it impossible for the state to win the loyalty of the public, while its resultant weakness again strengthened the family, the clientele and *mafioso* positions."[9]

Weakened by the absence of an absolutist and enlightened state tradition, the Bourbons, who ruled southern Italy up to 1860, were unable to force the dissolution of feudal political and economic arrangements. Feudalism had formally been abolished in mainland Mezzogiorno in 1806 under French dominion, and in Sicily in 1812 under pressure from the British government that then protected the island. After the 1815 Restoration the Bourbons rapidly completed, on paper, the transition from institutions of feudal type to those typical of an administrative monarchy. In reality, the change from the old to the new system was much more problematic: the new state structures proved to have only a weak territorial connection and to be largely inefficient for regulating society.[10]

For many decades after the 1860 Unification of Italy, the Italian government fared even worse than the Bourbon one. With its mixture of weaknesses and sudden outbursts of indiscriminate and barbarous repression, the government of the unified Italy quickly managed to alienate the southerners' sympathies and so prevented the development of any trust in the new state institutions. The incorporation into the national kingdom of Italy was thus largely felt, particularly in Sicily, as yet another invasion by a foreign power. The same provisions that were to ensure the penetration of state institutions provoked public dissatisfaction and hostility. The first call-up decree, for example, gave rise to particular indignation: since the people of the Bourbon

Kingdom of the Two Sicilies had for centuries not been subjected to compulsory military conscription, thousands of young people did not answer the government call but preferred to go to the mountains and become bandits. Likewise, the introduction of a new system that taxed income as well as landed property and land rents, produced widespread discontent.[11]

On the other hand, Italian state institutions for a long time proved unable to effectively penetrate large parts of the south and to guarantee public safety. Policemen and *carabinieri* officials were long considered alien bodies by the population who scarcely cooperated with them. The lack of adequate means of communication and the high rate of illiteracy prevented state institutions from permeating Sicily and Calabria. As Leopoldo Franchetti (a Tuscan aristocrat who wrote a famous inquiry on Sicily) put it, in the late nineteenth century western Sicily—but the same considerations may also be extended to southern Calabria—"was a society which has all its orders founded on the presumption that no public authority exists."[12] Likewise, Pasquale Turiello spoke about "a barbaric intolerance" in the whole south for the legal and impersonal domain of the state. Diffidence, fear, and resentment dominated the attitudes of the popular masses toward a public power that had never given signs of social solidarity or help, but rather had imposed heavy financial and material burdens, and appeared distant and unable to protect them.

In considerable parts of the Mezzogiorno the decline of feudal economic and political structures was not followed by the imposition of a centralized political authority. Thus, far from decreasing private violence, the abolition of feudalism made recourse to force more open and 'democratic.'[13] From the beginning of the nineteenth century, in both regions different actors exploited the power *vacuum* produced by the incapability of state institutions and arrogated to themselves the right to employ violence. Among these actors, there were land owners who saw their feudal privileges challenged by the modernization of the country, *civili* (that is, bourgeois) who used violence to support their social ascent, and members of the lower classes for whom violence presented a means of rapid enrichment.[14]

Despite what has been stated until recently by most researchers, these characters did not act alone, embodying "a heroic and anarchical form of individualism."[15] Whereas the land owners, particularly in Sicily, surrounded themselves with bands of violent *campieri* in order to defend their declining semifeudal authority, the second and third subgroups, often under the protection of the former ones, gave rise to associations for the promotion of their own interests through coordinated action which did not exclude resorting to violence. Some of these associations, particularly those that succeeded in stabilizing themselves, are the direct ancestors of Cosa Nostra and the 'Ndrangheta. These are the "brotherhoods," the "shady sodalities,"[16] the *camorre,* that were established in many towns and villages of Sicily and Calabria throughout the second half of the nineteenth century. Though denied in the first scientific studies on the Sicilian mafia in the 1960s, their existence has recently been proven by the inquiries of a new generation of historians. The latter have, in fact, retrieved from state archives a variety of scientific, literary, and official sources that date back to the period before the First World War and confirm the existence of well-structured mafia groups already in the last decades of the nineteenth century.[17]

The ideology further compounding state institutions' incapability to guarantee law and order was the code of honor. Such a code entails the power to make oneself respected and to defend one's person and entourage without recourse to the instrumentalities of the state. Hence, to be respected in traditional southern Italian societies meant to be entitled to the deference of others that came from the ability to use violence. Those who had a reputation for violence inspired respect: "the fact that before any other strikes the mind in hearing stories about Sicily and especially Palermo is the authority, not only material but also moral, that violent people have."[18] In the traditional southern Italian society honor was the key criterion by which to assess a man's value. It was not by chance that around such a code mafia associations have built their own collective identity: honor, in fact, justified the private use of violence, which is typical of *mafia* action. Thus, since the end of the nineteenth century members of mafia groups have defined themselves as "men of honor," and have called their association *Onorata Società*.[19]

Another byproduct of the weakness of state institutions was the diffusion of a "double morality." On the one hand, Sicilians and Calabrians carefully respected the norms of the in-group relationships—the relationship with the family, relatives, ritual relatives, friends, patrons and clients—even at the cost of many sacrifices, sometimes even self-sacrifice. On the other hand, they felt no loyalty towards the state, which they considered an abstract entity. Likewise, the concept of a social advantage superior to individual interests was absent in the majority of the inhabitants of the two regions. Nor could they conceive of a law inspired by such a criterion. "In all," as the police official Giuseppe Alongi affirms,

> ...a conviction took shape that private vendetta was the best way to ensure that one's own right counted, that laws and courts were an administrative pleonasm, an irony; that Government and rich people were allied so as to tyrannize the poor people for whom the only chance left was to become *facinorosi*, thieves, bloody in order to gain protection and impunity for misdeeds and, thus, improve their economic situation.[20]

Hence, mafia associations may be said to have emerged and prospered in the gap between the state as it ought to be and ought to function and the state as it actually was and actually functioned in the southern regions of the country, in the divergence between the official set of values and the unofficial but effective moral. Imitating its northern European counterparts, the Italian state formally subscribed to universal standards of bureaucratic honesty, recruitment by efficiency and allocation according to the needs of economic rationality. Nonetheless, particularistic categories of orientation and behavior long remained diffused in Sicily and Calabria as well as in most of the country, infiltrating the very structure of the state. Indeed, it was in this divergence between a "formal" and a "material constitution" that mafia associations were able to develop and thrive. These groups' collective identity and power founded on widespread subcultural codes—honor and the primacy of particularistic ties over universalistic ones—which were shared by consistent parts of the southern Italian population were subscribed to even by many politicians and state employees. Chiefs and members of mafia associations long fulfilled functions of social integration that state bodies were unable to fulfill. *Mafiosi* protected persons and property in their communities, repressed the most serious threats to the established order, countered behavior in conflict with subcultural norms, and mediated conflicts within the local society and the relations between that society and the outside world.[21] Thus, mafia power substituted for effective state institutions and perpetuated their weakness, preventing the diffusion of universalistic attitudes and practices and the strengthening and legitimization of the state apparatus in large parts of southern Italy.

The Liberal Age (1860-1922)

These two elements—the weakness of state institutions and the strength and legitimacy of mafia power—are the most important factors explaining the consolidation of the political-criminal nexus in the Liberal Age. Though formally condemning mafia violence and occasionally fiercely repressing it, state institutions throughout the second half of the nineteenth century usually came to terms with the representatives of mafia power and de facto delegated them the maintenance of public order in the territories under their control. A veritable "dual regime" was established.[22] Claiming a power over their homeland and effectively controlling a considerable amount of its human, social, and economic resources, mafia associations set their relationships with state institutions on an equal basis, almost like two sovereign entities, and saw their power recognized as legitimate, not only in the eyes of the local public opinion but also by state representatives and officials. As the *Commissione Parlamentare Antimafia* acknowledged in 1993:

> ...in practice, the relationships between institutions and mafia took place, for many years, in the form of relationships between two distinct sovereignties: neither would attack the other as long as each remained within its own boundaries...an attack (by state forces) would be made only in response to an attack by Cosa Nostra, after which they would go back to being good neighbors again.[23]

This relationship was eased by the *mafiosi* attitude towards state bodies and representatives: notwithstanding the proclaimed antagonism towards state authorities, the *capimafia*, once they had secured their power with violence, hardly ever put themselves in open opposition to state institutions or publicly fostered non-compliance with state laws. No matter how he had begun his career, the leader of a mafia group was no longer a bandit, an outlaw. Indeed, he portrayed himself as a man of law and order and paid formal respect to state authority. By the same token, mafia power was legitimized by state authorities in several ways. As late as 1958, for instance, Michele Navarra, the uncontested chief of Corleone, was granted the honorary title of *Cavaliere dell'ordine al merito della Repubblica italiana* two months before he died in a mafia ambush.[24] Similar honors were bestowed upon other mafia chiefs, such as Calogero Vizzini, Giuseppe Genco Russo, and Santo Flores. Such a process of "legalization" of mafia power often led to the roles of *mafioso* and state authorities coinciding. As a character of a novel written by the Calabrian writer Saverio Strati affirms:

> ...they all know who these *mafiosi*, these courageous men are. They are public characters: they occupy places in the Commune as assessors or even as mayors. Protected by the politicians—people whisper that even a Minister was present at a plenary meeting of the regional mafia.[25]

The complementary nature of mafia and state power was acknowledged time and again by public officials who openly protected *mafiosi* and defended their role as proxies for the state in the maintenance of order. In 1955, for example, on the occasion of Calogero Vizzini's death, one of Italy's highest legal dignitaries, Giuseppe Guido Lo Schiavo, attorney general in the Supreme Court of Appeals, wrote in a legal periodical:

> It has been said that the mafia despises the police and the magistracy, but it is incorrect. The mafia has always had respect for the magistracy and for Justice. It has submitted to its sentences, and has not obstructed the judge in his work. In the pursuit of bandits and outlaws it openly sided with the force of law and order.... Today, Don Calogero Vizzini's successor is making his reputation and in time he will succeed to his predecessor's authoritative position in the counsels of the secret conclave. May his labors increase in which the laws of the state are held, and may they be for the social betterment of all.[26]

The complementary nature of this relationship was strengthened by the total inclusion of mafia associations into the web of clientelistic relationships through which the central government integrated southern elites into the national political system and secured their invariable support for government majorities. From 1876, when the then-called Left came to power, the Mezzogiorno deputies became the mainstay of the "transformist" project first initiated by Agostino Depretis and continued by his successors up to the outbreak of World War I. This project aimed to control the threats posed to the northern bourgeoisie's dominion by peasants' protests and the urban masses.[27]

In such a system the clientele run by the *capomafia* and composed of his mafia consociates, his clients, and his blood relatives, represented "the specific application of a more general system. Its peculiarity distinguished itself for the fact that in this case one reached the extreme of the armed menace and the suppression of the antagonist and the opponent."[28]

It was, in particular, the extension of suffrage in 1882 that opened the season of a mutually profitable collaboration between politicians and *mafiosi* in Sicily and Calabria—a collaboration that, notwithstanding the turnover of regimes and parties, has lasted up to today. By lowering the census requirement and giving the vote to all literate men, the reform widened the electorate, previously restricted to a selected group of aristocrats and bourgeois (less than 2 percent of the overall population). Thus, the candidates were compelled to gain the votes of the lower and middle classes. As the Sicilian political scientist Gaetano Mosca noted:

> ...the *cosche* immediately understood the great advantage that they could draw from their participation in the political and administrative elections. This participation became more effective and active after the law widened the suffrage and gave the right to vote to the members of the *cosche* and to the classes in which they had greater influence and enjoyed prestige."[29]

In exchange for mobilizing their own clientele as well as for using violence to discourage opposing candidates or to convince uncertain electors, the *mafiosi* obtained all kinds of favors. Moreover, since electoral competition was fierce, the latter were often in a position of advantage and could bargain with the conditions to support this or that candidate. One of the first favors expected was protection from judicial investigations: if necessary the political patron was prepared to intervene with the responsible police officer or judge in order to guarantee a mild sentence, the revocation of an *ammonizione* (a formal police warning), the concession of an arms license, or similar acts. In addition, *mafiosi* were granted substantial contracts for tax collection and for public works. Occasionally the *capomafia* himself or more frequently his political patron even obtained the control of the town council through which they could further enlarge their following and consolidate their power.

Public offices were already at that time a crucial resource contested by *mafiosi*. Controlling these offices enabled *mafiosi* to manage public resources and so the *cosca* could provide jobs and revenue to a whole range of adherents as well as to the *mafiosi*'s relatives and clients. The account given in 1889 by Giovanna Cirillo, the widow of the Public Security delegate Stanislao Rampolla, about the mafia action in Marineo, a large center of the Palermitan province is emblematic in this respect.[30] The chief of the local mafia sect, which met under the front of the congregation of the Holy Crucifix, was the notary Filippo Calderoni, who was mayor of Marineo from 1860 up to 1866 and then again from 1879 to 1892. In such a position, Calderoni provided communal jobs and income to relatives and associates, many of whom were notorious evildoers, employed in the corps of field and communal guards. These positions were then "abusively" used by the mayor "in order to damage the properties of people belonging to the adversary party,"[31] and to extort kickbacks. Their activities were also particularly precious during election periods so as to persuade undecided voters or perpetrate blatant fraud. Moreover, according to a custom that has lasted to the present, public offices were used to increase one's own economic means and to consolidate one's position of power broker. Significantly, Calderoni channeled all the petitioners to his private notary office or to the legal bureaus of his two sons, where mediations and private *composizioni* of conflicts were offered without recourse to state bodies.

The services *mafiosi* provided to their political patrons were not limited to the elections. In an open-ended exchange, members of mafia associations provided all sorts of violent services, ranging from threats to extortions and even to murder. The cases involving lower- and middle-ranking victims are countless. Occasionally, however, if requested by their political patrons, the members of mafia associations also targeted aristocrats and high bourgeois. In February 1893, for example, the Marquis Emanuele Notarbartolo, former mayor of Palermo and former director of the *Banco di Sicilia* was killed, after he had denounced several illegal operations carried out by the bank, some of which included shady political contributions. The murder was carried out by two *mafiosi* from Villabate, most probably on the account of Raffaele Palizzolo, a national deputy of the regional party and one of the bank's governors, who was threatened by Notarbartolo's denunciations.

Notarbartolo's murder marks the first homicide of a high state representative carried out by the mafia. It is also remarkable for two other reasons. First, it shed light on the intermingling of mafia interests and political circuits and demonstrated the full compatibility of mafia actors into wider clientelistic practices. Second, the subsequent judicial proceeding fully revealed the collusive attitude held by the Sicilian landowning class and considerable sections of the national state apparatus towards the mafia at the end of the nineteenth century. Since the very beginning of the investigations, suspicion fell on Palizzolo himself and on the two above-mentioned mafia members, who were his clients and who were charged with the material execution of the murder. For six years, however, Palizzolo was kept out of the investigations thanks to his links with southern right-wing political leaders and his connections in the Palermitan public administration. Finally in 1902, in Milan, Palizzolo was condemned to thirty years' imprisonment, in spite of an attempted cover-up by some high prosecutors and the depositions of many prestigious Sicilians. As a consequence of this sentence, many influential members of the Sicilian economic and political classes organized a "Pro

Sicilia Committee," asking for the repeal of the sentence by the *Corte di Cassazione*. Their undertaking was successful and in a subsequent trial, held in Florence in 1904, Palizzolo was declared innocent because of insufficient proof and returned to Palermo as a triumphant hero.[32]

In the so-called "Giolitti Era" (1903-14), when the need to obtain southern votes grew as a result of another partial extension of suffrage and the rise of the Popular (Catholic) and Socialist parties, collusion between government candidates and the mafia frequently received the open support of state authorities and particularly of the Prefects who represented the central government on a local level. The malfeasances were so extensive that Giovanni Giolitti, who was almost uninterruptedly prime minister from 1903 to 1914, was called "the minister of the underworld." According to Gaetano Salvemini, Giolitti:

> ...exploits the miserable conditions of the *Mezzogiorno* in order to link the mass of southern deputies to himself: he gives them "white paper" in the local administrations; during elections he gives them the underworld and the *Questura*; he ensures them and their clients the most unconditioned impunity; he lets the electoral trials fall into prescription and intervenes with amnesties at the right moment; he leaves the mayors condemned for electoral crimes in office; he gives decorations to the guilty; he never punishes delinquent delegates; he deepens and consolidates violence and corruption, where the local misery develops spontaneously; he introduces them officially in the villages where they were before ignored.

The Hon. Giolitti is certainly not the first man of government of the United Italy that has considered the Mezzogiorno as a conquered land, open to all evil. But none has ever been so brutal, so cynical, so unscrupulous as he in founding his political power on the exploitation, the perversion and scorn of the Mezzogiorno of Italy; none has made more systematic and open use, in the elections of the Mezzogiorno, of this sort of violence and crime.[33]

Mafia infiltration into the political system was not uniform in the two regions. Especially in the most backward areas of Calabria, it was less pervasive than in the island. Up until the First World War, different tendencies coexisted in the 'Ndrangheta. Whereas some mafia families were inserted into wider political clienteles supporting candidates of the majority party, others only marginally participated in the political spoils system. The state presence was so weak in some villages of Calabria that local mafia groups could only marginally profit from collusion with state representatives. In both contexts, however, much more than in recent times, *mafiosi* tended to be in a subordinate position vis-à-vis their political protectors. Though several *capimafia* successfully integrated into the local ruling elites, the range of their power rarely exceeded the village and its surroundings: to influence decisions taken at the regional or national level, *mafiosi* usually had to turn to their political patrons. The superiority of the latter was reinforced by the fact that most of them came from a higher social background than the members of mafia groups. The hierarchical, unequal nature of these relationships also reflected relations of subordination in the economic sphere. The political patron was often the absentee landowner who lent his inland estates to the *mafia gabellotto* or hired *mafiosi* to supervise peasant labor.

As with most patron-client relations, however, the relationship linking *mafiosi* to their political patrons was inherently unstable. As *gabellotti*, many *capimafia* succeeded in accumulating considerable wealth at the expense of landowners and even in buying large properties themselves. Particularly in the years following the end of the First World War, when the repressive services provided by *mafiosi* became indispensable to control peasant protest, the *mafiosi* gained strength vis-à-vis their political and economic patrons, so much that the latter, feeling threatened, favored the rise of fascism to protect their social role and properties.[34]

Beyond the differences in power, an element of moral equality can also be traced. Throughout the Liberal Age, in fact, the relationship between *mafiosi* and politicians was largely founded on a common cultural background, on a shared system of values and codes that went beyond and, at the same time, reinforced the immediate exchange of favors.[35] Up to the early 1960s local and regional notables regularly accepted *capimafia* invitations to attend their major family celebrations, such as weddings and baptisms, and to act in these occasions as witness or godfather, thus establishing a lifetime relation of ritual kinship (called *comparaggio*) with the *mafiosi*. Banquets in country estates—called *schiticchio*—or in secluded places in Palermo and Reggio Calabria were also strategic occasions for establishing and maintaining ties between the mafia and its professional interlocutors.[36] The legitimacy of the mafia (meant as a system of values and not only as a criminal organization) was such that, in order to maximize their consensus, Sicilian politicians did not have scruples against defining themselves as *mafiosi*. In 1925, for instance, in a famous speech during the electoral campaign for the last free administrative elections before the full consolidation of the fascist regime, the Liberal deputy Vittorio Emanuele Orlando (who was also prime minister for a short time at the end of the First World War), was reported to have said:

> ...if by the word "mafia" we understand a sense of honor pitched in the highest key; a refusal to tolerate anyone's predominance or overbearing behavior...a generosity of spirit which, while it meets strength head on, is indulgent to the weak; loyalty to friends.... If such feelings and such behavior are what people mean by the mafia...then we are actually speaking of the special characteristic of the Sicilian soul. And I declare that I am a *mafioso*, and proud to be one.[37]

The Fascist Regime and the Second World War (1922-1945)

The fascist regime strongly hit the lower echelons of the mafia organizations both in Sicily and in Calabria. Particularly in the eastern Palermo province, where the anti-mafia campaigns staged in the mid-1920s by the "Iron Prefect" Cesare Mori were most violent, hundreds of *mafiosi* as well as their relatives and co-villagers were indiscriminately arrested, condemned to heavy imprisonment terms or sent to forced residence on isolated islands. Many others were forced to emigrate. The few who escaped arrest or returned home during the 1930s had to accept humble roles in village affairs. Nonetheless, though the scarcity of information does not allow certainty, there are indications that in the western Sicilian inland and even in southern Calabria the most educated and/or best-connected members of the mafia as well as the *mafiosi*'s unaffiliated patrons survived largely unscathed and often obtained positions of power and prestige within the regime itself. Calogero Vizzini from Villalba and Genco Russo from Mussomeli, for example, were hardly bothered by the anti-mafia repression, and in those years others, such as Michele Navarra from Corleone, built their own system of power.[38] In Raffadali the *mafioso* Vincenzo Di Carlo was an active member of the local fascist party and held relevant positions in the city administration.[39] When Mori in the late 1920s extended his investigations and denunciations to members of the aristocracy and high bourgeoisie, the campaign came to a brusque halt, Mussolini dismissed the Prefect, and the mafia was declared defeated.[40]

Fascism did indeed answer landowners' requests for protection and allowed them to refuse the impositions of the *mafiosi*. Nonetheless, it only provided a substitute: "it monopolized the use of violence without fundamentally changing the social milieu in which the mafia had flourished."[41] In the power vacuum that followed the collapse of the fascist regime and that the Allied Military Government of Occupied Territories (AMGOT) was unable to fill, mafia power rapidly re-emerged. Indeed, the AMGOT recognized mafia power.[42] Between 1943 and 1945, AMGOT appointed numerous *capimafia* mayors of several towns and villages of western Sicily and the Reggio Calabria province.[43]

The 1950s and 1960s

After the decline during the fascist regime, *mafiosi* again succeeded in securing a crucial role in the postwar political competition. The creation of the Republic and the rise of mass parties were not enough to destroy the clientelism used to obtain political consensus in the south. There was, indeed, a transformation from the traditional vertical clientelism, founded on notables, to a horizontal or bureaucratic one, capable of recruiting interest groups at the mass level through an organization of party officials.[44] But in such a system of mass patronage the associates of mafia families secured a role no less important than the one they had played vis-à-vis traditional notables. Indeed, universal suffrage in 1948 and the ideological split of the electorate along the left-right division made *mafiosi*'s intervention essential for the management of political clientele and the appropriation of public offices. At the same time, the "occupation" of government by the new post-World War II majority party, the *Democrazia Cristiana* (DC), and the devolution of huge resources to the enhancement of the industrialization of the south multiplied the possibilities of clientelistic exchange.[45] Thus, though many Sicilian *capimafia* supported the separatist movement right after the war, by the early 1950s the great majority had been co-opted into the DC. As Salvatore Cancemi, the former chief of the Palermitan Porta Nuova family put it, "Cosa Nostra's orientation has always been to vote the Christian Democracy party. Certainly in Cosa Nostra we have never voted for the communists and the fascists. If somebody preferred the exponents of smaller parties other than the Christian Democrats, this was allowed."[46]

The case of Palermo, Sicily's regional capital, exemplifies such a transformation well, anticipating processes that took place in other parts of southern Italy in following decades. Several prominent Palermitan politicians—elected at the local, regional, and national level—ritually affiliated "men of honor."[47] The leverage of mafia associations remained consistent even with respect to those politicians who were not formal mafia members—such as Giovanni Gioia, Salvo Lima, and Vito Ciancimino, perhaps the main figures in the DC occupation of the city administration. The three of them headed a group of Christian Democrat professional politicians who were tied to the faction *Iniziativa democratica* under the national leadership of Amintore Fanfani and which managed to occupy the Palermitan communal and provincial administration as well as the key positions at the regional level for about two decades, from the mid-1950s to the 1970s, after having ousted the old-style notables that had ruled in the immediate postwar years.[48]

For the members of this clique, mafia families continued to fulfill the crucial function of safeguarding political support and running party sections. During Fanfani's leadership, party sections had become "the keystone for control of the party because it is there that the *tesseramento* takes place."[49] Within the DC, in fact, ruling offices were assigned through elections, for which only the *tesserati* (that is, those who had a party card) were eligible. Thus, he who controlled the process of recruitment at the local level exerted a considerable influence in the selection of the party leadership at even the national level. It was exactly in this local grounding of the political power (at the local as well as at the national level) that the leverage of mafia groups lay. Though local politicians' power was enhanced by their relationship with the center (the Rome government) and, most notably, by their access to state patronage resources, the means by which that power was generated were local.[50]

Thus, notwithstanding the apparent disparity of power—the *Giovani turchi* (as the *fanfaniani* were called) in those years controlled all the fundamental levers of economic and political power in the region—the relationship between *mafiosi* and politicians was not characterized by the complete subordination of the former to the latter. The egalitarian character of such a relationship was favored by the common social origin of both *capimafia* and politicians. Unlike most representatives of the prewar southern Italian political class, who were aristocrats or high bourgeois, the Palermitan *fanfaniani* were *homines novi*: as many *mafiosi*, they came from a low or middle social background and had struggled to be fully integrated into the ruling elite.

The influence of Cosa Nostra on the Sicilian political world was remarkable: "The lists of candidates," recalls Gioacchino Pennino, the first politician, man of honor, who started to cooperate with the magistrates, "were decided by Lima, Pennino [uncle of the *pentito* and chief of the Brancaccio mafia family], and Brandaleone [one of Lima's followers and assessor in the Palermo administration as well as member of the Porta Nuova mafia family]."[51] Likewise, according to Buscetta, Pennino's house was "the natural seat of the DC."[52] According to a recent estimate (based on the political characters mentioned by the *pentiti*), between 40 and 75 percent of the Christian Democrat deputies and about 40 percent of all the deputies elected in Western Sicily between 1950 and 1992 were openly supported by Cosa Nostra.[53]

Thanks to their political protection, members of Palermitan mafia families managed to exert a heavy influence over four basic sectors of the local economy: the credit market, wholesale markets, the construction sector, and the labor market. Exploiting their political friendships, the *mafiosi* often obtained privileged forms of credit from large regional banks as well as the promotion or transfer of people that they had recommended. The career of Francesco Vassallo is exemplary: a man of humble origins who suddenly received a loan of 700 million Lira (then more than US $1.1 million) from the *Cassa di Risparmio delle province siciliane* without offering any form of guarantee and who became, within few years, one of the biggest building contractors in Palermo.[54]

Mafia influence was also pervasive in the Palermitan wholesale markets. The report of the subcommittee of the Parliamentary Anti-Mafia Commission appointed to investigate the wholesale market in Palermo ascertained that between 1963 and 1965, 18 mafia ex-convicts, denounced for delinquent association, were active in the fruit and vegetable market; 64 were producers, retailers, or merchants who had been the object of preventive police measures; in addition, 37 franchise holders and five fruit and vegetable wholesalers had criminal records.[55] The long-standing president of the wholesaler guild was Giacomo Alliotta, later targeted by a preventive police measure because he was suspected of the crime of mafia association.[56] The assignment of the stands, noted the above-mentioned parliamentary sub-committee, "was entirely left in the hands of the commissioners, with no interference of the institution in charge, the Palermo city council. This means that it was left in the hands of the strongest, that is the mafia *cosche* of the wholesale markets."[57]

Though in partnership with their political patrons, Cosa Nostra associates also dominated the labor market. The *pentito* Gaspare Mutolo recalls that "if one looked for a job, he did not go to the Employment Office but he tried through the *mafioso*, who, if it was opportune, talked with the man in charge of the Employment Office."[58] Mafia clients as well as *mafiosi* themselves usually found a job in the public sector, in which a relevant number of positions opened up in the first postwar decades. In Sicily, which was granted an autonomous status in 1946, an administrative apparatus counting several thousand clerks and officials—the *Regione Siciliana*—was brought into being *ex nihilo*, together with a whole range of public agencies whose purpose was to intervene in all the major sectors of the Sicilian economy. The employment of mafia affiliates and acolytes was greatly aided by clientelistic methods according to which recruitment was carried out: out of the 8,887 people hired by the region between 1945 and 1963, 8,236—that is, more than 90 percent—were employed without the usual public competition, "i.e., one must suppose on the basis of recommendations and relationships of friendship and power."[59]

Lastly, mafia acolytes established a tight control over the construction sector which, given the overall weakness of the manufacturing sector, accounted—and still today accounts—for a disproportionate share of industrial employment in all the Mezzogiorno.[60] Once again the mafia penetration in a key economic sector took place under the aegis of the Christian Democrat elite. By the early 1970s the construction industry in the city of Palermo was almost entirely in the hands of the mafia: "...mafia organizations completely control the building sector in Palermo—the quarries where aggregates are mined, site clearance firms, cement plants, metal depots for the construction industry, sanitary ware wholesalers and so on..."[61] When *mafiosi* did not succeed in getting a subcontract, they imposed the payment of a protection tax: "*mafiosi* or elements controlled by the mafia are generally the guardians of the building sites, of the areas, deposits and establishment of the suburb houses and the rural funds."[62]

The collection of revenue in all the island was also controlled by two ritually affiliated members of Cosa Nostra, the cousins Ignazio and Nino Salvo. Thanks to a shrewd exploitation of their political relationships, in the late 1950s the Salvos obtained the contract for revenue collection and won extremely favorable conditions. They were granted a 10 percent premium, as opposed to a 3.3 percent national average. They were able to become, and, up to their indictment for mafia associations in 1984, to remain two of the wealthiest and most powerful entrepreneurs of the island as well as the *domini* of one of the largest DC electoral clienteles.[63]

In other parts of Sicily and Calabria, the relationships between *mafiosi* and representatives of political authorities up to the late 1960s remained looser and less developed. In Calabria, for example, the fight was fierce at the local level and the *mafiosi* rushed to occupy the communal offices. A report written by the Reggio Calabria Prefect in 1955 pointed this out. In the towns, it said:

> the underworld controls the local activities and quite often the political activity (given that in these communes it is impossible to enter and to maintain oneself in the public administration without the support and favor of representatives of the local underworld, which is reciprocated with counter-services of both tolerances and abuses).

Thanks to such control, *mafiosi* were able to exercise a "systematic intervention...in rents, public tenders, service, concessions, the collection of civic rights and so on, from which they earn illicit profits."[64] Neither were the new bodies of *parastato* protected from mafia interference. In the Gioia Tauro plain, for example, the 'Ndrangheta attention was especially directed towards the *cooperative* which absorbed most of the citrus production and became the distribution seat of the subsidies granted by the state to the farmers.[65]

The cooperation with national politicians was, however, less systematic than in Sicily. Unlike Cosa Nostra members, the sympathies of the Calabrian men of honor were distributed to a plurality of parties: whereas many *mafiosi* were part of the clienteles of government party notables (particularly the DC and the Liberal Party, PLI), on the Ionic side several *'ndranghetisti* were members of the PCI (*Partito Comunista Italiano*) and were even elected mayors of their own villages in the Communist lists.[66] A third group, which formed in the late 1960s under the leadership of the De Stefano brothers, had connections with the Right, in all its political expressions (that is, from the official party, the *Movimento Sociale Italiano*, up to the extra-parliamentary movements) and actively supported them in the organization of the revolt that took place in Reggio Calabria in 1970 against making Catanzaro the regional headquarters.[67] Different political sympathies were sometimes found even within the same mafia group. "In Africo, for example, two opposing tendencies co-existed...the Bruzzanitis supported the PCI; the priest, don Stilo, instead, represented the DC, and both lived together in the *Onorata Società*."[68] Such a plurality of orientations was favored by the widespread conviction that a closer alliance with the parties holding the majority at the national level would not, in itself, offer advantages to the *cosche*. Meaningfully the postwar affiliation of many *'ndranghetisti* to the Communist Party is explained in the following way by the *pentito* Gullà:

> Even if it may seem a strange way of reasoning, there was indeed a historical moment when in many Calabrian villages, not to say in many areas, there were true zones of superimposition between the environment of the *Onorata Società* and the communist environment, since there was no unified political line in the 'Ndrangheta.
>
> Each of us went according to his own tendencies, his sympathies, not so much following economic interests, because there were not real economic interests in that period when the criminal level was archaic. There was no close relationship with the

public administration. The predominant economic sector was the agricultural one and the transformation of some products, such as, citruses. Hence there were not very relevant interests. In those times the 'Ndrangheta nursed agrarian interests, such as the *sensalia* [i.e., mediation] and the *guardiania* [i.e., protection of rural estates in exchange for a reward]. Everything turned out into a "systematic" extortion of these [agricultural] activities, given that there was only a little bit of construction, it was too early.[69]

Notwithstanding the local differences, in both contexts the connections with politicians and state officials—combined with the persisting legitimization of mafia groups among considerable sections of the local population and the indifference of the national public opinion towards the mafia problem— were sufficient to allow members of mafia groups to easily relieve themselves of law enforcement pressure. In those years *Mafiosi* on the run could comfortably hide at home, without taking any special precautions.[70] The only exception to such a pattern in Sicily was the five-year period that followed the massacre of Ciaculli on 30 June 1963: the murder of seven policemen had a sensational impact at the national level and led to a serious repressive campaign. Between 1963 and the end of the decade, all the leading figures of the Sicilian mafia found themselves in prison, in compulsory exile or on the wanted list. Nonetheless, most of them were freed for lack of evidence by the Catanzaro and Bari courts that held the two most important trials in 1968 and 1969.[71]

In Calabria the attention of law enforcement institutions was even more ephemeral: except for the so-called *operation Marzano* from August to October 1955, the *'ndranghetisti* were hardly aggravated by police officials and easily obtained passports, driving and arms licenses from the *Questura*, and absconded either on the Aspromonte or, more comfortably, to their homes. In 1955, the fugitive Vincenzo Romeo, from Bova, even succeeded in publicly marrying in his own town church, inviting "the chiefs of the Honored Society" to his reception.[72]

The attention of law enforcement bodies, furthermore, was limited to the persons who committed violent crimes and avoided completely the topic of mafia infiltration into the legal economy and political institutions. For example, it is striking that, notwithstanding calls from the First Parliamentary Anti-mafia Commission (1963-76), no investigation was started in those years on the activity of the Palermo Commune. Likewise, the Palermo Chief Prosecutor kept a report on irregularities in the management of the wholesale fruit market in a drawer for three years before starting an investigation on the matter. Though some police officials and prosecutors were most probably corrupted or threatened by the *mafiosi*, this judicial strategy can be fully understood only by keeping in mind that the law enforcement apparatus was largely an expression of the local bourgeoisie and reflected its moral values and its political sympathies. In such a *Weltanschauung*, mafia and clientelistic

practices were deemed acceptable and the *capimafia* and their protectors in
state bodies deserved respect and were thus considered to be not prosecutable
since they were members of the dominant power group.[73]

The Last Thirty Years

Following Palermo's example, from the mid-1960s all the *cosche* associated with the Cosa Nostra and 'Ndrangheta underwent an "entrepreneurial
transformation," attributing a growing importance to licit and illicit economic activities and orienting them towards rapid enrichment. This trend,
which has accelerated over the last three decades, was dictated by the progressive fading away of the subculture of honor in the society at large. Instead, in the eyes of public opinion in the 1960s and 1970s, wealth became
the basis of reputation, the most readily recognizable proof of success. To
possess wealth was imperative for anyone who wanted to enjoy a position of
respect.[74] In order to cope with this cultural change and not to lose their
preeminent position in the local communities, a growing number of mafia
associates have, in the last forty or so years, progressively used their brotherhood bonds for personal enrichment.

This adaptation process was greatly favored by two larger trends, which
provided mafia groups in Sicily and in Calabria with hitherto unforeseen
chances of enrichment: the expansion of world illegal markets (most notably
in tobacco and narcotics) and the growth of public spending in the
Mezzogiorno. Mafia groups' involvement into the international illegal markets largely took place independently of their connections with political
authorities (which remained, however, extremely important even in this field
to avoid penal prosecution).[75] However, the alliance with politicians and
state representatives has been fundamental to consolidate mafia groups' leverage over the public works market, an activity that has over the 1980s, been
producing profits "comparable to the illegal income from drug trafficking."[76]

As far as the involvement of mafia consortia in the public works market is
concerned, an evolutionary path can be drawn. Already in the 1950s, each
group of the two criminal networks imposed kickbacks on building contractors working within their territories. In the late 1960s, however, when large
sums of public money were devoted to the industrialization of the south,
mafia entrepreneurs did not content themselves with the parasitic collection
of a "protection" tax, but claimed a more direct involvement in the public
works, through the execution of subcontracts. Due to the weak opposition
shown by the large national companies working in the Mezzogiorno, which
usually preferred to come to terms with mafia power rather than denouncing
pressures and resisting extortion claims, the *mafiosi* obtained what they
wanted. A third phase opened in the early 1980s. Since then, in fact, mafia
bosses succeeded in being fully accepted in the so-called *comitati d'affari*

(business committees) made up of entrepreneurial groups, state representatives, and officials, which controlled the whole system of parceling out tenders at the outset of planning of the public investment. In a couple of important judicial inquiries, the Palermo prosecutor's office has been able to trace the mechanisms by which public money was maneuvered in Sicily during the 1980s, coming to the conclusion that:

> ...in the second half of the 1980s the mafia began to establish itself in a pre-existing system of illegal allocation of public contracts previously dominated exclusively by large-scale enterprises, politicians and public officials. This involvement over the years has progressively increased, tending to gain in some sectors a role of total and hierarchical control, in others, impinging on the space formerly reserved exclusively for the "business committees" and in others still, developing a kind of co-existence with these same "business committees."[77]

A sort of "duopoly" was established that sought to subject the public works market to the complete top-downwards control of two strong subjects—Cosa Nostra and the *comitati d'affari*—that had joined forces in a kind of symbiosis cemented by silence and complicity. The alliance between national construction companies and politicians, on one side, and mafia representatives, on the other, has been so tight that some northern entrepreneurs and several local politicians have been charged of the crime of mafia association (art. 416 *bis* Penal Code).[78]

In Calabria, too, a major investigation concerning the construction of the Gioia Tauro Power Plant that currently sees ENEL (the National Electricity Company) involved in one of the most clamorous scandals of the entire post-war period[79] demonstrated that the 'Ndrangheta took part in the direct management of the works and reached agreements with state officials, entrepreneurs, and politicians. As in Sicily, mafia conditioning no longer takes place only "downstream," at the end of the economic process of public investment—subcontracts and extortions—but, more seriously, "upstream" at the very beginning of the process, with decisions taken jointly by mafia representatives, ENEL, and the national building companies involved in the largest works, through the intermediation of a number of liaison elements. As the Palmi prosecutors stated, "there is a stable intertwining between mafia and political corruption. The relationship between the official economy and mafia economy has become organic."[80]

The case of the Gioia Tauro Power Plant is not an exception. The ability to exert a strong influence over the expense accounts of the local and national administrations is true of all the *cosche* in the province. In Reggio Calabria, where the stakes became huge in the late 1980s—the so-called "Reggio decree" provided 600 billion lira (then more than US $460 million) for the reclamation and the development of the city—mafia *cosche* went as far as murdering a politician, Ludovico Ligato, former president of the *Ferrovie dello Stato* (State Railway). By claiming a 10 percent kickback for himself, Ligato, who had returned in those years to Reggio Calabria, jeopardized the agreements that had already been reached between 'Ndrangheta groups and the local politicians.[81]

Growing involvement in economic activities succeeded in slowing the process of delegitimization of mafia power but not in stopping it entirely. Such a process, in fact, is the result of the contradictory but undeniable process of economic and cultural modernization that has overwhelmed the whole country in the postwar decades, reaching even the most peripheral areas of the Mezzogiorno.[82] The evolution of the larger social and cultural systems has progressively undermined the mafia "subsystem of meaning"—and *in primis* the code of honor—by which mafia chiefs had long legitimated their power both in face of the local communities and their own acolytes. Thus, notwithstanding the fortunes that mafia chiefs have accumulated over the last thirty years and the "military" arsenals that they have been able to build up, the authority of the mafia has decreased vis-à-vis the larger public and their subjects. Though the process was not immediately perceived, either by public opinion or by scholars and law enforcement officials monitoring the mafia phenomenon, the decline of mafia popular legitimacy continued even during the 1980s. Thus, this decade witnessed a "paradoxical" situation: what appeared outwardly as the apex of mafia economic and political mafia power carried the seeds of its future delegitimization and decay.

This contradiction clearly emerges in the relationship between *mafiosi* and politicians and state officials. On one side, the 1980s saw the highest moment of mafia leverage on the political world. The rise of the entrepreneurial mafia did away with the old subordination of the *mafioso* to his political patrons. What has been uncovered by judicial investigations throughout the Mezzogiorno can no longer be classified within the scheme of the traditional patronage system. Nor can it be described merely as an exchange of votes against public works between politicians and mafia entrepreneurs. What emerges is the existence of permanent and equal electoral and business pacts (often behind the cover of straw men) between politicians and modern *capimafia*. The inquiries carried out in the early 1990s by the Reggio Calabria and Palmi *Procure* have, for example, extensively proved that in Calabria the 'ndranghetisti not only exert a tight control on the political and administrative life of their communities[83] but, as in Sicily, they also play a decisive role in the selection and promotion of the candidates for the national Parliament. During the ninth legislature (1992-94), the Reggio Calabria prosecutors requested the parliament to authorize proceeding against four Calabrian members of Parliament (Dep. Riccardo Misasi, Dep. Sandro Principe, Dep. Paolo Romeo, and Sen. Sisinio Zito) on the ground of suspected criminal mafia association.[84] In March 1996, Giacomo Mancini, former national secretary of the Socialist party and Cosenza mayor, was condemned to a ten-year sentence for external support to a mafia association. Additionally, the investigation initiated by the Palmi chief prosecutor, who seized electoral material from the homes of well-known mafia bosses during the political elections of 5 April 1992, confirmed mafia interest in engaging in electoral campaigns so as to have candidates elected who would offer protection and support to their criminal activities.[85]

Indeed in Calabria, where the crime consortium enjoyed a persistent neglect by the national law enforcement headquarters and the public opinion, the intermingling between mafia consortia and clientelistic-business networks reached an unprecedented phase after the mid-1970s: the unification of the two power structures through the infiltration of state institutions by men formally affiliated to the mafia confederation. As Roberto Pennisi, a prosecutor of *Procura della Repubblica di Reggio Calabria*, stated in front of the *Commissione Antimafia,*

> ...often when we talk about the relationship between the mafia and segments of the state, of politics, of professions (physicians, lawyers, engineers and so on), we think that the mafia is on one side and all these other realities on the other and that these relationships are almost like rivers set up between these two entities. But, there are no rivers, because it is the same thing. The mafia has its own physicians, its own lawyers, its own politicians and, perhaps, its own segments of state institutions. There is no need to imagine a relationship.... The mafia has all these characters inside, it shapes them, they are its own, it does not need to get close to them or to entrap them, in order to get, and consequently do, favors.[86]

Over the last twenty years 'Ndrangheta families have been ever more successful in electing their own members to public offices, in an effort to foster their economic and political interests more effectively and cheaply. In some cases the *mafiosi*-politicians even held ruling positions within the mafia consortia. Since the death of Paolo De Stefano in 1985, for example, the two main chiefs of the Reggio Calabria clan have allegedly been the lawyer Giorgio De Stefano, who was for a long time a Christian Democrat representative in the city council, and Paolo Romeo, a member of Parliament for the *Partito Socialdemocratico Italiano* (PSDI) for several legislatures.[87]

In Cosa Nostra, instead, where the coincidence of the *mafioso*'s and politician's roles was already common in the 1950s, a reversal of power relations between Cosa Nostra and their political referents began to take place in the late 1970s. Emboldened by the millions of dollars accumulated in the transcontinental heroin trade,[88] Cosa Nostra chiefs increased their requests and began to exercise the control over the political life in their areas of dominion in an ever more pressing and arrogant way. Additionally, in the late 1970s Cosa Nostra started to kill politicians who did not honor pacts they had engaged in with the mafia in order both to punish them and to warn other mafia political associates. In March 1979, Michele Reina, the secretary of the Palermitan DC, was shot and a few months afterwards Piersanti Mattarella, the

DC president of the Sicilian Region, was murdered. After receiving mafia votes, Mattarella had been trying to free himself from mafia obligations and to launch a moralizing campaign inside his own party.[89] After the failed manipulation of the final sentence concerning the largest penal proceeding started by the Palermitan law enforcement agencies in the 1980s (the so-called first Palermitan *maxi-processo*), even Salvo Lima and one of his cousins, Ignazio (Nino had already died of natural causes in the late 1980s), were shot in March and August 1992, respectively.

On the other side, during the 1980s mafia bosses began to meet increasing difficulties in shaping public policy and, specifically, law enforcement action. Especially in Sicily, from the late 1970s a younger generation of prosecutors, judges, and police officials, who rejected an apologetic conception of the mafia, adopted new, empirical methods of anti-mafia investigation that began to produce considerable results. These southern state representatives also benefited from the successes of their northern counterparts in their fight against terrorism.[90] This struggle, in fact, not only increased the legitimacy of the law enforcement apparatus vis-à-vis the general population but also led to the accumulation of experience (such as working in "pools" and exchanging information among different prosecutors' offices) and the enactment of legislative measures (including the 1980 law that provided "compensation" for the members of underground organizations who cooperated with investigations) that turned out to be of great help for the new generation of magistrates and police officials committed to the prosecution of mafia crimes.

Unable to influence these new officials directly or through politicians, Cosa Nostra was obliged to resort to violence in order to neutralize them. From 1979 to 1982, more than 15 state officials and politicians were murdered in the Palermo province. In autumn 1982, in particular, the General Carlo Alberto Dalla Chiesa, who had three months before been sent to Sicily as prefect of the Palermo province and high commissioner against the mafia, was killed together with his wife and driver in Palermo.[91] The murder represented a turning point since it stimulated a large popular upheaval and a strong repressive reaction from state authorities. Two weeks after the Dalla Chiesa murder, the La Torre law, named after the Sicilian Communist leader who had also been killed by the mafia in April 1982, was passed.[92] It introduced the crime of delinquent association of mafia type (art. 416 *bis* Penal Code) and authorized the seizure and forfeiture of illegally acquired property of those suspected of art. 416 *bis*. Between 1982 and 1986 nearly 15,000 men were denounced in all Italy for criminal association of mafia type. Of these, 406 were brought to trial by a pool of Palermitan investigating magistrates (including Giovanni Falcone and Paolo Borsellino) in the so-called Palermitan *maxi-processo* or "maxi trial."

The state anti-mafia campaign was encouraged by widespread public support. Shocked by the murder of Dalla Chiesa, the *Palermitani* participated in unprecedented public demonstrations, including a spontaneous candlelight procession in honor of his memory. Since then a "protean and multifaceted anti-mafia movement" has developed.[93] In January 1984, representatives of the city party section and trade unions, responding to other assassinations, formed the so-called *Coordinamento Antimafia*, whose activities included organizing conferences and demonstrations on behalf of mafia victims. In 1985 Leoluca Orlando, a member of a reformist, left-wing faction of the Christian Democratic party who had taken a clear stance against the mafia, began to serve as mayor. During his administration the city hall became a focal point for the condemnation of mafia and its supportive political culture. For the multiplicity of activities that accompanied Palermo's maxi-processo, the mid-1980s were called "Palermo's springtime."

To punish the mafia traditional Christian Democrat associates who were accused of insufficiently protecting mafia interests by letting the *maxi-processo* take place, Totò Riina, Cosa Nostra supreme chief from the early 1980s onwards, ordered all mafia affiliates to vote for the candidates of the Socialist and Radical Party (PSI and PR) in the 1987 national elections. Even this maneuver, however, failed. The PSI exponents soon forgot the "guaranteeing" promises that had been made to *mafiosi* during the electoral campaign. The first degree trial of the maxi-processo ended in December 1987 with a ruling that meted out 2,665 years of imprisonment, 19 life-sentences, 11 billion lira of fines (at the 1987 exchange rate about US $8 million) and 114 acquittals. On 30 January 1992, despite the elaboration of a complex strategy of conditioning that saw the intervention of Salvo Lima, other members of Andreotti's faction in Sicily, and even the president of the first section of the *Corte di Cassazione*, Corrado Carnevale (now indicted for the crime of mafia association) (PrPA 1997b), the supreme judicial body, definitively confirmed both the interpretative scheme and most of the first-degree sentence convictions.

Not only did Sicilian *mafiosi* begin to face the first important setbacks in their influence of state decision making, but the quality of the relationships between mafia and political power also rapidly deteriorated. First, due to the decreasing legitimacy of mafia families, these contacts and exchanges have had to become more secretive. From the 1960s onwards, the mafia began to be condemned in ever-greater sectors of the southern Italian population. Consequently, open relationships with *mafiosi* progressively became a handicap for a man in politics. Once again, this trend can be detected in Sicily earlier than in Calabria. "Before 1963," noted the first Parliamentary Anti-Mafia Commission, "many *mafiosi* paraded their relationship with politicians and local administrators—and vice versa. At polling stations, *mafiosi*'s presence was impudent and aggressive. It is rare nowadays to see links between *mafiosi* and politicians openly manifested."[94]

The process of cultural modernization has also fostered the dissolution of the subculture shared by both *mafiosi* and politicians in the past. Consequently, the relationships among these subjects have lost their roots in a common subcultural system and have at the same time become primarily—if not exclusively—based on utilitarian calculations. Especially in Cosa Nostra's case, the consolidation of mafia leverage on the political competition has been accompanied by a growing distrust and lack of respect towards the political class. The change of attitude emerges powerfully from the comparison between the following two statements that refer to two periods separated by about thirty years. On one hand, according to Gioacchino Pennino, the relationships between Salvo Lima and his uncle, chief of the Brancaccio family, "were of great affinity both on a personal and a political level. Tommaso Buscetta and the brothers La Barberas were closely linked to both of them: they saw each very often."[95] The exchange of favors was thus inserted into a long-term relationship, which went far beyond the utilitarian moment but was based on friendship and bonds of mutual respect. On the other hand, totally different appears to be the attitude held by Totò Riina, Cosa Nostra head in the last fifteen years, in respect of politicians: as the *pentito* Balduccio di Maggio remembers:

> Riina Salvatore personally told me more than once that it is not possible that a politician at any level becomes a man of honor. It is not even possible that a man of honor starts a political career; on the basis of this rule that was stated to me in categorical terms, there is a substantial despite on the part of Cosa Nostra towards political men who are not regarded as serious enough to become part of the organization.[96]

To compensate the weakening strength of subcultural values, the relationships between *mafiosi* and politicians have been cemented by monetary rewards more frequently than in the past. Depending on the occasions, money has flowed in both directions. *Mafiosi* paid in order to obtain a favor, the adjudication of a tender or the adjustment of a process, politicians, on other hand, occasionally paid money in order to secure the support of a mafia family during electoral campaigns.[97] Betrayals and double games were then discouraged by the employment and the threat of violence on the part of mafia families: "We obviously give votes to politicians of our choice," states Di Maggio, "after a previous agreement with them, but they have to do what we say, 'otherwise we break them their horns'."[98]

Since the 1970s a powerful means to stabilize relationships between mafia and politics and at the same time to cope with the decline in mafia legitimization has been the Freemasonry. Up to the late 1960s the contacts between the Masonry and Cosa Nostra and the 'Ndrangheta were sporadic. In Sicily, according to various Justice collaborators, the relationship was originally characterized by the acknowledgment of the reciprocal spheres of autonomy and of the equality between the two brotherhoods. It was through Masonic channels that extreme right-wing movements asked Cosa Nostra to participate in the 1970 and 1974 subversive attempts. Then, from the mid-1970s the relationship became much closer. According to the Catania *pentito* Antonino Calderone, in 1977 a secret Masonic lodge asked Cosa Nostra to let two "men of honor" from each province join the Masonry. Allegedly, it was Stefano Bontade, through his brother-in-law Giacomo Vitale, who belonged to a Masonic lodge, that promoted this initiative and, by highlighting the great advantages connected to this, convinced the most influential Cosa Nostra chiefs to authorize the violation of the rule prohibiting the members of the mafia to adhere to other associations.[99]

The 'Ndrangheta, unlike Cosa Nostra, was, throughout all the 1960s, in a subordinate position to the Masonry. No *mafiosi* were affiliated to the Masonry but, according to the former 'Ndrangheta affiliate, Giacomo Lauro, the latter "acted as a connecting means with state institutions and...obtained a percentage from the businesses that brokered on our account."[100] Following the Reggio Calabria revolt of 1970, however, the relationship between the two associations was very much intensified and set up on a more equal basis: the close interaction between 'Ndrangheta bosses and heads of fascist movements belonging to the Masonry who managed the revolt promoted the affiliation of the former to the Masonry. The entrance of 'Ndrangheta chiefs into the Masonry was institutionalized with the creation of a secret rank within the Calabrian organization, named *Santa*. All the members of the *Santa* were authorized to join the Masonry and, indeed, most of them did, to the point that, according to Pasquale Barreca, a former high-ranking member of the De Stefano coalition, "in Calabria the 'Ndrangheta and the Masonry have become a 'single thing'."[101]

From the mid-1970s infiltration of the Freemasonry as well as of other lobbying networks came to play a crucial role in mafia associations' strategy of approaching and of penetrating into the political and institutional circles. It is increasingly through the Masonry and, above all, in the "covered" lodges, that *mafiosi* enter in illicit agreements with politicians, state officials, and professionals. On this theme, in a monumental request for warrants of arrest for almost 500 members of the 'Ndrangheta, the Calabrian prosecutors affirm that:

> ...the entrance into previously existing or *ad hoc* constituted Masonic lodges was the way to establish links with those social strata which traditionally adhered to the Masonry, that is, members of the liberal professions (physicians, lawyers, and notaries), entrepreneurs and politicians, representatives of state institutions, among them magistrates and members of the police forces. Through this link, the 'Ndrangheta was able to find not only new possibilities for economic investment, but previously unconceived political outlets. Above all, that "covering," accomplished in various ways and in various levels (diversions, lack of investigations, attacks of every kind to noncompliant magistrates, adjustments of trials, etc.), produced a substantial impunity, characteristic of this criminal organization, rendering it almost "invisible" to institutions, to such an extent that only a couple of years back it came to the

attention of the national public opinion and of the most qualified investigative bodies.[102]

The exploitation of the Masonic network by mafia confederations is undoubtedly facilitated by some specific features of this association. First of all, the bond of solidarity, brotherhood, and mutual aid to which the "brothers" pledge makes it easier for mafia members to ask for "favors," even from people belonging to the political and administrative community in the Masonic lodges. Secondly, and more importantly, the "confidentiality" that characterizes the Masonic membership makes it difficult to reconstruct the interpersonal relations that constitute the organizational foundation of the association. Secrecy is, in particular, maximized within "covered" lodges, which are created next to the regular ones to host the most prestigious affiliates, and by the possibilities of "reserved" affiliations for members covering delicate institutional roles, such as those *all'orecchio,* which are known only to the head of the lodge.[103] Third, Masonic rules provide both the *mafiosi* and their counterparts in illicit deals a well-founded expectation about the silence and the reliability of each other. Even if the Masonic politician or state official who is asked a "favor" by a Masonic/mafia brother refuses, he is still bound to keep silent so that the illicit request remains secret and is not denounced to the law enforcement agencies.[104]

For these reasons, the Freemasonry has from the early 1970s come to represent a privileged channel for Sicilian and Calabrian mafia associations to contact the representatives of the state. Though the subject is still partially veiled by secrecy, recent investigations have proved that many illicit deals have been made under the protective shield of the Freemasonry. Several investigations carried out by the Prosecutor's Offices of Palmi and Reggio Calabria have revealed that the selection of candidates for local and national elections, capable of promoting mafia interests took place within secret Masonic lodges.[105] It has been ascertained, furthermore, that Freemasons and in particular, Licio Gelli, the Grand Master of the Lodge P2 (Propaganda 2) were also involved in the electoral campaign of mafia-sponsored candidates in 1992 political elections in Calabria.[106] The conditioning of law enforcement action has also time and again taken place through Masonic or illicit lobbying networks, as *pentiti* both in Sicily and in Calabria refer. Significantly, Bruno Contrada, a high-ranking police official who was condemned for favoring mafia interests, was a member of a para-Masonic secret association, the *Ordine Equestre del Santo Sepolcro.*[107]

The Masonry has not only provided contacts with politicians and state officials. By enhancing contacts with members of the economic and financial establishments, affiliation with the Masonic network has also helped mafia members access new channels for the laundering and reinvestment of illicit proceeds and to enter into collusive agreements aimed at the control of the public works market. The contacts with both the financier Michele Sindona and Roberto Calvi were, for instance, at least partially mediated by the Masonry.[108] It was, for example, the secret Masonic lodge P2, headed by Licio Gelli, that allegedly acted as a guarantor in laundering the drug money of the Sicilian *cosche* carried out by Roberto Calvi, director of the Banco Ambrosiano.[109]

The range of services *mafiosi* may draw from their Masonic brothers is well illustrated by the case of Pino Mandalari, a well-known Palermitan accountant arrested by the Palermitan prosecutors in December 1994 for the crime of mafia association. Through a series of shell companies, Mandalari had administered the properties of Totò Riina, Cosa Nostra chief, and several other members of the Corleone family ever since the late 1960s. In addition to these financial tasks, Mandalari had founded and headed a secret Masonic lodge which, though not affiliated with any internationally recognized Masonic order, had attracted several members of the Sicilian establishment. It was through this network of contacts that Mandalari succeeded in securing good investments for his clients as well as representing the interests of Cosa Nostra in the circles of the Palermitan "high society." The network of affiliates was also employed to promote associated candidates in elections. In fact, several wiretappings carried out in the months before the 1994 national elections proved Mandalari's extensive commitment to several candidates of the right wing *Alleanza Nazionale* and *Forza Italia*.[110]

The Situation Today: Persistence and Vulnerability

By increasing the "invisibility" of the political-criminal nexus, entrance into the Freemasonry has successfully helped *mafiosi* and mafia-friendly politicians to counter the vulnerabilities that have emerged since the 1970s. With time, however, the latter have come to the fore. Weaknesses are in fact primarily related to the long-term process of mafia delegitimization begun in the 1960s. As a matter of fact, this process suddenly accelerated in 1992 and 1993 following the "terrorist" campaign staged by Sicilian Cosa Nostra. The murders of the magistrates Giovanni Falcone and Paolo Borsellino committed in rapid succession, and the bombs that exploded in some major Italian cities,[111] moved large strata of the Sicilian civil society and of the entire country against the mafia.

State institutions also reacted to these events with a strong counterattack, producing the highest peak of anti-mafia activities in the last thirty years. In the summer of 1992 a new anti-mafia act was passed, according to which most mafia chiefs were to be detained in special high security prisons, 7,000 soldiers were sent to Sicily to help civil police forces and anti-mafia investigations were substantially facilitated. The enactment of a law to protect "justice collaborators" and their families, the wide range of provisions foreseen by the

law of August 1992, as well as the successes of law enforcement forces, favored the growth of the phenomenon of *pentitismo*, powerfully intensifying the internal tensions and contradictions of mafia associations. As of 30 June 1996, former organized crime members cooperating with the judiciary numbered 1,177.[112] The declarations of informers made possible the widening and updating of the investigators' body of knowledge on the different facets of Italian organized crime and led to the arrest of fugitives, some of whom had been hiding for decades, and to the enhancement of investigations. The geography and the power networks of Cosa Nostra, the 'Ndrangheta, and the other major southern criminal coalitions were reconstructed. Murders and other serious offenses that had long gone unpunished were finally solved. Indeed, breaking the tradition that usually saw "excellent murders" unresolved, the Caltanissetta prosecutors were able to discover the instigators and executors of the Capaci and via d'Amelio slaughters where Judges Falcone and Borsellino lost their lives, together with the former's wife and eight policemen. A first-degree Court has already condemned most defendants. Thanks to the *pentiti*'s contributions, past cases that had been dismissed were reopened and the trials are underway.

Though it was until recently a sort of "national taboo," the existence of pacts between *mafiosi* and state representatives has also begun to be unveiled. In addition to Andreotti's trials, several other investigations of politicians and state officials are underway. Between 1991 and 1995 more than half of the deputies of the Sicilian Regional Parliament and 17 Sicilian deputies of the national Parliament were targeted by charges of mafia association and corruption. In particular, all the chiefs and main characters of Andreotti's faction in Sicily are either dead or are now facing trial. Furthermore, since the approval of the Law n. 221/91, "concerning the dismissal of the councils of communes, provinces and other local institutions following phenomena of mafia infiltration and conditioning," more than 110 communal councils have been dismissed in Campania, Calabria, and Sicily.[113]

The emotional reaction of state officials and public opinion alike to the terrorist strategy staged by Cosa Nostra is not enough to explain why the political-criminal nexus finally began to be revealed and severed in the early 1990s. Nor is it sufficient to recall the introduction of a set of new legislative tools right before and after the killing of Judges Falcone and Borsellino. (In addition to those already mentioned, a new specialized police force was set up to deal with organized crime—the *Direzione Investigativa Antimafia* (DIA)—in December 1991, and in 1993 the way was opened for penal prosecutions of members of Parliament).

To be fully understood, the detection and prosecution of the political-criminal nexus since 1992 need to be framed in wider historical processes. In a long-term, nationwide perspective, we ought, first of all, to mention the processes of social, economic, and cultural modernization that have changed

Italy since the end of the Second World War. Though with disparities and contradictions, a poor, predominantly agricultural, still largely illiterate country has, in about half a century, become the fifth richest nation of the world.[114] Moreover, economic development has been accompanied by deep changes in the social and cultural structure—such as the strengthening of the Italian civil society and the diffusion of universalistic codes and practices—which fostered the rise of anti-mafia movements since the early 1980s and which are the main cause of the process of delegitimization of mafia organizations and culture.

Faced with growing external constraints and the competition of developing countries, in the early 1990s Italy could no longer tolerate the distortions and wastes caused by the diffusion of corruptive and clientelistic practices. If these widespread practices had not been tackled, Italian development could not have proceeded any further. Indeed, in a systemic perspective, the anti-mafia and anti-corruption investigations carried out by the judiciary in different parts of Italy since 1992 may be seen as a reaction to these constraints, as an attempt to introduce more efficiency, fairness, and transparency into the relationships between the administration and the citizens and thus to eliminate a major impediment to the future development of the country.

Another large-scale factor to be considered is the fall of the USSR. With the end of the Cold War, the Communist Party (which in 1989 broke with its own past and took the name of *Partito Democratico della Sinistra*) finally gained full legitimacy vis-à-vis internal competitors, and the creation of a government coalition not including Christian Democrats (who had been part of government coalitions without interruption since 1948) became a real possibility. Likewise, the Christian Democrat and Socialist politicians that had in the past claimed immunity from investigations on the basis of their support for the Atlantic coalition, lost this blanket of legitimacy and became liable to inquiries concerning their bribes and shady deals.

Next to these two macro-changes, other more specific factors need to be considered. First, the growing independence of the judiciary was consistently enhanced by the successful campaign against terrorism staged in the 1970s and early 1980s. This factor, coupled with the strong backing of civil society, enabled prosecutors and judges to go on with their anti-mafia and anti-corruption inquiries even when these began to involve high-ranking politicians and state officials. In particular, the anti-corruption inquiries, which were autonomously started by the Milanese "Clean Hands" pool in early 1992 and which were also made possible by the above-mentioned long-term changes, provided a powerful backing to the investigations carried out by the southern Italian *procure* on corrupt exchanges between members of mafia associations, politicians, and state officials.

Another element worth mentioning is the growing international cooperation between the Italian judiciary, on one side, and its counterparts in the United States, Germany, Switzerland, and other European countries. Judicial collaboration with the United States goes back to the early 1980s and has ever since produced great results including the management of several joint operations (such as the so called "Pizza connection," "Irontower," and "Green Ice" to mention only the most famous) and the common handling of important mafia turncoats (including Tommaso Buscetta, the man of honor who first revealed the existence of Cosa Nostra to Judge Giovanni Falcone).[115] Likewise, Italian prosecutors have time and again exploited the mutual aid relations with their European counterparts to find proof of money laundering and corruption charges against a myriad of *mafiosi*, financial and business entrepreneurs, politicians, and state officials.

Finally, we need to consider changes within the mafia world and particularly within the Sicilian mafia confederation, Cosa Nostra, which has so far been the main target of judicial investigations. With their entrance into the transcontinental drug trade, both Cosa Nostra and 'Ndrangheta families acquired great wealth, which was unthinkable before the late 1970s when most mafia members were rather poor or only relatively well off. The drug trade profits were then invested in a number of legitimate businesses, thus allowing mafia members to exert an even tighter control over the licit economy of their own communities. New wealth and power, however, soon became liabilities.

The large money flows, new patterns of conspicuous consumption, and the acquisition of numerous legitimate businesses attracted the attention of the judiciary. Mafia families were also rendered more vulnerable by the growing intermingling with nonmembers imposed by the patterns and rhythms of the commerce in narcotics and other illegal commodities that reduced the homogeneity and cohesion of the inner group. Drug trafficking also caused bloody internal conflicts, frequently along generational lines. The opposition of elder affiliates to the involvement in the drug trade was frequently overcome with violence, which also unavoidably attracted law enforcement attention. In addition, dramatic executions of mafia bosses in public places were carried out to gain control of profitable rings in the drug trade, thus further increasing mafia visibility and vulnerability.[116] These public outbursts of violence, which also targeted several representatives of state institutions, severely affected mafia legitimacy vis-à-vis the general population. They also alienated the sympathies of the very politicians who had come to terms with them. After accepting mafia electoral support, many of them—ranging allegedly from high-ranking representatives of the Socialist Party to Andreotti himself—tried to distance themselves from mafia alliances and took measures that damaged mafia interests. (In Spring 1991, for example, then Socialist Justice Minister Claudio Martelli and Prime Minister Giulio Andreotti issued a special decree that sent more than a hundred *mafiosi* back to jail, after they had been freed by a corrupt judge on spurious grounds). Threatened and blackmailed by an ever more arrogant Cosa Nostra, a growing number of associated politicians and state officials decided that they could no longer afford to tolerate this parasitic and unpredictable rival.

It was the fortunate combination of these elements, coupled with the public outcry caused by Cosa Nostra's terrorist strategy that allowed anti-mafia and anti-corruption investigations to proceed in the early 1990s. Consequently, the room for discretion open to the corrupt representatives of the state has sharply diminished and the costs and risks of protecting mafia interests while holding political and institutional positions have grown considerably. The number of politicians willing to come to terms with the mafia has also decreased. As a consequence, over the last few years *capimafia* have found it increasingly costly to influence state action and decision making and their chances of obtaining what they want have rapidly diminished, thus further weakening the mafia chiefs' legitimization vis-à-vis their own subordinates.

Nonetheless, though endangered, the political-criminal nexus is far from being disbanded. Irrespective of the fact that the mafia consortia's complex network of political and institutional connections has begun to be targeted by judicial inquiries, a considerable number of politicians and state officials are still ready to advocate mafia interests. Members of the political and institutional establishment who have "recycled" themselves from 1994 in the so-called "Second Republic,"and who are subjugated to mafia interests represent the bulk of this group. Their political survival depends, in fact, on the cover-up of their past and present collusive agreements, whereas their physical well-being depends on the ability to refute accusations of betrayal by mafia members. Beyond monetary interests, the identification with mafia interests is for these actors almost complete.

This web of contacts and alliances was to have been exploited in 1993 to launch a separatist project that, by creating an independent state in southern Italy or at least in Sicily, would have enabled mafia associations to exert a stronger influence over political and judicial decision making affecting them. This project went through the first implementation stages and even obtained some promising initial success. At the election for the renewal of the Catania provincial council in January 1994, a separatist list *Sicilia Libera*, created by Tullio Cannella acting on the orders of the *Corleonesi*, gained about 9 percent of the vote. Initiatives to support such a plan were also taken by the bosses of the Calabrian mafia association with the meaningful support of several high-ranking Mason "brothers."[117] The plan, however, came to a sudden halt as Cosa Nostra and 'Ndrangheta bosses thought their interests could be represented at the national level by the alliance of center-right and right parties, which took shape in late 1993 under the leadership of television tycoon Silvio Berlusconi, that won the March 1994 national elections. As the Calabrian *pentito* Cesare Polifroni stated right after the elections:

> In this moment waiting for the politics of the new government is the prevalent attitude. I may say in this respect that there was the order of all the organizations in Sicily, Calabria, and Campania to vote either for Berlusconi or for Pannella, with the certainty that they were going to be the winning group. We believe that the new government will dismantle all the repressive legislation and go back to the "free state."[118]

Despite repeated attempts to discredit *pentiti* and to reform the anti-mafia legislation, the Berlusconi government, lasting only a few months, did not succeed in satisfying mafia expectations. Such a failure, however, has certainly not brought a halt to relationships between members of mafia organizations and representatives of the state. Although these relationships appear today much more fragile than in the past, since they no longer stand on a shared subcultural background and must be carefully hidden from the public view, they are perpetuated by the system of mutual rewards. Notwithstanding the growing distrust towards the political class, mafia bosses certainly cannot afford to loosen the contacts with politicians and indeed, are compelled, more than ever, to try to influence the political and judicial decision-making process.

Likewise, for some politicians and state officials, the risks of coming to terms with the mafia still appear lower than the potential monetary and electoral rewards and their moral restraints are not high enough to prevent them from entering into such deals. Some of them, furthermore, are blackmailed and intimidated by the *cosche* and are obliged by their own past choices to keep on promoting mafia interests. Although the base of mafia supporters in the political and institutional establishment is shrinking, the investigations going on in several parts of the country demonstrate that there are still politicians willing to make a "pact with the devil" in order to foster their political careers as well as by state officials ready to face the increased risks of mafia cooperation so as to integrate their income with occult rewards and gifts.[119] In April 1999, for example, Stefano Cusumano, a Sicilian Treasury undersecretary was arrested for allegedly providing a number of favors to a Catanese mafia group, including a large public contract for the construction of a hospital.[120]

The recent acquittal of Andreotti, moreover, reveals the difficulties of investigating the political-criminal nexus. Though the sentences are not yet known, in both Palermo and Perugia the judges most probably considered the evidence presented by the prosecutors inadequate to condemn one of the most famous political figures of the Republican era. Lacking written proof and photographic documentation, in fact, prosecutors had largely relied on the statements of mafia witnesses, many of whom repeated what other men of honor had told them. If many of the trials that are still pending end with similar verdicts, the whole anti-mafia and anti-corruption campaign may come in for sharp criticism by more or less disinterested sections of public opinion, and the risks associated with shady dealings may thus sink again rapidly, favoring the spread of old corrupt practices.

Thus, although the first half of the1990s has registered great successes in the fight against the mafia and the political-criminal nexus, it is too early to exult in our victory. It is true that Cosa Nostra's and 'Ndrangheta's ability to influence systematically the political and judicial decision-making processes at the national level has been consistently reduced. It seems highly unlikely that Sicilian and Calabrian mafia groups will again penetrate state institutions to the degree that they did in the past. Nonetheless, especially in Calabria, where antimafia investigations have met stronger resistance than in Sicily, the political-criminal nexus is still in place. The influence of 'Ndrangheta *cosche* on local political life remains pervasive. In the rare cases when they do not succeed in peacefully influencing public affairs, the *cosche* attack the public administrators with intimidations and threats. A recent victim of this strategy of violent influence has, for example, been the left-wing Reggio Calabria mayor, Italo Falcomatà, who, unlike his predecessors, has made anti-mafia commitment one of the characteristic traits of his administration.[121] Even in Sicily, notwithstanding the election of a new generation of committed anti-mafia mayors in the two last Sicilian administrative elections (1993 and 1997), elements of local and regional political life are still today controlled by people linked to traditional, clientelistic, and mafia-clientelistic ways of running politics. Furthermore, in both regions mafia groups are actively trying to weave contacts with the representatives of the left-wing coalition that has governed the country since 1996 and their efforts are at least occasionally successful, as Cusumano's arrest proves. Though in weaker, looser forms, the political-criminal nexus seems therefore bound to reproduce itself.

Notes

1. PrPA (1993a, b and c).
2. PrPA (1995). The indictment for the crime of mafia association was published in the volume edited by Montanaro and Ruotolo (1995). A synthesis can also be found in Arlacchi (1995). Other documents have been published by Santino (1995) and interpretations advanced by Macaluso (1995) and Lupo (1996). Lastly, see also Andreotti (1995).
3. Stanley (1999a and b).
4. Up to the early 1980s, the prevailing idea among social scientists was that the mafia had to be understood as an attitude and a behavior but that no mafia organization existed (Hess [1970] 1973; Blok [1974] 1988; Schneiders 1976; Arlacchi [1983] 1988; Catanzaro [1988] 1992).
5. Paoli (1997, 2000); Ministero dell'Interno (1994 and 1995).
6. Pezzino (1994); Romano (1963).
7. Hess ([1970] 1973); Blok ([1974] 1988).
8. Tilly ([1974] 1988: xxi).
9. Hess (1973: 25).
10. See Pezzino (1992a). Further, in both Sicily and Calabria the formal abolition of feudalism was largely insufficient to disrupt the extensive baronial property and succeeded only partially in giving incentive to a new modern landowning bourgeoisie willing to abandon the old and ineffective agricultural methods. The consequences were particularly irrelevant in Sicily where, even in 1860, the former feudal property, which included nine-tenths of all Sicilian land, was still undivided (Sereni [1948] 1968).
11. Hess (1973: 14-33); Renda (1984: 183-205); Marino (1986: 91 ff).
12. Franchetti ([1877] 1993: 14).
13. Ibidem.
14. Pezzino (1987).

15. Novacco (1972: 45).
16. Lupo (1988).
17. Pezzino (1987, 1990a and b, 1995); Lupo (1988, 1993); Fiume (1984).
18. Franchetti, (1993: 90).
19. See Paoli (1997); Marmo (1989). It is interesting to point out that the same concept is embodied in the word 'Ndrangheta. It derives from the Greek term andragaqos which meant "a noble, courageous man, worthy of respect as a result of his capacities." Thus, in the Calabrian dialect, strongly influenced by Hellenism, 'Ndrangheta is the society of the "men of honor," whereas 'ndranghetisti, valorous men, are its associates (Martino 1983).
20. Alongi ([1886] 1977: 16); see also Lorenzoni (1910: 678-85).
21. Schneiders (1976); Hess (1973); Blok (1988); Arlacchi (1988); Catanzaro (1992).
22. Sabetti (1984).
23. CPM (1993a).
24. Prefettura di Palermo ([1971] 1978).
25. Strati (1977: 9).
26. Lo Schiavo (1955).
27. Graziano (1980).
28. Romano (1963: 161). For up-to-date, sound "scientific" analyses of the rise of the Italian clientelistic system, see Graziano (1973, 1978, 1980) and Fantozzi (1993). The management of local power in Sicily and the relationships between mafia and politics are well described in Barone (1987), Chubb (1989), and Pezzino (1996).
29. Mosca ([1900] 1949: 243).
30. Cirillo Rampolla ([1889] 1986).
31. Ibidem, 54.
32. Barone (1987: 307-19); Lupo (1993: 67-81); see also Notarbartolo ([1949] 1994).
33. Salvemini ([1909] 1963: 137-8).
34. Blok (1988).
35. The diffusion of the duty of self-defense, independent from state intervention, is illustrated by the following episode. On receiving Emanuele Notarbartolo in his office, a man seeking justice for the murder of his own father, the Italian prime minister, the Sicilian Baron Di Rudinì, allegedly said: "But if you are sure that Raffaele Palizzolo is guilty, why don't you have him killed?" (Turone 1992: 72).
36. Schneiders (1997; 1984).
37. Quoted in Pallotta (1977: 81-83).
38. Lupo (1987: 402 ff).
39. CPMS (1971: 276-7).
40. Many books have been written on the fascist government's repression of the Sicilian mafia: among them, see Duggan (1989), Petacco ([1975] 1994), Porto (1977), and Tessitore (1994) as well as Lupo's long essay (1987). See also the volumes written by Mori himself: ([1942] 1993; [1923] 1988). On the anti-mafia action in Calabria, see Ciconte (1992: 216-36) and Gambino (1976: 113-19).
41. Blok (1988: 186).
42. The benevolent attitude of the AMGOT was allegedly facilitated by the services granted by certain American *mafiosi* and their Sicilian counterparts in the occupation of Sicily. Although this relationship has long attracted the curiosity of public opinion and the attention of journalists as well as serious scholars (Pantaleone [1962] 1972: 44-65; CPMS, 1976b: 966; Block 1985; Gentile 1993: 163-71), such cooperation should not be overemphasized. In fact, notwithstanding the Allies' reliance on *mafiosi* and large estate owners, it is evident that this factor alone cannot explain the re-emergence of mafia in Western Sicily (Mangiameli 1987; Pezzino 1995: 185-95; see also Ministero degli Affari Esteri 1978).

43. Mangiameli (1987); CPMS (1976a: 113-33); Renda (1987: 15-97).
44. Tarrow (1967); see also Fantozzi (1993).
45. See Gribaudi (1980) and Mastropaolo (1993).
46. PrPA (1995a, III: 35).
47. Those that the *pentito* Tommaso Buscetta remembers are the following: "the Monarchic Guttadauro Giuseppe (*rappresentante* of the Corso dei Mille family), the Christian Democrat Trapani Giuseppe (*consigliere* of my own family), Sorci Antonino (belonging to the Villagrazia di Palermo family, a namesake of the cousin said *'Ninu lu riccu'* [the rich one]), Cerami Giuseppe (who would become senator and was *combinato* in the Santa Maria del Gesù family). These last two Christian Democrats were in that period assessors or counselors of the Palermo commune, while the mayor was Salvo Lima and the construction assessor Vito Ciancimino. In that epoch, furthermore, both in the Palermo communal and provincial councils there were so many men of honor and I will be able to indicate them easily, as soon as I have the list of the people elected in that period. (...) Obviously there were also men of honor in the regional assembly—though in a smaller number" (PrPA 1995a, I: 103-5).
48. See Chubb (1982).
49. IbideM 64.
50. When the latent rivalry between Gioia and Lima exploded on the occasion of the parliamentary election of 1968, it was Lima who defeated his former patron, though Gioia's prestige and contacts in the national party organizations far surpassed Lima's. Thanks to his control of the local levers of power, in fact, and to his developed networks of personal loyalties, Lima, who was then virtually unknown outside Palermo, came in first among all DC candidates in the constituency of Western Sicily, outdistancing government ministers and undersecretaries, including Gioia himself. After this election Lima formally broke his partnership with Gioia and founded Andreotti's faction in Sicily, which, given his strength, attracted a great number of Gioia's supporters (Chubb 1980; Vasile 1994).
51. PrPA (1995a: 80).
52. Ibidem, 54.
53. Arlacchi (1995: 15-7).
54. CPMS (1976b).
55. CPMS (1970).
56. Questura di Palermo ([1970] 1978).
57. CPMS (1970: 40); see also Chilanti (1971: 79-90); Arlacchi (1994: 111-2).
58. CPM (1993c: 1222); see Fed. PCI-AG (1964: 56).
59. CPMS (1976a: 206).
60. The relevance of construction was, and still is, particularly evident in Palermo, where a large number of manufacturing firms produce supplies for the construction industry. Moreover, leaving aside state financed projects, the construction industry was the only one to expand significantly throughout the second half of the 1950s and all the 1960s. In Palermo "the economic miracle" merely consisted of an unprecedented and savage urban expansion that rapidly and drastically changed the face of the city within a decade. Such a trend was given further impetus by the rapid increase in the city population (between 1951 and 1961 almost 100,000 moved to Palermo) as well as numerous public housing projects and low-cost mortgages for regional employees (Chubb 1980; Cancila 1988: 525-42).
61. Falcone and Turone (1982).
62. TrPA ([1965] 1978: 663-4).
63. TrPA (1986, XXXII: 6826-6959).
64. Quoted in Ciconte (1992: 262).
65. Piselli and Arrighi (1985: 442-58).

66. Ciconte (1992: 261-79).
67. For a history of this revolt, which began as a popular movement and was then hegemonized by right-wing parties, see Lombardi Satriani (1971), D'Agostini (1972) as well as Walston (1988: 207-15).
68. PrRC (1995: 4755).
69. Ibidem, 343.
70. When he was in hiding, the *pentito* Gaspare Mutolo lived in his own neighborhood, a few meters away from his official address, sent his kids to the local school, accompanying them personally and giving the teachers his current address and telephone number (CPM 1993c: 1234-5, 1260). Likewise, as a fugitive, the former Cosa Nostra affiliate Tommaso Buscetta stayed at his son's house for a long time, and though this address was known to police authorities, nobody ever cared to look for him there (CPM 1992a: 365-6). Even more open, if possible, was the complicity inland: "in every town," Messina remembers, "the mayor, the marshal, and the *capomafia* command. The three of them are informed about the presence of a fugitive on their territory, policemen, and *carabinieri* meet him but they turn around ..." (CPM 1992b: 532).
71. One of the few pending cases, that of the *capomafia* Vincenzo Rimi from Alcamo, who had been condemned for the homicide of Lupo Leale on the grounds of the courageous statements by the victim's mother, was allegedly solved thanks to Andreotti's direct intervention. In 1971, in fact, the Supreme Court canceled the life sentences for Vincenzo Rimi and his son Filippo and ordered a new trial. In 1979 the Rome Court of Appeals absolved Filippo for insufficiency of proof (his father Vincenzo died in 1975 from natural causes). Furthermore, in order to have better penitentiary treatment, the Rimis obtained the intervention of a high magistrate of the *Cassazione*, Giuseppe Guido Lo Schiavo, the Ministry of Justice, Oronzo Reale, and three undersecretaries and a senator, Luigi Corrao, as denounced by the Right deputy Niccolai and written in the 1976 Minority Report of the Anti-mafia Commission (CPMS 1976c).
72. Ciconte (1992: 245-94).
73. Di Lello (1994).
74. Arlacchi (1988: 57-61).
75. On the matter, see Paoli (1997) and Ministero dell'Interno (1993 and 1994).
76. Ministero dell'Interno (1994: 195).
77. TrPA (1993a: 32); see also TrPA (1991).
78. See Ministero dell'Interno (1993: 85-97, and 1994: 370-40).
79. The multi-billion project, for many decades at the center of debates and polemics about the economic and productive development of Calabria, initially envisaged the coming into production of a steelwork center, complete with all the necessary infrastructure: in actual fact, only the port was built and was first used in 1995, more than twenty years after its construction began. When the project of the Fifth Steelwork Center was abandoned due to its clear unprofitability in the new international steel market, the government opted for the realization of a coal-fired power and heating station: the new project involved an estimated total expenditure of 5,000 billion lira (US $3,291 million at the 1983 exchange rate), including 1,000 billion for works to be subcontracted. For a synthetic reconstruction of the whole history, see CPM (1990: 59-64).
80. PrPL (1993: 1688); see also CPM (1990).
81. TrRC (1992); PrRC (1995: 1880-82); Ciconte (1994); Licandro and Varano (1993).
82. It must be emphasized that the cultural evolution as well as underlying social and economic developments have proceeded in an unsteady and nonlinear way. State

monopolization of violence, for example, to which the decline of the subculture of honor is primarily linked, has made, overall, a considerable advance throughout the postwar decades and recovered the gap lost in the years following the Allied occupation of the *Mezzogiorno* in 1943. Nonetheless, this trend has also been marked by considerable steps backward, by moments of carelessness and even shady pacts with illegal centers of power (including mafia organizations), "owing in part to the fact that what the Italian state accomplishes with one hand it often undermines with the other" (Schneiders 1994: 240). In the 1970s, for example, when law enforcement largely focused on terrorism, state monopoly of violence underwent a serious crisis in mafia-related areas, which was exploited by the Sicilian *mafiosi* to make unprecedented attacks against state officials.

Likewise, the same institutions—such as mass parties and unions—that challenged the mafia families' traditional function of regulation and representation of interests, frequently gave an ambiguous message: on one hand, in fact, they were the carriers of more universalistic instances of representation; on the other, they often incorporated mafia clienteles and relied on mafia methods, thus further perpetuating the power of the former and legitimating the latter.

83. Since May 1991, when the Law was enacted, 12 town councils have been dissolved in Reggio Calabria province for mafia conditionings. Among them, the most important are those of Gioia Tauro (18,497 inhabitants), Rosarno (13,032 in.), Taurianova (15, 919 in.) and Melito Porto Salvo (10,551 in.), that have twice been dissolved. According to the Palmi Chief Prosecutor, Agostino Cordova, for instance, "Rosarno municipality was a pure administrative projection of the mafia" (Forgione and Mondani 1994: 111). At the same time, over 400 Calabrian public administrators have been charged with severe offenses such as mafia association, murder and drug traffic.

84. PrRC (1992, 1993a, b and c).

85. Forgione and Mondani (1994).

86. CPM (1993a: 122-3).

87. PrRC (1993c).

88. On the basis of records of proceedings in Italian and American courts (TrPA 1982, 1986; Biden 1980) it has been estimated that between four and five tons of pure heroin were produced each year in the late 1970s by Sicilian laboratories. This quantity, largely exported to the United States, then represented some 30 percent of the total demand of that country. Subtracting the costs of production and transport, this gave a net profit of around 700 or 800 trillion lira (between US $700 and 800 million) (Arlacchi 1988).

89. PrPA (1995b).

90. P. Schneider (1997).

91. See Dalla Chiesa (1984).

92. Turone (1995).

93. J and P. Schneider (1994).

94. CPMS (1976a: 581).

95. PrPA (1995a, II: 80).

96. PrPA (1995, II: 66).

97. PrCL (1992).

98. PrPA (1995, II: 66).

99. CPM (1993b: 60-6 and 1993b-bis: 98-100); Violante (1994: 169-80).

100. PrRC (1995: 4933).

101. PrRC (1995: 5722); see Forgione and Mondani (1994). According to a hypothesis recently put forward by a *pentito*, one of the very few murders of a high-ranking

state representative ever committed by the Calabrian 'Ndrangheta—the homicide of Francesco Ferlaino, State General Advocate, the second Italian Judicial Authority after the General Prosecutor, which took place in Lamezia Terme in July 1975—was allegedly carried out to allow the infiltration of the 'Ndrangheta into the Masonry. According to Giacomo Lauro, a former mafia high-ranking member, "Judge Ferlaino was killed because the equilibria within the Masonry had broken. Ferlaino, who was Mason, opposed the new Masonic-business project, which started to root especially in the South, under the direction of Licio Gelli, foreseeing the hoarding of every profitable licit or illicit deal. Substantially Ferlaino opposed the degeneration of the Masonic structure from a licit to an illicit body" (PrRC 1995: 5754; see also PrPL 1993).

102. PrRC (1995: 4980-1); see also TrPA (1993b) and CPM (1993b: 60-6).
103. CPM (1993d: 65).
104. TrPA (1993b).
105. PrRC (1995: 5732 ff).
106. Forgione and Mondani (1994: 111-35).
107. TrPA (1992); see also PrRC (1995, XVIII).
108. Paoli (1993); TrPA (1986); TrMI ([1984] 1986); PrPA (1995a, ch. 18).
109. Paoli (1993); PrPA (1997a); see also Commissione P2 (1984).
110. TrPA (1994); Bonsanti et al. (1995).
111. Out of dozens of minor attacks, three episodes of this subversive strategy are particularly important. First, on 14 May 1993 a car bomb exploded in Via Ruggero Fauro in Rome, aiming at killing a popular TV journalist. Second, two weeks later, on 27 May, an even more devastating blast in Via dei Georgofili, in Florence's historical center, seriously damaged some halls of the adjacent *Museo degli Uffizi* and caused the death of five persons. Lastly, on the night of 27/28 July, three bombs exploded one after another near the Basilica of San Giovanni in Laterano and the ancient church of San Giorgio in Velabro in Rome, and in the gardens of the municipal villa in Via Palestro in Milan. These attacks killed six people, wounded many others, and seriously damaged several buildings.
112. Ministero dell'Interno (1996).
113. Ministero dell'Interno (1999); see Paoli (2000: 287).
114. Ginsborg (1990, passim).
115. Martin (1997).
116. See Paoli (2000).
117. Forgione and Mondani (1994: 129-32).
118. PrRC (1995: 5071). The reasons for Berlusconi's willingness to come to terms with the mafia become clear if one refers to the investigations opened by the Palermo prosecutor's office since 1993 on Berlusconi himself and Marcello Dell'Utri, one of his closest and earliest collaborators. For both of them the charge was of external concourse in mafia association. Whereas the inquiry on Berlusconi has been closed, at the beginning of 1997 the Palermitan prosecutors asked for and obtained the indictment of Dell'Utri, on the basis of the declarations of more than 20 *pentiti* and other investigations and inquiries (PrPA 1997a).
119. See Paoli (2000: 291-300).
120. *Corriere della Sera* (27 April 1999: 8).
121. *Corriere della Sera* (27 July 1997).

References

Alongi, Giuseppe. *La Maffia*. Palermo: Sellerio [1886], 1977.

Andreotti, Giulio. *Cosa loro. Mai v isti da vicino.* Milano: Rizzoli, 1995.

Arlacchi, Pino. *Mafia Business. The Mafia Ethic and the Spirit of Capitalism.* Oxford: Oxford University Press [1983, 1986], 1988.

_____. *Men of Dishonor. Inside the Sicilian Mafia:An Account of Antonino Calderone.* New York: William Morrow [1992], 1993.

_____. *Addio Cosa Nostra. La vita di Tommaso Buscetta.* Milano: Rizzoli, 1994.

_____. *Il processo. Giulio Andreotti sotto accusa a Palermo.* Milano: Rizzoli, 1995.

Barone, Giuseppe. "Egemonie urbane e potere locale (1812-1913)," in *La Sicilia,* ed. M. Aymard and G. Giarrizzo. Torino: Giulio Einaudi Editore, 1987.

Biden, J. R. "The Sicilian Connection: Southwest Asian Heroin en Route to the United States," Report of Senator J. R. Biden to the U.S. Senate Committee on Foreign Affairs. Washington, DC: GPO, 1982.

Block, Alan A. "A Modern Marriage of Convenience: A Collaboration between Organized Crime and U.S. Intelligence," in *Organized Crime. A Global Perspective,* ed. R. J. Kelly. Totowa: Rowman & Littlefield, 1985.

Blok, Anton. *The Mafia of a Sicilian Village, 1860-1960: A Study of Violent Peasant Entrepreneurs.* New York and Oxford: Polity Press [1974], 1988.

Bonsanti, Sandra, Maurizio De Luca, and Corrado Stajano. "Il caso Mandalari," *Dossier Libera* n.1. Roma: Libera, 1995.

Cancila, Orazio. *Palermo.* Bari-Roma: Laterza, 1989.

Catanzaro, Raimondo. *Men of Respect. A Social History of the Sicilian Mafia.* New York: The Free Press [1988], 1992.

Chilanti, Felice. *La mafia su Roma.* Milano: Palazzi Editore, 1971.

Chubb, Judith. *Patronage, Power, and Poverty in Southern Italy. A Tale of Two Cities.* Cambridge: Cambridge University Press, 1982.

_____. *The Mafia and Politic: The Italian State under Siege.* Ithaca: Cornell University Press, 1989.

Ciconte, Enzo. *'Ndrangheta dall'Unitá ad oggi.* Bari: Laterza, 1992.

_____. "Ludovico Ligato," in *Cirillo, Ligato e Lima. Tre storie di mafia e politica,* ed. N. Tranfaglia. Bari: Laterza, 1994.

_____. *Processo alla 'Ndrangheta.* Bari: Laterza, 1996.

Cirillo Rampolla, Giovanna. *Suicidio per mafia,* ed. G. Fiume. Palermo: La Luna [1889], 1986.

Commissione P2, Commissione parlamentare d'inchiesta sulla loggia massonica P2. *Relazione di maggioranza e Relazioni di minoranza,* doc. XXIII, IX Legislatura. Roma: Camera dei Deputati, 1984.

CPM, Commissione Parlamentare d'inchiesta sul fenomeno della mafia e sulle altre associazioni similari. *Relazione sulle vicende connesse alla costruzione della centrale termoelettrica di Gioia Tauro,* doc. XXIII, n. 24, X legislatura. Roma: Camera dei Deputati, 1990.

_____. *Audizione del collaboratore di giustizia Tommaso Buscetta,* XI legislatura. Roma: Camera dei Deputati, 1992a, 16 November.

_____. *Audizione del collaboratore di giustizia Leonardo Messina,* XI legislatura. Roma: Camera dei Deputati, 1992b, 4 December.

_____. *Audizioni in Calabria,* XI legislatura. Roma: Camera dei Deputati, 1993a, 29 January.

_____. *Relazione sui rapporti tra mafia e politica,* doc. XXIII, n.2, XI legislatura. Roma: Camera dei Deputati, 1993b.

_____. *Nota integrativa alla relazione sui rapporti mafia e politica del deputato Alfredo Galasso,* doc. XXIII, n.2, XI legislatura. Roma: Camera dei Deputati, 1993b-bis.

_____. *Audizione del collaboratore di giustizia Gaspare Mutolo,* XI legislatura. Roma: Camera dei Deputati, 1993, 9 February.

_____. *Relazione sulla Calabria,* doc. XXIII, n. 8, XI legislatura. Roma: Camera dei Deputati, 1993d.

CPMS, Commissione Parlamentare d'inchiesta sul fenomeno della mafia in Sicilia. *Relazione sui mercati all'ingrosso,* doc. XXIII, n. 2-Bis. Roma: Camera dei Deputati, 1970.

_____. *Relazione sull'indagine riguardante casi di singoli mafiosi,* doc. XXIII, n. 2-quater, V legislatura. Roma: Camera dei Deputati, 1971.

_____. *Relazione conclusiva. Relatore: Carraro,* doc. XXIII, n. 2, VI legislatura,. Roma: Camera dei Deputati, 1976a), 1-328.

_____. *Relazione di minoranza. Relatori: La Torre, Benedetti, Malagugini, Adamoli, Chiaromonte, Lugnano, Maffioletti, Terranova,* doc. XXIII, n. 2, VI legislatura. Roma: Camera dei Deputati, 1976b, 569-956.

_____. *Relazione di minoranza. Relatori: Nicosia, Pisanò, Giuseppe Niccolai,* doc. XXIII, n. 2, VI legislatura. Roma: Camera dei Deputati, 1976c, 959-1247.

D'Agostini, Fabrizio. *Reggio Calabria: i moti del luglio 1970- febbraio 1971.* Milano: Feltrinelli, 1972.

Dalla Chiesa, Nando. *Delitto imperfetto. Il generale—la mafia—la società italiana.* Milano: Mondadori, 1984.

Di Lello, Giuseppe. *Giudici.* Palermo: Sellerio, 1994.

Duggan, Christopher. *Fascism and the Mafia.* New Haven and London: Yale University Press, 1989.

Falcone, Giovanni, and Giuliano Turone. "Tecniche di indagine in materia di mafia," unpublished paper presented to the Convegno sulla mafia organizzato dal Consiglio Superiore della Magistratura. Castelgandolfo, 1982, 4-6 June.

Fantozzi, Pietro. *Politica, clientela e regolazione sociale. Il Mezzogiorno nella questione politica italiana.* Soveria Mannelli: Rubbettino, 1993.

Fed. PCI-AG, Federazioni del P.C.I. di Agrigento e di Sciaccia. "Memoriale per la Commissione Parlamentare Antimafia," enclosed to Commissione Parlamentare d'inchiesta sul fenomeno della mafia in Sicilia, *Relazione di minoranza. Relatori: La Torre, Benedetti, Malagugini, Adamoli, Chiaromonte, Lugnano, Maffioletti, Terranova,* doc. XXIII, n. 2, VI legislatura. Roma: Camera dei Deputati [1964], 1976c, 691-779.

Fiume, Giovanna. *Le bande armate in Sicilia (1819-49). Violenza ed organizzazione del potere.* Palermo: 'Annali della Facoltà di Lettere e Filosofia dell'Università di Palermo', 1984.

Forgione, Francesco, and Paolo Mondani. *Oltre la cupola, Massoneria, mafia, politica.* Milano: Rizzoli, 1994.

Franchetti, Leopoldo. *Condizioni politiche ed amministrative della Sicilia.* Roma: Donzelli [1877], 1993.

Gambino, Sharo. *Mafia. La lunga notte della Calabria.* Serra San Bruno: Edizioni quaderni Calabria-oggi, 1976.

Gentile, Nick. *Vita di capomafia. Memorie raccolte da Felice Chilanti.* Roma: Crescenzi Allendorf [1963], 1993.

Graziano, Luigi. "Patron-Client Relationship in Southern Italy." *European Journal of Political Research* 1 (1973): 3-34.

_____. "Center-Periphery Relations and the Italian Crisis: The Problem of Clientelism," in *Territorial Politics in Industrial Nations,* ed. S. Tarrow, P. J. Katzenstein, and L. Graziano. New York: Praeger, 1978.

_____. *Clientelismo e sistema politico. Il caso dell'Italia.* Milano: Franco Angeli, 1980.

Gribaudi, Gabriella. *Mediatori, Antropologia del potere democristiano nel Mezzogiorno*. Torino: Rosenberg and Sellier, 1980.

Hess, Henner. *Mafia and Mafiosi. The Structure of Power*. Westmead: Saxon House [1970], 1973.

Licandro, Agatino, and Aldo Varano. *La città dolente. Confessione di un sindaco corrotto*. Torino: Einaudi, 1993.

Lombardi Satriani, Luigi. *Reggio Calabria. Rivolta e strumentalizzazione*. Vibo Valentia: Qualecultura, 1971.

Lorenzoni, Giovanni. *Inchiesta parlamentare sulle condizioni dei contadini nelle province meridionali*, vol. VI: Sicilia, tomo I, "Relazione del delegato tecnico prof. Giovanni Lorenzoni." Roma, 1910.

Lo Schiavo, Giuseppe G. "Nel regno della mafia." *Processi*, 5 (gennaio, 1955): 21-5.

Lupo, Salvatore. "L'utopia totalitaria del fascismo (1918-42)," in *La Sicilia*, ed. M. Aymard and G. Giarrizzo. Torino: Giulio Einaudi Editore, 1987.

_____. "'Il tenebroso sodalizio'. Un rapporto sulla mafia palermitana di fine Ottocento." *Studi storici*, 29 (n. 2 1988): 463-489.

_____. *Storia della mafia dalle origini ai giorni nostri*. Roma: Donzelli, 1983.

_____. *Andreotti, la mafia, la storia d'Italia*. Roma: Donzelli, 1996.

Macaluso, Emanuele. *Giulio Andreotti tra stato e mafia*. Soveria Mannelli: Rubbettino, 1995.

Mangiameli, Rosario. "La regione in guerra (1943-50)," in *La Sicilia*, ed. M. Aymard and G. Giarrizzo. Torino: Giulio Einaudi Editore, 1987.

Marino, Giuseppe C. *L'opposizione mafiosa. Mafia politica stato liberale*. Palermo: Flaccovio, 1986.

Marmo, Marcella. "L'onore dei violenti, l'onore della vittime. Un'estorsione camorrista del 1862 a Napoli," in *Onore e storia nelle società mediterranee,* ed. G. Fiume. Palermo: La Luna, 1989.

Martino, P. "Storia della parola 'ndranghita," in *Le ragioni della mafia. Studi e ricerche di "Quaderni calabresi,"* ed. F. Faeta *et al.* Milano: Jaca Book 1983.

Mastropaolo, Alfio. "Tra politica e mafia. Storia breve di un latifondo elettorale," *Far politica in Sicilia. Deferenza, consenso, protesta*, ed. M. Morisi. Milano: Feltrinelli, 1993.

Ministero degli Affari Esteri. "Appunto in ordine alla ricerca di un presunto documento allegato all'articolo 16 del trattato di armistizio del 1943 tra l'Italia e le potenze alleate, trasmesso dal ministero degli Affari Esteri il 23 agosto 1974," in *Documentazione allegata alla relazione conclusiva*, ed. Commissione Parlamentare d'inchiesta sul fenomeno della mafia in Sicilia, doc. XXIII, n. 4, vol. IV, tomo I. Roma: Camera dei Deputati, 1978, 913-8.

Ministero dell'Interno. *Rapporto annuale sul fenomeno della criminalità organizzata per il 1992*. Roma, 1993.

_____. *Rapporto annuale sul fenomeno della criminalità organizzata per il 1993*, doc. XXXVIII-*bis*, n. 1, XII legislatura. Roma: Camera dei Deputati, 1994.

_____. *Rapporto annuale sul fenomeno della criminalitá organizzata per il 1994*. Roma, 1995.

_____. *Relazione sui programmi di protezione, sulla loro efficacia e sulle modalità generali di applicazione per coloro che collaborano alla giustizia - I semestre 1996*, doc. XCI, n. 1, XIII legislatura. Roma: Senato della Repubblica, 1996.

_____. "Consigli comunali sciolti ai sensi del decreto legge 31 maggio 1991, n. 164, convertito in legge 22 luglio 1991, n. 221." Roma, unpublished typescript, June 30, 1999.

Montanaro, S., and S. Ruotolo, eds., *La vera storia d'Italia. Interrogatori, testimonianze, riscontri, analisi*. Giancarlo Caselli e i suoi sostituti ricostruiscono gli ultimi venti anni di storia italiana. Napoli: Liguori, 1995.

Mori, Cesare. *Tra le zagare oltre la foschia.* Palermo: La Zisa [1923], 1988.

_____. *Con la mafia ai ferri corti.* Napoli: Flavio Pagano Editore [1932], 1993.

Mosca, Gaetano. "Che cosa è la mafia," in G. Mosca, *Partiti e sindacati nella crisi del regime parlamentare.* Bari: Laterza [1900], 1949.

Novacco, Domenico. *Mafia ieri mafia oggi.* Milano: Feltrinelli, 1972.

Notarbartolo, Luigi. *La città cannibale. Il memoriale Notarbartolo* (originally published under the title *Memorie della vita di mio padre Emanuele Notarbartolo di San Giovanni*). Palermo: Novecento [1949], 1994.

Pallotta, Cino. *Dizionario storico della mafia.* Roma, 1977

Pantaleone, Michele. *Mafia e politica 1943-1962. Le radici sociali della mafia e i suoi sviluppi più recenti.* Torino: Einaudi [1962], 1972.

Paoli, Letizia. "Criminalità organizzata e finanza internazionale." *Rassegna Italiana di Sociologia,* XXXIV, (luglio-settembre, 1993): 391-423.

_____. *The Pledge to Secrecy. Culture, Structure and Action of Mafia Associations.* Firenze: European University Institute 1997), Ph.D. dissertation.

_____. *Fratelli di mafia. Cosa Nostra e 'Ndrangheta.* Bologna: Il Mulino, 2000.

Petacco, Arrigo. *Il prefetto di ferro.* Milano: Oscar Mondadori [1975], 1994.

Pezzino, Paolo. "Stato violenza società. Nascita e sviluppo del paradigma mafioso," in *La Sicilia,* ed. M. Aymard and G. Giarrizzo. Torino: Giulio Einaudi Editore, 1987.

_____. *Una certa reciprocità di favori. Mafia e modernizzazione violenta nella Sicilia postunitaria.* Milano: Angeli, 1990a.

_____. "La tradizione rivoluzionaria siciliana e l'invenzione della mafia." *Meridiana,* 7-8 (1990b): 45-71.

_____. *Il Paradiso abitato dai diavoli. Società, élites, istituzioni nel Mezzogiorno contemporaneo.* Milano: Franco Angeli, 1992a.

_____. *La congiura dei pugnalatori. Un caso politico-giudiziario alle origini della mafia.* Venezia: Marsilio, 1992b.

_____. "Mafia, stato e società nella Sicilia contemporanea: secoli XIX e XX," in *La mafia, le mafie,* ed. G. Fiandaca and S. Costantino. Bari-Roma: Laterza, 1994.

_____, ed. *Mafia: industria della violenza. Scritti e documenti inediti sulla mafia dalle origini ai giorni nostri.* Firenze: La Nuova Italia, 1995.

_____. "Mafia e politica una questione nazionale." *Passato e presente,* XIV (38, 1996): 7-23.

Piselli, Fortunata, and Giovanni Arrighi. "Parentela, clientela e comunità," in *La Calabria,* ed. P. Bevilacqua and A. Placanica. Torino: Einaudi, 1985.

Prefettura di Palermo. "Fascicolo trasmesso il 5 giugno 1971 relativo alla concessione dell'onorificenza di Cavaliere al merito della Repubblica italiana al dottor Michele Navarra," in *Documentazione allegata alla relazione conclusiva,* ed. Commissione Parlamentare d'inchiesta sul fenomeno della mafia in Sicilia, doc. XXIII, n. 1/XI, vol. IV, tomo XVII. Roma: Senato della Repubblica [1971], 1978.

PrCL, Procura della Repubblica di Caltanissetta, Direzione Distrettuale Antimafia. *Domanda di autorizzazione a procedere in giudizio contro il deputato Maira,* doc. IV, n. 133. Roma: Camera dei Deputati, 1992, 28 December.

PrPA, Procura della Repubblica di Palermo, Direzione Distrettuale Antimafia. *Domanda di autorizzazione a procedere in giudizio contro il senatore Giulio Andreotti,* doc. IV n. 102. Roma: Senato della Repubblica, 1993a, 27 March.

_____. *Domanda di autorizzazione a procedere in giudizio contro il senatore Giulio Andreotti,* doc. IV n. 102, integrazione. Roma: Senato della Repubblica, 1993b, 14 April.

_____. *Domanda di autorizzazione a procedere in giudizio contro il senatore Giulio Andreotti,* doc. IV n. 102, 2° integrazione. Roma: Senato della Repubblica, 1993b, 20 April.

_____. *Memoria depositata dal pubblico ministero nel procedimento penale n. 3538/ 94, instaurato nei confronti di Andreotti Giulio* (1995a).

_____. *Memoria depositata dal pubblico ministero nel processo n. 3162/89 a carico di Greco Michele ed altri, relativa ai c.d. 'omicidi politici'* (cioè agli omicidi di Michele Reina, Piersanti Mattarella, Pio La Torre e Rosario Di Salvo) (1995b).

_____. *Memoria depositata dal pubblico ministero nel procedimento penale n. 4578/ 96, instaurato nei confronti di Dell'utri Marcello* (1997a).

_____. *Memoria depositata dal pubblico ministero nel procedimento penale n. 1866/ 93, instaurato nei confronti di Carnevale Corrado* (1997b).

PrPL, Procura della Repubblica di Palmi. *Richiesta di rinvio a giudizio, di misure cautelari e di archiviazione nei confronti di Galluzzo Vincenzo Rosario + 81* (1993).

PrRC, Procura della Repubblica di Reggio Calabria, Direzione Distrettuale Antimafia. *Domanda di autorizzazione a procedere in giudizio contro il senatore Sisinio Zito*, doc. IV n.30. Roma: Senato della Repubblica, 1992.

_____. *Domanda di autorizzazione a procedere in giudizio contro il deputato Sandro Principe*, doc. IV, n. 49 and n. 437. Roma, Camera dei Deputati, 1993a.

_____. *Domanda di autorizzazione a procedere in giudizio contro il deputato Riccardo Misasi*, doc. IV, n. 256. Roma: Camera dei Deputati, 1993b.

_____. *Domanda di autorizzazione a procedere in giudizio contro il deputato Paolo Romeo*, doc. IV, n. 465, XI legislatura. Roma: Camera dei Deputati, 1993c.

_____. *Richiesta di ordini di custodia cautelare in carcere e di contestuale rinvio a giudizio nel procedimento contro Condello Pasquale + 477* (1995).

PrRM, Procura della Repubblica di Roma. *Domanda di autorizzazione a procedere in giudizio contro il senatore Giulio Andreotti*, doc. IV n. 169 Roma, Senato della Repubblica, 1993, 9 June.

Questura di Palermo. "Segnalazione di proposta per l'applicazione della misura di prevenzione della Sorveglianza Speciale della P.S. a carico di Aliotta Giacomo," in *Documentazione allegata alla relazione conclusiva*, ed. Commissione Parlamentare d'inchiesta sul fenomeno della mafia in Sicilia, doc. XXIII, n. 1/VI, vol. IV, tomo XII. Roma: Senato della Repubblica [1970], 1978.

Renda, Francesco. *Storia della Sicilia dal 1860 al 1970, vol. I: I caratteri originari e gli anni della unificazione italiana.* Palermo: Sellerio, 1984.

_____. *Storia della Sicilia dal 1860 al 1970, vol. II: Dalla caduta della Destra al fascismo.* Palermo: Sellerio, 1985.

_____. *Un'interpretazione della Mafia.* Verona: Edizioni del Paniere, 1986.

_____. *Storia della Sicilia dal 1860 al 1970, vol. III: Dall'occupazione militare alleata al centrosinistra.* Palermo: Sellerio, 1987.

Romano, Saverio Francesco. *Storia della mafia.* Milano: Sugarco, 1963.

Sabetti, Filippo. *Political Authority in a Sicilian Village.* New Brunswick, NJ: Rutgers University Press, 1984.

Salvemini, Gaetano. *Il ministro della mala vita e altri scritti sull'Italia giolittiana.* Milano: [1909], 1963.

Santino, Umberto. "Guida al processo Andreotti," *Città d'utopia* (November 1995).

Schneider, Jane, and Peter Schneider. *Culture and Political Economy in Western Sicily.* New York: Academic Press, 1976.

_____. "Mafia Burlesque: The Profane Mass as Peace-Making Ritual," in *Religion, Power and Protest in Local Communities. The Northern Shore of the Mediterranean*, ed. E. R. Wolf. Berlin and New York: Mouton Publishers, 1984.

_____. "Mafia, Antimafia and the Question of Sicilian Culture *Politics and Society*, 22 (2, 1994): 237-58.

Sereni, Emilio. *Il capitalismo nelle campagne (1860-1990).* Torino: Einaudi [1948], 1968.

Stanley, Alexandra. "Andreotti Is Acquitted of 1979 Murder." *International Herald Tribune*, 25-26 September 1999: 1-5.

_____. "Andreotti Found Not Guilty of Protecting Sicilian Mafia." *International Herald Tribune*, 25 October 1999: 6.

Strati, Saverio. *Il selvaggio di Santa Venere*. Milano: Mondadori, 1977.

Tarrow, Sidney G. *Peasant Communism in Southern Italy*. New Haven and London: Yale University Press, 1967.

Tessitore, Giovanni. *Cesare Mori: la grande occasione perduta dell'antimafia*. Cosenza: Pellegrini Editore, 1994.

Tilly, Charles. "Foreword," to A. Blok, *The Mafia of a Sicilian Village, 1860-1960: A Study of Violent Peasant Entrepreneurs*. New York and Oxford: Polity Press [1974], 1988.

TrMI, Tribunale di Milano, Ufficio Istruzione Processi Penali. *Ordinanza-sentenza di rinvio a giudizio nei confronti di Michele Sindona*, luglio, published in *Sindona. L'atto di accusa dei giudici di Milano*. Roma: Editori Riuniti [1984], 1986.

TrPA, Tribunale di Palermo, Ufficio Istruzione Processi Penali. *Ordinanza-sentenza di rinvio a giudizio nei confronti di Torretta Pietro + 120*, in *Documentazione allegata alla relazione conclusiva*, ed. Commissione Parlamentare d'inchiesta sul fenomeno della mafia in Sicilia, doc. XXIII, n. 1/XI, vol. IV, tomo XVII. Roma: Senato della Repubblica [1965], 1978.

_____. Ufficio Istruzione Processi Penali. *Ordinanza-sentenza di rinvio a giudizio nei confronti di Rosario Spatola + 119* (1982).

_____. Ufficio Istruzione Processi Penali.. *Ordinanza-sentenza di rinvio a giudizio nei confronti di Abbate Giovanni + 706* (1986), November.

_____. Ufficio del Giudice per le Indagini Preliminari. *Ordinanza di custodia cautelare in carcere nei confronti di Morici Serafino + 4* (1991), 9 July.

_____. Ufficio del Giudice per le Indagini Preliminari. *Ordinanza di custodia cautelare in carcere nei confronti di Contrada Bruno* (1992), 23 December.

_____. Ufficio del Giudice per le Indagini Preliminari. *Ordinanza di custodia cautelare in carcere nei confronti di Riina Salvatore + 24* (1993a), 18 May.

_____. Ufficio del Giudice per le Indagini Preliminari. *Ordinanza di custodia cautelare in carcere nei confronti di Ferraro Pietro + 9* (1993b), 16 December.

_____. Ufficio del Giudice per le Indagini Preliminari. *Ordinanza di custodia cautelare in carcere nei confronti di Mandalari Giuseppe + 1* (1994), 17 December.

_____. Ufficio del Giudice per le Indagini Preliminari. *Ordinanza di custodia cautelare in carcere nei confronti di Mannino Giuseppe* (1995), 13 February.

TrRC, Tribunale di Reggio Calabria, Ufficio del Giudice per le Indagini Preliminari. *Ordinanza di custodia cautelare in carcere nei confronti di Battaglia Piero + 10* (1992), 1 December.

Turone, Giuliano. *Il delitto di associazione mafiosa*. Milano: Giuffrè, 1995.

Turone, Sergio. *Politica ladra. Storia della corruzione in Itali, 1861-1992*. Bari-Roma: Laterza, 1992.

Violante, Luciano. *Non è la priovra. Dodici tesi sulle mafie italiane*. Torino: Einaudi, 1994.

Walston, James. *The Mafia and Clientelism. Roads to Rome in Post-War Calabria*. London and New York: Routledge, 1988.

3

Drugs and Democracy in Colombia

Rensselaer W. Lee III and Francisco E. Thoumi

*The corruption of the Cali cartel is worse than
the terrorism of the Medellín cartel . . . terrorism
can be fought and faced; corruption has no
face.*
—*Alfonso Valdivieso, 1995*

Introduction

A succession of scandals that besieged the Ernesto Samper administration from the time it took power in August 1994 brought the country to the brink of a political and economic collapse. Tapes of telephone conversation made public immediately after Samper's election revealed that his campaign had been heavily funded by drug money. After a lengthy and traumatic legal process that indicted and convicted several important politicians, the president himself was exonerated on the grounds that the funding "took place behind his back." Independent of the president's verdict, the trial forced Colombians to acknowledge the existence of a very close nexus between politics and the illegal drug industry that polarized the country and weakened the government.[1] During the last few years guerrilla and paramilitary organizations gained strength relative to the forces of the state and became the recognized de facto power in many regions,[2] the level of violence increased dramatically, the vice-president resigned in protest against Samper, corruption charges were raised against several key government figures, and ministerial changes became common. The relations between Colombia and the United States deteriorated during the Samper administration to a point not seen since the independence of Panama in 1903.[3] (They have recovered somewhat during the Pastrana presidency). The traditionally resilient Colombian economy began to show signs of major strains as growth declined in the mid-1990s.

71

This trend was accentuated in 1998 and 1999, and Colombia may experience the first negative growth year since the end of the Second World War. Urban unemployment increased some 5 percent from the beginning of the Samper administration in 1994 to over 13 percent in 1997, reaching an unprecedented 19 percent in early 1999. Simultaneously, at the end of the Samper administration the fiscal deficit loomed out of control.

The political-criminal nexus in Colombia is a complex phenomenon, part of an ongoing Colombian drama in which many actors with various interests play a role: illegal drugs and other criminal organizations, guerrillas, paramilitary groups, the army and the police, the government and its bureaucracy, political parties, the United States government, civil society organizations (including the main legal economic interests of the country) and others. The nexus among these players is intertwined and difficult to ascertain with a high degree of certainty.

Using published sources and interviews with some of the main politicians of the country, including those in and out of jail, the authors seek to advance the understanding of these relationships. These interviews focused on the relationship between politicians and the illegal drug industry only. They dealt with other actors only marginally, and were aimed at identifying the structure of the political-criminal nexus, how it developed, the implications, and possible policy alternatives.[4] This discussion is divided into three sections: the conditions that favored the development of the nexus, followed by the development of the nexus itself, and finally the vulnerability of the nexus.

Conditions for the Nexus Development

Cocaine, heroin, and other illegal drugs are easy to produce. The technological skills required are relatively simple and well known. Still, some countries are more likely to produce drugs than others. The experience of countries or regions that today produce illegal drugs indicate that there are some underlying conditions that encourage production, and that there are other immediate factors that appear to trigger production.

Underlying factors

The nature of the political-criminal nexus depends on the structure and characteristics of the illegal industry. During the 1970s and 1980s Colombia possessed a significant array of underlying structural conditions that made the country the best place on the American continent for the industry to concentrate its manufacturing and export activities. Some of these causes are independent from the rest, but others interact with each other, enhancing their importance. The main underlying structural conditions in Colombia were: the delegitimization of the regime, the weakness of civil society, the widespread propensity to resolve disputes through violence, the geography of the country, the structure of the political system and parties, various obstacles to upward social mobility, the large scale of illegal economic activities, and the social acceptance of contraband and money laundering.

The Colombian regime has not been based on a social consensus about what society should be. It has been imposed by the traditional elites and has been perceived as ratifying the widespread "ethos of inequality" that prevails in society[5] and a lack of acceptance and legitimacy of "the Other" as a valid social actor.[6] There is a long history of arbitrary law enforcement, and the legal and judicial system has been used by those in power to extract benefits for themselves. During this century the traditional *hacienda-* and *minifundia-* based rural society changed as the country became urban, educated, and the manufacturing and tertiary sectors of the economy developed. These changes allowed many previously excluded from power to participate politically and to try to share in the benefits of economic development. Past experiences associated wealth with breaking economic laws and capturing rents. While in the past only the small elite could capture rents, a fight developed as social changes and development "democratized" rent seeking. The government exercised only intermittent control over large economic activities and areas of the country, and it never developed effective methods to protect property rights and to solve conflicts. A growing gap between de jure and de facto behaviors developed, legitimizing activities such as illegal drug production and marketing.

Colombia has many civil organizations, but their large number is deceiving in the sense that they do not impose constraints on individual behavior. National loyalty is almost nonexistent. Until the mid-twentieth century, political parties substituted as generators of deep loyalties for the country. Indeed, the great "irrational" violence experienced during mid-century can be explained only if one accepts that peasants had party loyalties comparable to national loyalties in other countries. Colombia did not have native communities that provided a sense of belonging to their members; the Catholic Church emphasized ritual compliance over behavior; and families became increasingly weak as migrations and modernization took place. Large urban growth and intra-city migrations prevented the development of neighborhood organizations by which peer groups exert social pressure. The result is a tragedy in which "there is capitalism but without its corresponding ethic of individual responsibility. It is thus a savage capitalism."[7]

Third, the growing illegitimacy of the regime and the weakening of civil society constraints have resulted in declining public support for key national institutions and the appearance of powerful nonstate actors like guerrilla and paramilitary groups and drug cartels.[8] Violence has been a very common means of resolving individual conflicts and capturing rents and wealth. Colombians' willingness to use violence is significantly more pronounced than that of other societies. Indeed, Colombia may be the most violent country in the world.[9] (Colombia's homicide rate at 78 per 100,000 in 1994 is seven times the rate in the United States, and comparable to that of Washington, DC). Violence has been used by Colombian traffickers to wrest control of the U.S. wholesale cocaine business from Cuban and organized crime trafficking syndicates.[10] It has been used to settle disputes between and within Colombia's major trafficking coalitions. The Medellín and Cali cartels have used violence to intimidate or to assassinate Colombian journalists, politicians, judges, congressmen, police, army officers, cabinet ministers, and other possible opponents. Yet this is not the only role played by violence in the development of the illegal drug industry. The violence of the 1940s and early 1950s, which was associated with peasants' fight for land, displaced many peasants who then fled to unsettled isolated areas of the country.[11] During the last twenty years, rural violence has continued to displace large peasant populations who have also settled in vacant isolated lands. Coca and poppy are the only crops that produce an income level sufficient to sustain the settlements. Thus, the failure of the land reform efforts is one of the main causes of the growth of illegal crops.

The geography of the country has also been conducive to the development of the illegal drug industry. The country's location between the traditional coca growing areas and the main cocaine market made the country a good transshipment site; also the large number of isolated, sparsely populated regions where there is very little government presence has made the country an excellent location for illegal drug manufacturing and smuggling. In such regions, laboratories, clandestine airstrips, and drug storage sites are relatively difficult to detect. Scattered central or local government representatives are also extremely vulnerable to intimidation and bribes.

The political party structure and the traditional parties' role in society have been conditioned by the country's geography. The weak physical integration of the country gave great autonomy to local leaders and governments. The two traditional parties developed with a very decentralized structure in which local leaders could exert power without central government controls. As observed in Leal (1989), weak central party organizations resulted in weak party ideologies and very pragmatic politics. In the first part of this century, local party leaders mediated between citizens and the state, and party loyalties substituted for loyalty to the Colombian nation since the presence of parties in many regions was stronger than that of the state. In the last fifty years this has led to the development of a strong clientelistic system in which the state has become a bounty to be distributed by local party leaders.

The political system was insufficiently open and democratic. The period of "La Violencia" (in effect, civil war between the Liberal and Conservative parties in the late 1940s and the 1950s) ended with the "National Front," an agreement between the two party elites to stop the killing and to distribute the state bounty. A constitutional amendment was passed that required the alternation of the presidency among the two parties for four periods and distributed all government jobs equally between the two parties. After the National Front formally ended in 1974, the political class refused to change the system, and it continued to operate informally. The National Front was, in fact, a cartel that monopolized power and excluded other political alternatives. One result of this agreement was the depoliticization of the two parties and their development into clientelistic electoral machines.[12] The system allowed for dissent within a party, but not for opposition. The party structure facilitated the development of relatively cheap support networks that have allowed the narcotics industry to operate in isolated regions; moreover, clientelism made local politics highly vulnerable to penetration by the illegal drug industry: once it is accepted that elections are won through direct or indirect vote buying, those who have the most money will control the political machinery.

Frustrated expectations of social mobility also contributed to the growth of the illegal industry. The weak state and lack of national identity and interpersonal trust were associated with extreme individuality and high transaction costs. These factors in turn produced a society in which cliques or mafia-like groups controlled business and political power. Within this context, social mobility requires the acceptance of strangers within those groups. There is no doubt that the success of the political system was due in part to the fact that some local and student leaders who became socially mobile were coopted. However, the possible social mobility channels were narrow to begin with, and as the level of education in the country soared, they became clogged.[13] For many young, frustrated Colombians the illegal drug industry was the easiest way to achieve social status. For others, the closeness of the political system also led to frustrations that were vented through illegal activities as a way to "get back at the system."

The amount of income and capital obtained illegally has grown significantly in Colombia during the last fifty years. This was a partial result and a confirmation of the growing gap between de jure and de facto behaviors and the weak state. Further, in this environment capital property rights were illegitimate and predatory behavior became widespread. The acceptance of illegal income and capital greatly increased.[14] Among the main illegal industries were emerald mining and exporting, diverse contraband imports, and contraband exports of cattle and coffee, through which Colombians developed foreign exchange, money laundering skills and international smuggling distribution systems. Contraband imports are estimated variously to account for 20 to 40 percent of legal imports. A large informal and illegal economy blurred any moral difference between drug generated income and capital and other income and capital, resulted in a widespread acceptance of contraband

and promoted the development of money laundering skills. All these factors contributed to the development of the illegal drug industry.

Trigger factors

Other factors coincided to trigger the growth of the illegal drug industry and facilitated the development of links with the legal economy and the political regime in Colombia. Among these are the decline of economic growth and the crises in certain industries, frequent tax amnesties, the international trend toward open market policies and the opening of the Colombian economy in the 1990s, the international drug industry trends and some of the anti-drug policies, the willingness of some high-profile Colombians to negotiate with drug entrepreneurs, and the industry's own initiatives to build links with the political regime, and more recently, the willingness of members of the political establishment to do the same.

The decline of Colombia's growth and the crises of some industries during the late 1970s and early 1980s also triggered the growth of the illegal drug industry and helped cement the industry's ties to the Colombian elite.[15] The main mafia organizations all developed in Antioquia, Valle and the North Coast, regions which had suffered a decline of industry and an increase in unemployment.[16] When Medellín's textile-dependent industrial sector collapsed in the 1980s, local businessmen turned to the cocaine industry for infusions of capital; some failed entrepreneurs even became traffickers themselves. In most parts of the world an economic recession does not in itself result in the growth of international organized crime. However, the presence of the structural elements discussed above turned the recession into a trigger for the illegal drug industry.

Second, in an attempt to increase government revenues, the government enacted tax reforms, accompanied by a tax amnesty in 1974. Successive governments have implemented tax reforms, most of which have included tax amnesties that under different rubrics allowed the repatriation of illegally held assets with "no questions asked." Such amnesties induced businessmen to keep some of their activities under the table, on the understanding that if needed, they could declare them openly. This kept money laundering costs low and permitted the illegal drug industry to establish links with the formal economy and the political system. In one notorious case in the early 1980s, Medellín trafficker Carlos Lehder founded a political party with illegal funds, the "Movimiento Latino Nacional." The money came from cocaine and marijuana transshipment activities in the Bahamas, and was brought back to Colombia under a tax amnesty declared by then-president Belisario Betancur.[17]

Third, from the point of view of drug control, macroeconomic policy strategies seem to have changed at the wrong time. The protectionist and interventionist policies of past Colombian governments encouraged illegal economic activities and helped develop skills used in the expansion of the illegal drug industry. If the economy had opened thirty years ago and de-personalized market mechanisms had been in place, the kinds of rent-seeking skills used to produce and export illegal drugs might not have developed to the same degree. Once the opening occurred in the early 1990s, however, the resultant liberalization of international trade and exchange increased the drug kingpins' opportunities to legitimize illicitly obtained wealth. How-ever, given the decline in growth during the 1980s, the large volume of contraband, world trends toward open economies, and the pressure put on the Colombian government by multilateral financial institutions and some U.S. government agencies, it is not clear that the Colombian government had any alternative but to open its economy. At most, it probably could have followed a different path, that is, opening the manufacturing sector first, while keeping the monetary sector partially closed for a time.

Some international drug industry trends and some of the anti-drug poli-cies outside Colombia also contributed to the growth of the Colombian in-dustry. For example, the marijuana eradication programs of the late 1960s in Mexico and Jamaica, and the Pinochet government's attack on the Chilean cocaine industry when he took over in 1973, were conducive to the develop-ment of the Colombian industry in the 1970s. In a sense, Colombia became "hooked" on drugs in this period. A fairly successful Colombian effort to eradicate marijuana in the late 1970s and early 1980s, the sharp increase in marijuana production in the U.S., and the development there of sinsemilla (seedless cannabis) growing techniques that enhance marijuana's drug con-tent merely encouraged the search for alternative drugs in Colombia. Part of the organizational and logistical infrastructure developed to export mari-juana was redeployed in the service of the cocaine industry, but most was not. The new cocaine industry required a more complex organization of produc-tion, generated far more income, and had a much wider national political impact than the more localized marijuana business.

Finally, Colombia's violent conflict with the Medellín cartel in 1989-93 played a significant if indirect role in shaping the political-criminal nexus in the country. The cartel's "absolute and total war" against the government punctuated by terrorist-style bombings in cities and kidnapping of members of the Colombian elite had two important consequences. One was to force the government into a de facto alliance with Medellín's chief rival, the Cali cartel. Cali maintained networks of informants within the Medellín coalition and also monitored some of Escobar's communications. Information obtained from these channels was passed to the police and the Department of Adminis-trative Security. This possibly proved decisive in the liquidation of Escobar and most of his trafficking empire in 1993. Not surprisingly, the common struggle against Escobar widened Cali's points of contact with and access to government officials and political leaders in Colombia. The Cali traffickers also wanted compensation for their contribution to the struggle in the form of judicial benefits, such as short sentences and house arrest instead of a jail cell, benefits which the government seemed willing to grant in the 1993-94 period.

A second important consequence was a preference for negotiating deals with drug criminals. Because of the weakness of the state and its criminal justice institutions, authorities in the Gaviria and Samper administrations felt compelled to make various legislative and judicial concessions to traffickers to purchase a modicum of social peace. In effect, violence diminished Colombia's drug fighting resolve, accelerated the delegitimization of the Colombian state, and strengthened the political-criminal nexus. The demise of extradition, the passage of extremely favorable (to criminals) plea-bargaining legislation, and the Colombian Chief Prosecutor's (1993-94) enthusiasm for face-to-face meetings with the Cali cartel leaders all reflect this unhealthy pattern of accommodation. The policy was to avoid a renewal of narcoterrorism at almost any cost. Ernesto Samper's defense minister Fernando Botero declared in a September 1994 speech in Cali defending the administration's conciliatory approach toward Cali's cocaine kingpins, "In no way will we allow the nation to fall again into episodes of war."[18]

Development of the Political-Criminal Nexus

Industry perspectives

Two aspects of the Colombian narcotics industry have contributed most significantly to the formation of the political-criminal nexus in Colombia. One is the industry's sheer size. Estimates of the size of the industry are uncertain, difficult to make, and vary within a wide range.[19] As of the early to mid-1990s, according to Clawson and Lee, the ten or fifteen main trafficking organizations in Colombia could have received net revenues (after payments to suppliers, transporters, and money launderers) of at least $3 billion to $4 billion annually from international sales of cocaine and heroin. More recent estimates have a somewhat lower bottom estimate.[20] Still, drug revenues for the cartels amounted to roughly 4 to 7 percent of Colombia's gross domestic product in the 1990s, which makes narcotics barons a dominant economic interest group in Colombia, particularly, because a large proportion of their sales result in profits. Colombian traffickers' large surpluses imply a significant capability for system penetration activities such as lobbying, bribes, and legal investments, as well as for the exercise of violence and intimidation against the Colombian state. Furthermore, narcotraffickers' accumulated wealth (as opposed to annual earnings) from trafficking and legal businesses is extremely threatening to the power structure. Independent of what estimates are used, narco-income and narco-wealth are so large relative to key economic variables in Colombia that they could easily alter the status quo of the economy and the political system.

A related problem is that traffickers need to buy high-level political support in order to launder their vast earnings in Colombia's relatively small economy. Large-scale transfers of funds and investments are necessarily conspicuous in such a setting and the dominant elites must acquiesce. As Thoumi observes, "for the most part the drug cartels require only local support networks to allow them to grow coca and poppies and to manufacture and export drugs. However, when it comes to laundering money these cartels often need to win favor with ranking officials of the central government. Such favor affords protection from the law. The reason that drug cartels have turned to corrupting high-level government officials involves the Colombian economy's modest capacity for absorbing and hiding illegal funds."[21]

For example, the profits of any mid-size export syndicate that exports sixty tons of cocaine a year are comparable to those of any of the largest financial conglomerates of the country. This indicates that any country's vulnerability to the corruptive capacity of the illicit drug industry is related to the industry's need to launder money and to the relative size and concentration of those illegal funds.

A second factor is the ability of Colombian traffickers to collaborate in influencing government policy, the law enforcement environment, and the political system generally. The original concept of a cocaine "cartel" referred mainly to economic behavior, especially cooperation among suppliers to rationalize the system of transporting cocaine. It was not about agreements to restrict supply and maintain price levels, and in fact, prices of cocaine declined steadily from the early 1980s to the mid-1990s. The idea was to maximize export volumes while reducing the risk to each participant. This included co-financing and co-insurance mechanisms as well as transport of large loads of cocaine to target markets via different conveyances and routes. Non-economic forms of collaboration, however, also became central to the cartel's activities as trafficking groups acquired more power and visibility, and as Colombian authorities (with some prodding from the Americans) sought ways to crack down on the drug trade. Trafficking organizations pooled information on law enforcement activities (such as planned raids on major leaders), developed joint counterintelligence and counter-enforcement strategies, jointly funneled cash to political parties and collaborated to improve their bargaining position vis-à-vis the state. To date, such patterns of cooperation have developed largely within specific regions, hence, the shorthand "Medellín cartel," or "Cali cartel."

However, narco-traffickers also exercised political influence at the national level. For example, in Cali, according to a *Miami Herald* report, major drug kingpins each contributed $200,000 per month to maintain a joint intelligence-gathering operation. Much of the money went to bribe police, army officials, and politicians. Cali leaders such as the Rodríguez-Orejuela brothers, José Santa Cruz Londoño, Helmer Herrera-Buitrago, and a number of smaller Valle traffickers reportedly established a common fund of some $8 million (in a special account in the Banco de Colombia in Cali) to influence the outcomes of the 1994 presidential and congressional election campaigns.[22] Also, in the late 1980s and early 1990s, leaders of the Medellín and Cali cartels negotiated as a group with the Colombian government in an effort to obtain collective judicial benefits such as short jail sentences, favorable conditions of incarceration, an end to extradition, and even amnesty for their crimes.

Finally, a leadership structure of sorts existed within Colombia's cocaine establishments, exercised by the heads of the dominant trafficking organizations. In Medellín, Pablo Escobar's pioneering role in establishing export routes, his access to the means of violence and his ruthless domination of smaller exporters held the coalition together and established its identity. In Cali, Gilberto Rodríguez-Orejuela retained what he called his "poder de convocatoria" (power of assembly) with other Valle drug dealers, and together with his brother Miguel defined the common position of the Valle group in surrender negotiations with the Colombian government in 1993-94.[23]

Trafficking groups also cooperate to inflict violence on their enemies. These include rival drug coalitions, leftist guerrilla forces and, in the case of the Medellín cartel, the Colombian power structure itself. For instance, Medellín kingpin Pablo Escobar successfully levied "war taxes" of $100,000 to $200,000 per month on Medellín cocaine shippers to support the cartel's political military activities, its war against the state and the economic and political elites, in the period from 1989 to 1993. These activities took a terrible toll in terms of casualties. At least 1,500 Colombians died, many of them civilians, and there was widespread damage to property and businesses. The Colombian establishment prevailed in the conflict, but the prolonged narco-violence weakened the state and widened opportunities for political corruption in Colombia.

Collusive Relationships

Organized crime's threat to the political order has proven greater than to the country's economic structure. The threat has been subtle and insidious rather than direct and overt, but it has been pervasive. Unlike terrorists or guerrillas who operate more or less outside the system and who may seek the overthrow of the government, criminals usually seek to manipulate the system from within. Indeed, well-organized groups conduct their businesses with the protection and sometimes the active support of governments.

Collusive ties between government and criminals are manifested in a number of ways. The most basic is the nexus of criminal money and functions of government. Corruption may be systemic, focused on influencing key officials, opinion leaders, politicians or legislators. The aim here is to protect the integrity of the organization and its leaders and to promote legislation favorable to criminal interests and generally to ensure a crime-friendly environment.

On an operational level, corrupted law enforcement officials allow individual illegal transactions such as drug processing or shipments to proceed unhindered. Officials provide their criminal clients with advance warning of government raids and dragnets. In Colombia, a case in point was the conspicuous failure of the government to arrest Pablo Escobar for many years, despite a series of encirclement campaigns conducted by thousands of soldiers and elite police troops. As a former Escobar associate remarked, "half of those who work for the government are protecting him while the other half are pursuing him."[24] The degree of social support that Escobar received in Medellín was also remarkable, and it was perhaps the main reason why it was so difficult to catch him. In *News of a Kidnapping*, García Márquez wrote that this was partly attributable to slum-rebuilding and other civil sector projects sponsored by Escobar in the early 1980s.

Similarly, judges and police officials on traffickers' payrolls made a mockery of the criminal justice system. Henchmen of the Medellín cartel reportedly offered judges trying drug cases '*plata o plomo*' (silver or lead), money if they let the trafficker go free, a bullet if convicted. Not surprisingly most judges chose the former option. The Cali cartel's technique was somewhat more refined: "We don't kill ministers or judges; we buy them," remarked Cali kingpin Gilberto Rodríguez Orejuela on one occasion.

Yet corruption, viewed broadly as an exchange of values between criminals and government or political authorities, has become almost inseparable from the activities and practice of statecraft in Colombia. Here the issue is no longer the delivery of specific services or favors in return for bribes but rather the management of relations with a powerful (if illegal) interest group to achieve specific political objectives.

Three specific examples of the collusive pattern can be mentioned: The first is the bizarre history of negotiations between the Colombian government and leaders of the Medellín and Cali cartels. In no other country has a government negotiated with criminals so openly and for such an extended period. In such negotiations (which have occurred sporadically since 1984) the government has sought various outcomes: to diminish the size of the drug trade, to reduce societal violence and "narco-terrorism," to achieve the release of kidnapped victims, and to bring traffickers to justice. The traffickers for their part have sought mostly guarantees of judicial leniency, non-extradition, amnesty or minimal jail time, and the chance for "reintegration" into Colombian society. Traffickers have made several grandiose (and probably insincere) offers to retire from the narcotics business, to dismantle trafficking routes, and to surrender assets such as laboratories, aircraft and weapons to the government. The Colombian government has viewed some offers with skepticism but, nevertheless, has found it expedient to maintain a dialogue with criminals who command significant economic and military resources.

Usually, government-trafficker negotiations have been initiated by the criminals, although the government at times has been an active and interested participant in such talks. The extreme violence of 1989-90, the period of most intense hostilities with the Medellín cartel, prompted prominent members of society to become intermediaries in the conflict. In 1990 a "Committee of Notables" consisting of three ex-presidents of Colombia, a former minister of government, a widely revered Catholic priest, and a leader of the leftist Unión Patriótica party attempted to negotiate peace and surrender terms on behalf of Medellín Extraditables. The notables, who were, in effect, representing the government, also sought and achieved the release of a number of hostages held by the traffickers, among them, members of prominent Colombian families. The activities of the notables and general popular pressure for peace prompted the government to issue a succession of decrees in late 1990 and 1991 that allowed traffickers to submit to justice under extremely favorable terms. Leading Medellín traffickers, including Escobar, took advantage of these concessions and turned themselves in.

In at least two recorded cases, in Panama City in May 1984, and in Bogotá in January 1994, cocaine kingpins held direct face-to-face meetings with government representatives. In Panama, leaders of the Medellín cartel, Pablo Escobar, Jorge Ochoa, and José Gonzalo Rodríguez-Gacha, presented a surrender proposal directly to Colombian Attorney General Carlos Jiménez-Gómez, following an earlier meeting with ex-president Alfonso López-Michelsen. (At the time, traffickers were on the run following a massive government crackdown mounted after the April 1984 assassination of Justice Minister Rodrigo Lara-Bonilla). During the early 1990s, Colombian Prosecutor General Gustavo de Greiff held successive private meetings with three important Cali chiefs: Helmer Herrera-Buitrago, José Olmedo Ocampo, and Juan Carlos Ramirez. The traffickers were seeking to clarify their legal status and to explore surrender options. Another source, former Cali cartel accountant Guillermo Palomari, claimed in a 1997 testimony in the United States that Gustavo De Greiff held seven meetings with Miguel Rodríguez-Orejuela in the presence of the latter's lawyer, Bernardo González, in a Rodríguez-owned apartment in Bogotá. This version is denied by De Greiff.[25]

A second politically noteworthy area of collusion was in Colombia's ongoing conflict with anti-government insurgent groups. Here the principal setting for the political-criminal nexus has been Colombia's guerrilla-infested countryside, where drug dealers have formed common cause with legal property owners and with the Colombian military. The focal point of cooperation among these groups has been paramilitary forces, in effect rural vigilante groups, which over the years have developed a broad anti-leftist agenda. This agenda includes not simply helping landowners defend themselves against predatory guerrillas but also actively rooting out and exterminating the insurgents' civilian support networks. Paramilitary groups receive significant funding from narcotics traffickers, who own an estimated 4 to 5 million hectares of the country's grazing lands (roughly 15 percent) and other agricultural lands in Colombia, and whose properties and cocaine laboratories are targets of guerrilla shakedowns.[26] In addition, the paramilitaries receive automatic weapons, training and intelligence information from local Colombian army units. Trafficker-landlords also have had their channels of communication with the army. For example, according to Clawson and Lee, in the 1980s drug lord Gonzalo Rodríguez-Gacha reportedly maintained direct radio contact with the military command center of the Army's Bárbula battalion in the Middle Magdalena Valley, a major counterinsurgency battleground in Colombia.[27]

To be sure, the Colombian pattern is not unique in the annals of statecraft. United States history offers several examples of government collusion with criminals to accomplish specific political or foreign policy objectives. In the United States, naval intelligence had an understanding with Lucky Luciano to help undermine the Fascist regime of Southern Italy. The CIA has dealt with Sam Giancana's organization in two assassination attempts against Fidel Castro, and the U.S. collaborated with Laotian warlords to fight the Pathet Lao Communists. Nevertheless, the trafficker-military-paramilitary nexus has more serious consequences in Colombia than in more stable countries. The effects are to exacerbate rural violence, to diminish government control over the hinterland, and to push the country toward de facto partition.

A third significant link in the political-criminal nexus in Colombia, and the one that has received the most public attention, is the pervasive influence of drug money in national presidential and congressional campaigns. As former vice-president Humberto de la Calle notes, "campaign finance is the principal point of entry into the political system."[28] Given the economic clout of the cocaine industry, contributions from traffickers can make the difference between success and failure for aspiring politicians in Colombia. In some parts of the country (Antioquia, Valle, and the North Coast) drug income is probably the leading source of private political funds. The current corruption scandal in Colombia suggests the dimension of the problem. At least twelve Colombian legislators, as well as an attorney general and a defense minister, were jailed for accepting money and favors from Cali traffickers in the 1994 elections. Santiago Medina, Samper's campaign treasurer believes that at least seventy congressmen were elected with funds provided by the cartel. The president of Colombia, Ernesto Samper, is widely believed to have solicited donations from traffickers although he was exonerated by the Lower House of Congress in an overwhelming vote (111 to 43) in June 1996.

Drug Money and Electoral Politics

Colombia's party structure and the clientelistic system described above has proven extremely vulnerable to the illegal industry. During the last fifty years political parties have become depoliticized and turned into electoral machines designed to distribute the state bounty. Widespread vote buying practices allowed the system to be controlled by those with the most money.

Electoral reform was one of the main concerns of those who wrote the new 1991 Constitution. Changes were designed to make the system more democratic and to make it more difficult to buy votes on election day. These included:

▫ Establishing two rounds of voting in presidential elections, requiring a runoff if no candidate won a majority of votes in the first round.
▫ Senators elected by all voters instead of by departments, to allow smaller parties to be represented in Congress.
▫ Changes in the voting system. Under the old system a voter was given a small envelope with his candidate's name written on a piece of paper inside it. This simple system made it easy to buy votes, and the envelope could be seen when it was placed inside the ballot box. Under the new system, the election witnesses give the voter a "tarjetón," a large paper with the names of all candidates among which the voter has to choose in private.
▫ Allowing paid political advertising in the mass media (TV, radio and newspapers). All interviewees concurred that before these changes Colombia was a country with cheap elections. The changes transformed it into a country of expensive elections. There is no doubt that those with greater capacity to fund elections have become more politically influential. These include the large financial conglomerates and the illegal drug industry.

Our interviews highlight two types of drug trafficking pressure on the system, reflecting the different goals of relatively prominent and relatively obscure drug entrepreneurs. In the past, the traffickers could be separated into extraditables (those singled out for eventual prosecution by U.S. authorities) and non-extraditables (those whose activities were sufficiently circumscribed to merit little attention by the United States). In small non-metropolitan areas, low and perhaps middle level participants in the drug industry do not feel threatened by extradition. They normally feel safe and do not seek any political favors from the political establishment. When they establish a link with the politicians their goal is usually social acceptance. According to Rodrigo Garavito,[29] "A typical narco has low education. His activity calls for force and valor. He comes from the middle or lower middle class. He first buys a house for himself, then one for his mother, then a car, and later on he buys a *finca*. Finally, he buys other urban properties. They want social acceptance. At banquets they want to be seated at a table near the politician." Their behavior is that of any other rich individual who wants to be active in his own community. They first approach the politician with support offers, and do not establish a direct quid pro quo. However, in case of a threat of arrest, they certainly will use whatever political clout they can muster. It is not known how many low-level provincial narcos there are but Zabludoff's work suggests that the number could be several thousand, large enough to influence local politics in most municipalities.

Politicians realize that some of their supporters have questionable associations, but they prefer not to probe too deeply into the origins of campaign funds. They are willing to accept illicit money but not the crime. At the same time, many campaign contributors prefer formal anonymity, that is, they want the politician to know who they are, but they do not want public disclosure. This is the case with large financial conglomerates that fund competing campaigns.[30] At local and provincial levels several systems have been used to maintain donor anonymity. One such system involves raffles. For example, a high-priced item such as a car is raffled. Most or all tickets are bought by a contributor, and the winner does not claim the prize.[31] Another, more overt system, is politician-issued "bonds," that is, bearer denominated receipts that are given in exchange for the contributions. These are "don't ask, don't tell," funding systems, that allow the politicians to receive questionable monies without having to acknowledge the source. The availability of illegal drug funding for political activities has increased demand. The use of drug funds has increased the level of campaign expenditures and tempted other politicians to seek or at least to be willing to receive them.

The need for formal anonymity and the danger of direct politico-narco contacts spawned the development of a whole industry of intermediates. The system is simple: the intermediary approaches a politician with an offer of funds from unknown rich contributors who want to remain anonymous. He lets the politician or his campaign manager decide whether to take the funds. Many times, after a deal is made and the money flows to the campaign, the intermediary takes a cut.

Larger and more important narcos are concerned that Congress does not pass strong anti-drug laws. They have been particularly but not exclusively concerned with extradition legislation. Their behavior towards Congress is similar to that of other powerful economic groups in the country. They contribute funds to political campaigns without making specific requests, but when relevant legislation is being discussed, they try to leverage their past contributions to seek favorable votes on those issues. Their contributions are like wild cards that they can use at opportune times. In this case, there is an implied threat of scandal or political ruin if the Congressman does not comply. On several occasions, narcos have funded lawyers who write memoranda in support of their desired legislation, and distribute them in the Congress. In this sense the narco lawyers function as staffers to the Congressmen.

Our interviews indicate that drug money has financed presidential political campaigns in Colombia during most of the last twenty years. Belisario Betancur's unsuccessful 1978 campaign received substantial funds from the illegal industry. Drug funds played an important role in the 1982 Belisario Betancur and Alfonso López-Michelsen's campaigns. Ernesto Samper, in his capacity as director of Alfonso López-Michelsen's 1982 presidential campaign, met with Pablo Escobar, Gonzalo Rodríguez-Gacha, Jose "Pelusa" Ocampo, and other Medellín kingpins in the "Medellín Suite" of the Intercontinental Hotel there. The outcome was that Samper obtained contributions totaling 19 million pesos ($317,000) from the businessmen.[32] Belisario Betancur, the winner in that election, is reported by his campaign treasurer in Antioquia to have received significantly larger sums. In the next two presidential elections in 1986 and 1990 it is likely that drug money played a smaller role because in both cases there was an ongoing war between the then dominant Medellín cartel and the government.

The 1991 Constitutional Assembly that made extradition of nationals unconstitutional, is frequently mentioned as having been highly influenced by drug money. Our interviews indicate that the situation was more complex. Pablo Escobar opted to pressure the establishment and society at large, but not the Assembly itself. His strategy was based on exploding bombs in heavily populated places and kidnapping important members of the establishment.[33] The Medellín cartel's terrorist activities, as well as Colombia's nationalist resentment against pressures from the United States had swayed most of the Colombian public against extradition. The Assembly also included a heavy leftist representation that opposed extradition on ideological grounds. The point is simply that most members of the Assembly opposed extradition, without any need for bribes by the drug industry.[34] This does not mean that there were no Assembly members who had strong contacts and links to the illegal drug organizations, or to the guerrilla movement for that matter.

After the new Constitution was approved, a special Congress known as "el Congresito," met to decide whether to approve decrees passed during the interim period while the new Constitution was approved. The interviews indicate that drug industry pressure there was significant as some of the decrees had to do with the "sometimiento" policy (legal procedures for surrendering drug dealers) of the Gaviria administration.

During the 1994 presidential campaign both main candidates were approached with offers of contributions from the Cali cartel. Pastrana refused them outright. However, his campaign was broken down into "his" central campaign in Bogotá and seven other conservative party campaigns in other regions of the country. This was probably done to circumvent the campaign spending limits, arguing that the regional campaigns were not part of his campaign. The central campaign rejected all drug contributions but it is not known what happened in the others, although the interviews indicate that there is a high probability that drug money did enter those campaigns.

The flow of Cali cartel funds into Samper's campaign has been the main political issue in Colombia for the last three years and has been the immediate cause of the political, social, and economic crises that the country is experiencing. Cali's contributions, which totaled at least 5 billion pesos ($6 million) played a very important part in the campaign and possibly affected the outcome of the election. The decision-making processes by which the money entered the campaign and the impact of the funds are not entirely clear. Accounts of various participants, however, seem to agree on the following:[35]

> The relationship was initiated by the Cali leaders. Funds were offered to Samper's campaign treasurer, Santiago Medina, in April 1994, roughly a month before the start of the campaign. A Colombian journalist with close ties to the cartel, Alberto Giraldo, communicated the offer to Medina in the latter's office in Bogotá. The offer was accepted by Samper's campaign manager, Fernando Botero (subsequently the defense minister in Samper's cabinet). To formalize arrangements for the donations, Medina traveled to Cali and met with Miguel and Gilberto Rodriguez and two other Cali leaders, Helmer Herrera and José Santacruz in early May. At the time, he asked for 2 billion pesos from the cartel and received 1 billion.

The campaign also solicited funds from the Cali traffickers. Samper and his campaign manager expected to win handily in the first round, but managed only a razor-thin margin of 18,000 votes over Pastrana. This failure confronted them with the need to spend large sums of money that they did not have during a three-week period before the second round. It appears that many in the campaign decided to ask direct support from the Cali cartel. Medina traveled to Cali in June to deliver the request and at the time received 4 billion pesos in additional funds from the traffickers. Some quid pro quo was involved in the campaign nexus. In contrast to the general pattern of drug-funded campaigns, Cali traffickers wanted specific understandings and assurances from the candidate in return for their donations.

To orchestrate the illegal fund operation, the campaign treasurer created what amounted to a double bookkeeping system. They set up a foundation, the Asociación para una Colombia Moderna to run the campaign's legal finances. The Asociación took checks and cash from legitimate donors up to 4 billion pesos, the prescribed campaign expenditure limits established by the National Electoral Council. A parallel system appears to have been established by Medina and Botero to receive and distribute illicit funds, including the donations from Cali. There is agreement that campaign expenditures exceeded the legal limits by significant amounts, and that drug money entered the campaign. The most likely version indicates that the excess expenditures were about 7.3 billion pesos (approximately $8 million); 5 billion of this could be attributed to the Cali cartel.[36]

The deal was a cash transaction. According to different sources, Cali's funds originated in the Banco de Colombia in the Cali account of a Miguel Rodríguez front company, Exportcafé. As noted earlier, that account had been set up by a coalition of Cali and Valle traffickers specially to support presidential and congressional campaigns.[37] The money reportedly was packed in boxes and gift wrapped (each box held 500 million pesos) in the presence of Rodríguez himself and then flown by private plane to Bogotá. Their cartel intermediary picked up the money and delivered it directly to Medina and Botero, who then arranged for the distribution of the funds to cover campaign expenses in different regions of the country.

The cartel's donation possibly made the difference between victory and defeat for Samper. Some of the money was used to cover media advertising costs (mainly TV), which, according to Medina's calculations, were 8 billion pesos ($9 million) during the campaign. Some was used for outright vote buying. One clear case was in the Córdoba Department where Samper received 31,000 votes in the first round of the campaign and 87,000 votes three weeks later!

In sum, campaign corruption, like other kinds of collusive behavior, represents an exchange of values. Campaigns are focused on raising money and winning elections. Traffickers, on the other hand, tend to have diffuse and generalized needs, not dissimilar to American corporate donors in U.S. elections. A bribe delivered to a judge, a police officer, or a government official implies an expectation that a specific service or favor will result from the action. Yet in donating to campaigns, traffickers want to create a relationship of goodwill that will pay off in subsequent access to the new incumbent. An apparent exception was the Samper presidential campaign, in which traffickers asked for and received general assurances relating to their legal status prior to giving money to the campaign. In any event, the entry of drug money into election contests itself establishes a nexus to the political elite. Traffickers, like large legal contributors, give money with the expectation that when there is specific legislation or a policy issue at stake, they can go to the politician and request particular favors. There the seeds of corruption are planted in the Colombian system.

The political-criminal nexus has conferred some benefits to both sides in Colombia. For the narcotics establishment generally, the benefits have included the opportunity to legalize drug earnings, to invest relatively openly in companies, real estate and rural land, to cultivate personal ties with political leaders and other establishment figures, and in general, to acquire a modicum of social acceptance and respectability. For traffickers under pressure from authorities, ties with the political system have paid off in relatively short prison sentences, favorable "plea bargaining" legislation (which allowed sentences to be cut by two-thirds or more under various pretexts), a constitutional ban on extradition in general and in individual cases, and the opportunity to rejoin society after serving time.

For the Colombian government the benefits have been less obvious: Surrender negotiations with traffickers have brought about a reduction in anti-state violence and also have incarcerated traffickers that the authorities were unable to apprehend. Yet such deals also have highlighted the weaknesses of the criminal justice system. The short sentences meted out to top Medellín and Cali kingpins, the farce of Pablo Escobar's "designer" prison in his home town of Envigado, which he could leave at will to attend soccer matches and carouse in local discotheques, and the apparent ability of Cali's Rodríguez-Orejuela brothers to run their trafficking empires from jail are testimonies to this unfortunate situation. In Colombia's troubled hinterland, traffickers' contributions to local security forces may have played a role in expelling guerrillas from some important rural zones in Colombia, like the Middle Magdalena Valley. Yet the narco-backed paramilitaries accentuate the problem of governability in Colombia even while performing positive security functions. Paramilitaries are in effect right-wing guerrillas who contribute to rural strife and instability. The traffickers' ability to buy the services of legislators and top government officials as well as the infiltration of drug money into political campaigns degrade the political environment in Colombia. The result is to underscore the government's weakness and to accelerate the delegitimization of the Colombian regime.

Finally, the 1994 campaign scandals and evidence of widespread corruption at the topmost echelons of Colombia's political system have complicated Colombia's international relationships, especially with the United States. For two successive years, Washington "decertified" Colombia as an unfit partner in the drug war, a decision that carries the possibility of economic and diplomatic sanctions. The Colombian government's inability to enforce the drug laws has increased its isolation domestically and in the international community, and appears to be leading the country to disaster.

Vulnerability of the Political-Criminal Nexus

Introduction

The issue of vulnerability comprises two interrelated questions: First, how can Colombia's drug trafficking establishment be dismantled or scaled back? Second, what opportunities exist to sever the linkages between drug criminals and the Colombian political system? Specific counterorganization approaches and possible strategies to limit traffickers' system-penetration activities are discussed.[38]

Counterorganization

Colombia maintains a fairly sizeable trafficking establishment. According to a careful study of the cocaine industry by a former CIA analyst, Sidney

Zabludoff,[39] the apex of the industry comprises some 500 entrepreneurs who handle most of the cocaine reaching U.S. and European markets. Below the top tier, approximately 6,000 people manage the day-to-day businesses of transport, overseas distribution, money laundering, and provision of security. This suggests that the cocaine trade is dominated by an elite and sub-elite of approximately 6,000 to 7,000 people. This group occupies a vital middle ground between the hundreds of thousands of Andean farmers and small processors and the millions of street dealers and cocaine consumers in the industrialized countries.[40] This analysis suggests significant parts of the establishment, much of the top elite and sub-elite, would have to be incarcerated, neutralized or induced to leave the business before an appreciable reduction in Colombian narcotics exports could occur. Such a scenario seems unlikely, given the progress of U.S. and Colombian law enforcement efforts to date.

The goal of disrupting trafficking organizations must be distinguished from the goal of disrupting the production and export of narcotics. Suffice it to say that U.S. and Andean supply control measures have been an utter failure, at least as measured by trends in the U.S. market. U.S. retail prices of cocaine and heroin have decreased by two-thirds since 1981, and cocaine and heroin purity have increased by 50 percent and 600 percent respectively, according to the White House drug czar's office.[41] Cutting off supply would require draconian measures, such as a massive aerial blitz against drug crops, which are technically difficult and extremely risky politically.

If controlling drug production is not a feasible goal, intelligent law enforcement can possibly have an effect on the actors in the narcotics business. Here the relevant objectives are to diminish the power and reach of the drug cartels and, where possible, to dismantle their component organizations and businesses. A general decentralization of the industry could be a political plus for Colombia even if exports cannot be reduced. It might be better to have 1,000 mom-and-pop refining and trafficking operations sending packages of cocaine to the United States via couriers rather than ten very large organizations, each with hundreds of millions of dollars in annual revenues, shipping tons of cocaine in containers or DC-9 airplanes, negotiating with governments, issuing communiques to the press, bankrolling political campaigns, and using violence as a political tool.

Past experience suggests that counterorganization strategies can yield significant benefits. Colombia, with U.S. logistical and intelligence support, virtually shut down the Medellín cartel in the early 1990s (admittedly, rival drug traffickers also contributed to this outcome, which later produced problems for the government). The onslaught against the Cali cartel in the mid-1990s disrupted the activities of that trafficking coalition, at least temporarily. A manifestation of this weakness is that Colombian traffickers increasingly are turning their distribution networks in the United States over to Mexicans.

Also, the Colombians exporting large quantities of cocaine to Mexico rather than to the United States are receiving a Mexican price of $7,000 per kilogram compared to a U.S. price of $14,000 to $15,000 per kilogram. All of this translates into a loss of profits in the U.S. market (and less narcotics income for Colombia) although Colombian dominance of growing markets in Europe and Asia and increases in Colombian heroin production might partly compensate for their losses.

More effective counterorganization strategies will depend on better intelligence about the inner workings of the drug business, laboratories, transit routes, money laundering mechanisms, and so on. Exploiting and manipulating rivalries among trafficking coalitions possibly can advance this objective. So also can plea-bargaining arrangements with high-level traffickers who could disclose significant details about their cocaine and heroin trafficking empires. Unfortunately, such strategies have not worked well in the Colombian context, mainly because of the weakness and ineptitude of the Colombian authorities. Colombia's de facto alliance with the Cali cartel in tracking down Escobar and his associates effectively strengthened the political-criminal nexus in Colombia, as already noted.[42] Colombia's criminal and judicial institutions clearly were not up to the task of negotiating deals with the cartels. The Colombian pattern was to give away judicial benefits while receiving little or nothing from the traffickers in return.

Breaking the Nexus

The prognosis for disrupting the political-criminal nexus in Colombia is poor, barring a major break up or decentralization of Colombia's cocaine multinationals. Colombia has enacted some relevant legislation (on illegal enrichment, money laundering and asset forfeiture), has increased maximum jail terms for traffickers (from 30 to 60 years) and continues to investigate political campaign contributions by drug dealers. But the problems, of course, lie much deeper. They reflect factors such as the weak development of civil society, clientelism and corruption in the Colombian party system, and widespread public tolerance for political-criminal ties. On the latter point, in a Gallup Colombia poll commissioned by Bogotá's *Semana* magazine in late 1996 respondents were asked whether Samper was guilty of soliciting drug money for his campaign, and whether Samper should resign the presidency. Almost 70 percent of those who responded with yes or no answers believed that Samper was guilty, but 55 percent said that he should not resign.[43] Such results attest to a weak anti-drug and anti-corruption consensus in Colombia. How the struggle against Colombia's criminal overlords and their henchmen in government will proceed under such circumstances is obviously difficult to predict.

Colombia's drug economy and the situation of the narcotics business in that country also need to be considered. Cocaine exporters' criminal net revenues amount to a significant percentage of Colombian GDP (4 to 7 percent) and that has allowed traffickers to accumulate significant wealth. As Thoumi notes, a single trafficking organization exporting 50 tons of cocaine a year can earn $500 million assuming export profits of $10,000 per kilogram.[44] By comparison, Bogotá's *Semana* magazine estimates that Colombia's four largest financial conglomerates earned profits ranging from $140 to $530 million respectively in 1995. Such numbers translate into wide economic influence for the cartels. This is reflected in the huge array of different business entities owned by the Cali cartel, some 60 companies according to the U.S. Treasury Department's Office of Foreign Asset Control. These provide cover and justification for cultivating close relations with the nation's power brokers. Indeed, Colombian politicians accused of illegal enrichment received money in the form of checks written on Cali-owned companies such as Exportcafé and Agrícola La Loma and have used such conduits as a means of legal defense. The companies had bank accounts, profit-and-loss statements, outstanding loans from Colombian banks and other attributes of legitimacy. The argument runs, "so where is the crime?"[45]

Still measures probably can be devised to reduce inflows of drug money into politics, at least at the national level. Targeted seizure of drug traffickers' assets, including companies used to funnel contributions to political campaigns, is one obvious approach. This, however, is easier said than done. Mechanisms for expropriation that do not destroy the value of assets or their production flows need to be developed. There is also the question of what to do with expropriated property. One of the political figures interviewed in the project, former prosecutor general Alfonso Valdivieso, believes that transferring property to (other) private hands would provoke retaliation by traffickers. He advocates the development of a special communal entity to handle the assets. Clearly, this is an issue that requires some thought in Colombia.

Other useful initiatives might focus on campaign finance reform. In general, there is a need to lower the costs of political campaigns (so that candidates do not have to appeal for illicit funds) and to increase the transparency of donations. Precluding privately paid TV, radio and newspaper advertising (which is 65 to 70 percent of campaign costs in Colombia) and funding campaign advertising exclusively from the state treasury would be an important step. A second would be to limit the duration of campaigns and shorten the time between the first and second rounds of voting.[46] (Former vice-president Humberto de la Calle recommends a three-month limit on campaigning.) Restricting the amounts of donations, perhaps as a percentage of total campaign inflows, by a single donor (person or corporations) would also help, as would listing publicly all contributors to campaigns and invalidating elections of candidates who are found to have received money from known drug dealers.[47] Such measures could make presidential campaigns less vulnerable to illicit drug funding; however, the effects of such reforms on congressional and local contests, which have a lower profile and are more difficult to monitor, are likely to be modest. (Most of our interviewed sources concurred on this point.) Nevertheless, campaign reform could be an important first step in breaking the drug criminals' hold on Colombia's political system, and hence, represents an urgent national priority.[48]

Notes

1. Investigative journalists Vargas, Lesmes and Téllez (1996) present a detailed chronicle of the events from 1994 to early 1996, when President Samper was close to resigning. López-Caballero (1997) studied Samper's trial in Congress. He argues, correctly, that what should have been a political trial became a weak legal trial in which the president was accused of non-legally defined crimes such as receiving checks from the legal bank accounts of legal companies. This led to his exoneration. Leal (1996) provides a more academic study of the crisis.
2. For example, in August 1996 a FARC guerrilla commando killed thirty soldiers and captured sixty more in an attack on a military post in Caquetá. Eight months later, after protracted negotiations with the government, they returned the captured soldiers after the government ordered its army to vacate, for about a month, a large area of the country where the guerrillas had been operating.
3. Colombia has been the first "friendly" country decertified by the United States for its lack of cooperation in the drug war.
4. During the last week of July and first week of August 1997, the authors interviewed the following actors in Bogotá: Horacio Serpa, perhaps the closest Samper associate, his former Minister of the Interior and currently the presidential candidate for the Samper faction of the Liberal party; Alfonso Valdivieso, former prosecutor general, and presidential candidate who is heir to the legacy of assassinated presidential candidate Luis Carlos Galán; Humberto de la Calle, former Samper administration vice-president who resigned in protest for the links of Samper's campaign with illegal drugs organizations; Felipe López, president of *Semana*, the country's most influential weekly magazine and son of former President Alfonso López-Michelsen; Manuel Francisco Becerra, former secretary of the departmental government of Valle del Cauca (whose capital is Cali), former representative and former governor of that department, former attorney general of Colombia and former Minister of Education, then awaiting sentencing; Rodrigo Garavito, Oxford-educated former representative from the Middle Magdalena region, then fighting money laundering charges on which he was found guilty; Santiago Medina, former treasurer of Samper's campaign, then under house arrest and now deceased; and Juan Manuel Avella, former administrative manager of Samper's campaign, then serving time at La Modelo jail in Bogotá. The interviews followed an open format designed to let the interviewees talk about a limited set of issues. Each interview lasted from ninety minutes to two hours. In one case the authors were asked to return for an extra hour. The authors agreed to use the interview findings with discretion, using direct attribution selectively.
5. Kalmanovitz 1989.
6. De Roux 1990.
7. Kalmanovitz 1989: 59.
8. Colombian intellectuals have focused their recent efforts on explaining the negative peculiarities of Colombian society and have defined its main problem as that of a

society in which people operate with a very effective individual logic but a disastrous social one (Gómez et. al. 1999).

9. Statistics show that Colombia has the highest rate of violent deaths among forty-three countries for which evidence is available (Ratinoff 1996). Colombia's rate circa 1990 was comparable to that of countries at war, and it was three times higher than that of Brazil, the second highest-ranked country. It is possible that the destruction of the social fabric in some African countries will lead to rates comparable to Colombia.

10. Gugliotta and Leen 1989.

11. Le Grand 1988.

12. Leal and Dávila 1990.

13. For example, thirty-five years ago 1.5 percent of the college age population was at school. Today, the figure is about 18 percent. There is no economy that can keep up relative salaries under such a large supply increase.

14. The interviews revealed a consensus that in Colombia there were many legitimate illegal activities such as contraband, tax evasion, bribery (in the public and private sectors) to achieve economic benefits, and that until the mid-1980s Colombian society had been extremely tolerant of illegal drug activities which had not been perceived as different from other "legitimate" illegal activities. Only when drug industry violence threatened the political and social establishment, did parts of society react against it.

15. Betancourt and García 1994.

16. Betancourt and García (1994: xxii) argue that during the 1980s, the economic crises experienced by "five large regions: Atlantic Coast (cotton), Antioquia (textiles), Valle (sugar), central (emerald zones of Boyacá and Cundinamarca) and eastern (bordering Venezuela), whose currency suffered a large devaluation at that time," triggered the development of illegal drugs centers.

17. Orozco 1987: 57-60, 162, 185; Lee 1990: 136.

18. As quoted in Vargas et al. 1996: 71.

19. Thoumi 1995a; Clawson and Lee 1996: 23-25.

20. Rocha 1997; Steiner 1996.

21. Thoumi 1997: 95.

22. Castillo 1996: 204.

23. Clawson and Lee 1996: 47, 55.

24. Escobar was finally tracked down and killed by police in December 1993, ten years after he became a fugitive in Colombia (Clawson and Lee 1996: 100).

25. Semana 1997: 35; De Greiff, a distinguished jurist, was a poor choice as a government negotiator. He was an open proponent of legalizing drugs, a position that undermined his credibility from the start. More importantly, prior to his appointment as prosecutor general, De Greiff had been a shareholder and the president of a company, Aerolíneas El Dorado, in which Gilberto Rodríguez had owned 42 percent of the shares. Certainly this is a possible case of guilt by association (see Castillo 1996: 52-53).

26. According to the CIA (1995) "meadows and pastures" in Colombia total approximately 30 million hectares. Reyes (1997) has produced the 4 to 5 million estimate.

27. Clawson and Lee 1996: 187.

28. Authors' interview. Humberto de la Calle, Bogotá, August 1997.

29. Authors' interview. Rodrigo Garavito, Bogotá, August 1997.

30. Since parties are depoliticized and devoid of ideologies, from the point of economic and social policies it really does not matter who wins. Since the main function of the parties has been to distribute the government bounty, what matters is to have supported the winner.

31. For example, Manuel Francisco Becerra explained in the interview that in Cali it became known among politicians that the drug store "La Rebaja," which belonged to the Rodríguez-Orejuela brothers, bought more raffle tickets than any other company in town, and from virtually any candidate.
32. Carlos Lehder reported contribution of $24 million pesos ($400,000). It is possible that the difference was taken by an intermediary.
33. "News of a Kidnapping," García Márquez' best selling book, tells this story.
34. It must be stressed that when it became known that extradition was going to be declared unconstitutional, there was no social or press outcry against the measure, which at the time was quite popular.
35. Principal sources include Samper campaign officials Juan Manuel Avella and Santiago Medina, interviewed in Bogotá in July-August 1999, and Guillermo Palomari, formerly Miguel Rodríguez's accountant who has recently testified in the United States under the witness protection program. Useful published material includes *El Tiempo* (1995: 8A-9A), *Semana* (1997: 34-38), Castillo (1996: 204-206), Vargas, Lesmes, and Téllez (1996: 112-150) and López-Caballero (1997).
36. It must be pointed out that most evidence about these expenditures is based on the testimony of individuals. Since most expenditures were in cash, it has been impossible to trace them. López-Caballero (1997) argues that in Samper's trial in Congress it was proven that only a fraction of those funds entered the campaign and that it is likely that Medina kept a large sum for himself.
37. Funds from the same Exportcafé account, some $250,000, also supported the congressional campaign of Orlando Vásquez-Velásquez who was later named attorney general. In August 1997, Vásquez-Velásquez was awaiting sentencing at a D.A.S. facility outside Bogotá.
38. The interviews revealed a consensus about the structural nature of the problem. Some interviewees simply gave up when we asked about solutions, indicating the need for profound social change before the illegal drug industry could be eliminated. Others, although skeptical of the possibility for change, ventured some policy suggestions to weaken the political-criminal nexus.
39. Zabludoff 1994.
40. Ibid.
41. The White House 1997.
42. University of Pittsburgh scholar Phil Williams suggests that U.S. and Colombian authorities made a strategic error by focusing obsessively on the recapture of Pablo Escobar after the kingpin's escape from prison in 1992. Instead, Williams argues, they should have allowed Escobar "to wage an effective campaign against his rivals in Cali." Weakening the Medellín cartel, he notes, simply allowed Cali to emerge as the premier trafficking coalition in Colombia (Williams 1995: 71).
43. *Semana* 1996.
44. Thoumi 1997a.
45. López-Caballero 1997; Procuraduría General de la Nación 1997: 6-20.
46. Eliminating the second round is also a possibility. However, one of the main reasons why the second round was established was to open up the political system allowing minority parties to form alliances and share power. This goal would have to be sacrificed if the second round is eliminated.
47. It is obvious that there are many ways to circumvent individual campaign contribution limits such as having several firms owned by the same person or group make separate contributions, but if the last two measures are implemented together, at least some large donors will be discouraged.

48. Interviews with Alfonso Valdivieso, Humberto de la Calle and Horacio Serpa. Bogotá, 1 August 1997.

References

Betancourt, Darío, and Martha L. García. *Contrabandistas, Marimberos y Mafiosos: Historia Social de la Mafia Colombiana* (Smugglers, Traffickers and Mafiosi: A Social History of the Colombian Mafia). Bogotá: Tercer Mundo Editores 1994.

Castillo, Fabio. *Los Nuevos Jinetes de la Cocaína* (The New Cocaine Cowboys). Bogotá: Editorial Oveja Negra 1996.

Clawson, Patrick, and Rensselaer Lee III. *The Andean Cocaine Industry*. New York: St. Martin's Press, 1996.

Central Intelligence Agency (CIA). *The World Factbook 1995-1996*. Washington, DC: Brassey's, 1995.

De Roux, Rodolfo R. *Dos Mundos Enfrentados* (The Clash of Two Worlds). Bogotá: CINEP, 1990.

El Tiempo. "La Indagatoria de Samper" (The Samper Inquiry), 3 August 1995.

García-Márquez, Gabriel. *Noticia de un Secuestro* (News of a Kidnapping). Bogotá: Grupo Editorial Norma, 1996.

Gómez Buendía, Hernando, et al. *¿Para Dónde Va Colombia?* (Where is Colombia going?). Bogotá: Tercer Mundo Editores, 1999.

Gugliotta, Guy, and Jeff Leen. *Kings of Cocaine*. New York: Simon and Schuster, 1989.

Kalmanovitz, Salomón. *La Encrucijada de la Sinrazón y otros Ensayos* (The Crossroads of Nonsense and Other Essays). Bogotá: Tercer Mundo Editores, 1989.

Leal, Francisco. *Estado y Política en Colombia* (State and Politics in Colombia), 2nd ed. Bogotá: Siglo Veintiuno Editores y CEREC, 1989.

_____ (ed.). *Tras las Huellas de la Crisis Política* (Following the Tracks of the Political Crisis). Bogotá: TM Editores-FESCOL-IEPRI (UN),1996.

Leal, Francisco, and Andrés Dávila. *Clientelismo: el Sistema Político y su Expresión Regional* (Clientelism: The Political System and Its Regional Expression). Bogotá: Tercer Mundo Editores and Instituto de Estudios Políticos y Relaciones Internacionales de la Universidad Nacional, 1990.

Lee III, Rensselaer W. *The White Labyrinth*. New Brunswick, NJ: Transaction Publishers, 1990.

Le Grand, Catherine. *Colonización y Protesta Campesina en Colombia 1850-1950* (Colonization and Peasant Protest in Colombia 1850-1950). Bogotá: Universidad Nacional de Colombia, 1988.

López-Caballero, Juan Manuel. *La Conspiración: el libro blanco del juicio al presidente Samper* (The Conspiracy: The White Book of President Samper's Trial). Bogotá: Editorial Planeta, 1997.

Orozco, Jorge Eliécer. *Lehder: el Hombre* (Lehder: The Man). Bogotá: Plaza y Janes, 1987.

Procuraduría General de la Nación. "Case against Rodrigo Garavito Hernández for Illegal Enrichment and other Crimes," Bogotá, 12 June 1997.

Ratinoff, Luis. "Delincuencia y paz ciudadana " (Crime and Civic Peace), in *Hacia un Enfoque Integrado de Desarrollo: Ética, Violencia y Seguridad Ciudadana: Encuentro de Reflexión*. Inter-American Development Bank, Washington, DC, 1996.

Reyes, Alejandro. "Compras de tierras por narcotraficantes" (Land Purchases by Drug Traffickers), in F. Thoumi (ed.), *Drogas Ilícitas en Colombia: su Impacto Económico, Político y Social*, Dirección Nacional de Estupefacientes and UNDP. Bogotá: Editorial Planeta, 1997.

Rocha, Ricardo. "Aspectos económicos de las drogas ilegales" (Economic Aspects of Illegal Drugs), in F. Thoumi (ed.), *Drogas Ilícitas en Colombia: su Impacto Económico, Político y Social,* Dirección Nacional de Estupefacientes and UNDP. Bogotá: Editorial Planeta, 1997.

Semana. "Por qué no se cayó" (Why Didn't He Fall), 10 December 1996; "La Película en Inglés" (The Movie in English), 28 July 1997.

Steiner, Roberto. "Los ingresos de Colombia producto de la exportación de drogas ilícitas" (Colombia's Revenues from Illegal Drugs Exports), in *Coyuntura Económica*, December 1996.

Thoumi, Francisco E. "Why the Illegal Psychoactive Drugs Industry Grew in Colombia." *Journal of Interamerican Studies and World Affairs*, 34, 3: 37-63, Fall 1992.

_____. *Political Economy and Illegal Drugs in Colombia.* Boulder: Lynne Rienner, 1995.

_____. "Derechos de Propiedad en Colombia: Debilidad, Ilegitimidad y Algunas Implicaciones Económicas" (Property Rights in Colombia: Weaknesses, Illegality, and Some Economic Implications). Bogotá: CEI-Uniandes, *Documentos Ocasionales,* 38, April-June 1995.

_____. "U.S. Colombia Struggle Over Drugs, Dirty Money." *Forum for Applied Research and Public Policy,* 12: 1, Spring 1997.

_____. "Introducción y Panorama," (Introduction and Overview), in F. Thoumi (ed.), *Drogas Ilícitas en Colombia: su Impacto Económico, Político y Social*, Dirección Nacional de Estupefacientes and UNDP. Bogotá: Editorial Planeta, 1997.

Vargas, Mauricio, Jorge Lesmes, and Edgar Téllez. *El Presidente que se Iba a Caer* (The President Who Was Going to Fall). Bogotá: Editorial Planeta, 1996.

White House, The. *The National Drug Control Strategy*, Budget Summary. Washington, DC, 1977.

Williams, Phil. "Transnational Criminal Organizations." *The Washington Quarterly*, 18, 1, Winter 1995.

Zabludoff, Sidney. "Colombian Narcotics Organizations as Business Enterprises." *Economics of the Narcotics Industry.* CIA-State Department Conference Report, 21-22 November 1994.

4

An American Way of Crime and Corruption

Robert J. Kelly

Introduction

Before discussing the political-criminal nexus, the etiology of the concept of "organized crime" and efforts to produce a workable definition of the phenomenon should be considered briefly. Theorists have often been perplexed by several issues, including:

1. Difficulties in reaching a consensus about objective aspects of organized criminal activity;
2. Formal universality of organized crime as a socio-cultural concept among modernizing and developed states, versus the apparent particularity and *sui generis* qualities of its concrete manifestations; and,
3. Extent of the political power of organized crime and the lack of strong coherent explanatory scientific traditions that make sense of it.

The tendency to raise organized crime to the status of a special criminal entity was encouraged in the past by government investigations (Kefauver, McClelland, President's Task Force) and by criminal justice bureaucracies (FBI, Department of Justice). Though it may have been politically advantageous to make organized crime synonymous with Mafia (La Cosa Nostra—as a sort of alien conspiracy contaminating the social structures of urban and minority communities) mainstream scholarship has all but abandoned this narrow and distorted view.[1]

An identified characteristic of many organized crime groups is a structure whose organizational elements include violence, corruption, continuity, structure, discipline, and multiple enterprises. Most are engaged in legitimate businesses as well as criminal enterprises. Those that have longevity and staying power and are identified by law enforcement as "organized crime" exhibit three essential characteristics: the capacity to corrupt police, politicians, and nongovernmental individuals; overlapping partnerships or interconnections among illicit entrepreneurial colleagues; and internal specializations and diversifications of members in terms of their skills and experience. This suffices to describe organizational attributes of groups or gangs achieving the status of "organized crime."

Another aspect concerning the activities of groups has to do with racketeering and the role of violence. Extortion looms as the basic organizing principle and sustaining force in criminal enterprises. Typically, crime victims and sometimes noncriminals have limited access to the law. To ensure a peaceful work environment, they must pay tribute ("criminal rent") or protection offered by criminal groups that introduce themselves into business milieus and enterprises. For extortion to function as a feasible operational currency, *the environments* in which illegality flourishes *need to be protected against law enforcement*. Thus, a precondition for the success and survivability of criminal enterprises is a capacity to neutralize or nullify law enforcement to some degree.

Several observers have pointed out that the political objectives and strategies of organized crime groups, formations, or networks are generally twofold:

□ To neutralize law enforcement threats to criminal operations; and,
□ To involve law enforcement and public officials in criminal conspiracies.

Thus, alliances and partnerships are the ideal arrangements criminals seek.

Criminal actors can facilitate the necessary degree of immunity from law enforcement in several ways. They can develop partnerships with law enforcement. Through diversification of activities where legitimate businesses are penetrated, or grafted onto criminal enterprises, they can also cloak crime with a veneer of respectability. The racketeer thus "disappears" and becomes barely discernible from ordinary business people.[2]

The political objectives of organized crime groups are *not* to compete with the established agencies of legitimate government. Organized criminal groups are not particularly interested (at least not in the USA) in political and economic reform. Their political objective is a negative one: nullification of government power to constrain, control and contain their operations.

The two levels at which such nullification may be sought are the law enforcement agencies and the administration of criminal justice. When a racketeer bribes a police officer or compromises a law enforcement officer (prosecutor, judge, or administrator) the object is to neutralize or invalidate the law enforcement process. When criminal conspirators support a candidate for political office, they do so in an attempt to increase illicit opportunities for profit and to reduce the impact of government activities that block opportunities for criminal involvement in business. At the level of legislative agencies (city councils, state government, etc.) the efforts are similar: to remove the intrusive presence of law enforcement in order to reduce its power to act.

The two levels are not discrete. A corrupted elected official—and this means an official who misrepresents his role to his constituents—may seek to insure that some laws are not vigorously enforced, or are enforced selectively. As long ago as 1952, the American Bar Association's report on organized crime concluded that the largest single factor in the breakdown of law enforcement dealing with organized crime is the corruption and connivance of many public officials.[3]

The other side of this problem is that the victims of corruption—law enforcement, the political system and the public—are too often willing collaborators in the linking nexus. To the extent that the public is victimized by partnerships with criminals, it may be asked what political needs criminals satisfy when liaisons are created with them.

Godson has pointed out that there is much to learn about how and why political-criminal relationships form, and the specific conditions that facilitate a political-criminal nexus (PCN)or lead to its breakdown.[4] The discussion is framed around a set of questions that:

□ Examine political, economic, and socio-cultural conditions that affect a PCN;
□ How these conditions develop and are maintained;
□ The dynamics and exchanges among the various actors;
□ The vulnerabilities of a PCN; and,
□ Oppositional strategies that may frustrate the emergence of political-criminal networks or weaken and destroy those that exist and are operative.

Factors Affecting the Formation of the PCN

In its Final Report on Corruption and Racketeering in the New York City Construction Industry (1990), the New York State Organized Crime Task Force identified the crux of the problem not solely in terms of individual career criminals and builders, but also incompetent and corrupted officials, and the dizzying array of laws, ordinances, and regulations governing the construction process as important considerations.[5] Putting up a building required more than 85 permits from state agencies, as well as union agreements, supplier contracts, and so on. The ordinances, designed to facilitate construction of safe structures and insure worker and occupancy safety, made construction unduly difficult. More important, this complex process created numerous opportunities for bribery, graft, and corruption. Compensating for the managerial defects of the construction industry and its inept state supervision, racketeers provided a "rationalizing" service that promoted a climate of stability by reducing uncertainties in a fragmented and fragile work environment. Twenty-five years ago in its report on police corruption in New York City, the Knapp Commission described the construction industry as a breeding ground of corruption and cited the same kinds of factors that precipitated criminal activity in the industry in 1990.[6]

The landmark police investigation by the Knapp Commission turned to the construction industry because the symbiotic links between politicians and gangsters were deep and obvious. Since the Second World War and the economic boom that followed, organized criminals have insinuated themselves into labor, business, and political circles as supporters and consultants to union bosses, business executives and political figures. The role played by the organized criminal groups has never been carefully documented though it is inconceivable that the massive public road construction, bridges, and public housing projects could have been completed without criminal participation.[7]

Postulating a theory of how corruption works, how it develops pathways that spread across the structure of institutions, will require documented hypotheses concerning ties among political, economic, and criminal power brokers and their personal and professional connections. In New York City, the phenomenon of police corruption serves as a "laboratory" in which corruption, a vital component of criminal patronage, operated across several public service institutions—not just the police—which not only enabled vice to flourish but also allowed criminals to penetrate legitimate industrial enterprises after law enforcement agencies had been compromised.

Moreover, apart from the persistence of a serious integrity problem with law enforcement and government oversight, there are conditions, circumstances, structures of certain activities, markets, and environments that tend to encourage organized criminality and the corruption of public officials. Many decades before compromised police enforcement and the collusion of public officials in widespread criminal activities were exposed by the Knapp Commission and Construction Racketeering Report, Lippman described the cultural and social structural contradictions that spawned organized crime in American society.[8]

As noted by Lippmann, much organized crime activity involves the supplying of illicit goods and services desired by a substantial part of the public with the consequence that support for law enforcement is diluted and weakened. Prohibition, for example, blurred the distinction between respect for the law and lawbreaking. A symbiotic relationship emerged among gangsters, their patrons and law enforcement which blocked the normal application of criminal labels. Corruption and the collusion of criminals, politicians and police were simply assumed in Lippman's analysis.

Weak state presence or controls often promote "informal" private solutions to problems (as with rural mafia *cosche* in the south of Italy nearly a century ago). In certain American industries, over-regulation, a state presence that is too strong, too intrusive in its oversight and regulatory functions, may be a source of problems. It appears that archaic laws and rules governing construction (a multi-billion-dollar business in New York City alone) promote organized criminal interventions and contribute to organized crime participation in the industry. The Wick's law, in particular, which obliges the state to award contracts to the lowest bidder within the parameters of engineering specifications, production costs, and timetables, appears to have encouraged the formation of an illegal cartel among contractors, as well as collusion with union racketeers. There is abundant data indicating that what was true in New York City in the 1980s had also been prevalent in many other American cities since the early 1900s. Repeating a much earlier analysis by Lincoln Steffens, Tannenbaum observed that:

> It is clear from the evidence at hand—that a considerable measure of the crime in the community is made possible and perhaps inevitable by the peculiar connection that exists between the political organizations of our large cities and the criminal activities of various gangs that are permitted and even encouraged to operate.[9]

The frequency of major scandals linking organized criminals with political and legal figures since 1938 suggests a general conclusion: while major cities such as New York, Chicago, Detroit, Miami, Boston and a hoard of lesser cities have been scandalized and cleansed innumerable times, organized crime persists and, in fact, thrives. Despite periodic forays, exposures, and reform movements prompted by journalists, and social activists, organized crime has become something of an institution in the United States.

At the turn of the century, Lincoln Steffens made a career of exposing corruption in American cities.[10] That task of exposure in recent years has fallen into the generally less daring hands of social scientists who, unlike their crusading predecessors in the press, have gathered their information from law enforcement agencies and criminal justice records. Unfortunately, this difference in the sources of information has probably distorted the description of organized crime. It almost certainly has led to an overemphasis on the "criminal" in organized crime and a corresponding de-emphasis on "corruption" as an institutionalized component of America's legal-political system. Concomitantly, this focus has obscured the perception of the degrees to which the structure of American law and politics—especially local political activity and organization—creates and perpetuates syndicates that conduct vice operations, extortion, and assorted crimes in major cities.

Organized crime is not a set of activities that exists exclusively outside law and government but is integral to them and may be a creation of them—a hidden but nonetheless functional component of governmental structure. Those identified by public investigations as criminal participants may technically be outside of government, but the nexus of which they are a part is organized around and conducted in the interests of not only criminal entre-preneurs but economic and political elites.

The focus here is on the infiltration of professional criminal associations into the legitimate sector. It sees organized crime as a phenomenon recogniz-able by reciprocal services performed by professional criminals for their cli-ents and politicians and examines their capacities to influence the criminal justice apparatus.

In studies of criminal penetrations of the legitimate economic sectors of the "upperworld," corrupted law enforcement agencies and officials and com-promised political actors function as "entry points" that define the bound-aries of vulnerability in the sectors of the legitimate side. The connective tissues of a nexus require that the concentration of criminal assets in the criminal milieu that makes up the bridge—the conduit—between politics, business, and crime be located. These linkages and connectives intertwine; they are complex and make charting the geography of criminal activity and influence difficult to identify. The world, or clandestine half-worlds of the criminal and the legitimate political/economic actor constitute a limbo re-alty of fear, suspicion, violence and ultimately betrayal while on the surface partnerships may appear stable and durable while beneath the appearance of normal reciprocal connections there is a torrent of uncertainty.

A major supposition of this essay is that as scientists achieve more preci-sion in their observations and descriptions of organized crime, it will become clearer that organized criminal activity itself is dependent upon the neutral-ization of law enforcement and a persistent demand for the illicit goods and services. Criminal syndicates appear to be tied to and in symbiosis with the political bureaucracies and regulatory agencies at all levels of government. And, the criminal operatives may be seen (and see themselves) as nothing less than power brokers and political middlemen whose power is predi-cated on their capacity to acquire, maintain, or manipulate control over segments of the economic clusters of activity linking criminal organiza-tions operating in local infrastructures and communities to the super-structure of the larger society. From this standpoint, organized crime is hardly a simple parable of criminal success or simple conspiracy, alien or otherwise. Rather, organized criminals symbolize the flaws in the competi-tive structures of business, commerce, and politics that occur in societies where political institutions are not particularly sensitive to or responsive to the needs of the public.[11]

The 1976 *Task Force Report on Organized Crime* notes that the "influence of organized crime in the political sphere . . . permits all of its operations—the legitimate and the illicit—to flourish." The Report continues that "the final explanation offered for the growth of organized crime and corruption con-cerns the structure of government in the United States—particularly at the state and local levels."[12] Further,

The American pattern of fragmentation of governmental authority tends to guarantee that attacks on crime syndicates. . .will be fragmented, that results will be delayed, and that most reform movements can be out waited. Although it might be argued that this fragmentation at least protects the public from a systematic tyranny by a corrupt leader, that same public must be prepared to pay the price of inefficient and protracted law enforcement efforts. Furthermore, in a nation divided into thousands of local governments, a crime syndicate that can buy control of key officials in just one police department can thereby secure for itself a base of operations for a gambling or drug network spanning an entire metropolitan area."[13]

Once established, the effect of criminal enterprises on the legal and political systems can be quite powerful. The law itself is compromised in the interests of the crime cabal/nexus with the political establishment. The legal system can be used in discretionary ways such that criminal activities are not easily detected and uncooperative police, prosecutors, officials, and citizens can be harassed with impunity. For example, in Chicago where almost 100 judges and other court personnel in Cook County were convicted of bribery to fix criminal cases, Mayor Richard Daley disbanded an effective Chicago police department investigative unit explaining that it was a cost-cutting decision.[14]

The establishment of a durable criminal enterprise (or syndicate) providing a range of goods and services (licit and illicit) requires the creation of symbiotic networks that contain representatives of all the leading centers of power. Businessmen must be involved. In New York City's construction industry businessmen used their influence and resources to facilitate the procurement of loans to expand the vice enterprises and the infiltration of the legitimate local economy by their professional criminal partners. Members of the banking and finance community can be considerable assets in a criminal enterprise.

The political influence of a criminal enterprise may be more directly obtained. As in the case of Al Capone, tax-free profits make it possible for a criminal network to support political candidates generously. Often the syndicate assists numerous candidates in an election, thus assuring itself of influence regardless of who wins. While usually there is a favorite, cooperative candidate who receives the greater proportion of the contribution, everyone is likely to receive something.

Neutralization or compromised police-organized crime control strategies may be achieved through corruption of police agencies with organized crime control missions. What would appear to be more effective is the deployment of corruption assets among public officials who determine law enforcement policies and budgets, promotions and the distribution of internal resources committed to organized crime control.

Influencing public officials with law enforcement responsibilities may not be that difficult because organized criminals are often well integrated into economic, political and occupational groups that they may no longer be easily recognizable as criminal enterprises.[15]

Machine Politics as Corruption Mechanisms

Some environments are particularly conducive to the creation of networks involving political actors and organized criminals. The political machine in urban politics has served as just such an instrument offering ideal conditions for generating and propagating liaisons between criminals and political officials.

As a generic type of social organization promoting the symbiosis of crime and politics the political machine has facilitated relationships between organized criminals with corrupt political structures in which success in one is heavily dependent on the right connections in the other.

The political machine is an ideal apparatus for meeting the latent needs of diverse subgroups in the community, including criminal organizations, that cannot be adequately serviced by larger legal social structures. Political machines derive their strength by meeting the specific needs of local communities and neighborhoods. The sociological intuitions of local political bosses can be seen in their recognition and definition of constituents as individuals with specific problems and personal wants that can scarcely be handled in the dispersed and circumscribed structures of bureaucratic power. The local political boss and his (or her) agents fulfill the important function of personalizing all manners of assistance to those in need.

Just as political machines have provided services (access to officials, government contracts, etc.) to legitimate businesses, they have also provided similar services for illegitimate businesses including rackets and vice industries. Morals and ethics aside, business is business.

The functions of political machines for criminal clients, according to Robert Merton, are to enable them to operate with the assurance that they can satisfy the economic demands of vice markets without interference from the government.[16] Just as legitimate business interests support machines to ensure representation and influence in government bureaucracies, so also do racketeers seek to minimize government interference in their operations. Machines then inevitably bring different groups and figures into political interaction; supporters are likely to include respectable business elements who are, of course, opposed to criminal rackets with individuals associated with the underworld. In this light, the presumption that legitimate and illegitimate groups are poles apart does not mean their status as social opposites fully determines their behavior and interrelationships. Both antipodal groups share common interests and the structural context of the political machine can provide "protection" for those who require an effective liaison of "business" with government.

To the extent that our concern is with the question about conditions that enable criminal elements to form relationships with state authorities and officials, this requires a sociological explanation. It does not seem as important to explain why one person, say, a James Marcus (a New York City Commissioner of Water Supply who steered reservoir construction and cleaning contracts to Cosa Nostra firms in lieu of gambling debts), or a Hugh Addonizio (a Newark, New Jersey Mayor who provided lucrative street construction contracts to Cosa Nostra associates) are corruptible and engage in malfeasance while others refuse to participate in wrong doing. It seems far more important to understand the characteristics of the social structure that create the institutionalization of corruption through organized criminality. If crime and corruption were simply the action of an occasional corrupt government official, focusing on individual motivations would make sense. When, however, it is ubiquitous and institutionalized, then answers are best found in the structural characteristics of the political, economic and social systems. Further, if we also think about organized criminal behavior as responsive and sensitive to the configuration of resources and constraints that exist in the social structure, then organized criminal activities may be understood as an outcome of processes reflecting people's actions as they adapt to those characteristics of the social structure that present obstacles and criminal opportunities.[17]

In looking at conditions that promote and energize a political-criminal nexus, the role of corruption appears to be central. But equally important are political/bureaucratic structures that threaten to strangle business operations with regulations (as in the construction industries in New York City) or function in too lax a manner. With the penetration of the Mayor's Office during John Lindsay's administration, La Cosa Nostra racketeers exploited the personal weakness of a top official who found himself in the pockets of gangsters. But not only individuals can be corrupted; entire administrations may be compromised by criminal elements. Some examples will follow. In this connection the discussion will turn to the second question concerning how a criminal/political nexus is developed and maintained.

Clientelist Politics and Organized Crime: Another Context for PCN Formation

Political elites consolidated in machines built around nonrepresentative clienteles provide opportunities for organized criminal groups to develop and expand—especially in minority communities and ethnic enclaves. Here, initially, the political-criminal nexus may be benign or nonexistent. Ethnic criminal groups, such as the Tongs in Chinatown, do indeed prey upon local businesses through extortion but also afford a cluster of stabilizing assets designed to encourage legitimate business growth. Private protection through "informal policing," and ready access to capital derived from vice industries may become available as legitimate business loans are circulated as investments offered through quasi-legal commercial entities and associations such as the Chinese Consolidated Benevolent Association (CCBA).[18] The CCBA emerged in Chinatown as an important political entity, a political brokerage, as it were, that even City Hall consults and confers with over policies affecting law enforcement and other community needs.[19]

Likewise in some Latino enclaves described by Portes and Bach organized criminal groups substitute as political entities that offer services similar to those that the Tongs provide in Chinatown.[20] Crime can be functional in ethnic communities where political machines are dominated by other non-representative ethnic groups and may be likely to adopt either predatory or standoffish postures toward entrepreneurs and political actors in the new neighborhoods. Moreover, amassing capital for some of the enclave members that facilitate their transition into mainstream legitimate business is a vital service criminal groups may provide.

It is well to remember that organized crime has not always functioned as an alternate government bridging the gaps between ethnic enclaves and mainstream institutions. Notable exceptions are found among first generation Japanese in Los Angeles and first generation Italians in San Francisco.[21] But even in these instances, circumstances and historical accidents occurred that promoted rapid social and economic assimilation into the mainstream. Actually, the availability of lucrative economic opportunities that managed to seep into and penetrate the ethnic enclaves connecting the latter to the larger community's economic infrastructures was largely fortuitous. And in these favored ethnic settlements many of the "state" functions that in other settings were instruments of, or partly aided by, organized criminal actors—namely welfare, governance, protection, and economic coordination—were assumed by legitimate political forces.

The dynamics of crime activity that may simultaneously inhibit and facilitate the processes of integration of ethnic enclaves dragging them into the legitimate political matrix creates a complex picture of modern minority communities and their relationships to organized crime. Today in many modern enclaves state-like services traditionally provided by organized criminal networks and their associated political machines are replaced by community police patrols, welfare, and other infrastructural services that tie the enclave to the larger society. At the same time, other economic forces such as the massive departure of city-based manufacturing help to strengthen criminal activities that serve as substitutes for legitimate economic activities. One might hypothesize that the more immigrant groups resemble a classical enclave, (i.e., the more isolated from the larger community and structures), the more likely substantial organized crime groups will operate as substitutes and alternatives to foreclosed external opportunities. Conversely, accelerated assimilation of minorities into the mainstream may serve to impede criminal development.

What this suggests is the complexity of a political-criminal nexus. They may develop and operate at various levels of the political stratum and hierarchies that overlay the socioeconomic structures of local communities, urban sectors, regional/state, and federal/national governmental entities. From the criminal activist's standpoint the goal is similar: power and control to manipulate the governmental social control apparatus. But the type of corruption and control may depend upon criminals' syndicates and groups mobilizing capabilities, their relationships to political entities, and the depth and range of influence required for criminal operations.

As the examples below illustrate, it may be more consistent with experience to suppose that there is not a monolithic "political/criminal nexus" but a plurality of possibilities and relationships at micro and macro levels of political/criminal collusion.

The fact that no unitary, single PCN has been identified may speak to the nature of the structure of the political economy of the United States. Since there is no command economy in America, there is no centralized, national administrative entity that superintends price controls, business activities organized around a uniform code, and so on, that can be targeted for criminal conspiracies and manipulations. Business and commercial activity is huge in the United States; it is often uniform and national in scope, but the political regulatory apparatuses with few exceptions do not exercise authority in every jurisdiction nationwide. Law enforcement itself is not administered naturally through a central bureaucracy; rather, it is a collection of quasi-autonomous agencies that can be put together in composite Task Forces to pursue organized crime control across several states. The FBI, DEA, IRS, Department of Labor, and various agencies with missions abroad do sustain organized crime units, but each pursues its particular objectives.

On the other hand, criminal syndicates in the USA have rarely achieved national coordination in criminal enterprises. Prohibition perhaps is the best example, because the social crisis Prohibition produced was national in scope and offered opportunities to criminal entrepreneurs to operate on a truly national scale. However, the law enforcement activity was in terms of its intensity, durability, and efficiency shaped and driven by local conditions and circumstances. There was no need to reach to the highest levels of national government or political power because enforcement and authority were mainly local activities.

Did organized criminal groups in the United States create a national-level PCN? The answer is that they have on several occasions with mixed results. There is some evidence that the director of the FBI, J. Edgar Hoover, resisted acting against organized crime because his gambling compulsions compromised his authority.[22] During the 1960 Presidential Campaign, there is evidence that various La Cosa Nostra bosses in New York City, Chicago, New Orleans, Tampa, Florida, Detroit and Cleveland assisted the democratic party by arranging for illegal votes which secured the election of John F. Kennedy. The gangsters and racketeers who arranged this voter fraud were betrayed by the Kennedy administration when it implemented a major attack on organized crime.[23] In the Prohibition era, the Volstead Act was a national piece of legislation but enforcement was localized and hence corruption and criminal conspiracies were local and regional, corresponding to criminal territorial organization of illegal alcohol production and distribution.

Organized Crime as a Response to Political Marginality

Where influence with government is an objective of organized crime groups operating in mainstream social environments adequately protected by law enforcement, in politically powerless communities (immigrant and minority communities) organized crime may take on different roles as quasi-governmental functionaries, as informal or alternate "governments" and policing agencies. In this sense, political parties and machines may actually encourage organized crime by ignoring the local ethnic/minority social and economic milieus.

Providing social stability and informal policing where political institutions are either dominated by other ethnic/minority groups in a spoils system, or where local inhabitants have been abandoned to economic predators and street criminals, may be a socially beneficial and useful function of organized crime groups. Organized criminals may act as political middlemen bridging the gaps between City Hall and the enclave. They may also amass capital (licitly and illicitly) in order to facilitate the transitions of their clients into legitimate businesses capable of competing outside the ghetto, or, short of that, operating profitably within the commercial sector of the local community. Thus, through organized crime an informally protected ethnic community may generate the assets needed to become internally productive and be poised to grow beyond the confines of the local community as opportunities present themselves.

These hypotheses focus on modern immigrant and minority communities, but clearly not all minority communities are victimized by the presence of organized crime, although it would seem that the more the migrant/minority group resembles a classical enclave, the more likely it is to have substantial organized criminality, since its external opportunities tend to be foreclosed and its residents more directly subject to the intimidation of powerful local criminals. Further, it seems worth considering to what extent commercial activities in comparatively apolitical enclaves are under the influence of organized crime, and whether the corollary theme—that the more isolated the enclave from political and cultural interaction with the larger society, the more some of its functions fall under the sway of organized criminals—empirically obtains. This seems prevalent in New York City's Chinatown and the Chinese enclave in San Francisco, California.[24]

A related issue concerns the degree to which ethnic/minority ghettos are politically assimilated into the larger institutional configuration. To the extent that they are not, it may be supposed that many state-like services may be furnished by criminal entrepreneurs and their agents acting in non-predatory roles as neighborhood governors, overlords and as police-like cadres creating some semblance of social order. This pattern, which was characteristic of traditional ethnic ghettos, seems less relevant in the life of modern enclaves where police routinely patrol, welfare agencies are active, and other infrastructural services tie (if only loosely) the community to the larger society.

Still, the variability in the ethnic enclave's politicization, its economic task environments, its core technologies, and specific political linkages may figure importantly in determining how deeply organized crime is entrenched and forms an invisible but nonetheless powerful government.

Political/Criminal Development and Maintenance

Criminal groups may be seen as decision-making units (or "firms" in economic language) where assets and resources are utilized and exchanged for services and goods they wish to acquire in order to facilitate their operations, enhance their wealth, and create a stable operating environment. In these respects criminal groups function much like legitimate businesses. Like legitimate companies, criminal enterprises can take a variety of forms and engage in activities quite similar to upperworld businesses in their search for markets and opportunities.[25]

Firms that conduct illegal enterprises may be quite variegated. They might be large and hierarchically structured (e.g., a "numbers" operation which may employ hundreds of runners and bankers and amass gross revenues of millions of dollars), or remain small in size, but powerful nonetheless (e.g., a group of extortionists and assassins who render services involving violence for a fee or provide violence as an appendage to an enterprise syndicate engaged in drugs, gambling, or racketeering). They can be short-lived (a drug trafficking network that dissolves after several shipments of heroin); or relatively durable (e.g., a loansharking operation that has successfully operated for years).

Whatever size, longevity, diversification, specialization in services or products, and whatever market share, a criminal firm possessing these characteristics experiences some constraints which are both internal and external. To avoid arrest and prosecution, criminal firms will seek to maintain secrecy and to avoid creating tangible evidence of their activities. Regardless of the shape, flexibility or complexity of firms, criminal firms require certain conditions, services and goods in order to conduct their business operations. (While La Cosa Nostra crime families have tended to vertically integrate services and capabilities [e.g., fences, fixers, gun dealers, assassins, thieves, informants, financiers, criminal brokers, and security personnel], not all criminal enterprises will develop the assets needed to insure their survival in an underworld governed by the gun and fear.) In the pre-Cosa Nostra period of the New York underworld, for example, a group labeled, rather luridly, "Murder, Inc." provided several criminal syndicates with highly skilled specialists in murder and mayhem. These individuals, whose sole task was to work exclusively for the criminal group favoring the syndicates, carried out contract murder, maimings, and beatings across the nation.[26]

Some conditions necessary to do business of any kind are so fundamental, and so easily available to legitimate firms that they are barely acknowledged in any survey of "factors of production" among upperworld firms. However, such fundamental, taken for granted conditions may be problematic for criminally oriented businesses. Since illegal organizations operate in the midst of criminals, and since neither police nor courts are available to respond to their complaints, it is an ongoing task fraught with danger for them to protect their assets and guarantee transactions.

Given the importance of protecting the basics needed to operate an illegal enterprise, criminal groups will have to devote their own resources to provide these conditions where, in contrast, legitimate firms may freely utilize the legitimate legal and credit apparatuses of the state (police, courts, insurance companies).

Beyond efforts to guarantee these basic conditions, criminal firms will need specialized services or products that are not customarily required for legitimate business enterprise. Many criminal groups will wish to buy "protection" from arrest or prosecution. From the perspective of legitimate society, this service, "corruption," and its ancillary procedures have been designed to try to guarantee that the service is not aggressively sold. Public efforts to discourage the practice have not eliminated it, but raised the price in an effort to dilute the value of the service. From the perspective of illegitimate society, corruption amounts to purchasing a "license" to do business which becomes a valuable component in the mix of "factors of production."

Corruption is, then, a practice that facilitates the basic operating conditions of illicit business. In many cases, the formation of a PCN involves members of organized crime groups, governmental officials, and private sector entrepreneurs who offer financial incentives for favored treatment in their business transactions. When we think about political-criminal coalitions, whether we know it or not, we are really focusing on the elements that make up organized crime: members of criminal groups like La Cosa Nostra and also members of the business, political, and law enforcement communities that encourage and/or tolerate criminal activity. Critical to the lifeblood of a crime network are collaborative political/legal actors. Perhaps the real significance of crime networks and their persistence has been overlooked for the most part because of the narrow focus on professional career criminals. Organized crime has been seen as consisting of organizations of criminals with names like Gotti, Bonanno, Gravano, and Gambino. The emphasis on the criminality of only a segment of those involved has meant neglecting other crucial participants in organized criminality and the crucial fact that criminal groups have been intimately tied to, and in symbiosis with, the legal and political bureaucracies and officials.

Aspects of the social structure that impinge directly on how people make a living, the work they do, and way they organize their labor to produce things that are useful and necessary constitute much of the substantive work of bureaucracies. Contrary to the prevailing myth that universal rules govern bureaucracies, the fact is that in day-to-day operations rules can—and must—be selectively applied. Consequently, some degree of corruption is not merely a possibility, but rather a virtual certainty built into the very structure of bureaucratic organizations, including law enforcement.[27]

The starting point for understanding this structural invitation to corruption is the observation that application of all rules and procedures comprising the foundation of an organization inevitably admits of a degree of discretion. Rules can only specify what should be done when the actions being considered fall clearly into unambiguously specifiable categories, about which there can be no reasonable grounds of disagreement or conflicting interpretation. But such categories in real life are a rarity. Instead, most events fall within the penumbra of the rules where the discretion of the official or office holder must hold sway.

Nothing illustrates this reality more dramatically than the career of John Nacrelli, mayor of Chester, Pennsylvania. A combination of corrupt politicians, criminals, and rogue law enforcement officers within the economically destitute small city bordering Philadelphia produced a sordid alliance that fed off itself and that became embedded in the political system like a parasite that thrives on a living organism. The combined influence of the PCN stretched beyond Chester and seeped into Delaware County. During his tenure in office and even after his racketeering conviction, Nacrelli treated the public trust of government as a form of private enterprise. For him politics was truly a personal business. Racketeers delivered money and provided services to officials in city government who controlled the police who, in turn, under orders from City Hall, either enforced the law or ignored criminal activity, no matter how blatant. Thus, a self-enclosed, self-generating political criminal machine thrived at the center of the government in Chester.

The modus operandi developed by Nacrelli was to saturate the city administration with hand-picked cronies and operatives who were chosen not on the formal basis of merit or technical competence but strictly in terms of patronage, as favors to allies, friends, and political supporters and as links to the criminal syndicate in the city. Public officials in positions to award contracts for city services would favor private contractors whose employees were friends and supporters of the Chester City administration. Less dramatic abuses, but in no small measure less corrosive of public confidence in government, involved routine misuse of the patronage system which undermined public efficiency by allowing civil service jobs to go unfilled or by appointing "temporary" provisional employees who became permanent by repeated re-appointment.

The criminal markets that emerged in video poker gambling, narcotics, and loan sharking, which were (and appear to remain) intertwined with law enforcement and the political machine, proved to be a sinister substitute for law enforcement and legitimate government. The outcomes were predictable in Chester: with police indifferent to crime or enforcing it in expedient, optional ways, crime settled into the community more deeply making it more difficult to control.[28]

While many approaches to the political-criminal connection describe the political and legitimate sectors of society as victims of criminal conspiracies, other accounts, do not. The spectacle of Chester exemplifies the point made alone that the putative victims in many instances function as active partners in criminal coalitions that seek to neutralize law enforcement, or to weaken the capacities of other firms and businesses to compete. Clothing manufacturing firms, trade unions, transport and construction businesses where criminals and legitimate businesspeople have collaborated in alliances in order to enhance their competitive advantages or to facilitate political careers of malleable officials through massive manipulations of electoral processes are not uncommon. Many organized criminals have survived and prospered because they have forged connections with influential politicians and law enforcement officials who themselves find their liaisons career enhancing and personally profitable.

What are the typical contexts in which corruption of political actors occur? A good example is Carlos Marcello who headed the Louisiana La Cosa Nostra. Marcello insisted on being identified as a successful realtor and businessman involved in numerous civic activities. Actually, his career was launched in the vice industries through which he acquired his considerable capital resources and then parlayed these into legitimate business assets. In order to protect his criminal enterprises he colluded with public officials at every level of government by direct cash payoffs, through huge campaign contributions, and by delivering large voting blocs for favored candidates. Typically, rather than choosing among candidates, his organization shrewdly backed all of them.[29]

Looking into the processes of corruption, it may well be tied to intermediary structures such as legitimate businesses. These appear to provide an ideal setting from which connections with government officials can be cultivated openly rather than surreptitiously. Legitimate businesses may be seen as the "delivery system" and natural bridge between gangsters and politicians. Packaging oneself as a "businessman" is a fairly common ruse of gangsters and may be more effective than anyone suspects. Among other things, the business identity affords racketeers a cloak of respectability, and makes it more feasible for legitimate people to deal with them or with their agents (attorneys). Politicians who would be embarrassed by organized crime connection, however remote, can always claim that they thought they were dealing with a respectable businessman.

As one of the most influential and durable La Cosa Nostra bosses in the United States, Carlos Marcello cultivated solid connections with many persons in high places. According to John Davis, whose research is based on FBI documents that include wiretap surveillance and undercover operations in Louisiana, Marcello's influence reached into the U.S. Senate, the U.S. Department of Justice, and the Governor's mansion in Louisiana. Still, there is no evidence that Marcello had direct connections with his corrupt political sponsors and partners. He utilized third-party intermediaries who would function as "go-betweens" carrying money and information back and forth among the principals. Marcello and the New Orleans LCN family would heavily finance a political campaign and turn out the vote. According to David Chandler, an investigative journalist for *Life* magazine, the quid pro quo among gangsters, lawmen, and politicians in Louisiana was simple: if they looked the other way as the crime machine chugged along, political support and money would be forthcoming. Of course, Marcello ensured stability in the underworld by using violence to quell other crime and to intimidate other criminal operators. In the mid- to late sixties, the flamboyant New Orleans district attorney, Jim Garrison, dismissed eighty-four cases brought against Marcello's men including attempted murder, manslaughter, kidnaping and illegal gambling.[30]

Garrison (who, incidentally, launched an investigation into the Kennedy assassination premised on the assumption that the CIA and its rogue operatives, not the underworld, murdered the president) was not the only high-ranking law enforcement official Marcello knew. As he admitted to two secretly wired undercover agents, Marcello had a connection via a third party to the Attorney-General of the United States; connections with high officials in the Immigration and Naturalization Service; friendships with several federal judges in New Orleans; personal relationships with the leadership of the largest and most powerful labor union in the United States (the Teamsters); and direct relationships with the heads of the Louisiana State Police, the chief of police of New Orleans, and the district attorney of New Orleans.

Within La Cosa Nostra, Marcello's standing was unique: he could "make" soldiers for his crime family without La Cosa Nostra Commission approval; and no underworld figure would dare to venture into Louisiana without his permission. Interestingly, his career moves and organizational elan which most law enforcement officials considered quite sophisticated goes back to the style of the New Orleans Matranga mafia cosche in the 1890s. In the early stages of his criminal career Marcello operated in the rural parishes surrounding New Orleans, Baton Rouge, and Shreveport; only later when he became a dominant figure and was firmly in control of the local underworld did he migrate into the cities and assume control of their vice industries.

Partners of Exchange and Collusion Between
Criminals and Political Officials

The venture capital Marcello raised from his illegal operations (illegal gambling, narcotics, prostitution, extortion, marketing stolen goods, robberies, burglaries and thefts) amounted to a criminal enterprise that required, according to Aaron Kohn, head of the New Orleans Crime Commission, a collusion with corrupted officials at every level including police, sheriffs, justices of the peace, prosecutors, mayors, governors, judges, licensing authorities, state legislators and members of Congress. The PCN Marcello nurtured and participated in enabled him to go beyond predatory, parasitic criminality and finance a sizeable array of legitimate businesses including motels, restaurants, taverns, banks, beer and liquor distributorships, shrimp boat fleets, shipbuilding, finance companies, taxi and bus firms, phonograph record companies, electrical appliance stores, and a tomato canning company. This last activity provided Marcello with his stock explanation for not having anything to do with organized crime. He stubbornly insisted that he was merely a $1,500 a month tomato salesman. Indeed, the Pelican Tomato Company, Marcello's firm, had the U.S. Navy as its biggest customer.

Money, votes, and immunity from prosecution are the "commodities" routinely exchanged in the nexus system of values. To operate criminal businesses required corruption and this meant alliances with politicians who provided a protective umbrella shielding the criminals. This could be accomplished in a variety of ways in Louisiana. In some cases there were direct cash payoffs; in others, huge campaign contributions were made. Sometimes, Marcello picked up virtually the entire tab in a campaign for governor or other statewide offices. In still other cases, he delivered large voting blocs to favored candidates. Marcello's shrewd techniques of political manipulation are instructive: in a hard fought gubernatorial election, the candidates in the Democratic primary (which was equivalent to election) were former Governor Jimmie Davis and the New Orleans Mayor de Lesseps Morrison. Typically, Marcello had maintained excellent relations with both Davis and Morrison and wished to keep things that way. Rather than choose between them, he found a way to back both of them. He himself became the chief contributor to Davis's campaign fund, and two of Marcello's associates became Morrison's main financial backers. Thus, no matter who won, Marcello was sure of keeping close ties with the incoming governor. Davis was elected and later took official actions that benefitted Marcello's empire by authorizing a publicly funded swamp drainage project that increased the values of Marcello's river front properties tenfold.[31]

Chicago along with Louisiana may be the other paradigm case of a criminal organization utterly smothering and compromising the legitimacy of the civil and criminal justice functions of government. Capone masterfully manipulated the highest local government officials, effectively neutralized them, and assimilated them into his networks.

It is fair to say that the public was at least ambivalent at first and stood by as a collective silent partner as local government was compromised and delegitimated. Only when violence became so indiscriminate and so intense did the public awaken and begin to support reform initiatives orchestrated by federal agencies determined to crush Capone and eliminate his political cronies.[32]

Capone's key henchman, Jacob ("Greasy Thumb") Guzik was the "connection guy" in the organization. Guzik supervised a group of Chicago gangsters whose prime function was to arrange the corruption of public officials and others.

In New York, the role of "middleman" that linked the political system with the crime syndicates was inhabited by Frank Costello who was known as the "Prime Minister of the Underworld."[33] Costello was an established gambler with a considerable record of involvement in bootlegging (who incidentally, also brought slot machines to Huey Long's Louisiana for a kickback). As a top mafia boss, Costello was a political broker and fixer for the New York mobs.[34] He succeeded in breaking the Irish domination over judicial appointments in Manhattan. In the 1940s, Tammany Hall Irish political chieftains turned to the increasingly Italian-controlled underworld for desperately needed funding. The "Mafia Plan" meant some risk for Irish politicians when Costello and his colleagues "decided to install their own Italian district leaders in Tammany clubhouses."[35]

Costello managed this sensitive transition skillfully and was able to secure judicial nominations to the New York courts where it was expected that jurists who owed their careers to Costello would take his suggestions in cases involving organized crime interests. With the power of the political machine at his disposal, Costello was able to assume the posture of a civic-minded public figure. Eventually, it all backfired with the exposures of the Kefauver Committee hearings in 1951 where he was mortified by questions concerning his criminal affiliations. His attempted assassination during an internal crime family struggle involving the leadership of the Luciano La Cosa Nostra family in 1957 (later to be called the Genovese Crime family) finally destroyed the credibility of his role as a civic-minded citizen and philanthropist.

What Marcello in Louisiana, Guzik/Capone in Chicago, and Costello in New York show is that the interactions between criminal organizations and political entities may be mutually beneficial, in the short run at least, and that the political organization under criminal influence becomes the mechanism for exercising both legitimate and illegitimate pressures to further the interests of the participants in the nexus. It also seems clear that manipulation of a political entity—whether party or elected officials—is feasible and more efficient in milieux where the political opposition is negligible or moribund and where conflicts between the law, what it forbids, and public appetites are apparent.

New York's Tammany Hall struck such notorious bargains between politicians and criminal elements that the Democratic machine was able to rule the city as a fiefdom for almost a century. In the 1930s, Dutch Schultz's influence with the Bronx Democratic party enabled him actually to deploy the police in an underworld struggle to take control of the black numbers rackets in Harlem.[36]

In these cases it seems clear that the relationship between the racketeer and the political machine is symbiotic. In Kansas City, the local La Cosa Nostra was an integral part of the Pendergast machine when the vote had to be "delivered" for a candidate. In return for support from gangsters who provided money and votes, police protection for their rackets was secured.[37] The alliance among politics, policemen, and their underworld allies required individuals who could deal with all the participants—the underworld, the world of business, the government—and who would not be identifiable solely as gangsters, but could masquerade as businessmen, or as ambitious politicians yet who were known, trusted, and respected by all. Credentials of the criminal/political middleman had to include knowledge of money; how to get it and how to use it. He had to be someone who appreciated the value and uses of graft and the bribe as well as creating and sustaining ongoing illicit secret partnerships. And he (or she) had to be a person who was amoral, not fearful of violence and its employment, and who projected a smooth polished front.

Not every criminal organization had to court reluctant politicians in order to forge partnerships. In 1970, Hugh Addonizio, mayor of New Jersey's biggest city, Newark, was sentenced to ten years imprisonment on kickback conspiracy charges involving La Cosa Nostra. Addonizio shared $1.5 million extorted from contractors through the services of Angelo DeCarlo, a Genovese crime family capo, for doing business with the city. Despite a steady stream of convictions including the mayors of Jersey City, and West New York, congresspersons from Bayonne, Fort Lee and officials in Hudson, Bergen, and Mercer counties, in November of 1984, Atlantic City mayor Michael Matthews was convicted after pleading guilty to accepting a $10,000 cash extortion payment from an undercover FBI agent. In July 1984, Matthews was removed from office as the result of charges that he conspired to sell the mayor's office of Atlantic City to the Scarfo La Cosa Nostra family of Philadelphia and Southern New Jersey. An organizer of Local 54 of the Bartenders Union in Atlantic City and an associate of Scarfo was also sentenced for his part in the conspiracy.[38]

What of today? Is the PCN functioning in much the way it did in the past? Is it more powerful than in the past or has the capacity of criminals to influence political actions, including law enforcement, diminished?

In the Gotti trials, informant Salvatore (Sammy the Bull) Gravano revealed that the Gambino Crime family had access to the federal prosecutor's office through an employee and had paid a police officer assigned to the Intelligence Division to provide information on police investigative activities. As for "political fixers" in the style of Frank Costello, whose influence reached directly and often openly into the political machine, that seems to be a thing of the past. Modern criminals operate through elaborate "fronts" and the subterfuges of the legitimate business entrepreneur image which Paul Costellano, assassinated head of the Gambino Crime family, sought to cultivate as his public persona.[39]

Marcello, Costello, and Guzik are no more than mostly forgotten hieroglyphs of the criminal past; they demonstrated that local political establishments were vulnerable to criminal manipulations. It was not until the post-Hoover era that the FBI became seriously involved in organized crime control. The passivity of the FBI before the Kennedy era may have contributed to the power of LCN and its success in forming political criminal networks. The federal effort added an important component to anti-crime efforts in several ways that weakened these linkages. Even before RICO, the resources of the FBI, then later the IRS, Treasury, and Strike Forces associated with U.S. attorney offices could mobilize manpower, forensic and investigative skills and needed resources seemingly untainted by local politics. RICO legislation, special prosecutors, federal grand juries, immunity provisions, and witness security programs were significant elements in strengthening organized crime control efforts that made the PCN more vulnerable.

Furthermore, the successful careers of organized criminals in corrupting and neutralizing the political structures in "one party states" such as Louisiana and in large metropolitan areas like Chicago, New York, Boston/Providence, and Kansas City suggest that the effectiveness of law enforcement against professional criminals may depend on political heterogeneous structures and the viability of jurisdictionally diversified law enforcement organizations. But, diversity can and has produced fragmentation when, for instance, agencies compete. On the other hand, when they cooperate in task force groups, they become quite formidable opponents of criminal organizations.

The "Fixer" and the PCN Operative

In criminal networks that are stable and durable such as vice syndicates, the role of the "fixer" defines the dynamics of the collusion that tie together elements of the political machine and criminal conspiracies. Jimmy Hines, a powerful political agent in Bronx County and in Tammany Hall, embodies the idea of the PCN.

Hines grew up in ward politics where politicians relied heavily on gangsters to win elections. So it was no surprise that, at the turn of the century, he staged his electoral campaigns for aldermen with the help of hoodlums such as Spike Sullivan and Harry "Gyp the Blood" Horowitz in the upper west side of Manhattan. As his career matured, Hines developed relationships with a broader, more powerful group of New York racketeers, including Arnold "The Brain" Rothstein, Dutch Schultz, Owney Madden, and Frank Costello, the Mafia's emissary to the political machines.

The extent of the ties between local politics and the mob is illustrated by the fact that when Hines attended the 1932 Democratic Party National Convention in Chicago that nominated Franklin Delano Roosevelt, Frank Costello shared his hotel suite. On Schultz's payroll alone, Hines received between $500 and $1,000 per week to protect the numbers rackets in Harlem and Manhattan and the bootleg operations in the Bronx. Hines's principal duty as the political agent of the mob was to see to it that police did not interfere with their rackets.

In 1935, Thomas E. Dewey became Manhattan district attorney and targeted key racketeers such as Schultz, "Waxey" Gordon, and Charles "Lucky" Luciano, along with their henchmen and partners in legitimate society. Dewey, a Republican and future presidential candidate, went after Hines, who was at one time the most powerful Democrat in New York State and Roosevelt's primary patronage dispenser in New York City. The first prosecution on conspiracies involving bribes paid to the judiciary and police ended in a mistrial. On 25 February 1939, Hines was convicted in a second trial and went to Sing Sing prison in 1940, where he served four years. Hines died in 1957, at age 80; he epitomized the political-criminal nexus that enables organized crime to exist.

In many corrupted urban political machines, the role of the fixer is vital for maintaining a smoothly functioning system. The police, the politicians, the local business elite, and organized crime cannot be seen together openly, so another, apparently independent party becomes the linchpin, the individual who can interact with each group without arousing too much suspicion. The fixer is like a thumb, able to touch the other fingers on a hand, enabling it to function. He (or she) is technically independent of government, an attorney in private practice, perhaps, who is intimately knowledgeable about the law enforcement community, the district attorney's office, the courts, the leading business groups and entrepreneurs in the community, and the organized crime bosses with vested interests in all sectors of the local society's power structure.

In New York during the 1930s, Jimmy Hines, the head of the Democratic Party machine in Bronx County, New York City, functioned as an influential fixer and go-between for the Dutch Schultz mob, the police, and the Democratic Party, which dominated the city's politics. In Louisiana, Carlos Marcello, a New Orleans La Cosa Nostra boss, utilized local attorneys to arrange graft, bribes, contributions to political campaigns, and secret business ventures. Sometimes a gangster will clean up his image and mix in with legitimate society, as in the case of Frank Costello, known in the mafia crime scene as the "Prime Minister of the Underworld." The public image of Costello was that of a philanthropist and charity organizer with powerful connections in politics and the judicial system. Over time many judges and politicians would owe their careers to Costello's influence. That influence (known as "juice") was used to secure court appointments of jurists and swing elections on behalf of mob-friendly political figures. For any durable crime organization, a fixer is a vital activity for the organization's security.

Vulnerabilities of the PCN

The question whether legal reforms and suppression strategies have been effective goes to the difficulties law enforcement officials and others have had in defining organized criminality. As it is often used, the term is both confusing and misleading. Ideally, a definition provides limits within which to focus inquiry and to isolate a relatively homogeneous set of phenomena that share certain characteristics from a wide variety of closely related but significantly different events. Several writers, and even the government it-self, observed that there is no acceptable definition of organized crime.[40] The GAO has suggested time and again that the root of the contemporary struggle against organized crime is hopelessly twisted because of the problem of mean-ing. During the 1960s there emerged the notion that organized criminality was an alien conspiracy and/or a bureaucratic monolith analogous to the structure of a corporation.

If, on the other hand, organized crime is defined as referring to those illegal activities involving the management and coordination of racketeer-ing (organized extortion) vice, then the framework permits us to think about a process of criminal activity without narrowing the notion to a static subset of professional career criminals. Who is involved is left open so that political actors may be included.

The empirical work referred to above is sensitive to a dynamic notion of "organized crime" showing the prevalence of crime networks linking profes-sional career criminals with political and legal figures.

As for the vulnerabilities of PCNs and preventative strategies that can weaken, destroy, or neutralize them, recent investigations may be illuminating.

Master Builders, Master Criminals: The New York City Construction Industry, Its Vulnerabilities, and the Political Ramifications

Corruption and racketeering in New York City's multi-billion-dollar con-struction industry dates back at least a century. Yet recent prosecutions, investigations, and studies by federal, state, and local commissions continue to document pervasive and systemic patterns of criminality and unethical conduct throughout the City's construction industry, particularly on public construction projects. The list of illicit activities is extensive: most common are racketeering, bid rigging, extortion, bribery of public officials, theft, fraud, falsification of business records, false filings with government agencies, and collusive bidding practices. In addition, organized crime's involvement is so effective that certain construction sub-industries are substantially mob-controlled.

In a report released in 1990, the New York State Organized Crime Task Force attempted to analyze the reasons for the industry's susceptibility to racketeering and corruption, and described how organized crime syndicates have exploited these facts. Although traditional criminal investigations and prosecutions play a critical role in identifying the particular industry traits that generate corruption, the report noted that law enforcement can play only a limited role in forcing reforms. It concluded that a comprehensive, multi-jurisdictional strategy to control organized crime ought therefore to look beyond prosecutions and incarceration, and use other means, including civil remedies, as well as legislative, administrative, and structural reforms.

Because such reforms often require altering fundamental ways in which an industry conducts its business, meaningful change may be difficult to achieve. In many instances, it requires modifying long-standing practices and procedures. Such institutional reform can be imposed through legislation, regulation, or judicial decision, but it stands a better chance of success if the affected institutions adopt these reforms voluntarily.

The Report's recommendations for containing official corruption included reform of electoral campaign finance laws. This implies that political will needs to be interjected into the reform process along with increased accountability among the agencies monitoring the vast industry. Whether detailed reforms will actually be addressed and implemented may be an indicator of the extent of criminal intrusion into the political system. Can the problems facing the construction industry be tackled by law enforcement alone? Probably not. The central problems developed in the Task Force analysis are, after all, political issues.

Strategies for Preventing and Weakening the PCN

New York City's school building and maintenance program has been one of the areas of the construction industry plagued by corruption, racketeering, fraud, bureaucratic inefficiencies, and abuse with particularly tragic consequences. In the past several decades, the Board of Education poured billions of dollars into school construction, often taking eight or nine years to build a single school at cost overruns of several hundred percent. The educational facilities of New York fell into a deplorable condition, leaving many schools unsafe and unhealthy.

In response, in 1989 the New York State Legislature created a School Construction Authority (SCA) charged with rebuilding the educational infrastructure of New York City. It was recognized that such an agency could be susceptible to criminal exploitation by La Cosa Nostra mobsters, labor racketeers, cartels of contractors and suppliers that operated in the construction industries at large. To deal with this threat, the Board of the SCA proposed an Inspector General Office within the agency to prevent corruption by blocking opportunities and reducing contractor incentives to act in a corrupt manner; to deter corrupt activity through investigation, prosecution, civil law suits and administrative sanctions, such as debarments from further work; and to provide opportunities for work among those contractors who believed that they had been unfairly restricted from competing for contracts.

The Inspector General's office represented an attempt to contain the threat of organized criminal involvement in public construction projects, by seeking deterrents through crime control efforts and by pursuing administrative remedies that could strengthen industry processes and block opportunities and occasions for racketeering.

The idea of an Inspector General stems from the practitioner-initiated approaches to apply the multi-jurisdictional perspective to organized crime control which includes efforts to detect and deter criminality by law enforcement investigation and prosecution, and to reform an industry by blocking opportunities for racketeering through administrative remedies.

The basis and rationale for the strategy is the assumption that law enforcement by itself is necessary but scarcely sufficient as a criminal deterrent. Moreover, as the Report of the New York State Organized Crime Task Force suggested, long-established policies and practices in the construction industry created opportunities for, and vulnerability to, criminal intrusions and therefore had to be changed. The challenge was then to determine the operational characteristics of the industry that led to crime.

The mandate of the Authority was to protect a $4.3 billion construction program from victimization by organized crime, crime monopolies and cartels, corruption, bribery, extortion, racketeering, and the other crimes endemic to the industry that also provide the occasions for creating or strengthening a PCN. The formation of the SCA flowed from the conclusions and recommendations of the study of corruption and racketeering in the New York City construction industry. As the Report observed:

> "The most promising antidote to fraud, waste, and abuse in public works is reform of the system of public contracting and better public administration. A city government poorly organized to carry out public works promotes delay, indecision, lack of accountability, and a culture of fraud, waste and abuse.

The city must invest greater funds and resources in auditing public works projects, and in investigating and punishing contractor fraud, both administratively and through the courts. Similarly, incompetent contract administration facilitates unnecessary and unjustified change orders...and unsafe construction. The solution is to overhaul and reform the public works process by abolishing the Wick's law, reforming the lowest responsible bidder system, improving auditing procedures.... Most of all, it means reforming the administration of public works."[41]

The Racketeering Report appeared on the heels of major scandals involving the construction industry in the city. Public officials and prosecutors acknowledged that law enforcement could not prosecute away the problems endemic to the industry. The inducements to corruption and racketeering were substantial (and appear to remain so) so investigation, prosecution, and deterrence can get at only a small fraction of the illegal behavior involved. In fact, by the late eighties with major prosecutions of crime bosses resulting in convictions, the media generated the impression that RICO-driven prosecutions finally put organized crime on the run. But many organized crime experts thought that this was illusory. New crime bosses emerged, different criminal monopolies formed and new mobsters were taking up the reins in unions where labor racketeers had been purged through criminal convictions. And, as Gravano revealed in his trial testimony and later in interviews, companies convicted of frauds and other economic crimes reappeared under new names with different corporate compositions.[42] Also testimony before Congress indicated as late as 1996, organized crime is still entrenched in the labor movement.[43]

Nor are the major institutions—whether public authorities or private real estate interests—necessarily equipped or inclined to take the sorts of measures that might be required to protect themselves and their ventures from racketeering. One reason, it may be supposed, is that they have limited information about contractors, union leaders and others affiliated with projects. Even after learning that some of these are mob-connected or controlled, builders may still have few compunctions about paying the high costs of doing business if delivery or performance can be reasonably guaranteed to meet schedules. Once again: the affected public may be ambivalent about criminal activity, as it was fifty years ago when crime syndicates selling vice flourished.[44]

Operational Strategy of the SCA

In order to achieve its goal of denying public contracts to individuals and firms that are mob-connected or otherwise corrupt, the SCA embraced a series of strategies which would join together investigative and prosecution efforts in crime control and deterrence with administrative remedies for reform. Thus, the strategy is one of "brokering" the interests and capacities of law enforcement on the one hand with the interests of a reform-minded public works program to find effective administrative schemes to build schools efficiently with a minimum of waste and fraud. However, brokering relationships among public agencies and private vendors is a management task that could prove difficult. Inducements to collaborate among agencies when an office lacks statutory authority to engage in what must be considered highly intrusive investigations can generate serious problems as happened with the New Jersey Casino Commission when it attempted to screen and license applicants for gaming licenses. New Jersey excluded known racketeers from casino ownership but it also led to concerted efforts by organized crime to position itself in the ancillary industries (labor, hotel work and construction, etc.) surrounding casino operations. In effect, the mobsters preyed more vigorously on the peripheries of the industry and exercised their influence indirectly but no less effectively.

While there is much to applaud in the motivation and goals of the SCA initiatives, they raise complex and difficult issues of governmental ethics, fairness, and efficiency. In August 1991, the New York City SCA announced that it was blacklisting for up to five years more than fifty construction firms. Nearly half of the disqualifications were based on purported mob ties or criminality—such as bribery of union officials or building inspectors, tax fraud, minority business enterprise fraud, and money laundering—not on poor performance or previous government contracts or demonstrated inability to perform future contracts.[45]

It can be agreed that firms that are unqualified should be denied contracts and, if possible, the right even to bid. Likewise, firms whose contract performance is unsatisfactory ought to be "debarred" from future public business. There are some questions as to the ethical viability and legitimacy of the policy. For instance, is such a policy capable of fair implementation? Would its costs in terms of administrative delay and reducing competition be worth the advantage of keeping government free of whatever taint comes from a contractual relationship with a firm associated with La Cosa Nostra regardless of whether they perform adequately? While the state's Task Force Report applauded the city's efforts to identify mob firms and recommended that debarment be used more liberally to eliminate undesirables, it did not recommend that government agencies deny contracts to firms who hire workers belonging to mob-controlled unions (which constitutes a very substantial number). Perhaps the State Task Force realized that such a policy could shut down public works altogether.

On its face, the recommendation that government agencies refuse to deal with companies run by racketeers looks uncontroversial. But will, "blacklisting" work as a crime-control strategy? Denying contractors work because of mob-influence is based on the belief that such a threat works as a deterrent. But blacklisted companies may continue to do business with the government under a different corporate identity and through different officers. Even if organized criminals could be purged from certain industries, does it follow that organized crime groups would be substantially? As a practical matter identifying and excluding criminally affiliated firms is an enormous administrative burden to shoulder. There are tens of thousands of city contractors. On what basis could a financially-strapped city government judge the moral character and associates of all these contractors, and at what costs? Further, even if government agencies had the time, resources, and expertise to investigate contractors, what standards should be set for disqualifications? Should the government exclude ex-convicts or "acquitted" criminals? Can it perform such an investigatory task—examining the backgrounds and records of thousands of employees, much less suppliers and subcontractors with whom firms do business? Isn't this the sort of exaggerated ambition that comes back to haunt government agencies when they are confronted with evidence of morally questionable individuals that somehow slipped through the security net?

Other questions suggest other problems. Assume that government agencies are justified in refusing to deal with "tainted" firms, then how are such firms to be identified? The obvious case is where a mafia don runs a company. But this possibility is farfetched because mafia dons don't serve as CEOs. Crime syndicates sell connections and protection and mob-controlled firms are operated by clean fronts and associates. How many La Cosa Nostra members, associates, relatives, or friends in a firm are enough to justify exclusion? Is it only La Cosa Nostra tainted firms that should be disqualified from government contracts? What of firms whose officers or employees are members of other crime groups? A principled policy would have to include organized crime groups other than La Cosa Nostra which might further paralyze the entire process.

The reasons for monitoring construction activities—organized crime control, clean government, and efficient contracting—are not easily balanced. The goal to protect government from criminal victimization seems sensible and companies that have in the past defrauded the city or have grossly failed to meet their contractual obligations ought not be awarded more work.

And even if crime control is the responsibility of all government agencies, it doesn't seem possible that public agencies other than law enforcement have the resources, experts or training of law enforcement professionals.

The drive to rid the construction industry of criminal influence is similar to other morality movements like the war on drugs. The whole enterprise simply bristles with questions about fairness and practicality.

In other settings where organized criminals have an interest, in waste collection and disposal, for example, similar problems abound in developing a "clean hands" policy where government enforcement strategies are designed to curb racketeering influence, and weaken the PCN. As might be expected there are pressures on regulatory agencies from powerful political and economic forces that control significant segments of the waste industry, including toxic and hazardous substances (which require special expertise, equipment and licensing), to be "reasonable" in their enforcement activities.[46]

Block and Scarpitti present a serious indictment against enforcement agencies including charges that their corruption extends through state agencies to the federal level. A significant part of the problem may be less the outcome of a broad, criminal conspiracy involving the collusion of waste haulers, dumpers, and regulatory officials, than the sheer size and complexities of the waste disposal problem in a period of environmental sensitivity where few technological advances have occurred or been implemented. True, the problem is compounded when organized crime figures are involved; and local investigative units will usually possess little knowledge or experience with organized crime operations. Investigating firms that use intricate techniques of disposal and are shielded by corporate veils and complex business relationships as well as political connections must prove irksome for even the most experienced police officers and prosecutors.[47]

Enforcement is weakened for other reasons that may indirectly attest to the subtle influence of a PCN in this area of the economy. The typical penalties for those few caught and prosecuted are relatively mild and inexpensive. The record also shows that jurists have yet to define illegal waste dumping as a serious criminal offense, either perceiving it apparently as another type of white-collar crime similar to offenses like fair trade violations and bid rigging or noticing that the compliance policies from the Carter administration through the Clinton administration have been low-key and minimal, so that the courts, ever sensitive to the political mood, do not take these matters with the seriousness they deserve.[48]

Another enforcement methodology used to circumvent the "normal" political system where a politicized criminal justice system appears unable to enforce the law or is unwilling to do so, has been the use of special prosecutors or supersession procedures which call for a special prosecutor to supersede a local prosecutor in a specific area of investigation. Such attempts at legal suppression of a corrupted or ineffective prosecutor form a part of the legal history of many metropolitan communities vexed by organized crime.[49] The Dewey prosecutions of Lucky Luciano, Lepke Buchalter, Waxey Gordon, and Dutch Schultz's associates in the police department and political establishment are among the best known. What these "crusades" did amounted to tinkering structurally with the PCN. Dewey's efforts produced sensational headlines, as did the Seabury investigation in the early thirties which uncovered pervasive and extensive corruption throughout the ranks of city government. All of these investigations and prosecutions reveal a PCN operating at full steam, but reform energies could not be sustained. Today, statewide crime commissions (many of which have been defended or discontinued after some initial successes in putting the spotlight on venal politicians and compromised police chiefs) along with federal investigatory committees produce some success against PCN structures or, more usually, against particular personalities; but the historical record shows that major victories against the participants in a PCN with their patrons and clients do not simply follow supersession efforts. Special prosecuting would seem to be most effective against a PCN when it is part of a broadly based reform movement. Conversely, the legal tool of the unfettered prosecutor is least effective when it stands alone at the culmination or climax of reform as it did in New York City from the 1930s through the 1970s. As it circumvents the officials in government, it stands theoretically apart and indeed often against many of the very arrangements developed by political power brokers that have been institutionalized within the criminal justice bureaucracies.

The irony in an otherwise useful exercise has been that the effectiveness of special prosecuting is mitigated by a return to political processes status quo ante. Rascals may be prosecuted, but if they are replaced within the regular criminal justice system through traditional means—even by reformers—the new appointees and politicians are exposed to the range of extralegal and informal channels of influence and accommodation. It would seem that the only fragile defense against the attractions of the PCN are personal integrity or a set of powerful structural disincentives to participate in a PCN.

Finally, there is the FBI. In the glow of incarcerations of major organized crime figures the public still does not seem assured that the "twilight of the Godfathers" is a reality. The link between jailing La Cosa Nostra figures and a reduction in crime and corruption may not be proved but the idea is certainly plausible, and there is circumstantial evidence for the notion that law enforcement has had a hand in cutting down on crime.

While skeptics have acknowledged law enforcement's role in reducing crime and weakening the PCN, some see its contribution as primarily putting more criminals behind bars. The strategy of the FBI and the Department of Justice may be precisely this: La Cosa Nostra members and nontraditional organized crime figures that ascend to leadership roles become the objects of intense surveillance, prosecution, and conviction. Though the organization may remain intact though shaken, the succession crises in leadership induced by law enforcement may result in a generational turn away from organized crime. As individuals rise in the ranks they eventually end up in prison. Thus (the theory goes), as individuals peripherally involved in organized crime witness others being killed or imprisoned they come to abhor further participation in crime.

This "little-brother syndrome" has not been explicitly acknowledged by the FBI but it may be an implicit feature of an operational strategy that is truly long term.

Summary

The 1967 Task Force Report on Organized Crime (TFR) found that "...all available data indicate that organized crime flourishes only where it has corrupted public officials."[50] From that standpoint, neutralizing local law enforcement would appear to be central to criminal operations. That conclusion would depend on (a) how one defines "organized crime" and (b) the assumption that organized crime described by the Task Force covers all cases and species of it including what is referred to as "non-traditional" organized crime. A conclusion that seems unchallengeable in the Report is the observation that it was impossible to determine "the extent of the corruption of public officials in the United States." The lack of information on this question was aggravated by the fact that many of those who provided information to the Task Force were themselves public officials.

The focus changed significantly years later in the 1986 President's Commission on Organized Crime report. There, the attention shifted to the less embarrassing topic of commercial corruption in banking and labor racketeering. Corruption was seen in 1986 not strictly in its political/law enforcement implications but as a problem prevalent in the private sector with the obvious possibility that there would be some spill-over effects involving public agencies. The approach in the 1986 Commission Report was cautious and noncommittal. In its recommendations, as with its 1967 predecessor, the Commission acknowledged indirectly the role of political corruption more as an outcome of criminal activity than as an engine driving it, and urged that more public funding be made available to organized crime control and that greater information-sharing and cooperation be encouraged as a priority in law enforcement projects. Still, as in 1967, the 1986 Commission was dominated by information and viewpoints provided by public officials and this probably worked against the development of a reasonable estimate of the true extent of official corruption related to organized crime.

Problems with Political Corruption and Organized Crime

Because the American political system depends so heavily on private financing in electoral campaigns, it is vulnerable as a matter of course to criminal intrusions. Part of the problem in understanding how organized criminals and politicians interact has to do with the complexities in the exchanges of money for political purposes. Helping to finance a political campaign means influencing it to varying degrees, and the current debates suggest that a sort of moral algebra that would differentiate legitimate campaign contributions from naked bribes has yet to be invented.

Conditions and Factors Favoring the Development of a Political-Crime Nexus

What can be learned from in depth investigations like that of the construction industry in New York City and other satellite businesses connected with

it including waste haulage, and scandals such as the Savings and Loan de-
bacle would seem to be that particular settings contribute to the emergence,
persistence and frequency of corruption among political actors, legitimate
businesspeople and organized criminals. A nexus may emerge as a solution to
problems associated with governmental bureaucracies that engender inefficiencies and that stymie commercial activity. Given the structure of the political system, politicians are susceptible to temptations that threaten to turn
their moral universes upside down.

Other conditions favoring the formation of political/criminal networks
may be found where political machines operate as organizations that help
individuals make accommodations to hostile and inhospitable economic environments. In this capacity political machines function as informal exchange
systems where the material advantages they can provide are traded for votes.

In social and economic conditions that exclude minorities and working
class people from opportunity, that tolerate bureaucratic ineptitude and in-
competence, and that oblige political actors to turn to the private sector for
resources and support in electoral campaigns—all are theoretically conducive to the formation of informal (and illegal) alliances among racketeers,
politicians and public officials.

Conceivably, these alliances when forged between ghetto criminals and
politicos operating on a larger scale on urban, state, and national stages may
function as stepping stones leading to the formation of more mature relationships that constitute a sophisticated PCN. In New York City, Prohibition
provided a rehearsal for liaisons with politicians that would enable racketeers
to diversify and move into labor racketeering and more sophisticated penetrations of the legitimate market place.

It is also evident that when organized criminals mask their identities and
masquerade as legitimate businesspeople they can reach into the government
more easily. Intermingling licit and illicit monies and creating a facade of
legitimacy are ruses that work and work with particular efficiency for the
deliberately gullible.

The Scale of the Political-Criminal Nexus

Political corruption in the United States seems more localized than in
other countries and that probably has to do with organizational realities
peculiar to the United States as a nation state. Apart from the FBI and DEA
which are offshoots of the Department of Justice, there is no centralized police agency or police function operating nationally, whose jurisdiction covers the entire country. Indeed, law enforcement targets of corruption have
been local and regional.

Even if regional federal law enforcement agencies and political units could
be compromised, as some were at various times in Louisiana, Pennsylvania,

Illinois, Kentucky, Ohio, Florida, and Texas, that did not precipitate an infectious spread of corruption throughout the entire federal apparatus of law enforcement investigation and prosecution. Indeed, the semi-autonomy of regional political structures in state governments and decentralized federal districts provides some degrees of insulary against corruption even if it should penetrate the hub of the central bureaucracies in Washington, DC. However, the converse of this arrangement also poses dangers to the integrity of law enforcement operations. In decentralized systems because of a lack of oversight, and because of multiple opportunities and resources, it might be easier for organized crime groups to corrupt officials functioning at lower levels. Whatever the configuration of law enforcement control strategies, there are inherent dangers and weaknesses in the structure. How law enforcement mobilizes itself will depend, it would seem, on how it assesses the threat.

With the inception of RICO, which became law in 1970, the picture has changed in some areas of the country rather dramatically. RICO has been a law enforcement tool that has enabled federal agencies to move more directly into regional areas and work jointly with local police.

It was not until the late 1960s during the Kennedy administration that the FBI publicly acknowledged the existence of La Cosa Nostra. The FBI director's opposition to the notion was notorious in refusing to use the FBI in organized crime cases. Hoover often asserted that the idea of a nationwide mafia operating as a national syndicate was nothing more than a myth concocted by journalists and sensation-mongering politicians. When Robert Kennedy became attorney-general he created units within the Department of Justice to investigate organized crime activities in various U.S. cities. Kennedy's initiatives spawned an array of control strategies and groups including Strike Forces—self-contained operational units attached to local U.S. Attorney's offices that concentrated on racketeering enterprises of the LCN. These and other components of the struggle against organized crime were coordinated within the Justice Department through the Organized Crime and Racketeering Section that collected and disseminated information nationally. Coupled with RICO, the immunity statutes, the Witness Security Program, money laundering legislation and the development of sophisticated electronic surveillance devices have had a significant impact on LCN operations throughout the country and indirectly but meaningfully against the larger PCN that provides the sustaining context for organized crime activities.[51]

If it is true that the variety and scope of organized criminal activity has changed and possibly expanded—and is still largely dependent upon corrupt officials in order to survive—then will its need to involve still more officials at every level increase accordingly as control strategies mature with experience and become even more sophisticated? (It should be noted parenthetically that "growth" is a problematic notion because it may be a misleading way of talking about another phenomenon, "regionalization" where the client population of criminals spreads out from teeming urban areas and ethnic enclaves and give the impression of economic expansion.) A dispersion of criminal activities need not mean that crime has substantially increased. A final issue to ponder is whether as government regulation stretches out into more areas of private and business activity, will the power to corrupt, or the candidates available for corruption increase, thereby affording corruptors with more opportunities to gain control over a greater number of governmental actors and bureaucrats? It would seem that this question must wait until a systematic evaluation of reform efforts is made to identify what strategies do and do not matter.

In thinking about the vulnerability of the PCN and strategies for preventing and weakening its emergence and growth, several recipes seem promising. First, public interest and faith must be re-kindled by policies and practices suggesting that something can be done to challenge these structures that promote pernicious criminal activity. The question is, how does government at all levels communicate these issues and create the means to interact with the public? The mobilization of the American public and its faith in government may be enhanced from lessons learned from the anti-mafia campaign in Italy. A spontaneous explosion of outrage, a collective emotional rejection of mafia occurred after the vicious murders of two leading anti-mafia magistrates in Sicily. But those feelings were not enough to sustain the movement; it had to be re-energized and carefully shaped to produce and maintain responses to mafia crime consistent with judicial integrity.[52] That may be a study case warranting serious attention by American law enforcement authorities.[53]

To what extent can government create opportunities against the PCN? Can information campaigns be developed to stimulate public interest? Policies to counter a political-criminal nexus depend on multifaceted approaches that understand that a PCN needs a hospitable societal climate to exist, that changes in societal attitudes are possible, and that public hostility to a PCN can be nurtured. With these matters in mind, the issue becomes one of asking what institutions can shape anti-PCN attitudes? Schools through crime education, a revitalized criminal justice sensitivity to the linkages between crime and politics, and a demand that public officials focus attention on these problems are potential candidates.

By way of a provisional conclusion, it may be appropriate to re-emphasize some general points of the discussion. The conceptualization of the Political-Criminal Nexus (PCN) is not conceived as an explanation of the socioeconomic bases of organized crime but as a means to understand how criminal entities manage to develop, survive, and perhaps flourish. Economic theories are well known and obviously of fundamental importance; cultural perspectives focusing on social and psychological factors clearly have a powerful impact on criminal organizational structures, territorial, and demographic issues; but in themselves none of these perspectives provides the framework for fresh appreciations of the phenomenon. Through the PCN, as the historical data cited above indicate, we can get a sense that events of the past are not separated from the present simply by the passage of time; rather, by its slowly focusing frame of analysis, the concept of the PCN as an intellectual tool directs attention to the range of necessary actors involved in organized criminal activity enabling us to see more comprehensively and clearly continuities, similarities, and differences that criminal formations exhibit and produce.

Notes

1. In *Theft of the Nation*, which puts La Cosa Nostra at the center of organized crime in the United States, and, in its way, provides a scholarly gloss for the Mafia dominance thesis, there is nevertheless a recognition of the role political corruption plays in organized crime. Cressey argues that the LCN is the most powerful corrupter of government, which is consistent with the Mafia dominance thesis, but is sufficiently formalistic and analytical to imply that in itself corruption and corrupted ties to government are necessary conditions for continuing organized criminal activities in general. See Donald R. Cressey, 1969, Chapter XI "Corruption of the Law Enforcement and Political Systems," in *Theft of the Nation: The Structure and Operations of Organized Crime in America* (New York: Harper and Row), pp. 248-289. For an in-depth discussion of the problems of defining organized crime, see Michael D. Maltz, "Defining Organized Crime," in Robert J. Kelly, Ko-lin Chin, and Rufus Schatzberg (eds.), 1994, *Handbook of Organized Crime in the United States* (Westport, CT: Greenwood Publishing), pp. 21-39.
2. Cressey, *Theft of the Nation*, pp. 248-289; and William J. Chambliss, 1978, *On the Take: From Petty Crooks to Presidents* (Bloomington: Indiana University Press).
3. American Bar Association, 1952, *Report on Organized Crime and Law Enforcement* (ABA, Washington, DC).
4. Roy Godson, Fall 1997, "Political-Criminal Nexus: Overview," *Trends in Organized Crime,* Vol. 3 (1), pp. 4-7.
5. New York State Organized Crime Task Force, December, *Final Report to Governor Mario M. Cuomo*; Peter Maas, 1997, *Underboss: Sammy the Bull Gravano's Story of Life in the Mafia* (New York: HarperCollins); New York State Organized Crime Task Force, 1988, *Corruption and Racketeering in the New York City Construction Industry: An Interim Report* (Ithaca, NY: ILR Press); Cressey, *Theft of the Nation*.
6. *The Knapp Commission Report on Police Corruption*, 1973 (New York: George Braziller), p. 125.
7. James B. Jacobs (with Coleen Friel and Robert Radick), 1999, *Gotham Unbound: How New York City Was Liberated from the Grip of Organized Crime* (New York: New York University Press).
8. Walter Lippmann, January/February 1931, "The Underworld as Servant," *Forum*, pp. 62-172.
9. Frank Tannenbaum, 1938, *Crime and the Community* (New York: Ginn and Company), p. 128.
10. Lincoln Steffens, 1966, *The Shame of the Cities* 1904 Report, (New York: Doubleday).

11. Robert J. Kelly, 1999, *The Upperworld and the Underworld: Case Studies of Racketeering and Business Infiltrations in the United States* (New York: Kluwer Academic/Plenum Publications).
12. National Advisory Committee on Criminal Justice Standards and Goals, 1976, *Organized Crime: Report of the Task Force on Organized Crime* (Washington, DC: U.S. Government Printing Office), p. 29.
13. Ibid.
14. William F. Roemer, 1995, *Accardo: The Genuine Godfather* (New York: Donald Fine), p. 125; Pennsylvania Crime Commission, 1989, *Report on Organized Crime* (Conshohocken, PA: Pennsylvania Crime Commission).
15. U.S. House of Representatives, 1997, Committee of the Judiciary, Subcommittee on Crime, 104th Cong., 2d sess., *Administrations Efforts Against the Influence of Organized Crime in the Laborers International Union of North America*, Hearings, July 24—25, 1996, (Washington, DC: U.S. Government Printing Office).
16. John A. Gardiner, "The Stern Syndicate in Wincanton, in John A. Gardiner and David J. Olson (eds), 1974, *Theft of the City: Readings on Corruption in Urban America* (Bloomington: Indiana University Press); and Robert K. Merton, "Some Functions of the Political Machine, in Gardiner and Olson, pp. 409-419.
17. Walter Goodman, 1971, *A Percentage of the Take* (New York: Farrar, Straus & Giroux); Thomas A. Hoge, 1972, "New Jersey—The Friendly State" in Nicholas Gage (ed.), *Mafia, USA* (New York: Playboy Press), pp. 272-282.
18. Robert J. Kelly, Ko-lin Chin, and Jeffrey Fagan, 1993, "The Dragon Breathes Fire: Chinese Organized Crime in New York City," *Contemporary Crises: Law, Crime and Social Policy* Vol. 19, pp. 245-269.
19. Ko-lin Chin, 1996, *Chinatown Gangs: Extortion, Enterprise and Ethnicity* (New York: Oxford University Press).
20. Alejandro Portes and Robert Bach, 1985, *Latin Journey: Cuban and Mexican Immigrants in the United States* (Berkeley: University of California Press).
21. Stephen S. Fugita and David J. OBrien, 1991, *Japanese American Ethnicity: The Persistence of Community* (Seattle: University of Washington Press); S. D. McLemore, 1980, *Racial and Ethnic Relations in America* (Boston, MA: Allyn and Bacon).
22. Athan Theoharis, ed., 1991, *From the Secret Files of J. Edgar Hoover* (Chicago: Ivan R. Dee); Richard Gid Powers, 1987, *Secrecy and Power: The Life of J. Edgar Hoover* (New York: Free Press).
23. Stephen Fox, 1989, *Blood and Power: Organized Crime in Twentieth Century America* (New York: William Morrow & Co.).
24. Ko-lin Chin, *Chinatown Gangs*.
25. Peter Reuter, 1985, *The Organization of Illegal Markets: An Economic Analysis* (Washington, DC: U.S. Department of Justice).
26. Burton B. Turkus and Sid Feder, 1974, *Murder, Inc.* (New York: Manor Books).
27. Dwight Smith, "Illicit Enterprise: An Organized Crime Paradigm for the Nineties," in R. J. Kelly et al. (eds.), 1994, *Handbook of Organized Crime in the United States* (Westport, CT: Greenwood Publishing), pp. 121-150.
28. Pennsylvania Crime Commission, 1991, *Organized Crime in Pennsylvania: A Decade of Change: 1990 Report* (Conshohocken, PA: Pennsylvania Crime Commission), pp. 311-318.
29. John H. Davis, 1989, *Mafia Kingfish: Carlos Marcello and the Assassination of John F. Kennedy* (New York: McGraw-Hill).
30. David Leon Chandler, 1975, "Louisiana in the Twentieth Century" in *Brothers in Blood: the Rise of the Criminal Brotherhoods* (New York: E. P. Dutton & Co.), pp. 172-194.

31. Michael Darman, 1972, *Payoff: The Role of Organized Crime in American Politics* (New York: David Mackay).
32. Laurence Bergen, 1994, *Capone: The Man and the Era* (New York: Simon and Schuster).
33. George Wolf (with Joseph Dammini), 1974, *Frank Costello: Prime Minister of the Underworld* (New York: William Morrow).
34. Ed Reid and Ovid Damaras, 1953, *The Shame of New York* (New York: Random House).
35. Steven P. Erie, 1988, *Rainbows End: Irish Americans and the Dilemmas of Urban Machine Politics, 1840-1985* (Berkeley: University of California Press), p. 122.
36. Paul San, 1971, *Kill the Dutchman: The Story of Dutch Schultz* (New Rochelle, NY: Arlington House).
37. Lyle W. Dorset, 1968, *The Pederast Machine* (New York: Oxford University Press).
38. Pennsylvania Crime Commission, p. 152.
39. Mass, *Underdogs.*
40. U.S. General Accounting Office (GAO), 1977, *War on Organized Crime Faltering* (Washington, DC: U.S. Government Printing Office), p. 8; Malt, "Defining Organized Crime.
41. See "Corruption and Racketeering in the New York City Construction Industry," p. 216.
42. See Mass, *Underdogs.*
43. National Advisory Committee on Criminal Justice Standards and Goals, *Organized Crime: Report of the Task Force on Organized Crime.*
44. Thomas D. Thacher, II, "Institutional Innovation in Controlling Organizing Crime," in Cyrilla Feigned and James B. Jacobs (eds.), 1991, *Organized Crime and Its Containment: A Transatlantic Initiative* (Amsterdam: Kluwer Academic Publishers), pp. 169-182.
45. Selwyn Raab, 27 August 1991, "52 Companies Banned from School Construction Bids," *New York Times.*
46. Alan A. Block and Frank R. Scarpitti, 1985, *Poisoning for Profit: The Mafia and Toxic Waste in America* (New York: William Morrow and Co.).
47. Robert J. Kelly, Winter/Spring, 1988, "Dirty Dollars: Organized Crime and Its Illicit Partnership in the Waste Industry," *Journal of Criminal Justice Ethics*, Vol. 7 (1).
48. Frank R. Scorpioid and Alan A. Block, "America's Toxic Waste Racket: Dimensions of the Environmental Crises," in Timothy S. Bynum (ed.), 1987, *Organized Crime in America: Concepts and Controversies* (Monsey, NY: Criminal Justice Press).
49. Alan A. Block, 1983, *Eastside-Westside: Organizing Crime in New York, 1930-1950* (New Brunswick, NJ: Transaction Publishers).
50. The President's Commission on Law Enforcement and Administration of Justice, 1967, *Task Force Report: Organized Crime* (Washington, DC: U.S. Government Printing Office), p. 6.
51. Between 1967 and 1971, the Organized Crime Racketeering Section of the Department of Justice (DOJ) established eighteen federal strike forces. They were staffed with DOJ attorneys and representatives from other federal investigations and law enforcement agencies. The strike forces operated for a decade in major urban areas where LCN crime groups had been identified. However, they were discontinued in 1977 after a Comptroller General (CAO) report which indicated that there was no national strategy on how to fight organized crime. Also, the U.S. Attorneys offices

around the country felt that Strike Forces were duplicating the work of their offices. See Patrick Ryan, 1994, "A History of Organized Crime Control," in Robert J. Kelly et al., *Handbook of Organized Crime.*

52. Pino Arlacchi, "A Tribute to the Work of Two Great Italians: Falcone and Borsellino," in Ernesto U. Savona (ed.), 1992, *Mafia Issues: Analyses and Proposals for Combatting Mafia Today* (International Scientific Advisory Council of the United Nations Crime Prevention Programme), pp. 47-52.

53. In the case of Chinese and Russians, obstacles in the way of establishing connections with a political institutional base are numerous but do not preclude future possibilities for these emerging groups. For La Cosa Nostra and other indigenous groups, powerful unions, low-technology industries composed of uneducated workforces, and insulated ethnic ghettoes have offered attractive milieux in which to acquire broad criminal influence. But with significant reductions in union strength, with a corresponding decline in American manufacturing coupled with vastly improved law enforcement anticrime technologies and crime control strategies, new groups must contend with formidable impediments in identifying and negotiating with opportunistic political operatives.

    Because they came later into a world where La Cosa Nostra had already succeeded and where law enforcement developed more formidable and sophisticated responses to political corruption, emergent groups can simply neither repeat this developmental process nor transplant the mafia model as their own. This may be seen as the ordinary logic of succession and the natural adjustment it entails, but earlier American criminal groups such as the LCN along with their political partners invented the nexus on which patents, so to speak, are impossible to preserve. Now that the tidal forces of the LCN have subsided, the question is whether the history of political-criminal alliances are there for the pirating. Can anything useful in terms of survival strategies be learned by newly emerging groups?

    Criminal organizations in Colombia and Italy nourished by revenues from drug trafficking and wide-scale extortion do show similar entrepreneurial capacities as the American La Cosa Nostra. However, unlike the LCN in the United States, neither Colombian nor Chinese gangs have branched out into other criminal activities beyond drug trafficking or extortion in the ethnic enclaves in the United States. The critical difference probably lies in the formation and role of systematic corruption through a PCN. It would seem that in addition to the intimidation of law enforcement in both Colombia and Italy, for example, the success of organized crime groups has been built on the purchase of broad political influence. Political corruption at home has doubtless enabled the top individuals in the cartels to invest with relative impunity in agricultural land.

    However, in the United States that sort of protection derivable from a functioning PCN has eluded newly merging groups—at least for the present. Neither Colombian cartel bosses and their American operatives, nor leaders of Chinese or Russian gangs in the United States have been able, at this juncture, to construct significant connections to political machines or develop alternative bases for expanded operations. Perhaps the Colombian case is special with regard to nontraditional groups taking on Mafia-like capacities. In contrast to racketeers in building construction, in trade unions, and retail businesses, drug dealers survive through discretion; they do not need the cover of legitimate fronts because they can traffic occasionally in varying locales which do not require regular police protection.

5

Slicing Nigeria's "National Cake"

Obi N. I. Ebbe

Introduction

In all contemporary regimes—democracies and dictatorships, industrialized and nonindustrialized nations, developed and underdeveloped societies, and capitalist and socialist economies—there are politicians and governments who ally with criminals as a means to amass wealth and to ensure their political survival. Such governments have been described as "predatory states."[1] A predatory state is a government that resorts to wholesale abuse of governmental power, and where the head of state rules and decrees much like the head of an organized crime "family," using criminal individuals and syndicates to loot his country's treasury. To that end, he uses government agencies, cabinet ministers, and directors of statutory corporations as bribe-collection agencies. In such a predatory regime, administrative checks and balances are rendered null and void. A cabinet minister or a chief executive of a statutory corporation in such a regime remains in his position only as long as he continues to funnel substantial sums of money budgeted for his department or corporation and kickbacks from contractors to the predatory head of state. It can be argued that Mobutu's Zaire (Congo), Duvalier's Haiti, Somoza's Nicaragua, Stroessner's Paraguay, Ferdinand Marcos's Philippines, and all military regimes of Nigeria, had indicators of a predatory state given the amount of money found to have been illegally laundered in foreign banks by the above leaders.[2]

Symbiotic relationships of varying degrees exist among some politicians and the criminals in a number of countries. However, predatory states are more likely to emerge in totalitarian regimes than in democracies. This paper will argue that totalitarianism leads to a predatory state; and a predatory state facilitates a political-criminal nexus, because totalitarian regimes lack the checks and balances found in democracies. Corrupt heads of state and their political parties can nullify the operation of these checks and balances.

The focus of this chapter is the political-criminal nexus in Nigeria. With the exception of the period from October 1979 to December 1983, Nigeria has been a predatory state since January 1966. The various forms of political-criminal relationships in a predatory state such as Nigeria and the modus operandi of such relationships are of great interest, not only because the government has operated like an organized crime syndicate, but also because, until now, the subject has not been systematically studied by anyone who was born into and has lived under such a regime.

Methodology

This study of Nigerian political-criminal relationships spans a period of over thirty years, from January 1966 through March 1999. The data were gathered by personal and telephone interviews, content analysis of Nigerian newspapers and magazines (*Daily Times* [1980 to 1997], *Punch, Vanguard, Guardian* [1980-1997], *West Africa* [1981-1994], *Nigerian Times International, The African Guardian, Newswatch Magazine* [1980-1997], *Nigerian Record, Nigerian News Update, Thisday, Nigerian Times*, the Internet *Naijanews*), and a review of relevant literature on corruption and political crimes in Nigeria, and by ethnographic observations.[3]

Personal and telephone interviews were carried out with eight self-exiled former cabinet ministers of Nigerian military and civilian regimes who are living in Europe and the United States; six ex-directors-general of military government departments (permanent secretaries); twelve ex-senior civil servants; seven Nigerian self-exiled renegades; seven self-exiled Nigerian senior military officials living in Europe and the United States; sixteen current senior civil servants, and ten senior law enforcement officers in the country. Additionally, the data include my personal experiences as a native of Nigeria with the various Nigerian governments, politicians, and the people of Nigeria. Lastly, twenty-eight "area boys" (unemployed youths who roam about the cities), who watch the young members of the "419" organized crime syndicates, were interviewed.

The data collection focused on the collaborative patterns of relationships between the politicians and the criminals. Also examined are the degree of involvement of past heads of state and cabinet ministers in using organized criminal syndicates to execute criminal schemes against the nation, the extent to which the Nigerian government is a predatory state, the place of the rule of law in a predatory state, and the role of social order in a predatory state such as Nigeria.

For purposes of defining the political-criminal nexus in Nigeria, the term "political authorities" in this study refers to state authorities in the executive, legislative, or judicial branches of government and political party officials. The term "criminals" refers to individuals who have an ongoing working relationship with each other, who make their living primarily from a variety of profit-making, covert activities the state deems illegitimate or criminal.

A political-criminal nexus spells organized crime. Just as the left hand and the right hand wash each other, similarly criminal syndicates and some politicians help each other in some countries. However, before embarking on an analysis of this symbiotic existence, the term "organized crime" must be explained. There are as many different definitions of organized crime as there are writers on the subject, and little consensus.[4]

Every criminal event is organized to some extent, but not every organized criminal activity is organized crime. This lack of an adequate definition makes the phenomenon difficult to study. As Howard Abadinsky notes, "the fact that organized criminal activity is not necessarily organized crime complicates the definition process."[5]

The definition of organized crime even varies among individual states in the United States. Taking two as an example, Mississippi law defines organized crime as "two or more persons conspiring together to commit crime for profit on a continuing basis." By contrast, California law states:

> Organized crime consists of two or more persons who, with continuity of purpose, engage in one or more of the following: (a) the supply of illegal goods and services, i.e., vice, loansharking, etc. (b) predatory crimes, i.e., theft, assault, etc. Several distinct types of criminal activity fall within the definition of organized crime. These types may be grouped into five general categories: (1) Racketeering—criminal activities organized. (2) Vice operations—continuing business of providing illegal goods and services, i.e., narcotics, prostitution, loansharking, gambling. (3) Theft/fence ring—groups organize and engage in a particular type of theft on a continuing basis such as fraud and bunco schemes, fraudulent documents, burglary, car theft and truck hijackings, and purchasing stolen goods. (4) Gangs—groups who band together to engage in unlawful acts. (5) Terrorists—groups of individuals who combine to commit spectacular criminal acts, example, assassination, kidnapping of public figures to undermine public confidence in established government for political reasons or to avenge some grievance.[6]

California's definition emphasizes the types of illegal activities that fall within the generic term "organized crime," and is therefore very relevant in the investigation of the political-criminal nexus in Nigeria. All the illegal activities that fall under organized crime in California are also crimes in Nigeria. However, there is no underlying concept of organized crime in Nigerian law. Instead, the Nigerian Criminal Code and Penal Code clearly defines those illegal activities that fall under organized crime in California as felonious offenses. Additionally, by decrees, the Nigerian military government defines narcotics possession and smuggling, counterfeit currency trafficking, smuggling contraband, bank fraud, and terrorism as special tribunal miscellaneous offenses punishable by life imprisonment. Nigeria has no law specifically targeting organized crime, because Nigeria has a law against conspiracy, and in every organized crime event, there is a conspiracy.[7]

The findings in this study are presented in six parts: the first discusses the etiologies of the political-criminal nexus in Nigeria with regard to political, economic, sociocultural, and external factors. The second analyses how a political-criminal nexus develops and is maintained. Third, the patterns of exchange between the parties and what the politicians and the criminals seek to gain from the relationship is then examined. The vulnerabilities of the political-criminal nexus in Nigeria is explored in the fourth part. The fifth presents strategies for destroying and preventing the emergence of political-criminal nexus in Nigeria, and finally, there is a discussion of the negative consequences of political-criminal nexus in general.

The Emergence of the Political-Criminal Nexus in Nigeria

Political Conditions

Nigeria is not a single national entity, but an amalgam of nations designed by a colonial power to serve its own interests. Even during the colonial administration (1849-1960), especially when the British administered Nigeria directly (1900-1960), the three major ethnic groups (Hausa, Ibo [Igbo], and Yoruba) did not unanimously consent to the idea of "one Nigeria" as a united country. Each occupies a particular region of Nigeria: the Hausa-Fulani in the north, the Ibo in the east, and the Yoruba in the west. There were clearly defined natural boundaries. The colonial administration redefined the boundaries of the three regions, effectively remaking Nigeria.

Nigeria's national resources, which were controlled by the colonial administration, and later by the federal government following independence in 1960, are often referred to as "the national cake." Throughout the colonial administration, the three regional representatives were competing and struggling with each other to get a larger share for their regions or ethnic groups. What happened after independence was predictable.

Once the administration of the Nigerian federal government was handed over to Nigeria on 1 October 1960, and all British colonial administrators in government agencies departed, the struggle by each ethnic group for its share of the "national cake" intensified. Each politician representing his own region/ethnic group in the federal administration resorted with impunity to embezzlement of federal property entrusted to his care.[8] In effect, expropriation and appropriation of the "national cake" became the sport for every federal government office holder. The politicians led the way, and the civil servants followed. Effective law enforcement was impossible, because the centralized Nigerian Police Force (NPF) was also ethnically divided. In effect, despite the laws against bribery and stealing from the government, there was no sense of guilt in graft, pilferage, and wanton malfeasance among some politicians and top civil servants.[9] Consequently, corrupt activities went unchecked.[10] The inability of the government to control the wholesale criminal activities of the politicians and top civil servants led to public agitation for a change of government, and the military overthrew the elected government of Nigeria's first prime minister, Abubaka Tafawa Balewa, in a bloody coup d'état on 15 January 1966.

The overthrow of the Balewa administration on charges of wholesale corruption, and hostilities against the Ibos of Eastern Nigeria, led to the collapse of "one Nigeria" on 30 May 1967, and to the secession of the Eastern Region of Nigeria, which declared itself the Republic of Biafra. The secession of Eastern Nigeria led to the Nigerian Civil War (6 June 1967-12 January 1970). Biafra lost the war and Eastern Nigeria was brought back to the fold of "one Nigeria."

The ostensible reason for the Nigerian military's overthrow of the Balewa regime was to erase corruption. Unfortunately, the military themselves, once in power, became even more corrupt. The same extreme ethnic allegiances that fueled corruption in the Balewa administration also haunted the military regimes.[11]

The overthrow of the Balewa administration was led by an Ibo army major, Chukwuma Kaduna Nzeogwu. In the coup, many top politicians of Hausa and Yoruba origins were killed, but not a single Ibo politician lost his life. Many Hausa and Yoruba people, therefore, perceived it as an "Ibo coup" to take over leadership of Nigeria. Additionally, after the 15 January 1966 coup, the most senior army officer in the Nigerian army at the time, Major General Thomas Umunnakwe Aguiyi Ironsi (an Ibo), was installed as military head of state. On 29 July 1966, a company of Hausa army officers attacked and killed him and installed their own man, Major General Yakubu Gowon, in August 1966. It was the cold-blooded assassination of Major General Ironsi by the Hausa soldiers, the genocidal massacre of the Ibos living in the north and west of Nigeria in August 1966, and the consequent failure of the Aburi accord that led to the secession of Eastern Nigeria and the consequent Nigerian Civil War.

From August 1966 through December 1998, Nigeria has had seven military regimes and only one democratically elected civilian regime—the Second Republic (1 October 1979-October 1983). Every one of the six military regimes (Gowon, 1966-1975; Mohammed, 1975-1976; Obasanjo, 1976-1979; Buhari, 1984-1985; Babangida, 1985-1993; Abacha, 1994-June 1998); and General Abubakar, June 1998-present), behaved like an organized crime family. They nullified the role of the Nigerian Police Force, ruled by martial law, and consigned the rule of law to oblivion. What would have constituted a Third Republic was overthrown by General Buhari in December 1983. Each regime appointed its own Inspector General of Police who would not check, monitor, or investigate malfeasances and syndicated criminal connections in the government.[12]

The "national cake," controlled by the federal government, was seen by every politician and top civil servant as something "up for grabs." The various ethnic groups devised criminal techniques to secure their own share. The military head of state represents his own personal interests and the interests of his ethnic affiliation. Patriotism has been forsaken. The concept of Nigeria as a nation, of a people with a destiny, faded, and became an increasingly distant memory. Many Nigerians seeking outlets for their talents, found none, and instead experienced mounting feelings of hopelessness. On the other hand, for past and present military heads of state, their cabinet members and military warlords, the politicians chosen on the basis of their ethnic status, and the members of the criminal syndicates, every day was pay day.

Ethnic rivalries in both colonial and post-colonial regimes prevented the rise of nationalism and loyalty to the state. A study of the short-lived democracy of the years 1960-1964 may reveal that no political-criminal nexus existed because opposition parties and ethnic watch-dogs prevented it. Corruption did exist then, but it did not rise to the level of a political-criminal nexus. The Second Republic was corrupted by the military that preceded it because they continued to exert a great deal of influence on the leaders and ministers.

Every military regime in Nigeria suspended the Constitution and ruled by martial law. The first six Nigerian military regimes also suspended the rule of law.[13] In other words, martial power was used to overthrow the rule of law. Like an organized crime family, each regime ruled by intimidation, threats, and murder. Journalists and politicians who criticized the military leaders' policies and flagrant criminal activities were either assassinated, detained, imprisoned after trial on trumped-up charges, or driven to self-exile. Some regimes have been referred to as "Bida Mafia" and "Kaduna Mafia" by Nigerian journalists and the people.[14] The assassination of the famous Nigerian journalist Dele Giwa is remembered by many Nigerians. A letter-bomb was dispatched to him by top army politicians because he exposed their illegal narcotics trafficking, which they operated through organized criminal groups.[15] The military regimes had no need to obey the laws because the decrees in existence were their own decrees and enforced by them. They were judges in their own cases. Nobody had either the courage or the will to charge them with legal violations. The judiciary is not independent of the military warlords either. In effect, the judiciary is intimidated and rendered incapable of performing its legal duties. The population in general lacks social and moral controls. This has a profound effect on Nigerians in general and especially on young people of both sexes who resort to the criminal lifestyle of their national leaders. Nigeria has become a disorganized society where law has little meaning. The laws are not enforced because of bribery and corruption among the national leaders and the law enforcement agencies.

The Nigerian Police Force is impotent because it is controlled by the military and used by them to realize their criminal and noncriminal interests. The successive military regimes failed to attend to the welfare and interests of the junior police officers and other ranks, so that some have resorted to begging for money in the streets and on highways. Others use extortion and robbery to get by. The military turned the newly formed, strategic law enforcement units into witch-hunting units for their own political advantage.[16]

Even the only elected civilian government of Shehu Shagari (October 1979-December 1983) collapsed because the predatory state of the previous military regimes swept into the civilian government.[17] This was not surprising since some of the top politicians in the Shagari administration were accomplices in the criminal enterprises of the previous military regimes. During the civilian government of Shehu Shagari, the political-criminal nexus reached epidemic proportions because the seeds of a wholesale predatory state of organized crime had been sown by the military regime. Under the civilian regime, the top military warlords had nothing to fear by continuing their organized criminal ventures. The military and the top politicians became allies in wholesale organized crime. (See interview responses of eight ex-officials, and six ex-ministers of Shagari administration.)

The political upheavals in Nigeria have shown that the British colonial administration had imposed some degree of order in the country, which the post-independence governments, even the military ones, were unable to accomplish. There were criminal groups in the colonial days, but they were not connected to the colonial government. The links between the government and the criminals were forged when the military took over the government.

Economic Conditions

Another factor that has contributed to the emergence of the political-criminal nexus in Nigeria is the neglect of the agricultural sector. Most Nigerians are engaged in subsistence agriculture using tools that are local and almost primitive. They produce very little for the market beyond subsistence. Mechanized agriculture is too remote for most farmers. Even so, prior to the mid-1970s, Nigerian farmers were producing enough for the Nigeria population at the time. All of the traditional export crops, cocoa, palm produce, ground nut, cotton, soya-beans, copra, etc., were being produced and exported throughout the 1950s and up to the mid-1960s when the military seized power. In fact, throughout the 1960s, Nigeria was still exporting agricultural products such as palm produce, and cocoa and competing internationally. But the irrational economic and political policies of the military regimes coupled with the appearance of the "oil boom," destroyed the Nigerian agricultural economy.

When the military regime failed to develop the agricultural economy, the young and the old left the rural towns in large numbers and migrated to the urban areas in search of jobs that were not there.

▫ *The Oil Boom*

The sudden discovery of more oil in the delta region in the early 1970s and a sharp increase in worldwide oil prices at the same time, boosted Nigeria out of the ranks of poor nations. The military regime, however, did not invest this surplus wealth in the traditional agricultural base that had long sustained Nigeria nor in building small-scale industries that could produce basic needs for the people, but instead resorted to personal enrichment and conspicuous consumption through graft, embezzlement, and blatant malfeasance.[18]

Every top army, navy, or air force officer was also a politician. Each established his own criminal gangs to secure some of the federal government revenue through one or more of the federal government corporations, agencies, or departments.[19] The military head of state was involved in the mass expropriation of the "national cake," and it was he who appointed the senior military officers who accepted bribes from contractors and embezzled money entrusted to their care.[20] He demanded his own share of their booty, and, of course, they obliged in order to retain their lucrative appointments. When the head of state leads the way in corruption and malfeasance, who will control the law breakers? Top police officers, too, were drawn into the criminal conspiracy.[21] Civilian politicians without federal or state office allied themselves with top army officers, and became registered contractors without any obvious expertise for the work.

Before the Nigerian Civil War, the military regimes, and the oil boom, organized crime in Nigeria was at an elementary stage. The end of the Civil War and the emergence of the oil boom brought a high degree of sophistication to domestic and international organized crime in Nigeria.[22] When the war ended, the Ibos returned to Nigeria. It was an uncomfortable reunion with the Ibos for the Yorubas and Hausas, because the Ibos had the reputation of amassing huge wealth from little capital. Consequently, the Yorubas and Hausas, who were in control of the Nigerian economy and who also had the political power, resorted to intensified expropriation of federal properties before the Ibos had a chance to assert themselves. In the process, the Yorubas and Hausas became enemies and remain so. The Ibos were observers until 1975, when General Murtala Mohammed overthrew the government of General Yakubu Gowon and gave some Ibo politicians political offices. The old three-way, interethnic struggle for the "national cake," began again in earnest. At this stage, in the mid-1970s, the military politicians and their cronies developed various forms of organized crime strategies to amass wealth. These went far beyond the "national cake," which nevertheless remained a target.

◻ *Military Politicians and Organized Crime*

In the wake of the oil boom, organized crime activities developed in the context of various relationships and enterprises that can be summarized as follows:

1. Governor/Minister—Domestic contractors, and organized crime.[23]
2. Governor/Minister—Foreign contractors, and organized crime.[24]
3. Minister—Federal agencies graft gangs.[25]
   Passport Office, Citizenship Office, Immigrant Visa Office, Customs and Excise Office, Nigerian Airways Corporation, Nigerian National Petroleum Corporation (NNPC), Nigerian External Telecommunication (NET), etc.
4. Military/Politicians—vice operations.[26]
   Brothels, gambling casinos.
5. Illegitimate Enterprises:[27]
   Child trafficking and slave labor, trading body parts, narcotics trafficking, illegal importation of certain goods, counterfeit currency dealing.
6. Legitimate Enterprises:[28]
   Illegal diversion of government property, illegal contracts and ghost contractors.

Among the above activities, numbers four to six involve career or professional criminals who were already engaged in criminal enterprises before allying themselves with politicians. The activities in categories one, two, and three involve mostly career civil servants. Most of the civil servants belong to the same ethnic group with the politician-boss who masterminded the graft and criminal conspiracy.

The following examples illustrate how the military-politician organized crime syndicates operate.

◻ *Ministers and Domestic Contractors*

The minister is a career army, navy, or air force officer appointed by the military head of state to direct a federal government department or a department of the army, air force, or navy. The department may have a director general (Permanent Secretary) who is under the minister. Both the minister and the director general work hand in hand in every large project in the department including criminal schemes.[29] They select building and other project contractors, as well as supplies and service contractors. Before bids are even invited, they will have already made an agreement with other contractors, usually members of the same ethnic group as the minister or the director general.[30] The project costs are always overestimated.[31] The contractor, the minister, and the director general all know what the real amounts are, and they share the difference among themselves, with a designated amount going to the military head of state.[32] There is no fear of government audit because the Federal Audit Department is like a toothless bulldog. It operates in fear of the top military officials,[33] as does the Nigerian Supreme Court.

Some of the contractors in this organized crime enterprise may even be nonexistent, "ghost contractors,"[34] who are "awarded" contracts by the minister and the director general. On behalf of the federal government, the minister and the director general sign false papers certifying that the job has been completed and paying the "contractor"—themselves—for this fraudulent scheme. According to some self-exiled ex-ministers, the military head of state takes up to 50 percent of "ghost contractor" payment.[35]

❑ *Minister-Foreign Contractor*

Contract awards to foreign construction or service companies work in much the same way. The foreign contractor is informed of the conditions under which the contract will be awarded. These include signing over a certain amount above the true cost of the project, often millions of dollars or British pounds, to all the top officials involved in the illegal contract award. This money is then deposited in the officials' Swiss or British bank accounts. Many foreign contractors willingly participate in such criminal conspiracies.[36] That is the reason why the amount of money left in foreign banks by Nigerians living in Nigeria today is more than the amount of money in circulation in Nigeria.[37]

In situations in which the minister awarded a contract without involving the director general, the native or foreign contractor must pay the director general 10 to 15 percent of the value of the contract before the director general will sign a check for payment on the contract work completed. Such practices make some foreign contractors understandably nervous.

❑ *Minister-Federal Agencies Graft Gangs*

Every one of the nine federal agencies listed in item three has a director appointed by the military head of state. The director is answerable to a federal department minister under which the agency operates.

(a) Passport Office, License Office, Citizenship Office, and Immigrant Visa Office
Based on my personal observations during 1973, 1979, 1984, 1986, 1988, and 1993-1997, the directors in each of these agencies employ young men

and women as agents. These agents who are not federal government employees, accost visitors to the Passport, Citizenship, and Immigrant Visa Offices to find out why they are there. If they are seeking a passport, business license, citizenship certificate, or visa, the agents take the individual aside and explain how much it will cost. The agents emphasize that there is no other way to get the documents. Once the applicant hands over the money demanded by the agent, the document applied for arrives, often in less than an hour. Applicants who refuse to pay never get their documents. Sometimes they are told that their application files are missing and to reapply, a bribe must be paid to obtain the forms. To get the actual documents will cost more. To understand the scale of this graft, one would have to imagine that Americans paid one thousand five hundred dollars ($1,500) for a passport. A Nigerian passport costs around fifteen thousand to twenty-five thousand Naira. Two-thirds of Nigerian workers do not make fifteen thousand Naira in a year. For foreign nationals or those who have dollars or pounds, Nigerian passports are cheap because of the weak Naira. Nigerian passports are easy to get because nobody investigates the real nationality of an applicant once the bribe has been paid.[38]

Every Nigerian knows that it is impossible to get federal documents without bribing the agents. Many Nigerians already know who the agents are and even go to their homes or offices to deliver the bribe money. The agent simply obtains the data needed for the application, and takes the information and the money to the federal agency concerned. Two to three hours later the document is handed to the applicant.

There are other rackets in all four federal offices that deal with passports, immigrant visas, import licenses, business licenses, and citizenship certificates. The federal government issues only a certain number of official documents to each state office, and most of the time it is less than the number of applicants. So the state office simply produces its own certificates, licenses, passports, that are identical to the genuine ones issued by the federal government.

(b) Customs and Excise Office

The minister, other politicians, and top military officials employ gangs of smugglers who are guaranteed free passage at the Nigerian Customs checkpoints.[39] These privileged smugglers are not checked at ports of entry. I witnessed these gangs on several occasions arriving at the Nigerian Murtala Mohammed International Airport with loads of heavy cartons and boxes of contraband goods. A senior army officer or Customs official was standing nearby, and raised his baton swerving it to his left or right side as a sign to let the smuggler pass without being checked. Sometimes the goods are piled up at one side of the luggage claim area until other passengers have left. Then the smuggling agents move the contraband goods without anybody asking any questions.[40]

Direct bribes to customs officials at ports of entry are paid by individual smugglers not affiliated with a politician or military or customs officer. These smugglers pay bribes because it is easier than going through the process of assessment to determine how much duty is to be paid.[41] The only smugglers who get arrested by customs officials are those who are unaffiliated or who refuse to pay bribes.[42] All bribes received by Customs officials are shared by the officers at that port, as well as the director of Customs and the minister of Internal Affairs.[43]

(c) Nigerian Airways, Nigerian National Petroleum Corporation, and Nigerian External Telecommunications

In all three federal corporations, the directors engage in embezzlement, contract fraud, overvalued contract awards to domestic and foreign contractors, and pilferage through intermediate and subordinate employees.[44] The proceeds are shared with whomever is the military head of state.[45]

Today, to my personal knowledge, every Nigerian who has been a director of the Nigerian Airways Corporation owns either an airline enterprise or is a partner in a private airline in Nigeria. The Nigerian Airways Corporation has been led into bankruptcy. However, there was no probe into the activities of these former directors because the military head of state was a party to the conspiracy to bankrupt the Corporation.[46]

Nigerians in all walks of life know that all federal statutory corporations are sources of illegal money for the military head of state and his cronies.[47] The federal government pumps oil money into the corporations every year to support them, but the public and the federal government get nothing back in return. Where, then, do the profits of these corporations go? The money given to the corporations each year by the federal government to support operating costs, as well as the annual profits, are embezzled by the directors, the head of state, and the minister under which the corporation is administered. No one looks out for the interests of the people, and the nation deteriorates further.[48]

(d) The Judiciary

As the members of the judiciary at the federal courts are handpicked by the military head of state, they are not prepared to cite the illegality of his actions and decrees. Instead, the judiciary's response has been to resort to wholesale corruption.[49] Whoever pays the larger kick-back wins the case. Almost every judge at the federal and state courts has agents who offer financial propositions to the parties in a case.[50] In June 1996 and January and 1997, I observed these agents at work at the Nigerian court buildings. Every land case has its price. Even child adoption has its price, and nobody adopts any child at a State Court without paying a specified bribe to the agent of the judge.

□ *Military/Politicians—Vice Operations*

The vice operations involve brothels, casinos, and bootlegging. Based on my own investigations, the illegal import and sale of alcohol are not enterprises run exclusively by top politicians and military officials, but casinos and brothels are. These politicians and military officers are the real heads of the criminal enterprise, but like organized crime bosses, they stay away from the everyday activities of the enterprise. When politicians are partners in vice operations, the other partner is not a politician. The politician partner uses his position to protect the illegal enterprise from police harassment and law enforcement. This manifestation of the political-criminal nexus is widespread, although not as highly integrated with the upper echelons of government. The ties to the head of state and to the inspector general of the Nigerian Police Force may not be very strong. For this reason this kind of criminal enterprise is vulnerable to action by the police or any other federal law enforcement agency.

Prostitution is illegal in Nigeria, but many politicians and top military officials own brothels in various cities, including so-called "call-girl" brothels. These are prestigious hotels, but call-girls are permitted to frequent the premises. In some hotels, only call-girls who are working for the politician-owner are allowed. Occasionally, in cities like Onitsha, Aba, Jos, Kano, Port Harcourt, Lagos, Enugu, Ibadan, and Benin the police raid brothels owned by lower-class businessmen who refuse to pay bribes. They arrest both the prostitutes and the owner. On the other hand, brothels owned by politicians and businessmen who pay are never raided or harassed. Similarly, casino and liquor businesses owned by politicians and military officials are left alone, despite the fact that it is illegal to operate casinos in Nigeria.

Unlike in the United States and other industrialized nations of Europe and Asia, vice operations in Nigeria are masterminded by the individuals who supposedly make policies for their control. This corruption of the Nigerian leadership is rooted in an obsessive desire to amass wealth, to be superior to all other entities in the country , and also to gain ethnic domination of the political and economic sectors of Nigerian society. In effect, customs and police officials do not see any reason for stringent enforcement of the law as long as the smuggler or bootlegger is willing to give them a bribe. Five customs officials that I interviewed in Lagos in 1997 said that "the leaders of the nation violate the laws with impunity, why then should a small man be prosecuted for the same offense? Unless the small man refuses to offer a bribe, then we get him arrested, and he will end up in prison."

□ *Illegitimate Enterprises*

Only a few Nigerians without political and military connections were involved in illegal business activities during the oil boom. However, in the mid-1980s, when the oil industry collapsed, many Nigerians got into illegal arms smuggling, narcotics trafficking, counterfeit currency trafficking, smuggling of all sorts of prohibited textiles and foods, trading in body parts, and trafficking in children for slave labor and prostitution.[51]

Several developments led to this huge growth in illegal activities. By 1985, the Babangida administration had devalued the currency and introduced the Structural Adjustment Program (SAP) which gave Nigeria easy access to foreign currencies. The politicians and military officials who were already in the illegal enterprises were forced to lure some unaffiliated smugglers to run their illegal activities for them, with guarantees of protection from prosecution if they got caught crossing the Nigerian borders.[52] It was during this period that new organized crime groups emerged and came to be known as the "419" syndicates. The name, pronounced "four-one-nine" came from a government decree that prohibited, among other things, illegal transfer of money to foreign banks. The "419" syndicates, under the camouflage of legitimate business, built their own banks, hotels, and other enterprises. The banks were more like loansharking operations, lending money at a rate of interest more than 15 percent higher than government regulations. This underground banking system also facilitated money laundering. The bankers "maintain ledgers in code so that no official paper trail is created."[53] The speed, simplicity, and confidentiality of these transactions made them attractive and safe.[54] The trusted brokers at the receiving end know that the money is from an illegal source. Some senior police officers, politicians, and military officials are friends of the "419" syndicates and guarantee them protection against criminal prosecution, in exchange for money and personal security from time to time. Others have established regular business alliances with the "419" syndicates.[55]

The syndicates also run illegal casinos. With friends or partners in high places, the casinos operate without licenses or interference from the police. According to unsolicited statements of some associates of "419" elements, some politicians, top military officials, and contractors provide the money for the illegal enterprises of "419" syndicates.

Some of the joint activities by politicians and the "419" organized crime syndicates are associated with high levels of violence and/or do profound harm to innocent Nigerians. These include narcotics trafficking in cocaine, heroin, and marijuana; theft and distribution of stolen property; child stealing; kidnapping; trading in body parts; illegal manufacture of drugs for medical use; production of counterfeit medicines; forging foreign trade-marks for Nigerian-made goods that are later sold as "foreign made imports," and racketeering.[56]

There are three principal types of organized crime syndicates: the traditional criminal syndicates of the 1960s to the present, the "419" syndicates of the 1980s to the present, and the secret societies of the past and present. Each type of organized crime syndicate has its own specialty. Unlike organized crime operations in the United States, there is no division of territory, nor is there a common bond among them. This is partly because the head of state is a participant in the illegal enterprises and no Nigerian head of state remains in that position for very long. When a regime is toppled, it spells the end of the associated criminal enterprises. Nigerian organized crime groups, a fairly recent phenomenon, generally lack the well-established organizations of La Cosa Nosta in the United States, for example, and cannot survive such upheavals.

Both the traditional organized crime groups in Nigeria and the "419" syndicates engage in the same kinds of criminal enterprises. Both are involved in drug smuggling and both have female members. Unlike the traditional Nigerian organized crime groups, the "419" syndicates also have branches in London and Paris, and in major cities of the United States, India, Pakistan, Bangkok, Thailand, Brazil, Colombia, Ethiopia, Italy, Ghana, Cameroon, Kenya, South Africa, Namibia, and Zimbabwe, while they maintain their base of operations in Nigeria.[57]

The traditional organized crime and "419" syndicates have rings specializing in stealing cars, artworks, and valuable domestic and office items. They distribute the stolen items across Nigerian borders in Africa, and smuggle the artwork overseas.[58] Both engage in "the sale of children into bonded labor, prostitution, and domestic slavery." [59] According to a leading Nigerian human rights group and the Constitutional Rights Project Report:

Middlemen go out scouting for families with more children than they can care for. They convince such families of the juicy employment opportunities for their wards in the city, inside Nigeria and outside Nigeria.

Ten-year-old Chukwudi Joseph was recruited and shipped to Gabon to work for a logging company. After three years, Gabonese authorities deported him to Nigeria. He had never been paid.

Thirteen-year-old Tope came from neighboring Benin (Republic) on the promise of work, but when she arrived in Lagos (Nigeria) found that work was in a brothel. When she became pregnant she was abandoned on the street. [60]

An even more horrific fate awaited those children and adults killed by "419" syndicates for their "body parts." [61] In fall 1996, in the city of Owerri (Imo state of Nigeria), the police found body parts in a freezer at the Otokoto Hotel. The hotel owner, Mr. Otokoto, a local government official from the Ikeduru area, was arrested after being implicated by a tip-off from other "419" syndicates. The investigation had been triggered by the disappearance of the son of a very wealthy Owerri citizen. The police also forced Otokoto to show them where the bodies of the persons whose heads, liver, kidney, penis, and genitals, were found in the freezer, had been buried. Sixteen human bodies without heads were exhumed near Otokoto's home and he later confessed to selling body parts since 1976. Nigerian newspapers reported that some politicians were involved with the "419" criminal activities and in the selling of body parts.[62]

Immediately after the arrest of Otokoto, unemployed youths, some of them university graduates, known as "area boys," went on the rampage and burnt the Otokoto Hotel to the ground. Next they torched all residential buildings, hotels, and businesses known to be owned by "419" syndicates. Whether or not they were related to Otokoto, the "area boys" knew that every "419" group is an organized crime group. The relatives of Otokoto were subsequently excommunicated by the people of Imo state.[63]

Trading in body parts went unnoticed by the public in Nigeria for many years, because some politicians and some very wealthy persons were said to be involved. Since those elites also control the police, there were no investigations.

There are some "exclusives" even in Nigeria. Eighty-five percent of the "area boys" interviewed in Owerri said that the "419" syndicates are not in the bootlegging business. Bootlegging is the exclusive business of the traditional Nigerian organized crime groups and their political affiliates. They supply contraband liquor and distill and sell it without a license. However, both "419" and traditional syndicates are racketeers. Fraud is the most lucrative business of "419" syndicates,[64] and the federal government of Nigeria is most often the victim. Some politicians, executives of statutory corporations, and top civil servants are privy to these fraudulent schemes.[65] Other "419" fraud victims include other governments in Africa, foreign companies, and individuals and businesses in the United States, Canada, Britain, France, Germany, Japan, India, and Pakistan.

The "419" syndicates are also deeply involved in document fraud and currency counterfeiting, especially Nairas, U.S. dollars, and British pounds. They use their own banks and corrupt bank managers in other commercial banks to put the counterfeits into circulation. They operate in collaboration with some top federal government officials to fake business certificates and Nigerian passports as well as those of other countries.[66]

□ *Organized Crime in Legitimate Enterprises*

Organized crime elements pose as legitimate business in the construction industry, banking, and manufacturing. Activities in these areas are also masterminded by politicians and military officials. In the construction industry, organized crime groups including "419" syndicates register themselves as contractors. Some "419" companies are registered as legitimate companies, but they use illegal methods in the contracts awarded to them. They either perform the contract fraudulently or do not carry it out at all, but still collect their money in full from the government as if they had satisfied all the terms. Either the head of state is a member of the conspiracy or a top politician is privy to the fraud, so the syndicates gets away with it. In some situations, both the head of state and a minister of a government department are part of a fraudulent deal. All of them share the millions of dollars usually involved. In operating the legitimate enterprises, the "419" syndicates resort to assassination of competitors, terrorism, and tax evasion. They also underpay or even *never* pay their workers, knowing that since a politician is a partner in the enterprise nobody will do anything.

There are cases of "419" contractors who ally with politicians and directors general and receive contracts on a continuing basis. As noted earlier, some of the contracts are performed and some are not, but are still paid by the federal government or state government.[67] The politicians and the directors general get their share of the money and nobody questions the contract non-performance contract or poor performance.[68]

The scale of bribery in private and statutory corporations and the manufacturing industry, demonstrates that the traditional organized crime groups have effectively nullified government regulation by bribing the federal agencies assigned to enforce the regulations.[69] If the head of state is the owner of the enterprise, no police officer or regulatory agency will enforce the law against him. If the enterprise is owned by a politician and his criminal partners, the influence of the politician on the inspector general of police or on the individual police officers in the area will accomplish the same end. These organized crime manufacturing enterprises avoid paying taxes by keeping two sets of books, one for government inspection which determines the taxes to be paid, and another for the company's own use to evaluate productivity and overall profit. Government inspectors are bribed not to ask for production records.[70]

In Nigeria, banks fail frequently due to wholesale fraud by "419" groups and bank managers and their collaborators outside the bank. As of 15 June 1997, more than 2,000 bank managers and their chief accountants have been in detention for over six months without trial. And between January 1995 and January 1996, over 188 bank managers and accountants were sentenced to prison terms ranging from seven years to twenty-one years.[71] The bank managers' conspiracies include some military officials, politicians, "419" syndicates, and big businessmen.[72] The bank managers were jailed or detained indefinitely for awarding fraudulent loans or for embezzlement. However, most of them came from commercial banks that were not in the head of state's personal "portfolio." His were largely untouched.

Sociocultural Factors

Three important sociocultural factors facilitated the development of the political-criminal nexus in Nigeria and led some Nigerians to use all means available to "make it" economically. They are first, the interethnic scramble for a share of the "national cake"; second, the concept of extended families, of being one's brother's keeper, and the expectations thus raised; and, finally, a culture that honors conspicuous consumption.

The expectations of the extended family system and the cultural requirement of sons to take care of aged parents create enormous pressures. Public opinion holds that "what belongs to the government also belongs to everybody." To steal from the government is a minor abuse of power at best. So a son with a government position who fails to expropriate from the government that which belongs to the government to help his relatives and members of his constituency is regarded as weak and wicked. Government workers who try to live by the rules are worthless to the community. They may be nicknamed "Holy Nweje," a colloquialism that means a false holy person in the eyes of God. Similar expectations about government service can be found in all ethnic groups in Nigeria, and in all African societies south of the Sahara.

The pressures of these cultural expectations and the desire to succeed economically led some to join secret societies that guarantee members opulence and prosperity. There are many secret societies in Nigeria, but only two types are directly involved in organized crime: "wealth-oriented secret societies" and "Untouchable (osu) sorcery society."

The "wealth-oriented secret society" resembles a satanic cult in certain respects whose adherents will to do anything to amass wealth in their business enterprises. Members must be willing to sacrifice their nearest and dearest to the satanic entity who, in return, will make them fabulously rich. This might mean a wife, son, daughter, mother, father, or a friend, whoever is held most dear and is acceptable to the entity. Demands might also extend to the member's own body, anything short of life threatening—an eye, a hand, a leg. Once a member has confronted the satanic oracle there is no going back. The principles, rules, and missions of the cult are secret. From time to time, however, members attempt to leave and enter spiritual churches in an attempt to protect themselves. It is then that some of the secrets are revealed. The existence of this type of cult is general knowledge in Nigeria and throughout African societies, and is well documented in African law and literature about Nigerian customs. Although some members of the wealth-oriented secret society belong to the Untouchable (osu) caste, others have joined since Christianity emerged in Nigeria in the 1860s. If a cult member becomes a politician, he is protected by the cult through its chief priest. This protection may increase motivation to engage in the activities of the political-criminal nexus.[73]

This wealth-oriented secret society is the oldest type of traditional organized crime in Nigeria. Its members run all kinds of businesses, both legitimate and illegitimate, without any government intervention. Like organized crime groups in the United States, they support political candidates who can protect their enterprises. Politicians know them and respect them for their fabulous wealth.

The Untouchable sorcery society has its roots in Eastern Nigeria, especially among the Ibos, and has since grown to embrace others with similar life experiences in various parts of Nigeria. Individuals become members by virtue of their status as outcastes or "osu." They are not freeborn by birth. Their ancestors committed atrocities and were dedicated to the gods. They worshiped the holy shrine (god) to which they were dedicated.[74] Their descendants also became outcastes or untouchables simply by being born into such a family, and were treated accordingly.[75] There is a certain injustice in the culture which punishes someone for the crimes of one's ancestors.

Unfortunately, forming a secret sorcery society became a kind of coping mechanism for the untouchables. Today, they claim to use witchcraft to fight against the freeborns, even those who had not wronged them in any way. In Eastern Nigeria some people believe that untouchable sorcery society members also use witchcraft to destroy the businesses of the freeborn and that their gangs of murderers assassinate the men and women who segregated them, or freeborn politicians who opposed their members in their constituencies.[76] Politicians who are from untouchable families may be more prone to join the political-criminal nexus and the money-making opportunities associated with it, since they believe that wealth and opulence will lead to general acceptance and positions of authority in the country.

The untouchable sorcery societies are known to engage in assassinations, and since the 1970s, they have killed many prominent Ibos and non-Ibos in Eastern Nigeria. Their methods are well known, but nothing can be done, because many of them are in political leadership of Nigeria, some in the topmost echelons.[77] Their members in the media prevent adverse reporting on their illegal activities. Some are highly educated as they were the first to go to church and school when the Europeans came to Nigeria.[78] Among their ranks are lawyers, judges, medical doctors, professors, engineers, and other professionals. They identify their own through a "password" or sign that acknowledges membership of the outcaste (osu) institution, even if they are meeting for the first time.

External Forces

The oil boom of the 1970s attracted many foreign industrialists to Nigeria, and with their arrival a large market for Western manufactured goods sprang up. Some foreign companies and foreign contractors who were prepared to launder illegal money in overseas banks amassed fabulous wealth through illegal business deals with Nigerian politicians and military war lords. Some specialized in carrying out illegal and fraudulent business transactions with Nigerian politicians as part of a Nigerian organized crime partnership operating across the Atlantic and Indian Oceans.[79] Throughout the 1970s and 1980s, every major bank in Western Europe, Japan, and China had Nigerians as customers in both legal and illegal bank accounts.[80] There are laws against money laundering in Nigeria, but like most Nigerian business laws, they are not enforced.

How the Political-Criminal Nexus Developed
and is Maintained in Nigeria

As noted earlier, Nigeria is a predatory state in which the head of state has allied himself with criminal elements to amass wealth and retain political power. However, the activities of the head of state, insofar as they relate to the political-criminal nexus, can be differentiated from the activities of others. The head of state uses his aides, the "419" cliques, and his cabinet ministers to amass wealth. His aides run illegal activities and businesses for him, such as withdrawing millions, and sometimes billions of dollars from the Nigerian Central Bank and laundering the money in overseas banks. The "419" connection undertakes other illegal business activities for him such as smuggling narcotics and other contraband goods, and assassinating opponents. His cabinet ministers give him a percentage of the money budgeted for their government department every year.

A somewhat different type of political-criminal nexus functions at the cabinet minister-director general level. This has two subcategories: one is based at each government department. In the department, the minister (political/military official) and the director general act as the masterminds of the organized crime enterprise. The intermediate civil servants who are deployed at the key revenue sources act like lieutenants of organized crime funneling bribes to the director general and the minister. Other intermediate civil servants at the revenue sources, and the noncivil servants who are field agents act like the commission agents in American organized crime.[81] If a department's business involves contract awards, it is handled by the director general and the minister of the department personally.

There are also independent criminal groups outside the government department who undertake illegal activities for their own benefit as well as for the heads of government departments.[82] This relationship involves laundering money and cooperating with them to defraud the Nigerian government and its people. In most cases, it is the minister and the director general who initiate the request to the outside criminal group, which might be a legally registered company or a contractor.[83]

The second subcategory is the "politician-'419'" connection." Interviews with the "area boys" indicate that most of the "419" groups operate with the support and interests of some politicians and top military officials. In some cases, the "419" leader makes an illegal proposal to the politician, and the illegal enterprise takes off from there. In some situations, it is the politician that initiates the connection. The only intermediary between the politician and the "419" leader may be the director general. In other cases, it is a top businessman who happens to be a friend of the politician. The negotiations about the division of the illegal profits and the modus operandi of the illegal scheme take place between the politician, the director general, and the "419" leader.

Patterns of Exchange Between the Politicians and the "419" Syndicates

The "419" syndicates are sources of income for some politicians. Their connections involve defrauding national and foreign governments, banks and businesses, money laundering for the politicians and the military officials, and running illegal businesses such as brothels and casinos for the politicians. The "419" groups often register hotels and other forms of businesses under fictitious ownership names for the politicians or military officials. The latter, in return, provide the "419" syndicates immunity from police harassment and prosecution.[84]

Some "419" syndicates specialize in providing personal security to the politicians. Politicians with strong influence in the Customs and Excise Department secure easy and uninterrupted passage across Nigerian borders with contraband goods for the "419" syndicates.[85] In all cases, both financial and nonfinancial favors are exchanged in an atmosphere of mutual respect. When "419" members are prosecuted, their protectors come to their aid and the case may die without any further court action. For instance, Mr. Otokoto has still not been tried, because it is alleged that a top Nigerian politician was involved in the Otokoto "body parts" business.

Other "419" organized crime syndicates also engage in terrorism. Politicians who want to be rid of their political opponents or business competitors pay the "419" syndicates and guarantee them immunity from prosecution. The assassinations of Chief Obi Nwali in Port Hacount (River State) in 1994, and Mrs. Kudirat Abiola, the wife of Chief M. K. O. Abiola, in Lagos (1996), have been described by some Nigerian newspapers as the work of "419" syndicates.[86]

During 1996, many politicians escaped assassination attempts. In the case of the former minister of justice, Dr. Onagoruwa, the "419" gangs killed his son instead.[87] In January 1997, Chief Abraham Adesanya, the deputy chairman of the National Democratic Coalition (NADECO), a pro-democracy movement in Nigeria that is against military rule in Nigeria, escaped an assassination attempt while driving to work in Lagos.[87] Also between 3 January 1997 and December 1997, there were six bomb explosions in Lagos, three in Abuja National Capital, and two in Onitsha, Anambra State. The targets were the military, but the bombs took the lives of innocent passersby and wounded over sixty.[88] The last assassination attempt in Nigeria in 1997 was on General Oladipo Diya, the Nigerian vice president. A bomb killed his security officer.

The attacks were said to be the work of "419" organized crime gangs hired by some politicians excluded from the current military regime and by top military officials seeking to secure their own positions by eliminating their fellow officers.[89] These political assassinations and assassination attempts in Nigeria are somewhat reminiscent of the ancient Roman Senate.[90]

Vulnerabilities of the Political Criminal Nexus

Not all Nigerian officials accept bribes. For example, some customs officials and police officers arrest smugglers and other criminals whenever they catch them. This deters some "419" members and some criminal politicians from engaging in criminal conspiracies. Similarly, some soldiers who are not involved in the political-criminal nexus have become whistle-blowers and testified against their senior officers. This patriotic attitude on their part is, of course, disturbing to those involved in criminal activities.

As Table 5.1 shows, 4,745 politicians and army officers were charged along with other criminals, and 4,578 others, including governors, were dismissed at the federal level. Table 5.2 shows that at the state level, 4,784 politicians and army officers were charged with other offenders. Also, at both the state and federal levels, many politicians and army officers were sentenced to prison terms and some were retrieved with or without benefits. These punitive efforts have had a deterrent effect on the political-criminal nexus in Nigeria.

The fact that international organizations such as the Commonwealth of Nations, OPEC, and foreign corporations, can impose sanctions on Nigeria for wholesale political corruption is also a threat to the political-criminal nexus. Fear of a negative portrayal of Nigeria in the foreign press because of political corruption and its effect on world opinion also keeps the political-criminal nexus in check to some extent. Lastly, "419" gangs and their erstwhile protectors who have been displaced by cabinet reshuffles lurk as an ever present threat to those who seek to establish new political-criminal connections in the government.

Strategies for Preventing the Reemergence and Weakening the Political-Criminal Nexus in Nigeria, and Ultimately Destroying It

Controlling the political-criminal nexus in Nigeria will require a total reorganization of the Nigerian police, adoption of adequate pay scales and creation of an intelligence unit totally unaffiliated with the police to investigate allegations against the police. Furthermore, the relationship between the police, other law enforcement agencies, and the politicians must be weakened so that the law enforcement agents can go about their work without fear of retaliation by politicians. Also needed is a well-trained, nonpolitical intelligence agency charged with investigating and controlling organized crime in general, and the "419" type of organized crime in particular.

Table 5.1
Federal Government Officials Found Guilty of Bribery, Graft, Embezzlement, Fraud, and Other Malpractices from 1981 to 1995*

TYPE OF PUNISHMENT

	DISMISSED	RETIRED WITHOUT BENEFITS	RETIRED WITH BENEFITS	PRISON SENTENCE	POLITICIANS & ARMY OFFICERS CHARGED WITH CRIMINALS
State Governors	10	—	—	—	10
Directors of Statutory Corporations	38	—	—	3	—
Commissioners	8	—	—	—	8
Directors General or Permanent Secretaries	7	3	4	2	11
Other Civil Servants	2,310	91	18	142	2,419
Officers of Federal Statutory Corporations & Federal Agencies	2,205	27	22	188	2,254
TOTAL	4,578	121	44	335	4,745

Source: Tallied from *West Africa*, October 1981-December 1989; *The African Guardian*, January 1989-December 1989; *Nigerian News Update*, January 1992-December 1995.

The Nigerian police should also be decentralized, with each state allowed to set up its own force. At present, Nigerian police are often posted to states where they do not speak the language of the people, thus severely limiting their effectiveness. Under the auspices of the federal government a nonpolitical intelligence unit for controlling organized crime, white-collar, and political crime should be established. The main obstacle to controlling organized crime in Nigeria is that many top Nigerian politicians are privy to organized crime activities. Consequently, Nigeria always has leaders and politicians who run with the hare and hunt with the hounds,[91] a state of affairs reminiscent of what Richard Quinney termed "contradictions of capitalism."[92] These relationships between Nigerian leaders and organized crime make control of the political-criminal nexus very difficult.

Corruption is a cancer that weakens and kills governments. More deadly to statehood than corruption is when a government is a predatory state like the military governments of Nigeria have been since 1966. Efforts to combat

Table 5.2
State Government Officials Found Guilty of Bribery, Graft, Embezzlement, Fraud, and Other Malpractices from 1981 to 1995*

TYPE OF PUNISHMENT

	DISMISSED	RETIRED WITHOUT BENEFITS	RETIRED WITH BENEFITS	PRISON SENTENCE	POLITICIANS & ARMY OFFICERS CHARGED WITH CRIMINALS
Directors General or Permanent Secretaries	32	26	18	8	47
Directors of Statutory Corporations	8	—	—	6	8
Other Civil Servants	2,830	977	196	39	3,912
Officers of State	2,310	91	18	142	2,419
Statutory Corporations & Federal Agencies	728	78	11	88	817
TOTAL	5,908	1,172	243	283	7,203

Source: Tallied from *West Africa*, October 1981-December 1989; *The African Guardian*, January 1989-December 1989; *Nigerian News Update*, January 1992-December 1995.

*These data should be used with caution since there may be other cases that were not reported in West African Magazine and other the Nigerian media sources cited. There is also the possibility that some cases were counted more than once.

corruption in Nigeria must be swift and stringent and come from the very top. Any head of state who is sincere about ending the political-criminal nexus and wants to be taken seriously must declare his assets on taking office, and clean his household of corruption and of all criminal connections.

Essential reforms must also be instituted throughout the legal system. As Robert Leiken has suggested, legal reforms including laws against illicit enrichment, required financial disclosure for all public office appointees and holders, anti-bribery legislation, extradition of self-exiled corrupt officials, and stringent enforcement of money-laundering laws bolster the system against corruption.[93] There should also be horizontal accountability in judicial reforms. The judiciary must be assured of independence and personal security. Codes of ethics for judges must be stringently enforced, and, to rid the ranks of corrupt judges, their activities need to be regularly monitored. In addition, increased investigative capacity of strategic law enforcement agencies will be required, as well as witness protection programs. A separate, well-trained, anti-corruption agency with specialized sections to deal with the various types of corrupt activities known to exist in different government departments will help root out criminal dealings and clean up the civil service.

Administrative reform of the Nigerian civil service will require a series of broad ranging initiatives including constant independent auditing, adopting and enforcing uniform standards of conduct, merit-based entry examinations and promotions, removing politics from the civil service, ending quotas, and creating performance-based incentives in both the civil service and the statutory corporations.

Other measures will also be needed. The entire procurement system in the government departments and statutory corporations should be overhauled and a transparent bidding system adopted. Anti-bribery pledges should be required of officials in government departments and statutory corporations. A reorganization and restructuring of all federal agencies, especially customs and immigration, should include the creation of independent, anti-bribery enforcement units, not associated with the departments or agencies. Economic reform is needed to privatize some statutory corporations, initiate equitable tax collection procedures, end corrupt practices, stabilize the Naira currency, and improve road transportation, air transportation, and telecommunication (domestic and international) systems.

Finally, there should be vertical accountability involving community participation in policing, anonymous tip telephone hotlines to inform law enforcement agencies of legal violations in government departments and statutory corporations, support and protection for "whistle-blowers" against politicians, directors general, and military officials in government departments and corporations, and last, but not least, freedom of the press.

The international community can help. Many Nigerian politicians have fled Nigeria with millions of dollars stolen from the Nigerian government and later settled in Europe or the United States. This capital flight can only be stopped by international cooperation.

Conclusion

Organized crime activities flourish in Nigeria because law enforcement is weak or nonexistent at all levels. The police were corrupt even before organized crime emerged in its present form in Nigeria. Since "corruption is necessary for the successful operation of organized crime,"[94] the structure and operation of the Nigerian police, together with the activities of corrupt heads of state and corrupt politicians, made Nigeria fertile ground for organized crime. When those who make the laws and those who enforce the law are shamelessly corrupt, then the entire society is corrupted. These leaders are supposed to be the role models of the younger generations in Nigeria. Instead, they represent what Gresham Sykes and David Matza have termed the "appeal to higher loyalty"—a technique for rationalization of wrongs by underprivileged elements of Nigerian society who willingly engage in criminal activity.[95]

Nigerian politicians became involved in organized crime for the same reasons as the leaders of most organized crime syndicates—to amass huge wealth and for the power money can buy—both political and economic.[96] However, the Nigerian case is made worse by an almost total absence of accountability, oversight, or enforcement. Some wealthy individuals have vast holdings in real estate or manufacturing, but nobody ever asks them how they came by it. Then there is the extraordinary example of directors of Nigerian Airways who all either own an airline or have a controlling share in one. Nobody questions how they got the money because some past and present Nigerian heads of state are privy to the criminal conspiracy.

What is needed to end the Nigerian political-criminal nexus is a total reorganization of society through value reorientation. However, in a country like Nigeria where no drafted constitution works, the anomie and social disorganization which favors political-criminal nexus will always rein supreme and render all efforts for crime control fleeting at best.

The validity of the data on the political-criminal nexus in Nigeria presented here is supported by the fact that in 1996, the present head of state of Nigeria, General Abacha, gave back to the Nigerian people and government all money and properties he acquired illegally and ordered all members of his cabinet, other politicians, and directors of statutory corporations to do the same. Also in 1996, General Abacha's government mounted a thorough investigation into the operations of "419" organized crime syndicates and the activities of senior bank officials while he was a participant in "419" enterprises. The result was the arrest of over 2,000 bank managers and bank accountants on charges of fraud, embezzlement, and illegal financial manipulation.[97] In principle, the Nigerian military governments have not supported organized crime and the political-criminal nexus. While this may appear to be inherently contradictory, it is important for understanding how the political-criminal nexus works in Nigeria. The head of state had his own criminal connections, while his cabinet ministers also had criminal connections but in different enterprises. For instance, General Abacha withdrew hundreds of millions of dollars from the Nigerian Central Bank as if it were his personal investment. Since he died six months ago, many of his aides have been arrested for keeping hundreds of millions of dollars in their homes. They subsequently revealed how the money was withdrawn on the general's orders. At the same time, however, General Abacha was trying to control political-criminal nexus in some government departments. Not every "419" bank manager is affiliated to a politician, and the Nigerian government is not, as a rule, affiliated to "419." However, the head of state was affiliated to some "419" banks. When there was a huge public outcry against some fraudulent bank failures, he found himself in the uncomfortable position of having to enforce the national law against the "419" banks.

Instituting democratic government in Nigeria may eliminate the predatory state, and the checks and balances of democracy would have a deterrent effect. The opposition parties could become watchdogs, and freedom of the press would help ensure that the political-criminal nexus is exposed. Under the most recent military dictatorship there was no press freedom,[98] no real accountability, and no effective and consistent law enforcement. The political-criminal nexus cannot be significantly reduced in Nigeria unless these essential elements are in place. Until then it remains viable.

Unfortunately, the hope that the new government of Nigeria elected in March 1999 would be democratic and would eliminate the political-criminal nexus has already been shattered. The winner, General Obasanjo, a retired former military head of state, was supported by the military government of General Abdulsalam Abubakar and all the retired generals. There was considerable public agitation against General Obasanjo's run for the presidency of the Federal Republic of Nigeria. In spite of this, and aided by the $2.3 million he gave to the People's Democratic Party (PDP), he pushed aside the party's founder, Dr. Ekwueme, and formed a new civilian government.

It was General Obasanjo who in 1979 handed over a predatory state to the civilian democratic government of Shehu Shagari. For three years prior, the general had fostered the political-criminal nexus in all government operations. Now some twenty years later, he again inherits a predatory state. General Obasanjo has already said that he will not investigate the military high command who have amassed enormous wealth while in power. This gained him support from the military for his political campaign, and some protection for himself since he, too, came by his fortune illegally. His cabinet will contain many of the retired military generals who have contributed to the political-criminal nexus in Nigeria in the past. Its demise seems unlikely for the foreseeable future.

Notes

1.   Douglas Marcouviller and Leslie Young, "The Black Hole of Graft: The Predatory State and the Informal Economy," *The American Economic Review* 85 (June 1995): 630-646.
2.   See "Bad News for the Rich," *West Africa* (23-29 January 1989): 121. British Prime Minister Margaret Thatcher threatened to publish names of Nigerian politicians with foreign bank accounts. "Foreign Bank Accounts," *The African Guardian* (15 May 1989): 11-14.

3.   The following sources of data are Nigerian newspapers: *Daily Times, Punch, Vanguard, Guardian, Nigerian Record, Nigerian News Update, Thisday,* and *Nigerian Times.* The following are magazines: *West Africa, The African Guardian, Nigerian Times International, Newswatch, The News, New Breed, African Concord,* and *Africa Report.*

4.   Howard Abadinsky, *Organized Crime,* 3rd ed. (Chicago: Nelson-Hall 1990). Also see Jay Albanese, *Organized Crime in America* (Cincinnati, OH: Aderson Publishing Company, 1985); also, Jay Albanese, ed., *Contemporary Issues in Organized Crime* (Monsey, NY: Criminal Justice Press, 1995); Rufus Schatzberg and Robert J. Kelly, *African-American Organized Crime: A Social History* (New York: Garland Publishing, Inc., 1973); and Gary W. Potter, *Criminal Organizations: Vice, Racketeering, and Politics in an American City* (Prospect Heights, IL: Waveland Press, 1994).

5.   Abadinsky, op. cit. p. 2.

6.   Abadinsky, op. cit. pp. 2-4.

7.   Albanese, op. cit. pp. 8-9, *Organized Crime in America.*

8.   Obi N. I. Ebbe, *Strategic Approach to Control of Organized Crime, White Collar Crime, and Political Crimes in Nigeria* (Ada: Ohio Northern University Printing Press, 1982). Also see Onyema Ugochukwu, "The Return of the Military," *West Africa* (9 January 1984): 53-56.

9.   See "Background to Nigeria's Coup," *West Africa* (9 January 1984): 51. Also see "British Trial Reveals £7m Fraud," *West Africa* (27 April 1987): 840.

10.   Robin Theobald, "Lancing the Swollen African State: Will It Alleviate the Problem of Corruption," *The Journal of Modern African Studies* 32 (1994): 701-706; also see Onyema Ugochukwu, "Nigeria: The Trials Begin," *West Africa* (21 May 1984b): 1056-1057; Niik Bentsi-Enchill, "Poverty and Politics," *West Africa* (22 November 1982): 3018-3019; Kay Whiteman, "Policeman Jailed," *West Africa* (14 December 1981): 3012; Enukora Joe Okoli, "Opening Up Tender," *West Africa* (12 July 1982): 1812-1815; Robert L. Tignor, "Political Corruption in Nigeria Before Independence," *The Journal of Modern African Studies* 31 (1993): 175-202; S. Pedder, " A Survey of Nigeria: Anybody Seen a Giant?" *The Economist* (21 August 1993): 3-14; and Richard W. Wilson, "Political Pathology and Moral Orientations," *Comparative Political Studies* 24 (July 1991): 211-230.

11.   See "Jobs for Sale" in the Nigerian Government. *The African Guardian* (15 January 1990): 17. Also see "Corrupt Politicians List Out Soon," *The African Guardian* (6 February 1989): 17. This refers to Nigerian politicians who have accounts in Swiss Banks; Chukwuemeka Gahia, Emenike Okorie, Ray Echebiri, and Tunde Oguntoyibo, "Changing Tidal Waves: Nigeria Britain Brace up for New Ties— Special Report, " *The African Guardian* (15 May 1989): 11-14.

12.   See "Why Oyakhilome Was Removed," *New Breed* (1 April 1991): 5-26. The Nigerian head of state, Babangida and his wife were implicated in a narcotics deal by the only non-Hausa senior police officer, Deputy Inspector General (DIG) Oyakhilome. Oyakhilome was removed so that the Inspector General of Police and his other senior police officers could suppress evidence already exhumed by Oyakhilome.

13.   A journalist and individuals who criticized the military regime were arrested and thrown into jail without trial for months and years. See "Detained Journalist in Court," *West Africa* (11 June 1984): 1239-1240; "Press Decree Published" and "Journalist Held," *West Africa* (23 April 1984): 900; "Sword Against the Pen," and "Why Five Journalists Are Held," *West Africa* (7 May 1984): 960 and 964, respectively.

14. See "Who Killed Dele Giwa?" *West Africa* (19 October 1987): 2089; "Fawehinmi in Dele Giwa Court Battle," *West Africa* (2 March 1987): 436. Also see "Senator Obi Wali Murdered," *Nigerian News Update* (13-16 May 1993): 2. See also "Assassins on the Prowl Again in Lagos: Gunmen Attack NADECO Chief," *Daily Times* (15 January 1977); and an attempt to assassinate the Chief Justice of Nigeria, Mr. Onagoruwa, which led to an assassination of his son. See "General Abacha Comforts Onagoruwa," *Daily Times* (14 January 1997): 1.

15. Onome Osifo-Whiskey and Kola Ikori, "Deaths That Defy Defection: Mysterious Killings Send Shock Waves into a Hitherto Peaceful Community," *Newsweek* (13 June 1988): 8-15, also see Mike Ubani, "War Against Drugs," *The African Guardian* (16 April 1990): 15.

16. Whiteman, op. cit; p. 3012, and Ugochukwu, op. cit., pp. 53-56 (1984a).

17. Ugochukwu, op. cit., pp. 53-56 (1984a).

18. Okoli, op. cit., p. 1812; Ugochukwu, op. cit., p. 53 (1984a), p. 1056 (1984b); Bentsi-Enchill, op. cit., p. 3018; Whiteman, op. cit., p. 3012. Also see Onyema Ugochukwu "Nigeria: A Parade of Gubernatorial Convicts," *West Africa* (2 July 1984c): 1349-1351.

19. See "Tribunals Move Center Stage" and "Illegal Importation of Goods" and " Illegal Transfer of Money by Politicians" in *West Africa* (11 June 1984): 1204-1205.

20. Gahia et al., op. cit., pp. 11-14. Also see "Extradition Bid Fails," *West Africa* (20-26 February 1989): 289; and "Extra Misled: Iwuanyanwu to Government," *Thisday* (31 December 1997): 1.

21. See "Buhari's New Year Broadcast" *West Africa* (9 March 1984): 56-57; Also see "Towards 1992 Corruption and Indiscipline," *West Africa* (31 August 1987): 1688-1690; and "Kaduna, Police Corruption in the State," *West Africa* (2 March 1987): 438.

22. Okoli, op. cit., pp. 1812-1815.

23. Ugochukwu, op. cit., pp. 53-56, (1984a), pp. 1056-1057 (1984b), pp. 1349-1351 (1984c); Okoli, op. cit., p. 1812; Gahia et al., pp. 12-17, Also see Janet Mba-Afolabi, "Haven for Fraudsters," *Newswatch* (4 December 1957): 17-18; see "Public Fund Recovery Panels Findings: Contract Awarded Twice, Different Letter-head Paper Used," *Nigerian International Times* (15 January 1997): 5. Also see where the head of state was involved in illegal contract deal—"The Panoco Connection," *West Africa* (7 December 1987): 2410. Also see "Extradition Bid Fails," *West Africa* (20-26 February 1989): 289. Also see "Ex-governor Jailed for 21 Years," *West Africa* (25 June 1984): 1329.

24. Okoli, op. cit.; p. 1813. Also see Onyema Ugochukwu, "Nigeria: And Now for the IMF," *West Africa* (23 April 1984d): 866-867; see "Bank Summons on JMB Scandal," *West Africa* (30 January- 5 February 1989):158, where some Nigerian politicians and their Nigerian business friends conspired to defraud the Nigerian government using a British company, Johnson Mathey Bankers (JMB), in falsification of import documents. See "184 NET (Nigerian External Telecommunication) Officials Sacked," *West Africa* (30 April 1984): 950. Also see overvalued contracts in "Banchi" *West Africa* (14 December 1981): 3013.

25. Tim Whiteman, "Nigeria: Red Alert on Oil Fraud," *West Africa* (10-16 April 1989): 546-547; Mike Ubani, "The Aba Ring," *The African Guardian* (13 February 1989): 25-26; Alain Adesokan, "A Horrifying Miasma," *Newswatch* (10 January 1994): 13-16; see "Passport Office Minister hits out," involving middlemen in Nigerian passport and visa racket, *West Africa* (4 July 1983): 1579. Also see "Gongola Audit Reveals Embezzlements," *West Africa* (23 November 1981): 2807;

"Immigration Department Fights Passport Rackets," *Nigerian News Update* (15 January 1993): 6; "Audu Ogbe Indicted," *The African Guardian* (1 May 1989): 14; "Fraud Probe at NEC" (Nigerian Electoral Commission), *West Africa* (20-26 February 1989): 289.

26. Oladipo Adamolekun, "Sense and Nonsense," *West Africa* (12 May 1986): 992-994; see the following: "Politicians Not Mentally Healthy," in *West Africa* (23 April 1984): 900. "Crude Oil Racket," in *West Africa* (22 August 1988): 1547; Toxic (nuclear) waste imported from Italy—"Mysterious Exits from the Country," *West Africa* (23-29 January 1989); "Last Batch of Toxic Waste Removed," *West Africa* (29 August-1 September 1988); and, "Police to Try Pornographic Violent Films' Dealers," *The Guardian* (15 January 1997 6.

27. Kunle Jenrola and Felix Obanya, "Deals...Dirty Deals: Sharp Practices Rob Nigeria of Invaluable Petroleum Revenue," *The African Guardian* (5 March 1990): 19-25; John Nwaobi, Paul Nwachukwn, Debo Adesina, Abdul Oroh, Wale Akin Aina, and Ben Akparanta, "Hitting a Dangerous High: Hard Drugs Threaten Menacingly Society Looks on Helplessly," *The African Guardian* (25 September 1989): 12-15; Mike Ubani and Billy Okonedo, "Furor Over Frisking: Nigeria Airways, Customs Find No Alternative to Crude Searching Methods," *The African Guardian* (13 March 1989): 15; Wale Akin Aina, "The Quandary of the Judiciary," *The African Guardian* (10 July 1989): 18; Mike Ubani and Adegbe Onu Adegbe, "Worms in the Apple: Smugglers Smile, the Nation Bleeds," *The African Guardian* (13 February 1989): 19-23; Chukuemeka Gahia, "The Making of a Scandal: Nuclear Waste Dumped in Nigeria," *The African Guardian* (28 June 1988): 12-17; Mike Ubani, "In the Pangs of Crisis: Awka-Etiti Communal Feud Deepens Following Another Murder," *The African Guardian* (7 May 1990): 8-11; Stephen Agwudagwu, "Jail Bonanza," *Newswatch* (13 June 1988): 37; Olaniyi Ola, "Smugglers Paradise," *West Africa* (27 March-2 April 1989): 468; Seye Kehinde, "Guilty as Charged," *African Concord* (4 November 1991): 42; see the following: "Ex-Commissioner Denies Drug Deal," *West Africa* (11 June 1984): 1240. Over-invoicing by licensed importers—"Smuggling problems," *West Africa* (4 January 1982): 19; "Illegal Miners Arrested," in *West Africa* (16-22 January 1989): 80; Illegal drug trafficking—"Kenyan and Three Nigerians Sentenced to 28 Years for Drug Trafficking" in *Nigerian Times* (15-30 September 1995): 8; Currency trafficking—"Nigeria Impounded a Large Amount of Cash at Airport," *Nigerian Times* (1-14 September 1995): 23; Smuggling Contrabands: "Billy EKO Panel to Report," *West Africa* (11 May 1987): 935; "N. A. Acts Against Drug Smugglers," *West Africa* (27 April 1987): 840; "Diplomat Held over Drug Smuggling," *West Africa* (19 September 1983): 2204; "Trouble at High Commission" (drug smuggling), *West Africa* (14 December 1981): 3012; Licensed importers smuggling—"Smuggling Problem," in *West Africa* (4 January 1982): 19; "Smugglers to Face Life Jail," *West Africa* (4 January 1989): 2459; "Nigeria's Illegal Gems Behind the Precious Stones Boom," *West Africa* (23-29 January 1989): 96-97; "Timber Smuggling," in *West Africa* (23-29 January 1989): 122; Cocoa smuggling—"Anti-Smuggling Task Force," in *West Africa* (11 January 1988): 53; "Renewed Effort to Combat Smuggling" in *Africa Report* (March-April 1982): 35; "Customs Seize Petroleum Products from Smugglers," in *Nigerian News Update* (14-27 December 1993): 10; "Customs Seize 130,000 Liters of Petroleum Products at Seme," *Nigerian News Update* (2-15 November 1993): 8; "NDLEA (Nigerian Drug Law Enforcement Agency) Arrested 243 Traffickers," in *Nigerian News Update* (2-15 November 1993): 11; "Alleged Drug Baron Appears in Court over $20 Billion Heroin Import," *Nigerian News Update* (7-20 February 1994): 2; "NDLEA Arrest

20 for Drug Offences," in *Nigerian News Update* (24 January-6 February 1994): 3; "Nigeria Loses $50 Million Daily to Oil Smuggling," in *Nigerian News Update* (15-30 March 1993): 9; "Former Army Major Arrested with Drugs," in *Nigerian News Update* (14-28 December 1992): 4; "Drug Agency Prosecutes 1,285," *Nigerian News Update* (14-28 December 1992): 4; and Counterfeiting currency— "Nigerians Gaoled in Taiwan," *West Africa* (30 April 1984): 951.

28. Okoli, op.cit., pp. 1812-1815.

29. Ugochukwu, op.cit., p. 1056 (1984b) and p. 1349 (1984c) Adamolekun, op. cit., p. 992.

30. Kaye Whiteman, "475 Detainees—Idiagbon," *West Africa* (19 March 1984): 638.

31. See "Bank Summons on JMB Scandal," note 24.

32. Ugochukwu, op.cit.; pp. 53-56.

33. Sunny Biaghere and Mazino Ikime, "The Wig and the Gun," *The African Guardian* (20 November 1989): 8-9.

34. See "Vast Probe" for ghost workers and ghost contractors, *West Africa* (19 March 1984): 637.

35. Gahia et al., op. cit., pp. 11-14. See the following: "Ex-military Governor Restricted," in *West Africa* (11 June 1984): 1239; "Extradition Bid Fails," *West Africa* (20-26 February 1989): 289.

36. See "Bank Summons on JMB Scandal," *West Africa* (30 January-5 February 1989): 158; a British financial institution, Johnson Mathey Bankers, was implicated in falsification of import documents that led to millions of British pound sterling losses to the Nigerian government. A total of 86 percent of all present and ex-government officials interviewed testified to this in an interview.

37. Uzoma   Onyenaechi,   "Fraud   in   Nigeria,"   Internet   News (UZO@alumni.sil.umich.edu), 1996.

38. Mazino Ikime, "Still Walking on Crutches: NIPOST Remains Unreliable in Spite of Public Criticism," *The African Guardian* (5 March 1990): 12.

39. Jenrola and Obanya, op. cit., pp. 19-25. See Nigerian passport rackets, note 25. Also see "3,000 Civil Servants Dismissed," *West Africa* (23 April 1984): 900.

40. See "Customs Men Questioned," *West Africa* (30 January-5 February 1989): 162.

41. John Mukum Mbaku, "Bureaucratic Corruption and Policy Reform in Africa," *The Journal of Social, Political & Economic Studies*, 19 (Summer 1994): 149-175; Wilson, op. cit., p. 211; Thesbald, op. cit., p. 701; Marcouiller and Young, op. cit., p. 630; Tignor, op. cit., p. 175; Pedder, op.cit., pp. 3-14.

42. See note 27. Also see "Customs Seize 18 Drums of Petrol," in *West Africa* (30 November-13 December 1993): 9.

43. William J. Chambliss, *Whose Law ? What Order?: A Conflict Approach to Criminology* (New York: John Wiley & Sons 1976), 127.

44. See note 24. Also see "Farewell Nigeria Air Waste," *West Africa* (27 February-5 March 1989): 304.

45. All of the ex-cabinet ministers interviewed agreed on this point.

46. K. Whiteman, op.cit., pp. 5-7; see the "Bida Mafia," "Kaduna Mafia," and "Coup Plotters Arrested," *West Africa* (6 January 1986): 5-7.

47. Pedder, op.cit., pp. 3-14; Tignor, op.cit., p. 175.

48. See "£5bn (5 billion pounds) Racket, Government Steps-in," *West Africa* (19 September 1983): 2204. Also see "National Seminar on Corruption," in *West Africa* (2 May 1983): 1089. The money stolen by the politicians including the head of state is smuggled out of Nigeria by their agents. See "Illegal Dealing in Naira," in *West Africa* (2 May 1983): 1093; "Nigeria's Foreign Exchange Crisis," in *West Africa* (10 May 1982): 1274.

49. Biaghere and Ikime, op.cit., pp. 8-9.
50. See "NBA (Nigerian Bar Association) Chief Urges Judiciary to Redeem Image," *The Guardian* (15 January 1997): 6. Court "Judge and Deputy Jailed for Bribe," *West Africa* (20-26 February 1989): 289.
51. Jenrola and Obanya, op.cit., pp. 19-25; Njadvana Musa, "Curbing Smuggling," *The African Guardian* (24 April 1989): 5; Woani, op.cit., pp. 19-23.
52. Ugochukwu, op.cit., pp. 53-56 (1984a); Ola, op.cit., p. 468; see notes 25 and 27. Also see *Democrat & Chronicle*, 10 August 1997: A6.
53. Margaret E. Beare, "Money Laundering: A Preferred Law Enforcement Target for the 1990s," in *Contemporary Issues in Organized Crime*, ed. Jay Albanese (Monsey, NY: Criminal Justice Press, 1995), p. 183.
54. Ibid., pp. 171-187.
55. Boniface Chizea, "Bank Fraud: Who Is to Blame," *Newswatch* (4 November 1991): 61; T. Whiteman, op.cit., pp. 546-547.
56. See "Nigeria Loses $50 Million Daily to Oil Smuggling," *Nigeria News Update*, (15-30 March 1993): 9; "Notes for Nigerian Creditor," in *West Africa*(6 April 1987): 677, and "Plateau, N5-6 m Rice deal," *West Africa* (30 April 1984): 951.
57. James Webb, "Nigerian Drug Ring," (Naija News, Internet, 1996); see "Women Deported for Prostitution in Italy," in *West Africa* (29 August-4 September 1988): 1592.
58. See "Police Recover Computers Worth N40 Million," in *Nigerian News Update* (7-20 February 1994): 13. Also see "Robbery by Military Personnel on the Rise," *Nigerian Records* (January 1995): 12.
59. Matthew Torstein, "Child Slavery: Nigerian Human Rights Group Reporting" (Lagos, Nigeria: Press Digest 1996).
60. Ibid., Emma Eke, "Ripples of Otokoto Rock Aba," *The Guardian* (12 January 1997): 2. See *Democrat & Chronicle*, (10 August 1997): A6. Also Naijanews@Umich.edu,1996.
61. Iyabo Modupe, "God Is on Our Side: Otokoto Family Members Say as They Relocate to Lagos," *Sunday Vanguard*, (12 January 1997): 1-2; Abuchi Anueyiagu, "Nsukka Gripped by Otokoto Saga: A Six-Year-Old Boy Escapes Kidnap," *Thisday* (4 January 1997): 1-2.
62. Eke, op.cit., p.2; Modupe, op.cit., p. 1; Anueyiagu, op.cit., p. 2.
63. Modupe, op.cit., p. 2; Anueyiagu, op.cit., p. 2; see "Hotel Proprietor's (Otokoto) Son Implicated in Owerri Riot," in *The Guardian* (15 January 1997): 4.
64. Kunle Jenrola, "The Seamy Side of Banking: Fraud and Bad Loans Cause Problems for Financial Industry," *The African Guardian* (23 April 1990): 11-14; Mbo-Afolabi, op.cit., pp. 17-18; Chizea, op.cit., p. 61; Jenrola and Obanya, op.cit., pp. 19-25; see the following "419" cases of fraud: "FIIB Arrested Three Who Tried to Dupe a German of $141,000," *Nigerian News Update* (7-20 February 1994): 13; "Colombian and Six Nigerians Arrested over Diversion of NITEL's N26 million," *Nigerian News Update* (7-20 February 1994): 14; "Maritime Fraud Cost Nigerian N5 Billion in 5 Years—Insurance Association Boss Says," *Nigerian News Update* (10-23 January 1994): 8; "Fraud Suspects Face Tribunal," *Punch* (10 January 1997): 7. "NITEL duped of N2.5 billion," *Daily Times* (14 January 1997): 1; "Two Arraigned over N3 M Fraud," *Daily Times* (10 January 1997): 4; and, "N5.9 Billion Lost to Bank Fraud," *Nigerian Times* (1-14 October 1995): 4.
65. Ejike Okpa, "I Am Not One of the Corrupt Nigerian Military Officers," *Nigerian Times* (1-14 September 1995): 9; Jenrola and Obanya, op.cit., p. 19; see "Nigeria Airways Top Staff Fired," *Nigerian Times* (15-30 September 1995): 12; "28 Abandoned Government Vehicles Recovered," *Daily Times* (10 January 1997): 1.

"Kaduna: 26 Officials Sacked over N38.83 Million Fraud," *Nigerian News Update* (7-20 February 1994): 7; "Ministry Investigates Fraudulent Practices of Officer," *Nigerian News Update* (24 January-6 February 1994): 4; "Adamawa: Administrator Orders Arrest of Auditor-General," *Nigerian News Update* (7-20 February 1994): 6; "Ondo: Government Recovers N4 Million from Former Commissioner," *Nigerian News Update* (24 January-6 February 1994): 6; "17 Workers in Trouble over Fraud," *Nigerian News Update* (30 November-13 December 1993): 5; "Ex-accountant General Charged with Fraud," *Nigerian Times International* (16-31 December 1995): 11.

66. See "Nigeria's Currency Change," in *West Africa* (28 May 1984): 1103. Also see note 27.

67. Ugochukwu, op.cit., p. 53 (1984a), p. 1056 (1984b), p. 1349 (1984c); see "Attempt to Detect Ghost Workers May Be Foiled," *Thisday* (31 December 1996): 10; and "Extra Misled: Iwuanyanwu to Government," *Thisday* (31 December 1996): 32; see "Contract Awarded Work Not Performed But Paid For," *West Africa* (2 January 1984): 42.

68. Ugochukwu, op.cit., pp. 53-56. Also see *Thisday* (30 November 1998). General Abacha illegally withdrew $832 million (N71.6 billion) from the Nigerian Central Bank.

69. Ugochukwu, op.cit., pp. 1056-1057; Adamolekun, op.cit., p. 992.

70. Abdul Oroh, "One Coup, Many Issues," *The African Guardian* (7 May 1990): 23-24; Chukwuemeka Gahia, "Why They Struck: Coup Plotters Flaunt Their Reasons to Unseat Ibrahim Babangida," *The African Guardian* (7 May 1990): 21-22; Aina et al., op.cit., pp. 14-20.

71. Jenrola, op.cit., p. 11; Chizea, op.cit., p. 61.

72. See "Nigeria recovers assets from detained bank chiefs" which amounted to $8.75 million (N700m) in *Nigerian Times* (1-14 September 1995): 8; "Bosses of failed banks on trial for fraud," involving $3 million (N242 million) *Nigerian Times* (1-14 September 1995): 29; "New Law against Money Laundering Underway," *Nigerian News Update* (15 January 1993): 8.

73. Taslim Oluwale Elias, *The Nature of African Customary Law.* (Manchester: Manchester University Press, 1956), 126-127; 224-227; 259. Also see Daryll Forde, "Justice and Judgment Among the Southern Ibo Under Colonial Rule," in Hilda Kuper and Leo Kuper (eds.), *African Law: Adaptation and Development* (Los Angeles: University of California Press, 1965), 10, 81,84, and 91. The existence of this type of cult in Nigeria is transmitted by oral history from generation to generation. Their members are easily identified in every community in which they live. It is a common knowledge in Ibo (Igbo) communities.

74. Chinua Achebe, *Things Fall Apart* (New York: McDowell, Obolensky, 1959).

75. Obi N. Ignatius Ebbe, *Comparative and International Criminal Justice Systems: Policing, Judiciary, and Corrections* (Boston: Butterworth-Heinemann, 1996), 7-8.

76. Onome Osifo-Whiskey and Kola Ikori, "Deaths that Defy Defection: Mysterious Killings Send Shock Waves into a Hitherto Peaceful Community," *Newswatch* (13 June 1988): 8-15; Akpos Balebo, Obinali Nwafor, and E. V. M. Pauls, "Dele Giwa Affair," *Newswatch* (10 January 1994): 6; Ubani, op.cit., p. 15; see "Senator Obi Wali Murdered," *Nigerian News Update* (13-16 May 1993): 2. Also see the following: "Businessman, 50, Shot Dead by Hired Killers in Abeokuta," *Vanguard* (31 December 1992): 2; "Assassins on the Prowl Again in Lagos: Gunmen Attack NADECO Chief," *Daily Times* (15 January 1997): 1-2; "General Abacha Comforts Onagoruwa," *Daily Times* (14 January 1997): 1; "Adesanya Survives Gun

Attack," *The Guardian* (15 January 1997): 1-2; "Ume-Ezeoke Recovering in London," in *West Africa* (12 December 1983): 2911; and "Eight Set Ablaze," *West Africa* (12 December 1983): 2150.

77. There may be other persons charged or dismissed that were not reported by *West Africa* and other Nigerian publications.

78. Achebe, op.cit.

79. Gahia et al., op.cit., pp. 11-14; Mba-Afolabi, op.cit., pp. 17-18; Ugochwuemeka, op.cit., p. 53-56 (1984a), pp. 886-886 (1984d).

80. For evidence of General Abacha illegally withdrawing billions of dollars from the Nigerian Central Bank disclosed, see Emeka Nwankpa, "Two Abacha Ministers, Kin Share $2 billion," *Guardian News* (Thursday, 3 December 1998). Bola Olowo, "Banking Controversy," *West Africa* (31 August 1987): 1676-1677; Wale Akin Aina and Ahmed Zaka Tulfare, "Satan Will Never Hold Me: Jailed CBN Legal Adviser on the Run," *The African Guardian* (4 December 1989): 16-17.

81. Mba-Afolabi, op.cit., pp. 17-18; see "Buhari Decries Wanton Corruption in Government," *Nigerian News Update* (21 February-7 March 1994): 1; "FG (Federal Government) Probes Five Former Acting Military Administrators," *Nigerian News Update* (10-23 January 1994): 3; "Niger: Secretary to the Government, Three Others Arrested over Sale of Generator" *Nigerian News Update* (10-23 January 1994): 6; "Government May Set up a Body to Battle Corruption," *Nigerian News Update* (1-15 February 1993): 1-7; "Jobs for Sale," *The African Guardian* (15 January 1990): 17.

82. See notes 11 and 72. Also see "Corrupt Practices," *West Africa* (19 October 1987): 2089.

83. Gahia et al., op.cit., pp. 11-14; Aina and Tulfare, op.cit., pp. 16-17; Wale Akin Aina and Billy Okonedo, "Narcotic Blues: Rise in Drug Trafficking Turns the Red Light on Airport Security," *The African Guardian* (10 July 1989): 18.

84. Ubani, op.cit., p. 15; Jenrola, op.cit., pp. 11-14; Musa, op.cit., p. 5.

85. Ubani, op.cit., pp. 25-26; Nwaobi et al., pp. 12-15.

86. Ubani, op.cit., pp. 8-11 (1990b); See note 76.

87. Ibid.

88. Ibid.

89. Ibid.

90. Louis Proal, *Political Crimes* (New York: D. Appleton and Company, 1898), 19-21.

91. Okoli, op.cit., pp. 1812-1815; Ubani, op.cit., pp. 8-11 (1990b); Ubani and Adegbe, op.cit., pp. 19-23.

92. Richard Quinney, *Class, State, and Crime: On the Theory and Practice of Criminal Justice* (New York: David Mackay and Company, 1977).

93. Robert Leiken, "Strategies for Controlling Corruption," paper presented in a colloquium on Challenge of Corruption, Hacienda San Antonio, Mexico, 6-8 March 1997: 2-4.

94. Ralph Salerno and John S. Tomiki, "Protecting Organized Crime," in *Theft of the City: Readings on Corruption in Urban America*, ed. John A. Gardiner and David J. Olson (Bloomington: Indiana University Press, 1974).

95. Gresham M. Sykes and David Matza, "Techniques of Neutralization: A Theory of Delinquency," *American Sociological Review* 22 (1957): 644-700.

96. Nicholas Gage, "Organized Crime in Court," in *Theft of the City*: op.cit.; Gardiner and Olson, op.cit.; Gary W. Potter, *Criminal Organizations*, op.cit.. Abadinsky, op.cit., pp. 45-101; Albanese, op.cit., pp. 29-64; Gary W. Potter and Larry Gaines, "Organized Crime in 'Copperhead County': An Ethnographic Look at Rural Crime

Networks," in *Contemporary Issues in Organized Crime*, ed. Jay Albanese (Monsey, NY: Criminal Justice Press, 1995).

97. Mba-Afolabi, op.cit., pp. 17-18; Agwudagwu, op.cit., p. 37; Chizea, op.cit., p. 61; Aina et al., op.cit., pp. 14-20; Jenrola, op.cit., pp. 11-14.

98. See the following: "Nigeria: Decree 4 Under Trial," *West Africa* (25 June 1984): 1324; "Sword Against the Pen," *West Africa* (7 May 1984): 960; "Why Five Journalists Are Held," *West Africa* (7 May 1984): 994; and "Blow for Press Freedom," *West Africa* (23-29 January 1989): 121.

References

Abadinsky, Howard. *Organized Crime,* 3rd ed. Chicago: Nelson-Hall, 1990.

Achebe, Chinua. *Things Fall Apart.* New York: McDowell Obolensky, 1959.

Adamolekun, Oladipo. "Sense and Nonsense." *West Africa* (12 May 1986):992-994.

Adesokan, Akin. "A Horrifying Miasma." *Newswatch* (10 January 1994):13-16.

Agwudagwu, Stephen. "Jail Bonanza." *Newswatch* (13 June 1988):37.

Aina, Wale Akin. "The Quandary of the Judiciary." *The African Guardian* (10 July 1989):18.

Aina, Wale Akin, and Ahmed Zaka Tulfare. "Satan Will Never Hold Me: Jailed Ex-CBN Legal Adviser on the Run." *The African Guardian* (4 December 1989):16-17.

Aina, Wale Akin, and Billy Okonedo. "Narcotic Blues: Rise in Drug Trafficking Turns the Red Light on Airport Security." *The African Guardian* (1 May 1989):12-13.

Aina, Wale Akin, Kunle Jenrola, Abdul Oroh, and Okey Acacia. "Twelve Hours of Madness: How Nigeria's Bloodiest Coup Was Foiled." *The African Guardian* (7 May 1990):14-20.

Albanese, Jay. *Organized Crime in America.* Cincinnati, OH: Anderson Publishing Company, 1985.

Albanese, Jay (ed.). *Contemporary Issues in Organized Crime.* Monsey, NY: Criminal Justice Press, 1995.

Anueyiagu, Abuchi. "Nsukka Gripped by Otokoto Saga: A Six-Year-Old Boy Escapes Kidnap." *Thisday,* 4 January 1997:1.

Balebo, Akpos, Obinali Nwafor, and E.V.M. Pauls. "Dele Giwa Affair." *Newswatch,* 10 January 1994:6.

Beare, Margaret E. "Money Laundering: A Preferred Law Enforcement Target for the 1990's," in *Contemporary Issues in Organized Crime*, ed. Jay Albanese. Monsey, NY: Criminal Justice Press, 1995.

Bentsi-Enchill, Niik. "Poverty and Politics." *West Africa*, 22 November 1982:3018-3019.

Biaghere, Sunny, and Mazino Ikime. "The Wig and the Gun." *The African Guardian*, 20 November 1989:8-9.

Bonger, Willem Adriaan. *Criminality and Economic Conditions.* Translated by Henry P. Horton. Boston: Little, Brown and Company, 1916.

Chambliss, William J. "State-Organized Crime—The American Society of Criminology, 1988 Presidential Address." *Criminology* 27 (Spring 1989):183-207.

Chambliss, William J. "Vice, Corruption, Bureaucracy, and Power." *Wisconsin Law Review* 4 (1971):1150-73.

Chambliss, William J., and Milton Mankoff (eds.). *Whose Law? What Order?: A Conflict Approach to Criminology.* New York: John Wiley and Sons, 1976.

Chizea, Boniface. "Bank Fraud: Who Is to Blame." *Newswatch*, 4 November 1991:61.

Daryll, Forde. "Justice and Judgment Among the Southern Ibo under Colonial Rule," in *African Law: Adaptation and Development,* ed. Hilda Kuper and Leo Kuper. Los Angeles: University of California Press, 1965.

Ebbe, Obi N. Ignatius. *Comparative and International Criminal Justice Systems: Policing, Judiciary, and Corrections.* Boston: Butterworth/Heinemann Publishers, 1996.

Ebbe, Obi N. I. *Strategic Approach to Control of Organized Crime, White-Collar Crime, and Political Crimes in Nigeria* (a monograph). Ada: Ohio Northern University Printing Press, 1982.

Eke, Emma. "Ripples of Otokoto Rock Aba." *The Guardian,* 12 January 1997:2.

Elias, Taslim Oluwale. *The Nature of African Customary Law.* Manchester: University of Manchester Press, 1956.

Gahia, Chukwuemeka. "The Making of a Scandal: Nuclear Waste Dumped in Nigeria." *The African Guardian*, 28 June 1988:12-17.

Gahia, Chukwuemeka. "Why They Struck: Coup Plotters Flaunt Their Reasons to Unseat Ibrahim Babangida." *The African Guardian,* 7 May 1990:21-22.

Gahia, Chukwuemeka, Emenike Okorie, Ray Echebiri, and Tunde Oguntoyibo. "Changing Tidal Waves: Nigeria—Britain Brace up for New Ties—Special Report." *The African Guardian*, 15 May 1989:11-14.

Gage, Nicholas. "Organized Crime in Court," in *Theft of the City: Readings on Corruption in Urban America*, ed. John A. Gardiner and David J. Olson. Bloomington: Indiana University Press, 1974.

Gardiner, John A. *The Politics of Corruption: Organized Crime in an American City.* New York: Russell Sage Foundation, 1970.

Gardiner, John A., and David J. Olson (eds.). *Theft of the City: Readings on Corruption in Urban America.* Bloomington: Indiana University Press, 1974.

Haffar, Enis. "Nigeria Needs Accountability." *West Africa,* 23 May 1983:1248-1249.

Ikime, Mazino. "Still Walking on Crutches: Nipost Remains Unreliable in Spite of Public Criticism." *The African Guardian*, 5 March 1990:12.

Jenrola, Kunle. "The Seamy Side of Banking: Fraud and Bad Loans Cause Problem for Financial Industry." *The African Guardian,* 23 April 1990:11-14.

Jenrola, Kunle, and Felix Obanya. "Deals.....Dirty Deals: Sharp Practices Rob Nigeria of Invaluable Petroleum Revenue." *The African Guardian,* 5 March 1990:19-25.

Kehinde, Seye. "Guilty as Charged." *African Concord,* 4 November 1991:42.

Mba-Afolabi, Janet. "Haven for Fraudsters." *Newswatch,* 4 December 1995:17-18.

Marcoviller, Douglas, and Leslie Young. "The Black Hole of Graft: The Predatory State and the Informal Economy." *The American Economic Review* 85 (June 1995): 630-646.

Mbaku, John. "Bureaucratic Corruption and Policy Reform in Africa." *The Journal of Social, Political Economic Studies* 19 (Summer 1994): 149-175.

Modupe, Iyabo. "God Is on Our Side: Otokoto Family Members Say as They Relocate to Lagos." *Sunday Vanguard,* 12 January 1997:2.

Musa, Njadvana. "Curbing Smuggling." *The African Guardian,* 24 April 1989:5.

Nwankpa, Emeka. "Two Abacha Ministers, Kin Share $2 Billion." *Guardian News,* 3 December 1998.

Nwaobi, John, Paul Nwabuikwu, Debo Adesina, Abdul Oroh, Wale Akin Aina, and Ben Akparanta. "Hitting a Dangerous High: Hard-drugs Threaten Menacingly, Society Looks on Helplessly." *The African Guardian,* 25 September 1989:12-15.

Nwokoro, Jullet. "Privatising Without Cash." *The African Guardian*, 6 March 1989:28-29.

Ojukwu, Dili, and Grace Ama. "Justice for Sale." *The African Guardian,* 10 July 1989:16.

Okoli, Enukora Joe. "Opening Up Tender." *West Africa,* 12 July 1982:1812-1815.

Okpa, Ejike. "I Am Not One of the Corrupt Nigerian Military Officers." *Nigerian Times,* 1-14 September 1995:9.

Ola, Olaniyi. "Smuggler's Paradise." *West Africa*, 27 March-2 April 1989:468.

Olowo, Bola. "Banking Controversy." *West Africa*, 31 August 1987:1676-1677.

Omoifo, Isa, Abdul Oroh, Tayo Afolabi, John Nwaobi, Debo Adesina, and Paul Nwabuikwu. "Judges with a Blindfold: They Neither See, Hear, Nor Talk of Evil in Governments." *The African Guardian,* 10 July 1989:12-17.

Onabanjo, Bisi. "Quote Me." *The African Guardian*, 10 April 1989:19.

Onyemaechi, Uzoma. "Fraud in Nigeria." Naijanews at University of Michigan. (Internet News: Uzo@alumni.Sils.umich.edu), 1996.

Oroh, Abdul. "One Coup, Many Issues." *The African Guardian*, 7 May 1990:23-24.

Oroh, Abdul, Wale Okey, Seun Ogunsellan, and Augustine Anyanna. "The Toxic Bug: After Koko, Poisonous Waste Continue to Threaten Nigeria Like a Saga." *The African Guardian*, 4 December 1989:20-23.

Osifo-Whiskey, Onome, and Kola Ikori. "Deaths that Defy Detection: Mysterious Killings Send Shock Waves into a Hitherto Peaceful Community." *Newswatch*, 13 June 1988:8-15.

Pedder, S. "A Survey of Nigeria: Anybody Seen a Giant." *The Economist*, 21 August 1993:3-14.

Potter, Gary W. *Criminal Organizations: Vice, Racketeering, and Politics in an American City.* Prospect Heights, IL: Waveland Press, 1994.

Potter, Gary W., and Larry Gaimes. "Organized Crime in 'Copperhead County': An Ethnographic Look at Rural Crime Networks," in *Contemporary Issues in Organized Crime*, ed. Jay Albanese. Monsey, NY: Criminal Justice Dress, 1995.

Proal, Louis. *Political Crimes.* New York: D. Appleton and Company, 1898.

Quinney, Richard. *Class, State, and Crime: On the theory and Practice of Criminal Justice.* New York: David Mackay and Company, 1977.

Shelley, Toby. "Privatisation—Fad or Panacea?" *West Africa*, 20-26 February 1989:260.

Salerno, Ralph, and John S. Tomiki. "Protecting Organized Crime," in *Theft of the City: Readings on Corruption in Urban America*, ed. John A. Gardiner and David J. Olson. Bloomington: Indiana University Press, 1974.

Schatzberg, Rufus, and Robert J. Kell. *African-American Organized Crime: A Social History.* New York: Garland Publishing, Inc. 1996.

Sutherland, Edwin. *On Analyzing Crime*, ed. Karl Schuessler. Chicago: University of Chicago Press, 1973.

Sykes, Gresham M., and David Matza. "Techniques of Neutralization: A Theory of Delinquency." *American Sociological Review* 22 (1957): 644-700.

Theobald, Robin. "Lancing the Swollen African State: Will It Alleviate the Problem of Corruption." *The Journal of Modern African Studies* 32, (1994): 701-706.

Tignor, Robert L. "Political Corruption in Nigeria Before Independence." *The Journal of Modern African Studies* 31, (1993): 175-202.

Tosterni, Matthew. "Child Slavery: Nigerian Human Rights Group Reporting." Lagos, Nigeria: Press Digest, 1996.

Ubani, Mike. "The Aba Ring." *The African Guardian*, 13 February 1989:25-26.

_____. "War Against Drugs." *The African Guardian*, 16 April 1990a:15.

_____. "In The Pangs of Crisis: Awka-Etiti Communal Feud Deepens Following Another Murder." *The African Guardian*, 7 May 1990b:8-11.

Ubani, Mike, and Adegbe Onu Adegbe. "Worms in the Apple: Smugglers Smile, the Nation Bleeds." *The African Guardian*, 13 February 1989:19-23.

Ubani, Mike, and Billy Okonedo. "Furor Over Frisking: Nigeria Airways, Customs Find No Alternative to Crude Searching Methods." *The African Guardian*, 13 March 1989:15.

Ugochukwu, Onyema. "The Return of the Military." *West Africa*, 9 January 1984:53-56.

_____. "Nigeria: The Trials Begin." *West Africa*, 21 May 1984b:1056-1057.

_____. "Nigeria: A Parade of Gubernatorial Convicts." *West Africa*, 2 July 1984c:1349-1351.

_____. "Nigeria: And Now for the IMF." *West Africa*, 23 April 1984d):866-867.

_____. "Withdrawal of the Naira." *West Africa*, 30 April 1984e:912.

_____. "Nigeria: Stories from the Currency Exchange." *West Africa*, 28 May 1984f:1106-1108.

Webb, James. "Nigerian Drug Ring." *Naija News*. Internet, 1996.

Whiteman, Kaye. "Policeman Jailed." *West Africa*, 14 December 1981:3012.

_____. "475 Detainees—Idiagbon." *West Africa*, 19 March 1984:638.

_____. "Coup Plotters Arrested." *West Africa*, 6 January 1986:5-7.

Whiteman, Tim. "Nigeria: Red Alert on Oil Fraud." *West Africa*, 10-16 April 1989:546-547.

Wilson, Richard W. "Political Pathology and Moral Orientations." *Comparative Political Studies* 24 (July 1991): 211-230.

6

Mexico's Legacy of Corruption

Stanley A. Pimentel

This chapter examines the associations between organized crime and politics in Mexico from the 1960s to the mid-1990s. To understand these developments, the historical and cultural contexts of the evolution of this nexus will be examined. In the contemporary period, the organized political and criminal elements came together to work in a collaborative pattern. Organized crime was, for a time, controlled and managed by the political authorities. A theoretical framework developed by Peter A. Lupsha is particularly helpful in interpreting the Mexican case.[1]

Three centuries of occupation, exploitation, and civic neglect by Spain, and a century of local dictatorships by revolutionary leaders could not evolve into a democratic civic society overnight. An agreement by several competing factions to put aside their weapons and come together under the rule of one political umbrella, beneficial to all, began with the formation of an official party in 1929, which subsequently evolved to become today's Partido Revolucionario Institucional (PRI). The PRI, a political monopoly, has been a "patron-client," authoritarian type of system for seven decades and has used its social control forces (military, police, and internal security agencies) to control, tax, and extort from the organized criminal elements. The political authorities provided immunity from prosecution for the criminal elements, while obtaining money for development, investment, and campaign funding for the party, as well as for personal enrichment. The criminals were expected to pay and obey the authorities; if they became a liability or could no longer produce, they were either liquidated or incarcerated.

Over time, however, these relationships between political officials and criminal groups were altered dramatically by several factors. Concern for human rights have come to the fore, the North American Free Trade Agreement (NAFTA) was passed; global communications have become a reality; a

175

more educated middle class demands democracy; and, the opposition parties began to win important positions. The political authorities in power can no longer control the organized criminal elements. As a result, the criminals are on the offensive, killing anyone seen as going against them, including law enforcement officials and prosecutors. With no professional law enforcement or an effective system of laws capable of combating these criminals, the results are proving disastrous to Mexican society. Drastic measures must be taken by the Mexican government to combat these organized criminal elements and to successfully destroy the political-criminal nexus that has endured. Creating an elite professional law enforcement task force working with a national criminal intelligence clearinghouse is a beginning. Empowering this elite group with the proper tools, equipment, and laws so that they can actively pursue the organized criminals is also needed. Their task will be to identify and attack the weaknesses of these organized criminals and their partners, such as seizure of their assets and lengthy prison sentences in order to break the cycle of the political-criminal nexus.

Historical Legacies of Authoritarianism and Instability

Speaking at a bankers' convention in Cancun, Quintana Roo, Mexico, on 7 February 1997, President Ernesto Zedillo promised to make Mexico a "country of laws" and to build public confidence in the justice system. He stressed that one of his top goals is to shore up Mexico's democratic institutions. He went on to state that "we do not have conditions now guaranteeing our security nor have we achieved the full state of law that is required for Mexico's development." In an interview with the *Chicago Tribune* published on 20 July 1997, President Zedillo spoke of the urgent need to introduce a "government of the rule of law" and expressed his desire to free the country of official corruption. He went on to say, "Corruption is not a phenomenon that came about a few years ago, but unfortunately, has been around since the colonial times within our cultural traditions and certain practices."

The Mexican political system, "New Spain," evolved out of three centuries of occupation, exploitation and civic neglect by the European colonial powers, and a century of local dictatorships. The basic fact is that Mexico was under the "paternalistic and repressive control of Spain which discouraged political self-government, stifled individual economic initiative and suppressed intellectual ambition."[2] Spain was interested in souls, gold, and silver, but not necessarily in that order. For generations, Mexico was ruled by a viceroy who ran the colony as the personal representative of the Spanish Crown. "He lived in a palace, maintained a court and all forms of royal pomp and prestige, and appointed all officials with the king's authority, and supervised economic, religious, intellectual, and social affairs. The viceroy headed the colonial government, was supreme judge, and made, and enforced the laws. To see that he functioned honestly and efficiently, the viceroy was often spied upon by a 'visitor general' sent by the Crown to report on colonial matters."[3] (To this day, many of Mexico's government agencies continue to have a "visitor-general," analogous to an "inspector general," to report irregularities to the cabinet minister; sometimes the holder of this position acts as the "hatchet man" or "bagman" for the superior.) The Spanish colonials became the propertied class, along with the Catholic Church, whose mission system provided the means of administration and social control in the outlying areas. While the viceroy and governorships were initially in the hands of Iberian-born, and later local Creole elites (those born in Spanish America of European parents), administrative units, town, and city councils, and magistrates were run by *mestizo* (mixed indigenous-European) elites. Limited and weak administrative control by Spain, harsh topography, and slow communications allowed for local autonomy and upward mobility among the mestizo leadership, as well as the evasion of royal edicts and taxes. In spite of all the Spanish laws imposed on New Spain, "political corruption flourished, especially when the Spanish Crown, after the sixteenth century, decreed that public offices could be sold at auction to the highest bidder. In this way, many incompetent and corrupt individuals got into colonial offices."[4]

At the same time, local corruption and the sale of offices allowed the landed oligarchy to gain control over the rural administrative offices as access to higher positions. Once entrenched there, nepotism and graft extended into the patron-client system, which became the embedded norm, and the motto "*Obedezco pero no cumplo*" (I obey but do not comply) became the cry of the leaders of New Spain. As a result of these systems of control, the "inevitable outcome of three centuries of exploitation and repression by the Spanish was revolution, which stirred Mexico to its foundation and resulted in the severing of ties"[5] to the motherland. Four centuries of authoritarian rule could not be transformed into a democratic civic culture overnight. It is a struggle that still confronts and configures Mexico today.

> [Its]...beginnings as an independent nation in 1821, when she cut her last ties to Spain, were inauspicious. Because of the lack of self-rule under Spain, the general poverty and illiteracy of the inert masses, and the preponderant economic and political powers of the army, and the Church, Mexicans were not prepared to rule their own house. The shift from a colony to a republic meant only a change of rulers for the common man...the tensions merely shifted...[6]

from the Spanish born to the Creole and from the Creole to the mestizo. Roughly a century of instability, foreign invasion, dictatorship, and revolution followed Mexico's independence in 1821. First came a "war of reform" that led to nationalist rule by Benito Juarez, followed by a brief period of the European-imposed ruler, Maximilian (1864–1867). After this came Juarez's efforts to implement liberal laws in a period called the "Restoration" (1867–

1876), which led into the dictatorship of Porfirio Diaz (1876-1910), who fortified Mexican unity. Unity collapsed into revolutionary convulsions (1910–1920), during which period a succession of *caudillos* (strongmen) fought for control of the national government and the promulgation of the 1917 Constitution. Out of this instability came the creation, in 1929, of the ruling party, initially known as the Partido Nacional Revolucionario (PNR, National Revolutionary Party), the forerunner of today's PRI.

The current political system in Mexico began in 1928–29 after the assassination of Alvaro Obregón, the revolution's victor, its strongman and president. The incumbent president, Plutarco Elías Calles, and his successor, Emilio Portes Gil (1928–1930), worked together to convince "all political factions into one imposing party, the PNR, which was financed by a 'kickback' from the pay envelope of every government employee."[7]

> Calles recognized the historic opportunity and his unique responsibility to achieve a comprehensive political agreement, create the new political institutions for a modern Mexico, and leave behind the raw violence that had characterized personal politics...to establish and maintain control over the main forces and actors in Mexican politics. To achieve it, all the accesses to decision-making centers and all the roads to economic, social and political mobility passed through the party, the formal and operating structure of the 1929 political agreement. The party became the only gatekeeper of access to power, closed and out of reach to those on the outside who would never enter. A monopoly of access to power was created.[8]

For the next seven decades, the PRI, operating under a patron-client hierarchy, distributed via its governors, trade unions, and occupational associations, patronage, contracts, jobs, educational opportunities, social services, and other benefits to its loyal adherents. Various power centers, cliques, and alliance systems within the oligarchy would vary positions and offices in alternate administrations, all with a strong "splash" down to the people. Upward mobility, education and economic opportunities were available to the loyal who attached themselves to the right patron and were able to stay in the stream of rising party stars.

Presidential control over the succession, influence over gubernatorial selections and state financing, and what amounted to a "rubber-stamp" legislature and judiciary, all contributed to centralized power in the PRI and Los Pinos (the presidential residence). The presidential clique and the party leadership, together with the security apparatus (formal security agencies, the police, the attorney general's office, and the military), possessed both the power and capacity to make their collective will felt throughout the country. A term frequently used to describe Mexico's political system,

> ["presidentialism"]...has caused so much harm to the country, particularly in the last few *sexenios* (six-year presidential terms) and is a product of the control the president of the Republic has exercised over PRI congressmen and senators. The

authoritarianism, the discriminatory application of the law, the centralism, the corruption and the impunity are all products of placing all the state power in one solitary person: the president of the Republic.[9]

During the PRI monopoly of power, actors such as the media and the Catholic Church have been co-opted and have become part of the political system. Early on, the PNR removed the Mexican military from the center of power by promising great rewards, exercising civilian oversight over their food and supplies, and rotating the zone commanders every two to three years. "Senior officers were encouraged to enrich themselves with assorted business opportunities, sinecures and favors, and even illicit activities, such as contraband, drug trafficking and prostitution, were tolerated.... At the same time, the government protected the armed forces from media criticism..."[10] The military thus became something of a "sacred cow."

Also at the disposal of the president was the Secretaría de Gobernación (Ministry of Government, or Interior), the second most powerful position next to the presidency, "with its broad responsibility for preserving the country's political stability...in charge of managing the political arena where both the opposition and the PRI perform."[11] Within this ministry was the Federal Security Directorate (DFS), responsible for investigating matters affecting national security and other duties as directed by the president. This agency, consisting of members of the elite presidential Military Staff Guards (EMP) and paramilitary experts, was ready to do as the president commanded, or to use the president's name when it suited their purpose.

With these tools at their disposal, and with their many coalitions of interest groups, and alliances with other powerful institutions, the president and the PRI leadership enjoyed near absolute power. "Myriad pyramids of power are thus superimposed on the larger hierarchical pyramid: everyone except the president is both boss and servant... (where) the process spawns political cliques—known as mafias—that are loyal to the president but compete fiercely with each other. Without them, the system of loyalties could not work."[12] As a result of these loyalties to bosses and ultimately to the president, institutions have not become professionalized, nor can there be any checks and balances to offset the corruption and complicity ingrained in this system. The PRI has successfully permeated the entire system in Mexico. Everyone from the lowly police officer on the street, to the mayor of the city, the governor of the state, to the minister of finance, or the attorney general himself, are all indebted to the party bosses, and ultimately, to the president. No controversial action was taken by one patron, without checking with his/her patron, and on up the line. Many decisions that normally would be made by a deputy secretary would be referred to the president, who appointed that individual, for the final say. And since there is "No Re-election" of the president, governors, mayors, congressmen and senators, everyone must "make hay while the sun shines" so that he/she can have a larger "nest egg" when no longer in a position to obtain the benefits of office. Carlos Hank Gonzalez, former secretary of agriculture in the Carlos Salinas administration, former mayor of Mexico City, and a well-respected PRI stalwart, probably said it best when asked about his accumulation of wealth and his status as one of Mexico's richest men: "A politician who is poor, is a poor politician."

The Political-Criminal Nexus: Theory and Practice

Peter A. Lupsha has developed a theory that helps interpret political-criminal relationships in the Mexican case. He posits two basic patterns of criminal-political relationships: the "stage-evolutionary model" and the "elite-exploitation model." According to Lupsha's "stage-evolutionary" model, the most common progression in the relationships between organized crime and the political system, most organized crime groups tend to evolve through three stages: the predatory, the parasitical, and the symbiotic. In the predatory stage, the criminal group is usually a street gang or group rooted in a particular territory or neighborhood, such as the gangs in Los Angeles, Chicago, or New York. Criminal gangs evolving from the predatory stage into the parasitical stage have developed a corruptive interaction with the legitimate power centers. La Cosa Nostra did this during Prohibition in the United States in the 1920s. Political corruption, which accompanies the provision of illicit goods and services, provides the essential glue binding the legitimate sectors with the underworld criminal organization. The third or symbiotic stage evolves when the criminal organization and the political system become one of mutuality, where the political and economic systems become dependent upon and subject to many of the services the criminal organizations have to offer. In New York City, La Cosa Nostra's control of the Fulton Fish Market, or the construction industry and garbage collection are prime examples of this stage.[13]

This dynamic evolution of organized crime in the "Stage-Evolutionary" model is one in which the criminals follow an illicit parallel ladder of upward mobility and over time seek to achieve legitimacy in their wealth and status for themselves and their children. These criminals actively seek niches in the interstices of the law where they can enrich themselves and at the same time buy into the political and economic systems to minimize the risks of arrest and loss of wealth. From governmental and citizen perspectives these organized criminal enterprises provide desired economic services, such as gambling, prostitution, illicit alcohol, and drugs, yet are part of an underworld that is accepted but not catered to.[14]

Lupsha's second model of organized crime, the "elite-exploitative," is one in which the organized crime enterprises are not treated as useful or necessary evils but rather as "cash cows," to be manipulated and exploited by political authorities. This model most usefully describes what we observe in Mexico, where organized crime becomes a source of funding and illicit enrichment for the political elite and their social control agents. Drug traffickers in these settings, after achieving some entrepreneurial successes, are sought out by the system and taxed and disciplined into their role within the system. While corruption is a key factor in both of these models, in the "stage-evolutionary" model, it is initiated by traffickers in pursuit of insurance and protection. The legitimate social control actors in this model may accept payoffs, and even seek them, but they rarely become the initiators of trafficking or its reinforcers.[15]

In the "elite-exploitative" model, the traffickers are under pressure from the legitimate social control agents, indeed forced, to accept and sell loads of seized drugs, and are constantly threatened and taxed by those agents who are passing percentages of this tax to officials higher up. These criminals are rarely permitted to retire; they are either killed or imprisoned while other family members are allowed to take over. In this model, the organized criminal system is called upon to support the oligarchy. Control and initiation comes from the top, from the so-called legitimate power holders and their social control agents, and the drug lords, like good "cash cows," are protected, milked (taxed), and when no longer useful, are imprisoned or sent to the slaughter.[16] "Nevertheless, these groups continue to work with renewed efforts, which demonstrate that, contrary to common belief, the drug trafficker's power is limited; they are disposable elements, and as part of the unwritten rules, are utilized for convenience, either by the State or their real bosses."[17]

Mexico appears to be a good fit with the "elite-exploitative" model. Political authorities used social control agents to organize and regulate drug trafficking. Traffickers were manipulated and disposed of to suit the needs of political officials. Over time, however, traffickers grew more powerful and the political system became more pluralistic, but not institutionalized. In these circumstances, drug traffickers gained greater autonomy of action—and became more violent and aggressive in their dealings with both state and society.

The case can probably be made that the first association between an organized criminal group and a politician in Mexico occurred when Hernan Cortes and his marauding band of soldiers from Spain marched into Tenochtitlan (present-day Mexico City) and captured the Aztec capital and its emperor, Moctezuma. Despite the fact that Moctezuma had previously offered Cortes and his organization gifts of gold, silver, and jade in hopes that they would leave, Cortes is said to have remarked, "The Spaniards are troubled with a disease of the heart for which gold is a specific remedy."[18] The evolution of the criminal-political nexus in Mexico can be seen clearly for the first time during the early 1900s when the United States attempted to put a stop to the contraband trade of drugs, whiskey, and arms with its Mexican neighbor.

> The business was so lucrative that it raised the attention of several powerful politicians such as...Colonel Esteban Cantú, Governor of the Territory of Baja California Norte from 1914 to 1920. In Customs reports from Los Angeles in 1916 sent to the Department of the Treasury, he was mentioned as one who gave out concessions to exploit the opium trade in exchange for important sums of money. The cost of a concession was $45,000 (U.S. Dollars) and the monthly rent was between $10,000 and $11,000.[19]

As long as there has been a United States-Mexican Border, there has been smuggling and contraband trade. From Mexico came marijuana, heroin, and more recently, cocaine into the United States, while refrigerators, televisions, automobiles, and weapons crossed in the opposite direction. Average citizens purchased many such goods; however, the bulk was smuggled by organized crime elements that have conducted family-run businesses for generations. These same families have produced all the major organized crime figures, such as Miguel Angel Felix Gallardo, Rafael Caro Quintero, Juan Garcia Abrego, Amado Carrillo Fuentes, the Herrera family, and the Arellano Felix brothers of the present day. Most got their modest start in the 1960s in the drug trade.

Opium poppy and marijuana were grown in abundance in the western parts of Mexico where "politicians, business people, police and peasants all knew who was planting poppy seed.... [T]he police knew who were the producers.... [T]he Chief of Police was the one who controlled the 'percentage' in exchange for tolerating (the trade) or for support.... [K]nowing the Chief of Police meant closeness to the Governor..."[20] What began as a local, home-grown organization's paying off the officials of the local "plaza" (town), grew into a national organized crime organization's paying off high-level political authorities. Originally, under the concept of the "plaza," the drug trafficker or smuggler bought his or her "license" to operate from the local police chief, military commander, the mayor, or the individual who had been given authority in that area by the PRI."...[P]ayments went to locals who passed part of it up to the patrons to whom they owed their positions. Should a trafficker have a major business success with resulting notoriety, he would then likely be visited by the '*judiciales*' (state level agents of law enforcement) and later by '*federales*' (agents of national police agencies) and operating 'franchises' would have to be also purchased directly from these agencies."[21]

One of the sources interviewed for this chapter reported that the Mexican government, particularly the Ministry of the Treasury (Hacienda), has not provided a budget to other government institutions, such as the Mexican Attorney General's Office (PGR) or the Federal Judicial Police (PJF), and these agencies have had to seek out their own ways of obtaining operating funds. For so many years, these agencies have assigned their personnel to their offices (plazas) throughout Mexico, expecting them to perform their duties with honor, while providing little or no funding to operate their offices. These officials arrive at their new posts and must find ways to "earn" money so that they can pay for personnel, office expenditures, and at the same time be able to survive on their meager salary. According to Source "A," it was generally through the arrests of organized crime figures and the seizures of their contraband goods (whether these were stolen cars, drugs, weapons or television sets) that these individuals were sent to jail and their goods confiscated and turned over to Hacienda. The drugs would then be turned over to the prosecutor for destruction, while Hacienda would sell the contraband items and provide 40 percent of the profits of these sales to the federal law enforcement officials. That was how the police survived. Source "A" indicated that the police official in charge of the area would simply confiscate contraband from the crime figure and submit the goods to Hacienda for a payment, while requiring the crime figure to sign over the deed or title of his house or car to the law enforcement official or a relative. Source "A" blamed the Mexican government for not providing the law enforcement officials with the funds, training, and equipment to perform their duties in an honorable fashion. According to "A," the hierarchy has deliberately looked the other way while its personnel were extorting monies, properties, and gifts to administer justice, and illegally enriching themselves.

Source "A" further observed that, since the PGR/PJF hierarchy in Mexico City was not in a position to earn a decent wage, the commanders in the field would donate to "La Copa" (essentially "passing the hat around"), by which means a percentage of the field profits was sent to superiors in Mexico City, usually on a monthly basis. Source "A" explained that since Mexico City was declared a free zone (not controlled by anyone), the hierarchy in the Federal District relied upon donations from the field commanders to supplement their incomes. This tradition had been carried on for decades and it was not until approximately the mid 1980s, with the establishment of the National Commission on Human Rights and with the complaints lodged by criminals against the PGR/PJF officials, that the custom changed. Source "A" indicated that until this time, the police or military had dictated the terms of the "plazas" to the organized crime figures and had exerted control over these. However, when human rights became an issue, the police and military commanders could no longer exert control over the criminals, and many of the experienced commanders resigned for fear of going to prison. Thus, many "plaza" holders went to work for the crime figures and became part of the organized crime scheme, rather than the attempt to control or prosecute the criminals.

Source "A" advised that in the late 1940s, President Miguel Aleman "devalued the Mexican Generals" by creating 300 new generals where before there had been only 20, vastly enlarging the group looking to share "the spoils" of the country. As has previously been stated, Military zone commanders obtained monies and gifts from drug traffickers and other organized criminals within their zones in exchange for protection and/or immunity from prosecution. The zone commanders have generally coordinated through intermediaries with the PGR/PJF officials on the "levies of funds" to be obtained from organized crime.

A second informed source, "B,"stated that the PGR Ministerio Público Federal (MPF) (federal prosecutor), who is typically assigned to one location from four to six years, is generally the intermediary between the drug trafficker, the PGR/PJF hierarchy, and the Military. It is usually through the attorneys working for the drug traffickers or organized criminals that this arrangement is made. Rarely are senior government executives involved in direct negotiations with criminals. Suitcases of money are passed from the criminals through their lawyers to the MPF. The prosecutor then passes the money on to his superiors, who, in turn, deliver it to their superiors as far away as Mexico City. Both "A" and "B" advised that while the PJF was directed by Rodolfo León Aragón and Adrián Carrera Fuentes (1990–1994), they regularly sent their immediate subordinates in official PGR aircraft to pick up the suitcases filled with money and gifts obtained from the organized crime elements by the PGR/PJF "plaza" holders throughout Mexico.

The contents were later disbursed among themselves, to their superiors in the PGR/PJF, and ultimately to Los Pinos (presidential residence) to a "slush fund" account. Details of this slush fund were brought out during the extradition hearings of former PGR Deputy Attorney General Mario Ruiz Massieu in U.S. District Court, Newark, New Jersey, in 1996. When questioned about the source of money in a seized Houston bank account, Ruiz Massieu claimed that he had received a number of bonuses from President Salinas, the larger being 800,000 pesos (approximately $240,000 at the 1993 exchange rate). Documents presented at the extradition hearing by the PGR attested to the presidential accounts and the awards of bonuses to PRI members.

Source "A" continued that many believe the Mexican military has been exempt from complicity with organized crime. However, evidence to the contrary is the February1997 arrest of the former division commander, and former commissioner of the PGR's National Institute to Combat Drugs (INCD), General Jesús Gutiérrez Rebollo, who was charged with protecting the major drug cartel leader, Amado Carrillo Fuentes and his organization. Allegedly, in exchange for gifts such as luxury apartments, vehicles, jewelry, and money, Gutiérrez provided protection to the Carrillo Fuentes organization, while attempting to dismantle the rival Arellano Felix drug trafficking organization of Tijuana. Witnesses have testified at the Gutiérrez Rebollo hearings that drug trafficker Amado Carrillo Fuentes was in possession of PGR credentials allegedly provided by Gutiérrez Rebollo. (Carrillo Fuentes died at a clinic in Mexico City on July 4, 1997, while undergoing surgery to alter his appearance.) The role played by the PJF and former DFS agents with organized crime has been abundantly portrayed in the media. However, "the information about the military collusion with drug traffickers is less known...and surely, their participation is more than what has been 'filtered' by the media...the 'generals' are not necessarily those who are the visible heads."[22]

Source "A" advised that "La Copa" has been a traditional means of corruption within the law enforcement institutions of Mexico. However, in the mid-1970s until the early 1980s, the DFS, in the name of national security and with total impunity granted by the presidential office to attack the enemies of the system, took the concept of corruption to a new level with its greed and dictatorial powers. "DFS's primary mission in the 1960s was as an anti-guerrilla force to combat the National Revolutionary Civic Association (ACNR), and later the Party of the Poor and the Mexican People's Party. As the guerrilla organizations mobilized in the cities, DFS formed the White Brigade (La Brigada Blanca)...to neutralize them...the White Brigade is said to have tortured, killed and "disappeared" hundreds of Mexicans considered threats to the regime.[23] While getting rid of the guerrilla threat to the country, the DFS personnel with its "death squads" combined its counterinsurgency activities with active participation in the drug trade, particularly in the Guadalajara region.

> From its inception, DFS had interactions with drug traffickers...Antonio Zorrilla (Director of the DFS in the 1980s) signed the DFS and Gobernación Agent Identification cards that Rafael Caro Quintero and other members of the Guadalajara cartel were carrying when they were arrested. According to the revelations of the Camarena trials (the DEA Agent kidnaped, tortured and killed by drug traffickers in 1985), DFS Comandantes and ex-Comandantes even became participants and investors in the Guadalajara cartel's plantations and trafficking ventures.[24]

Once the guerrilla movement was quashed by the DFS, in the mid-1980s the complicity between the drug traffickers and the DFS reached unprecedented levels. Mexican newspaper reporter Manuel Buendía was killed in May 1984, and DEA Agent Enrique Camarena Salazar and his pilot were murdered by traffickers the following year. Buendía allegedly came into possession of a videotape showing high-ranking government officials meeting with drug traffickers. Buendía was ordered killed by his friend and confidant, Jose Antonio Zorrilla Pérez, the then head of the DFS. Zorrilla Pérez was said to be politically linked to the Interior Minister when Buendía began publishing details of the drug traffickers' connections to high-level police, politicians, and businessmen in a Mexican newspaper.[25]

Source "A" noted that Zorrilla's predecessors had been of military backgrounds, and therefore disciplined, and had kept in check the many organized crime figures. According to this source, Zorrilla, as head of the DFS and a career politician, believed himself an all-powerful and untouchable executive of the PRI. He ordered the assassination of Buendía and was even rewarded by the Interior Ministry and designated a candidate for a PRI federal deputy position. However, "A" advised that public opinion and a presidential decision by then-President Carlos Salinas de Gortari ordered that Zorrilla be tried for the Buendía murder. Zorrilla was sentenced to forty years in prison.

As a result of these two well-publicized events and at a time when the media were linking governors, military officers, and even President Miguel de La Madrid to drug traffickers, in late 1985, de la Madrid ordered the dissolution of the DFS. As a result, several ex-DFS commanders continued their involvement in drugs. In particular, Rafael Aguilar Guajardo would become a major drug cartel leader in Juarez, Mexico. He was murdered in 1993 in Cancun.

Source "B" has stated that until approximately the mid-1980s, the local "plaza" dealt with the organized criminal elements in the region, and these in turn, dealt only with the authorities of that area. The "plaza" holder generally received instructions from Mexico City, either through the mayor, the governor, or from the director of the PJF, or DFS. The financial terms would be dictated to the organized crime figures. However, Rafael Caro Quintero, head of the Guadalajara drug cartel, broke all the rules by personally approaching the secretaries of defense and interior. According to "B," no organized crime figure had ever dared approach a high-level government official before, and all negotiations between Mexico City and the plaza had been through intermediaries of the region. "A 1988 District Court affidavit in the State of Arizona states that in 1984 an informant told the DEA that a consortium of traffickers including, Rafael Caro Quintero, Juan Esparagoza Moreno, Jaime Figueroa Soto, Manuel Salcido, and Juan Quintero Paez paid ten million dollars to the Mexican Secretary of Defense General Juan Arevalo Gardoqui for protection..."[26] A note from the Second Section (Intelligence Section-Mexican army) to the secretary of defense, dated March 4, 1997, lists persons linked to drug traffickers in the 15th Military Zone, Guadalajara, Jalisco. During an investigation carried out by the military in 1991, the former brother-in-law of former President Luis Echeverría, Ruben Zuno Arce, was found to have been involved with drug traffickers.

> General Juan Felix Tapia, formerly in charge of the 15th Military Zone, now retired, was an associate and protector of Ernesto Fonseca Carrillo, alias Don Neto, and has received monies and gifts directly from him or through the intermediary, Lt. Colonel Jorge Garma Diaz (fired), or through another drug trafficker, Roberto Orozco. It is said that Rafael Caro Quintero gave him (General Felix Tapia) a dark red Grand Marquis and another to Colonel Beltran Guerra. It has also been noted that General Arévalo ordered that Garma Diaz be given access to a car and driver, and that Felix Tapia was closely associated with Ruben Zuno Arce.[27]

In the summer of 1990, Zuno Arce was convicted of complicity in Camarena's murder by a federal court in Los Angeles, and is presently incarcerated in the United States.

A third informed source, "C," advised that for approximately the past thirty years, the seeding, cultivation, transportation, and sales of marijuana, heroin, and cocaine have been carried out by reputed Mexican drug traffickers; however, all these were acting in concert with the governing powers of the state, namely the governors, the military, and police forces, and these in turn collaborated with their patrons in the hierarchy of the PRI. Source "C" stated that *no one could act without protectors (nadie sin protectores)* in the patron-client relationships, which have existed within the PRI for the past seventy years. Source "C" noted that for the past thirty years, politicians and organized crime figures have worked hand in hand, the politicians providing organized criminals with protection from prosecution or competition from rivals in exchange for money and gifts. Oscar Lopez Olivares, alias El Profe, a lieutenant of former drug kingpin, García Abrego, stated that:

> Drug trafficking...is a matter completely handled by the government, from the protection that is given to the marijuana cultivations, everything is duly controlled, first by the Army, next by the Federal Judicial Police, and even the fumigators of the PGR'...there is no doubt that police agencies have been the protective arm of the principal drug barons...at the same time, these (barons) have received protection from high level politicians...[28]

Source "C" continued that those who fall out of line or are not in agreement with the governing forces are jailed or killed, while new clients are found to provide the "protectors" with the necessary cash and gifts. Source "C" maintained that nothing happens in Mexico that is not known by the "protectors" and, therefore, when a government official states that the whereabouts of a wanted fugitive are unknown, it is a lie. As an example, all three informed sources agreed that certain officials within the Mexican government knew where the Gulf Cartel leader and former FBI Top Ten Fugitive, Juan García Abrego, was in the 1990s, and could have detained him when he was being sought by U.S. authorities. However, these officials chose not to because García Abrego was paying them directly or indirectly and he had not yet become expendable. It was only after García Abrego became a liability to the Mexican government that he was allowed to be captured and turned over to the U.S. Government in January 1996. PGR officials familiar with the capture of Juan García Abrego allege that the PJF commander in charge of the García Abrego investigation received one-half million dollars and a new bullet proof Grand Marquis vehicle from another major cartel leader for arresting Garcia Abrego. The informed source "B" reported that this PJF commander was assigned to Tijuana after the arrest and expulsion of García Abrego, with orders to prosecute the Arellano Felix drug trafficking organization. Instead, he received several million dollars from them to allow them to continue their operations in Tijuana.[29] There is also the view of Figueroa based on her study of the García Abrego organization that "no one doubts that the Gulf Cartel

(García Abrego) is a part of the power group. It is impossible to move tons of cocaine, launder thousands of millions of dollars, maintain a clandestine organization of several hundred armed persons, without a system of political and police protection...(it is) a clear example of how a criminal organization interrelates with a power group."[30]

The three informed sources separately corroborated that the sale of offices within the PGR/PJF has generally been accomplished through a deputy attorney general, who was purposely selected by the PRI hierarchy and named by the president. (One Mexican attorney general informed the writer that President Salinas did not allow him to select his own deputy attorney general.) In addition, one former PGR delegate (who functions much like an United States attorney for a district) informed the writer that a deputy attorney general informed him that the plaza he was taking over would cost three million dollars, plus a payment of one million dollars per month rent, and that he should pay up front. The delegate advised that he told the deputy attorney general that since the president had selected him, he was not going to pay. Two of the informed sources pointed out that during his tenure former President Carlos Salinas selected three individuals to coordinate Mexico's counterdrug efforts. The three have been reportedly linked to drug traffickers by the media. Important positions such as the delegate or deputy delegate in Tijuana or Juarez could cost up to three million dollars for the "concession." The delegate, in turn, would pay one million dollars per month, payments to be made to the PGR hierarchy, and, ultimately, to "Los Pinos." These monies were provided, of course, by the organized crime elements. Source "C" confirmed that portions of the payments collected during the Salinas administration by the PJF directors would ultimately reach President Salinas' private secretary, where the monies would be placed in secret accounts to be used as the president or the PRI hierarchy saw fit. Positions in other non-drug-producing or less populated states cost only $30,000 for the concession, plus a few thousand dollars per month payments to the higher ups. Sources "A" and "B" report that the sale of offices continues to this day in the PGR/PJF.

Two of the informed sources corroborated that selective law enforcement of organized crime activities took place during the past thirty years. Organized crime figures went to prison only after much hue and cry from the United States, and when the individual had become a liability to the Mexican government, such as in the case of García Abrego. Or, if the political situation warranted, such as in the weeks prior to the "certification process" by the U.S. Congress by March of each year, a "sacrificial lamb" was provided to appease the United States government. The sources reported that as long as the criminals maintained a low profile, paid their "dues" each month, and did not create any problems for the police, the law enforcement authorities would not prosecute them.

In Mexico, control was in the hands of the State...which in determined circumstances...especially when there are political pressures from the United States...(Mexico has been) obligated to sacrifice laborers (who are) easily replaced, but without weakening to the point of placing its (drug organization) existence in danger...[31]

Two sources state that 1992 marked the beginning of the "limousine service" in which the military, the PGR/PJF, and State Judicial Police officials began providing protection for drug shipments to the border area. Most often, the roadblocks implemented in an area by the military, the PGR/ PJF, or the local authorities, are to safeguard the passage of the shipments, and not necessarily for the detection of contraband. Through intermediaries, the "plaza" holder will be notified when a drug shipment is expected and instructed to set up the checkpoints. The sources indicated that one "plaza" holder would not necessarily know that another "plaza" holder in another state or region has coordinated the shipment of drugs to the next area. To facilitate smooth operations, orders will come from Mexico City to the appropriate "jefe" in the "plaza" to supervise and ensure the safe transhipment of the "merchandise" through his/her area.

The sources continued that not only was organized crime expected to pay consistently, but they had to continually keep the "plaza" informed of their activities, their associates and their rivals, particularly those who were not paying or had not received the authority from the "plaza" to operate. The three sources stated that once a productive relationship had been developed between the organized crime figure and the "plaza," the crime figure would try to keep that individual in place for a long period by making the "plaza" holder look good in the eyes of his superiors. "The trafficker was expected to assist the police and the political system by providing grist for the judicial mill, (i.e., pinpoint or inform on rival traffickers) as well as public relations materials to give the U.S. drug enforcers. Thus, while the trafficker could gain protection and warning information, the police could gain credit, praise, and promotions; the political system gained campaign monies and control; and the U.S. obtained statistics, to justify a job well done."[32] Source "B" advised that many organized crime members are marrying police officers and/or prosecutors to further protect themselves from persecution and prosecution. The three sources noted that organized crime leaders have insulated themselves further by recruiting family members, trusted friends, and others, through intimidation exerted by their attorneys and enforcers to carry out their trade. Sources "B" and "C" advised that most of the organized crime figures' money does not leave Mexico, but rather is invested in real estate, apartments, houses, financial markets, construction and road building firms, drug stores, tourism projects, and, of course, paying for protection.

If the Mexican government has been a patron-client type of system, who is the ultimate patron? One informed source stated that the person manipulating or orchestrating the PRI hierarchy behind the scenes, much like a puppe-teer, is a former secretary of interior, who has maintained extremely powerful control over the principal members of the PRI through favors, promotions, and blackmail. This individual has been able to manipulate and control the PRI hierarchy for so many years because of his astute ability to play one political interest against the other, and yet maintain the loyalties of the play-ers. Other sources agree that this individual is powerful; however, they sug-gest that a select few long-time, central figures of the PRI have also exerted control over its members for the past forty years.

"Traffickers have been perceived as creatures used by the dominant politi-cal class to do its dirty work, (and) not as independent social agents or barbar-ians trying to take by force the strength of the State through corrupt strategies directed at unpolluted officials at different levels."[33] Organized crime figures are in business for the money. The more money they can make, the more they can legitimize their status in the community, the region, and the nation. The Mexican drug traffickers are known to have built roads, churches, schools, and medical centers in their communities. Others, like García Abrego, sent their children to the United States to be educated. In this way, they can legiti-mize their status in the region, and, at the same time obtain protection and immunity from the authorities. According to the informed sources, these or-ganized crime figures have not sought political positions nor do they seek publicity in the media. Cartel leaders such as García Abrego and Carrillo Fuentes bought newspaper and magazine businesses to try to keep their names out of the press. PGR officials advised that they have established that many in the print media receive salaries from organized criminals for the purpose of not printing stories about them, just as the PRI has bought off newspaper reporters to publish stories favorable to that party.

Disorder in the Political-Criminal Nexus

On July 6, 1997, a new era began in Mexico. For the first time in almost seventy years, the PRI no longer held a majority in the Chamber of Delegates; it also lost two governorships to the opposition PAN (the National Action Party), and the mayoralty of Mexico City to the Revolutionary Democratic Party (PRD). The PRI would now have to learn how to share legislative pow-ers with the opposition parties and not be a "rubber-stamp" for the president, as it had for so long. At the same time,

> [Mexico has undergone a]...significant erosion of institutional authority. There is less power at the center, even in the presidency, than there used to be.... [I]n effect, Mexico has been witnessing political disintegration at two distinct levels—among its uppermost institutions, and within the political class. These developments intersect with each other and multiply their mutual effects. In this fashion, they set the scene for the ascendancy of the country's new-age drug barons...the deterioration of

Mexico's long-standing system tends to magnify the political significance of drug traffickers, since they face relatively few constraints on their action.[34]

At present, the stark truth is that no one is in charge. The traditional methods of control from the president on down through the PRI hierarchy, and through the social control agents control over organized crime, have deteriorated to the point where criminality is rampant, a number of political murders have not been resolved, and kidnapings for huge ransoms have gone unresolved for years. The transition from authoritarianism to democracy in the last five years has been extremely difficult to navigate. Organized crime figures, watching this breakdown, know that they are out of reach of the lawful authorities for the moment. They have seized the opportunity to go after their competitors and are assassinating the police officers and prosecutors who do go after them. So "no one is confronting the mafias or serious crime for one simple reason; everyone, in whatever police agency, knows who is killing whom and why. But they will not investigate for one simple reason: it is better to delay it (investigating) or face assassination by one's own police comrades."[35]

The mass firings of federal, state, and local police in the 1990s aggravated the situation by placing more individuals on the street hungry to "make ends meet" at any cost. They have joined the criminals or banded together to form their own enterprises. "By 1995, according to an internal Interior Ministry report, there were an estimated 900 armed criminal bands in Mexico of which over 50 per cent were made up of current and retired members of law enforcement agencies."[36]

Because of the well-established "patron-client" systems that ruled Mexico for so many years and kept major crime in check, there was no perceived need for a career civil service system. Therefore, with the exceptions of the army, Foreign Service, and the Bank of Mexico, no professional government institution exists today. That lack of a professional career and a civil service system for the police and judicial services has placed an unfair burden on those who administer justice. The lack of training, decent wages, or possibility of promotion, and the institution's inability to provide the necessary tools for an investigation (i.e., cars, phones, gas, per diem, as well as adequate laws) leads to corruption in the institution. When the institution does not provide the tools for the official to carry out his/her duties, then he/she must seek other ways, generally through corrupt practices, to pay for his/her services to the public institution. Through intimidation, coercion, and bribery of judges, major criminals are having serious charges dismissed, allowing them back on the street to continue their criminal activities. The authorities at the state and national levels are "outgunned, outmanned," and undercut by the corruption and intimidation of the criminals. President Zedillo has repeatedly stated that criminals present the number one threat to the national security of Mexico. In addition, urbanization, multinational corporations, global communications, internationalization of finance and financial controls, the North America Free Trade Agreement (NAFTA), the creation of an educated and viable middle class with democratic expectations, have all contributed to weakening the authoritarian system of governance in Mexico.

For almost seven decades, and accompanied by relative calm, it was true that, "corruption enables the system to function, providing the 'oil' that makes the wheels of the bureaucratic machine turn and the 'glue' that seals political alliances."[37] That alone was no longer enough.

> Corruption and complicity appear to have been carefully organized. If this is so, they have to be considered as institutions serving precise and specific goals of the existing Mexican political system.... They integrate the political elite, reward loyalty to the Presidency, serve as real and permanent threat for those not conforming to the rules and provide a vehicle for economic and social mobility. However, the set of institutions created in 1929 no longer respond to the needs of a society in the process of modernization. Many of the institutions that had functioned in the past, have become dysfunctional and now threaten to thwart Mexico's further development.[38]

Indeed, the change from authoritarianism to democracy will be a difficult challenge for Mexico and there could be a period of ungovernability as we are witnessing today. A recent newspaper article aptly stated:

> There currently exists in Mexico an alarming political vacuum. We are trapped in the midst of a transition from a presidentialist and centralist system that no longer functions, toward a plural democratic system that has not been consolidated. The violence, the insecurity, the lack of dialog, and the permanent political tension that we live are all products of that power vacuum and from the lack of a profound democratic reform.[39]

For Mexico to regain its streets and the confidence of the public, drastic judicial and law enforcement changes must be implemented. First the social control agencies and the judiciary need to be professionalized. Secondly, the laws need modification to attack the organized crime problems effectively and efficiently. At the helm of the PGR, PJF, and other national law enforcement agencies must be strong, honest, and experienced individuals with equally strong and honest staffs experienced in law enforcement and willing to be career professionals. The professionalization of law enforcement is critical. To achieve this, the recruitment, selection, and training processes must be upgraded and maintained, with better salaries, incentive programs, and career opportunities. These institutions must operate with checks and balances to ensure that the performance and integrity of public officials will be above board and open to public scrutiny. An impartial device for monitoring the performance of public officials, with the power to discipline and punish offenders of the public trust must be established. Legislative oversight must be implemented to ensure compliance, public scrutiny, and continuity in the professionalization of police and law enforcement. The operations of law enforcement must be transparent and coordinated to address the major crime problems of the community. Task forces must be established to attack organized crime elements, gather intelligence on corrupt organizations and dismantle these by seizing their assets and incarcerating their members. Profits realized from the seizure of assets should be returned to the police to augment its budget for training and equipment. Judicial reform is a must in order to attack organized crime. Passage of legislation to utilize undercover agents, informants, electronic monitoring devices, and effective witness protection programs, as well as provision of funding for such initiatives is required. Banking laws must be strengthened to make money laundering and fraud serious criminal offenses.

There is no respect for law enforcement authorities in Mexico. The community needs to have a sense of trust that each citizen can expect respect, honesty, and integrity from public servants. The institutions must work with the community to improve relations and to build up public trust toward the police. On the other hand, the police and the prosecutors must work to gain that trust by making it known that they will not take bribes, by being professional and courteous, by respecting the civil rights of each citizen, and by working with the community to create a secure environment for everyone. Extensive crime-prevention programs that address all age groups should be sponsored and implemented by the government and the private sector.

President Ernesto Zedillo, in an address to the nation on 30 November 1997, stated that he shared the nation's indignation over rising crime and pledged to crack down on organized criminals and police corruption. He promised to send draft legislation to the Congress that would reform the Constitution and Mexico's antiquated laws to stiffen penalties against criminals and make it more difficult for criminals to avoid judicial actions. He announced his intention to launch a nationwide crusade against crime and violence by: (1) promoting rigorous laws that would punish the criminals; (2) profoundly transforming the law enforcement institutions and their personnel; (3) greatly increasing financial resources for law enforcement efforts; (4) mobilizing society toward a culture of lawfulness; and, (5) instilling in society an awareness that all crimes must be punished, whether at the local, state, or national levels.

The future of Mexico is fraught with peril, and with many competing interests. On one hand are those who seek democratic change with equal participation of all political parties; on the other are the so-called "dinosaurs" of the PRI who do not want change under any circumstances and who will fight change with their customary methods of corruption and complicity. Also resisting change are the organized criminals, competing among themselves for fiefdoms through kidnapping and murder. The majority of hardworking and honest Mexican citizens striving for tranquility and justice are caught in the middle. As Mexico's Nobel Laureate, Octavio Paz put it:

> ...we are witnessing the end of the PRI system, which could pave the way to a multiparty system; but if we don't achieve that, if the different forces don't succeed in agreeing on a peaceful transition toward a new political situation, we will have demonstrations, possible violence in the countryside and the cities, internal fighting, or something like that...in the long run, the forces of openness, modernization, and democracy will prevail, but it will be a very painful, very difficult road.[40]

Appendix

Comparative Models of Organized Crime

Model One: The Stage-Evolutionary Model of Organized Crime

1. *The Predatory Stage*:
   Exemplars: Street gangs, outlaw motorcycle gangs (early period); Vietnamese gangs.
2. *The Parasitical Stage*:
   Exemplars: Italian-American organized crime in general; many Colombian organizations; many Bosnian groups.
3. *The Symbiotic Stage:*
   Exemplars: Italian-American organized crime in private carting, Fulton fish market, and New York city construction industry; certain labor unions; Japanese Yakusa; Chinese triad organizations in Southeast Asia; Cali cartel in Valle de Cauca.

Model Two: The Elite-Exploitation Model of Organized Crime *

1. *Entrenched Dominant Elites*:
   Dominant political party, military, political-economic, security apparatus. Russian Nomenklatura; key regime actors; serious criminal communities.
2. *Tax And Extort:*
   Major national, transnational, and regional organized crime groups and drug traffickers.
3. *For Hard Currency, Internal Development and Investment, Campaign Funding, and for Personal Enrichment.*

*This system is controlled by operators and collusion at the top: Exemplars include Myanmar, Mexico, Pakistan, and Russia.

Some Indicators of the Elite-Exploitation (E-E) Model Compared with the Stage-Evolutionary Model of Organized Crime*

▢ Organized crime entrepreneurs are viewed as "cash cows" to be "taxed," exploited, and manipulated by the political system's agents and institutions of social control.

▢ Organized criminals are rarely permitted to retire from the game. If they are, other family members take their place in the system.

▢ The children of organized criminals rarely establish legitimate careers totally separated from the business of crime. Money laundering fronts are about as far as they get.

▢ The agents of state institutions of social control plan and initiate criminal acts ranging from sale of seized drugs to murder.

▢ Extrajudicial acts and actors are a basic part of the system.

▢ Seized drugs and other contraband tend to be used and sold not destroyed, despite "Potemkin-like" displays of destruction.

▢ When elites change, organized crime group leaders tend to be replaced, and the old leader is arrested, extradited, or killed.

▢ When contraband seizures are made, generally no arrests are made.

▢ When arrests are made, these are generally the lowest level of personnel of the criminal organization.

▢ Offices (positions) are sold, especially those in lucrative ports of entry in drug/contraband/ import areas.

▢ The elite's willingness to commit crimes and use threat and torture creates a conspiracy of silence among organized criminals even after arrest or extradition.

▢ There are embedded expectations of kickbacks and payments up the chain of command. Thus, extortionate behaviors permeate every level of organization and spread across the system.

Little of the above is commonplace in the stage-evolutionary model.

The above models and indicators were developed by Professor Peter A. Lupsha.

Notes

1.   I wish to express my gratitude to Peter A. Lupsha, professor emeritus, University of New Mexico, for providing a first draft of this material. I would also like to thank many current and former members of the Mexican government, who do not wish to be identified, and who gave of their time and expertise to assist in this project. I have relied particularly on three sources in this chapter that have provided reliable information in the past, and are well placed in the system. To the extent possible, others have corroborated their information.

2.   A. Curtis Wilgus and Raul D'Eca, *Latin American History* (New York: Barnes & Noble, 1963), 3.

3.   Ibid., 67.

4.   Ibid., 67-73.
5.   Ibid., 115
6.   Hubert Herring, *A History of Latin America* (New York: Alfred A. Knopf, 1962), 300-302.
7.   Ibid., 372-373.
8.   Roberto Blum, "Corruption and Complicity: Mortar of Mexico's Political System?" (Institute for Contemporary Studies, National Strategy Information Center, Hacienda San Antonio, Mexico, 1997), 8.
9.   Demetrio Sodi de la Tijera, "1997, The Year of the Democratic Change," *El Universal* (Mexico City), 3 January 1997. (Translated by writer).
10.   Alan Riding, *Distant Neighbors* (New York: Vintage Books, 1989), 91.
11.   Ibid., 95.
12.   Ibid., 77.
13.   Lupsha, "Transnational Organized Crime versus the Nation-State" in *Transnational Organized Crime*, Volume 2, no. 1 (Spring 1996), 21-48; London, see especially pp. 30–32. Also see appendix for a further comparison of these two models of organized crime provided by Lupsha.
14.   Peter A. Lupsha and Stanley A. Pimentel, "Political-Criminal Nexus," (Institute for Contemporary Studies, National Strategy Information Center, Hacienda San Antonio, Mexico; Washington, DC, 1997).
15.   Ibid., 8-9.
16.   Ibid., 9-10.
17.   Yolanda Figueroa, *El Capo del Golfo* (Mexico D. F.: Editorial Grijalbo, 1997), 71. (Translated by writer.)
18.   Riding, 27.
19.   Luis Astorga, "Crimen Organizado y Organizacion del Crimen" (Mexico D. F.: Instituto de Investigaciones Sociales de la Universidad Nacional Autonoma de Mexico, 1998), 6-7. (Translated by writer.)
20.   Luis Astorga, *El Siglo de las Drogas* (Mexico D. F.: Espasa-Calpe, 1996), 81. (Translated by writer.)
21.   Peter A. Lupsha, "Drug Lords and Narco-Corruption: The Players Change but the Game Continues," Reprinted from *War on Drugs* (Westview Press, Boulder, San Francisco, Oxford, 1992), 179; quoting Terrance E. Poppa, *Drug Lord: The Life and Death of a Mexican Kingpin* (New York: Pharos Books, 1990), 41–42.
22.   Luis Astorga, *El Siglo...*, 161. (Translated by writer.)
23.   Peter Lupsha, "Drug Lords....," 180, quoting from *Proceso*, a Mexican weekly magazine.
24.   Ibid., 180-181, quoting from *Proceso* (5 August 1985) and *Penthouse* (December 1989).
25.   Ibid., 183; quoting from Rogelio Hernandez, *Zorrilla: El Imperio del Crimen* (Mexico City: Editorial Planeta, 1989).
26.   Ibid., 188.
27.   Carlos Marin, "Military Intelligence Documents Entangle High Ranking Chiefs, Officers and Army Troops in Narcotics Trafficking," *Proceso*, no.1082 (27 July 1997), 19. (Translated by writer.)
28.   Figueroa, 69. (Translated by writer.)
29.   The Commander was fired by Attorney General F. Antonio Lozano Gracia in September 1996.
30.   Figueroa, 137.
31.   Astorga, *El Siglo...*, 166. (Translated by writer.)

32.   Lupsha, "Drug Lords...," 182.
33.   Astorga, "Crimen Organizado...," 8. (Translated by writer.)
34.   Peter H. Smith, *Drug Trafficking in Mexico* (Washington DC: Institute for Contemporary Studies, National Strategy Information Center, 1996), 14–16.
35.   J. Jesus Blancornelas, *Una Vez, Nada Mas* (Mexico D. F.: Editorial Oceano, 1997), 143. (Translated by writer.)
36.   Andres Oppenheimer, *Bordering on Chaos* (New York: Little, Brown & Co., 1996), 301.
37.   Riding, 114.
38.   Blum, 12.
39.   Sodi de la Tijera, "Power Vacuum," *El Universal* (Mexico D. F.) 2 January 1998. (Translated by writer.)
40.   Oppenheimer, 318.

7

Russia and Ukraine: Transition or Tragedy?

Louise I. Shelley

Symbiotic relationships between government officials and criminals are a potent legacy of the Soviet period. No successor state to the USSR has escaped the phenomenon. These relationships, carefully masked in the Soviet period, have surfaced publicly with a striking intensity in both Russia and Ukraine. Although both countries emerged simultaneously from the USSR, significant differences in the political-criminal nexus are apparent in the short period of Russian and Ukrainian statehood. The divergence of these two societies from the Soviet model suggests that specific political, social and economic conditions have a decisive influence on the evolution of the nexus.

In all societies, the political-criminal nexus is harmful because this coalition places its financial interests above those of the citizenry or the long-term objectives of the state. This cancer within a transitional society is particularly devastating because the nexus develops in tandem with the state, denying the construction of a healthy nation.

Russia and Ukraine are societies in transition, their situations contrast sharply with many of the countries addressed in this study. Their laws, economic system and governmental institutions are in a period of profound change. Whereas Russia lost its empire, Ukraine was unexpectedly created without the institutions needed to run a country of 40 million people. During the major transition in both societies, the political-criminal nexus of the Soviet period expanded.

After the collapse of the USSR, Russia needed to downsize its institutional capacity. In contrast, Ukraine needed to immediately create laws and a bureaucracy capable of governing a highly complex society in economic crisis. These institutional demands coincided with the need to build an identity as a Ukrainian state. Inheriting a potent political-criminal nexus with an inferior capacity to cope with organized crime, the nexus poses an even greater threat to Ukrainian state development than in Russia.

Russia with a more developed civil society and diverse political environment is more capable of defending itself against the political-criminal nexus than Ukraine. On a more practical level, Russia also has a greater capacity to combat organized crime because it inherited most of the Soviet Union's specialists in the field of organized crime and its institutional experience. The headquarters of the Ministry of Interior and the KGB, which had responsibility to study and address organized crime, were in Moscow and therefore inherited by the Russian state. Many of these officials are corrupt and they are concentrated in Moscow. Therefore, the inheritance is not a pure advantage to the Russian state. The political-criminal nexus, however, grows unimpeded in Ukraine because the new state has neither the political will nor the trained specialists capable of controlling the problem.

Contrary to expectations, the privatization of the Soviet state did not lead to a free market economy or a democracy. The process was hijacked from its inception by the political-criminal nexus which appropriated the vast wealth of the state by acquiring the banks, natural resources, and enterprises that had once been government property. With their new-found wealth, the new financial elite acquired power in a new form. Their power is not based on the military power of the Soviet state. Rather it is economic and political power that can still operate internationally. Those who dominate the Russian and Ukrainian economies are not only a financial oligarchy. They acquired and retained their enormous wealth in illicit ways that have much in common with those of organized criminals. Nor are they necessarily the energetic entrepreneurs depicted in the Western press.[1]

The economic costs for the citizenry are clear. Lacking capacity to control the criminal-political nexus in this transitional period, state property in Ukraine and Russia has been distributed almost exclusively to the former *nomenklatura* (the party elite) and their criminal associates. As a consequence, the ordinary citizen has become the big loser in the property grab that accompanied the collapse of Soviet power. Most Russians and Ukrainians have almost no equity stake in the future. Instead, millions of citizens in both countries are not paid for months at a time, social services are bankrupt, and the military is on the verge of collapse.[2]

Property redistribution in Russia and Ukraine is accompanied by large numbers of killings because crime groups have defended the property interests of the ruling elite. Minister of Interior Kulikov reported that there were 560 contract killings in 1996 of which only 15 percent had been solved by Soviet law enforcement authorities.[3] Many abhor the violence but few understand the long-term consequences of the merger of crime groups and the political structure for the citizenry, the press, or the emergent democratic institutions.

In Russia, privatization was more rapid, inspired by the belief that Communism could be made irrevocable only with the return of property to private hands. At the end of the first five years of statehood, the Russian government owned less than 20 percent of the country's economy, a transfer of property on a scale not seen since the Bolshevik Revolution.[4] Western assistance focused almost exclusively on promoting privatization with little attention paid to the legal framework needed to guarantee the fair distribution of property or secure property rights.[5] The West failed to acknowledge or criticize the criminalization of the privatization process. Domestic criticism was muted because many high-level Russian officials were complicit in the illegal property grab "prikhvatizatisiia" (a word play on privatization). Increasingly all forms of mass media were acquired by the new financial oligarchy, thus precluding the free discussion of the sale and redistribution of state property.[6]

In Ukraine, privatization is occurring more slowly. But as in Russia, there have been no safeguards over the process permitting spontaneous privatization of state assets to occur. Without controls, the Ukrainian privatization process has also been hijacked by a political-criminal coalition. Nationalism, potentially a potent force for state construction in Ukraine, cannot alone counteract the corrosive impact of crime and corruption. The pride in having an independent state cannot counteract the personal avarice of many with access to national resources.

The development of the political-criminal nexus is shaped by the political and economic realities of the successor states. The long-term development of the nexus depends not only on the domestic environment but pressure by foreign countries to address the problem. The pressure is being placed strongly on Ukraine but to a very limited extent on Russia by foreign aid donors and international organizations. Ukraine depends on large-scale foreign aid for its survival. The political-criminal nexus is, therefore, a double threat to Ukraine's independence. The domestic drain on its natural resources and the loss of foreign aid undermine its financial and political viability.

The Causes of the Political-Criminal Nexus

Lord Action has written that "absolute power corrupts absolutely." The absolute power of the Communist Party in both political and economic terms explains much of the observable corruption. But there were several unique aspects to Soviet governmental corruption, not the least of these being the crucial alliances which existed with the shadow economy and the criminal underworld.

Several important conditions facilitated the development of the political-criminal nexus. First, throughout the Soviet period citizens were severely restricted in their acquisition of private property. As Locke has pointed out, property is the citizens' bastion against state authority. Second, state interests were always supreme over those of the individual. Third, the rule by law was valued for the maintenance of order and the protection of citizens.[7] But the rule of law where property rights are valued and the state maintains a commitment to legality was absent.[8] Fourth, civil society was totally destroyed precluding the existence of any groups outside of government-controlled institutions. Citizens lacked the financial resources or the ability to join private associations which would have allowed them to check the symbiotic relationships that developed between politicians and criminal groups.[9]

Soviet communism created unique preconditions for the development of the political-criminal nexus. In contrast to other societies where personal wealth or the existence of civil society can serve as a bastion against state authority, there were no independent forces to check the growth of the corrupt ties in the USSR. In the absence of a free media, civilian watchdog organizations, or financially independent individuals who could afford to oppose the government, there was nothing to impede the growing links between corrupt officials and participants in the illegal economy. In Poland independent trade unions were checks on the government. The mobilization of workers at the end of the Soviet period never translated into a movement that could help curb governmental corruption.

The law was used to force compliance with state objectives. In the absence of the rule of law, political pressure was applied to all branches of the legal system to produce politically desirable outcomes. Under these circumstances, law and justice were not respected as ends in themselves but merely as tools to achieve ends sought by the state.[10]

Legal officials had value not as objective enforcers of the law but only as persons who could achieve tangible results. Legal authority was personalized. The source was not the law, but the bureaucrat who held the position of responsibility.[11] There was no concept of the independence of the judiciary; the judge was valued for his/her ability to bend the law and adjust to the circumstances.

Legal officials were part of a state bureaucracy where corruption in the post-Stalin period was pervasive and citizens expected to be able to influence officials. Within the Ministry of Interior, certain law enforcement personnel were known to serve as go-betweens for the criminals who sought to influence investigators, prosecutors, and judges and to have contact with state bureaucrats. Not all the personnel needed to be corrupt as the cases needed to be redirected only to individuals who could provide a favorable resolution.

While the Communist Party required certain standards of Party members, there were numerous cases in which Party officials and members of the *nomenklatura* (Party appointees to political and governmental positions) escaped sanction for serious offenses. Party members enjoyed an immunity from investigation and prosecution unless the Party authorized legal officials to proceed.[12] Investigations were often halted even in serious corruption cases because the guilty officials were deemed to be essential economic managers.[13]

The Party was supreme over the government. Therefore, there was no independent governmental oversight over the Party. With a legal system subordinated to the Party, corrupt officials could justifiably feel that they were above the law. The absence of an adequate system of checks and balances contributed to a system where many officials believed that all was possible and there were no limits to their exercise of power. There was little to constrain individuals in a culture where political expediency was preferred over the pursuit of justice.

The Communist Party existed in power for seventy years with no challenges to its authority. The endemic corruption was not unique to the former Soviet Union. Profound corruption has also been observed in other societies dominated by a single political party, such as the PRI in Mexico or the Liberal Democratic Party in Japan. Deep-rooted corruption also existed in Italy where a dominant political coalition ruled until it was rooted out by the clean hands investigators in the early 1990s. In Japan, Mexico, and Italy the mid- to late 1990s has revealed the strength of the political-criminal nexus.

A second economy arose to satisfy the unmet consumer needs of the population.[14] In a centrally planned economy geared to the needs of the military rather than the citizenry, there were chronic shortages and the infamous waiting lines that characterized daily life. The sizable shadow economy, run largely by members of ethnic minorities, had long-standing relationships with governmental officials. These relationships were almost never disrupted because loyal Party members could expect to serve without challenges to their authority. The shadow economy required the participation of government and law enforcement officials who were complicit in its existence.

In parts of the former Soviet Union, particularly in the Caucasus and Central Asia, positions in commerce were already being privatized by corrupt officials in 1970s. For example, crucial positions in the trade network were selling for as much as $100,000 in the republic of Georgia during these years. Individuals who became Ministers of Trade or Light Industry could subsequently sell positions under their control.[15] In turn, those who acquired these positions maintained continuous, unofficial financial arrangements with members of the underground economy, the Party bureaucracy, and the legal establishment.

The reason for this prevalence of illicit activity was that even after years of Soviet rule, the trading culture among Caucasians, Jews, and Central Asians was not eliminated. These ethnic groups, excluded from positions of power in the central government and circumscribed even at the local level, continued to pursue their financial interests outside of established state structures. As in many countries, where organized crime is dominated by different ethnic groups that are precluded from legitimate social mobility, the Jews and Asian groups were significant figures in the shadow economy.

Individuals operating in the second economy were vulnerable to intimidation by the KGB. Some agreed to serve as informers for the security police in exchange for protection from prosecution. After the collapse of the Soviet Union, there were legitimate opportunities to participate in trade. But overseas trade, particularly the lucrative areas of import and export, were often dominated by former and current KGB personnel who had developed ties overseas over the course of many years. Therefore, the intimidation of the emergent international trading class by members of the security apparatus continued. In cases, partnerships were formed between the semi-licit business class and members of the KGB.

With the advent of *perestroika* and the collapse of the USSR, there was a breakdown of the official governmental institutions but not of the unofficial relationships which existed. Not only did the social control apparatus of the state collapse but also its administrative capacity. Citizens remained totally unserved by the government which ceased to ensure their employment or the provision of goods and medical services.

The problems of corruption were rampant and provided fertile soil for the further development of organized crime. Citizens needed to provide bribes to obtain even the minimum of social services from the government. The problems observed in the USSR were by no means unique to that society. A comparative analysis of socialist economies reveals the close links between major economic transition and organized crime. These problems were already evident in a variety of socialist countries before the collapse of the Soviet Union.[16] These problems became even more acute when privatization occurred without adequate legal safeguards over the process of transfer of state property. According to Maria Los, a long time observer of the illicit elements of socialist economies, traditional property is entrenched in space and time whereas the privatized property of former socialist states has become virtual property that is "Fluid, easily disposable, convertible, invisible, or hidden behind false names or short-lived fronts."[17] With these qualities, it can easily be shipped overseas and laundered to other countries.

Market-oriented reforms in former socialist societies expand the opportunities for illegal opportunities. Criminals stand to benefit because they can insure that the economic transformation occurs in ways favorable to their financial interests. In contrast to healthy market economies, where criminals and corrupt officials have only a peripheral impact on the economy, in the Russian and Ukrainian cases their impact is very significant. The criminalization and corruption of these two economies reveals the inherent limits of transforming unreformable economies. "Quasi-market reforms blur the ideological distinction between legal and illegal markets and between their respective laws."[18] The trajectory of this transition was already evident well before the socialist system collapsed.

The underground economy and the markets for their products rely on unofficial networks and exchange relationships. They exist alongside the official legal system. As a parallel legal system, they challenge the official state authority. As Los has explained,

> Informal networks are crucial for organized crime, but they have to cross the lines between the second and the official hierarchies. In the end—states the USSR Deputy Prosecutor General—"underground millionaires and policemen, thieves and prosecutors, judges and speculators, Party-workers and 'godfathers' frequently wind up on the same side of the fence." Nepotism, mutual protection and development of stable patron-client relationships are crucial to the success of the operations.[19]

Over time these relationships become institutionalized. They existed as a parallel power to the state. In the late 1970s and early 1980s, the Party leadership did not authorize legal authorities to move against the criminals or their partners in the political apparatus. By the late 1980s, the leadership of the USSR had enjoyed relative impunity for more than a decade. The punishments meted out by the judiciary and by the Party against high-level officials who abused their authority became increasingly rare. The increasing corruption at the highest levels of authority, unimpeded by any official measures, contributed significantly to the collapse of the Soviet Union. The Soviet state survived the end of the Brezhnev era by less than ten years, in part, a consequence of a weak state failing to counteract the rise of political-criminal ties.

Methods

Different methods of study are available for the Soviet and Russian periods. More direct forms of analysis and social science methods can be applied in the contemporary period when scholars have greater access to information.

The analysis of the political-criminal nexus of the Soviet period requires application of the tools of the historical method. Analysis of the political-criminal ties can be done by examining career paths and patterns of association. To understand the relationships from the side of Party officials, an analysis can be done of their posts, patrons and the regions of the USSR where they served. For example, unraveling the political-criminal nexus of the Ministry of Interior officials in the Brezhnev era requires an understanding of their career trajectory and family ties to the Brezhnev family which will be discussed in greater depth later. The minister of interior, N. Shchelokov, had worked closely with Brezhnev for almost his entire career. His vice-minister was Brezhnev's son-in-law. Yuri Churbanov obtained this position after his marriage to Brezhnev's daughter, Galina. The leadership of the so-called "Uzbek Mafia," leading Central Asian officials were exploited to promote their economic and political interests. Regional and local officials, linked to the local criminals paid large bribes to the leading government officials to achieve autonomy.[20]

To analyze the relationships for the other end of the chain one needs to understand the milieu of the criminals—their family associations, particularly of members of ethnically based groups, and their periods and places of confinement. Individuals from the underground economy were often recruited as informants by the police and the security police while they were under investigation and in confinement. These ties which existed between the criminals and members of the law enforcement and security community have resurfaced in the present environment. They are sometimes exploited by the former law enforcement personnel who now prey on the businessmen who operate on a large scale in the post-Soviet era.

The prison subculture is crucial to an understanding of the political-criminal nexus. Sentences in the Soviet period were so lengthy, the ties that developed in prison equaled or often surpassed those with family members. They became part of a criminal subculture (*urka*). Increasingly, as the Soviet period progressed, this subculture had high political ties.

Analysis of the political-criminal nexus is facilitated by the transnational nature of post-Soviet organized crime which allows wiretapping of conversations across borders. This permits members of various intelligence communities to do this analysis, but such information is not available outside this closed community. The trial of Ivankov, a thief-in-law, recently convicted in a federal case in New York revealed his criminal associations which dated back to his lengthy confinement in Siberian labor camps.[21] Wiretaps on his telephone, however, also identified links to high-ranking present-day government officials. A visiting high-level Russian law enforcement delegation was informed of these wiretaps by a high-level official in the FBI. As a member of the delegation reported at a conference in Moscow, the conversations stopped even before the delegation returned to Moscow. This revealed that the political-criminal nexus operated continuously and the criminals received information from law enforcement even while they were traveling in the United States.[22]

Studies of elites and their associates are another way of approaching the topic. Kryshtanovskaia's research on Russia's elite led her to the study of organized crime. This study was not intended as a study of the criminal world but as she has explained, analysis of the elites led inevitably to their links with the criminal world. The KGB lost 50 percent of its personnel in Moscow and these individuals acquired positions in the banking sector, as executives of the independent security services and some acquired key positions in privatized heavy industry.[23] Studying the social patterns and associations of members of the political and economic elite resulted in a detailed analysis of the political-criminal nexus.[24] Other work to map the elite clans also focuses on the fruits of the corruption.[25]

Historical Background: Origins

The relationships between the political and economic elites and crime groups have deep roots in Soviet society. The literature on the corruption of the Soviet state focuses on the post-World War II period and the rise of a consumer culture in Russia. But the origins of the political-criminal nexus go back much farther in Soviet history and are tied to a much darker period of Soviet history.

In the revolutionary period, the Bolsheviks used released offenders for their own objectives. Links by the Soviet state to the criminal culture were enhanced in the 1930s. The absorption of the criminal subculture into the state bureaucracy began in the 1930s as criminal elements and homeless youth (*bezprizorniki*) were brought into the security apparatus as enforcers by the state. In addition, long-term links were established between state officials and criminals as the professional criminal class became the enforcers for government officials in the massive system of labor camps. Large numbers of criminals were sent to the labor camps where they helped maintain order. The literature of former political prisoners such as Solzhenitsyn reveals much of the close relationships that existed between the brutal professional criminals and the labor camp administration which teamed up against the politicals.[26] These ties between the criminals and the authorities subsequently provided for further links among other officials, the criminals and law enforcement personnel who were often the conduits.

When the criminal underworld and the homeless youth became enforcers for the state, it expanded the Soviets' capacity to intimidate and eliminate enemies. They were able to coopt violence outside the state, thereby increasing the state's monopoly on violence. This kept the political-criminal nexus contained within state structures during the Soviet era.

The nexus between the criminal world and officialdom evolved over the seventy years of the Soviet period. While Ministry of Interior officials estimate that as little as 3 percent of the professional criminal class survived the Stalinist labor camp system, the thieves-in-law, the elite of the criminal underworld, reconstituted themselves in the post-World War II period.[27] Increasingly, these individuals performed the dirty work for state law enforcers. Unlike in the Stalinist period, they generally remained outside of state structures contributing to the rise of the political-criminal nexus.

Throughout the Soviet period, state interests were supreme over those of the citizen. During the Stalinist period, many remained committed to Bolshevik ideals. After the revelations of the Khrushchev era, commitment to state ideology declined. Many leaders of the USSR, disillusioned with the state ideology, increasingly viewed the state less as an abstract ideal but instead as concrete institutions which could provide them tangible benefits. Although they were only managers rather than owners of state property, they used their

influence over state resources to amass wealth. The possibilities for enrichment increased as the shadow economy grew to satisfy consumer demands
unmet by the state.[28]

The shadow economy involved politicians from the local, regional and
national level. It joined the traders and entrepreneurs of the second economy
with the law enforcers meant to circumscribe their behavior. This curious
alliance had to bribe members of the party apparatus who had oversight over
the justice system and the centrally planned Soviet economy. Prosecutions,
however, were frequently of the business people rather than their official
associates.[29] The pervasive circumvention of legal norms associated with the
shadow economy, undermined the already limited respect for law within the
Soviet state.[30]

Managers of the Soviet economy were also active participants in the second economy as they siphoned off state resources to establish private factories, trade in consumer items and provide a small service sector. These were
highly organized schemes in which goods were diverted by managers to the
black market in conjunction with the drivers, guards of the warehouses and
other employees.[31] The crime groups running these operations often existed
for several years until they were disrupted by authorities.[32] Criminals exploited their knowledge of economic abuse by party officials to establish
mutually beneficial relationships. Party member's behavior was often indis-
tinguishable from the criminals who demanded tribute.

The political-criminal nexus provided many advantages for its participants on both sides. The advantages of this relationship differed during various Soviet periods. For example, during much of the Soviet period, political
connections provided criminals less harsh treatment by the then very brutal
criminal justice system. Because so-called "telephone justice" was a central
element of the criminal justice system, a call from a highly placed official
could be essential in halting an investigation or leading to favorable treatment by the courts.[33]

The illicit behavior was not without risk. Corrupt officials could be sanc-
tioned by the Party, a more frequently applied tool than penal measures.
These penalties provided a limited deterrent for many officials. In Azerbaidzhan
in the early 1980s, then Party Secretary Aliev closed the law schools to the
offspring of law enforcement personnel because their ties to the shadow
economy were making them a financial elite.[34] Draconian penal measures
were infrequently applied to members of the state apparatus although several
labor camps, as previously mentioned, existed throughout the USSR to house
law enforcement officials convicted of abuse of their positions.

Many economic trials of the 1960s and 1970s revealed the varieties of
illicit business activity.[35] Lengthy labor camp sentences were meted out to
the managers and entrepreneurs who were tried. Minority members— Caucasians, Central Asians, and Jews—peoples with long histories as traders, were

the most frequent scapegoats in these prosecutions of underground business. Theft from the state was punished more severely under the socialist system than theft from private citizens. Members of the second economy consequently served long terms in labor camps along with thieves-in-law and other professional criminals. Confined in the same camps for years on end, they developed close ties enduring to the present.

During the Brezhnev years, the prison and labor camp population totaled at least one and a half million individuals.[36] Sentences were long and many lost touch with their families. The criminal ties that developed often became more important than the familial.[37] For this reason it is hard to speak of a crime problem confined to Russia or Ukraine because the criminals' ties stretch across the whole former Soviet Union. The ties that formed between the ordinary criminals, the trade sector who, in turn, were linked to the *nomenklatura* (the party elite) have emerged in the post-Soviet period as the contemporary political-criminal nexus.

The Brezhnev period saw a rapid rise in the political-criminal nexus with the crony politics he epitomized. As previously mentioned, the Ministry of Interior was corrupted at the top. The minister, a close friend of Brezhnev and the vice-minister, his son-in-law, had lucrative links with many crime groups. After Brezhnev's death, his son-in-law, Yuri Churbanov, was sentenced to many years of confinement, following his conviction for accepting large-scale payments from the Central Asian mafia. The nine-month trial closely followed by the mass media highlighted the links between governmental officials and crime groups in Central Asia. The former minister of interior, Nikolai Shchelokov, a close friend of Brezhnev's and Churbanov's superior, escaped conviction only through suicide.[38]

The Churbanov trial was only the tip of the iceberg. The political-criminal nexus had expanded significantly during the Brezhnev period because there was little deterrence. The risks associated with corruption and criminality declined. There were a few visible investigations carried out by the security police, the KGB, in the mid-1960s to the late 1970s, exposing the relationships between the underworld and the ruling elite in several Soviet republics. The prosecuted cases were far from Moscow and did not affect the central government leadership.[39] Apart from these, there was little effort by law enforcers such as the Ministry of Interior or the Procuracy to break the ever-strengthening ties among the political elite, the underground economy, and the underworld.

The ultimate costs of this political-criminal nexus became apparent only in the final years of the Soviet period when the vast wealth of the Soviet state was finally privatized. As one popular news account reported, "The old bureaucrats dominate much of the privatization process, for example, often deciding who gets what at what price."[40] As one of the leaders of the privatization process, Yegor Gaidar noted, the *nomenklatura* (party elite) "acted gropingly, step by step exploring what it could get away with, not in accordance with a well-considered plan, but obeying a deep instinct. It followed the scent of property as a predator pursues its prey."[41] In Russia, corrupt links were noted in many regions between governmental officials and territorial committees to promote privatization.[42] The source of the capital for privatized enterprises often came from "shadow economy activity—speculation, racketeering, extortion, looting."[43]

The establishment of cooperatives in the late 1980s allowed wealth to be laundered into businesses.[44] The strict controls on the establishment of cooperatives meant that officials could control who was able to move their wealth into the legitimate arena. Often these cooperatives permitted officials to set up their relatives in business. But it also fostered the political-criminal nexus by permitting select criminals to move into legal businesses. They subsequently owed a debt to the officials who allowed them to establish these businesses. The criminals also thrived by having new structures on which to prey.

The political-criminal nexus permitted both the officials and the criminal world to acquire the privatizing property. State officials lacked the financial means to buy the privatizing property because in the Party system their privileges were based on access rather than actual sums of money. Bribes and pay-offs helped officials acquire the assets they would need to acquire the new wealth. Party funds gave Komosomol and Party officials the assets to establish banks and acquire further assets. Former members of the security police assumed an especially critical role in the banking sector. Their links with the shadow economy and the criminal world gave them the money to buy the apartments, cars and to establish the businesses and the front companies which have become such a central aspect of the acquisition of wealth in the post-Soviet period.[45]

The members of the shadow economy and criminal world, through their associations with the managerial and Party elite, were able to secure part of the state property that was open for redistribution. Often the new business class served as the intermediaries between the politicians and the law enforcement community which had ties with the criminal world. These links with government officials existed in such crucial sectors as banking, transport, construction and the system of distribution of consumer goods.[46]

Government officials who were privatizing the state's mineral and other natural resources needed to transport these goods to ports and other destinations. Organized crime helped organize the shipment of goods and their delivery in an insecure environment where these valuable loads could easily be hijacked. They also helped enforce the contracts to supply raw materials and distribute raw materials and finished goods. Their role of enforcers of contracts has resulted in parallels being drawn to the Sicilian mafia.[47]

The political-criminal nexus developed because there were mutual advantages. It allowed both the criminals to have access to state property and to deliver these goods to markets. Both groups chose to export most of their capital overseas rather than to reinvest it within the successor states.[48] The process of mass transfer of capital overseas accelerated after 1987 when export licenses began to be awarded on a large scale to politicians and leaders of crime groups. This was particularly pronounced in mineral rich regions where local and regional leaders licensed exports in exchange for significant payments and other benefits.[49]

By the end of the 1980s, *Pravda*, the official government newspaper, was reporting that organized crime and corruption were being fused in the arena of socialist entrepreneurship. The means by which socialist entrepreneurship facilitated this development, the creation of commercial entities and joint ventures both with companies inside the USSR and with partners abroad allowed illicit relationships to be legitimized.[50] There was a reshaping of traditional alliances from relationships based on power to those based on money and access to state resources.

Andropov, Brezhnev's successor in 1982, attacked the political-criminal nexus vigorously. Almost as soon as Andropov became Party secretary, he attacked corruption at high levels prosecuting individuals who had been spared because of their high-level connections. His attacks on corruption ended prematurely with his death in 1983 and some have speculated that this stopped a series of show trials in the corruption area.[51] Chernenko, in his brief period in office, did not pursue the investigations initiated under Andropov; he was tied too closely to Brezhnev's old guard.

Gorbachev was more focused on opening up the society than prosecuting abuses. Russian data for the decade from 1986 to 1996 show a marked decline in the registered number of offenses for embezzlement by officials (33 percent decline), bribery (17 percent decline) and misuse of official position (33 percent decline). While the reports of crimes declined, the actions taken against offenders declined even more appreciably. Those sentenced for the crime of official embezzlement declined ten times. Whereas in 1986, 26,507 persons were convicted of this offense, in 1994 the number was 2,747. Convictions for bribery went down three times in the same time period.[52]

In contrast to the law enforcement apparatus, the journalists of the perestroika era did much to expose the pervasive corruption and criminalization of the economy. The Party system which gave rise to the political-criminal nexus was to be transformed. Gorbachev did not feel there was a need to clean house before reform was initiated. The system was exposed but not eliminated leaving a dangerous legacy for successor states. The political-criminal nexus had, in part, supplanted the state. It created a variety of tangible and intangible benefits for its participants. The acquisition of money was central. Some of this money was to increase influence by buying newspapers and influencing election campaigns. But some of this was money for money's sake, stored offshore in safe havens. The money was laundered outside of Russia and Ukraine by the criminalized banking sector, multiplying the effects of the political-criminal nexus.

The nexus increased the physical insecurity of both the business and the entrepreneurial elites. The relationships developed between the criminals and the political elite helped eliminate political threats, as seen in the killing of legislators, as well as business competitors. The privatization of law enforcement personnel and of organized criminals, often in the same private security firms, helped enhance the personal security of criminals, businessmen and politicians. These same privatized police organizations could also be used for blackmail, extortion and physical intimidation.

The funding of election campaigns gave the criminals power over the politicians. This gave them an immunity from prosecution. But even more important, the ability to shape legislation in the transitional period. Unlike in many societies, the criminals did not have to neutralize the enforcement of the laws. Instead, they only needed to ensure that laws and oversight mechanisms were not adopted. The political-criminal nexus, therefore, distorted the development of democratic institutions and a free market economy.

Russia and Ukraine: Points of Similarity

With the collapse of the Soviet Union, both Ukraine and Russia inherited the Soviet legacy of a political-criminal nexus. The nexus endures because there has not been lustration, the removal of former government or Party officials in Russia or Ukraine. Government officials of the Soviet period enjoy an even more economically privileged position in the successor states because as property is redistributed in these countries without conflict of interest laws or laws to stem corruption, key officials in the national and regional bureaucracies benefit enormously.[53]

The corruption of governmental officials in both countries is extremely serious, according to World Bank research. Surveys in these countries reveal that government credibility is lower than in any other region of the world surveyed. This widespread corruption contributes to weakness of the rule of law and undermines the predictability of the judicial process.[54] The corruption undermines the certainty of business transactions making businesses vulnerable to exploitation by organized criminals. Ukrainians believe that their country has a more severe problem with corruption than Russia and other successor states.[55]

Electoral and Legislative Processes

The political-criminal nexus in Ukraine and Russia has several important similarities. It has a major impact on the electoral and legislative processes by sponsoring candidates for Parliament and pressuring individuals within the legislatures to develop policies that serve their interests. The criminalization of legislatures is a problem both at the national and at the regional level. There is also serious concern that the nexus permeates the highest reaches of power in the administrative branches of government.

Former Ukrainian Prime Minister Lazarenko reportedly made tens of millions annually through his company's license to import natural gas and oil.[56] He is now a member of Parliament and the leader of the Hromoda movement. In December 1998, he was arrested by Swiss authorities for money laundering and was subsequently released on multimillion dollar bail. The Swiss seized bank documents and tens of millions of dollars following repeated inquiries from Ukrainian authorities. The prosecutor-general has accused Mr. Lazarenko of receiving kickbacks to provide private companies the right to exploit Ukraine's natural gas.[57]

Prime Minister Chernomyrdin in Russia, according to intelligence sources, has accumulated millions abroad from the privatization of Gazprom, the Russian gas industry.[58] These industries are backed by their own private security forces which have close ties to the security apparatus, the police and the military and often as well to the criminal world. The largest are attached to the banking and oil and gas industries.[59]

Officials in both Russia and Ukraine aid their long-term associates from the shadow economy with whom they are inextricably linked in complex financial relationships. Sometimes this assistance is not financial but protects them from the application of the criminal law. For example, in the summer of 1997, Russian Minister of Justice Yakovlev was forced to resign after videos of him were released by the Ministry of Interior revealing him in a bath house of the Solntsevo crime group with several prostitutes.[60] Pressure for his resignation was strong because many felt his indiscretion made it impossible for him to apply the rule of law with objectivity.

This link is common because as a leading Russian sociologist has explained, the criminal world established informal contacts with politicians. This is done through their traditional meeting places such as tennis courts, bath houses, tennis courts, sanatoria, and summer houses. Criminals and politicians can easily meet in sports clubs where they both naturally gravitate.[61] Yeltsin's sports trainer and sport associates have figured in high level corruption.[62] The National Sports Fund under their command was investigated for depriving the state of millions of dollars while failing to provide services to the citizenry. The quantity of money resulted in violence and links to the criminal world.[63]

The link of crime and sports makes it hardly surprising that many crime bosses head sports clubs that are frequented by politicians and their associates. The associations developed here are often translated into support for election campaigns or for the pursuit of particular interests by the legislature.

In both countries, the legislative process is undermined by the political-criminal nexus. This is particularly crucial in these two transitional societies which need to pass the legal frameworks to develop and regulate a market economy. According to the Ukrainian security service, forty-four people with various degrees of criminal activity have already been elected to local political bodies.[64] Penetration also existed at the ministerial level according to Ukrainian President Kravchuk already in 1993.[65]

In October 1995, Russian Interior Minister Kulikov reported that the MVD had assembled a list of eighty-five individuals with criminal records running for Parliament.[66] President Yeltsin's representative in Novosibirsk declared in late 1997 that criminal elements were competing for seats in the Novosibirsk Oblast Soviet. He asserted that he could document these charges with documents.[67]

A national parliamentary deputy, Yevchen Scherban, one of the richest men in Ukraine was killed in 1996. His death was linked by many to his association with Donetsk governor Volodomyr Shcherban who had made the region's industrial sector one of the most privatized in Ukraine.[68]

In Russia, the impact of criminals on the politicians and the political process is evident from a variety of sources. A procurator general of a major Russian region was pressured to release a serious organized crime figure after a visit from the executive assistant of a member of the Duma, a noted economic reformer. Immediately after his election, he sent his representative because the politician's campaign had been supported financially by the crime group and they had also helped deliver the vote.

One of the members of the Duma's powerful Committee on State Security has twice been incarcerated for serious offenses, according to an advisor to the committee. Neither of his offenses were linked to the shadow economy but instead were crimes characteristic of members of the criminal world. Records kept by the Ministry of Interior of his incarceration have disappeared and requests to solicit his court record have been deflected.

In both Russia and Ukraine, individuals pursue parliamentary careers because this gives them an immunity from prosecution. Politicians are very reluctant to lift their colleagues' immunity even when confronted with overwhelming evidence of their criminality. This was the case with Mavrodi, the head of the pyramid scheme MMM, who defrauded millions of citizens in 1994 and 1995 in a gigantic pyramid scheme.[69] He subsequently resisted many attempts within the Russian Duma to deprive him of his parliamentary immunity.

The legislative corruption exists not only on the national level in Russia. The links exist not only with regional and local legislative bodies but can stretch across the entire country. This was recently shown when a member of the Moscow City Duma established many links with crime elements in Sakhalin, the Russian Far East, a region with a highly criminalized economy.

The highly respected reporter from the Far East who documented these ties commented that individuals hardly differentiate the criminals from the politicians.[70]

Political-Criminal Nexus Overseas

Links with politicians are being established by Russian organized crime groups overseas as they replicate their domestic practices in other countries. A 900-page investigation by the Italian government revealed the links established by a Russian crime boss residing outside Rome with former members of the Italian security service and the former director of one of Italy's largest state-owned companies.[71] The deputy director of the Italian police in hearings before the U.S. Congress confirmed the serious nature of the links being established in Italy by Russian crime figures.[72]

In Israel, top Russian mafiosi are having contacts with government officials and have been accused of financing campaigns of candidates for the Knesset, Parliament, in the 1996 elections. As one Israeli analyst explains, the groups "have representatives in Israel who make connections with Israeli businessmen, lawyers, and local and national politicians."[73]

Patterns of Exchange: Economic Relations

The unique aspects of the political-criminal nexus in Russia and Ukraine is the possibility of obtaining enormous financial assets in this transitional period. Unlike in other societies, where the majority of property already is in private hands, in Russia and Ukraine, almost all property was collectively held. The benefits for the political-criminal nexus was not only the receipt of funds but the control of the privatization process and dominance over the banking sector and emerging financial markets.

Privatization

Privatization has allowed for the enrichment of the nomenklatura of the Soviet era who have moved from being directors of enterprises to owners of enterprises they once controlled. Privatization does not simply mean that individuals acquire goods in an orderly distribution of state property. The criminal-political nexus is central to the manner in which property is redistributed. Much of the property is acquired by combining access to information or goods with use or threat of force by crime groups.

The Russian minister of interior in early 1998 commented that state officials who participated in the privatization process accounted for a large part of the 30,000 crimes that were recorded in this area. As he stated, "The state's property transformation process into other kinds of property turned out to be the center of the criminals' interests." Significant economic damage, according to Kulikov, was inflicted when the criminal structures and corrupted officials merged. At present, in Russia, those who acquired property in this illicit manner are now trying to legalize their property and penetrate state power structures.[74]

Ukraine has faced this problem most acutely in former centers of Party power in Donetsk and Dneprpetrovsk where conflicts over the redistribution of property have led to numerous contract killings.[75] Official privatization of the economy of Ukraine has proceeded more slowly on the official level than in Russia. But government officials and crimes groups have appropriated significant state resources often exporting their ill-gotten gains overseas. The illicit privatization has occurred in mineral rich regions of Ukraine, at military bases in factories and in cities with valuable real estate.[76] Blatant legal violations by the Ukraine State Property Fund were detected. Symbolic sums were paid for valuable state property and the funds gained from these sales were misused.[77] The same process and problems occurred in Russia.

In Ukraine, major conflicts have occurred over shares in the gas and metal-lurgy monopolies. Shcherban's killing is tied to the conflict among Donetsk, Dneprpetrovsk, and Moscow groups for parts of these privatizing enterprises.[78] It is these lucrative state resources and franchises that have seen the most abuse in the privatization process.

In Russia, organized crime groups used intelligence, false documents and violent tactics to acquire controlling blocks in fifty-three firms in St. Petersburg and Murmansk. Bureaucrats and bankers were bought off. The personnel of the mafia boss would show up at a firm, state they were distributing humanitarian aid and obtain the addresses of retirees. The retired employees would then be intimidated or given a small sum of money and their shares would go to the crime group. The heads of personnel departments of the firm, either through bribes or threats, would be forced to provide the lists of employees. The same tactics were used with them as with retirees. Management was offered special deals or, if intractable, were intimidated. Registration of these business transactions went on with the knowledge and acquiescence of governmental officials.[79]

Both countries have done little to solve the contract killings or stem the violence accompanying the property redistribution. This impunity has contributed to a sense of frustration among the citizenry and made the new propertied class feel extremely vulnerable as numerous bankers in both societies have been killed.

Banking and Financial Markets

The political-criminal nexus is strongest in the banking sector in both Russia and Ukraine. State funds flow through banks enriching the bankers and the crime groups that control or extort money from the banks. The criminalized banking sector provides many opportunities for money laundering by both domestic organized crime groups and foreign groups which choose to move their money through banks in Russia and Ukraine. The large number of casinos and exchange bureaus facilitate large-scale money laundering by drug traffickers and others.

The lack of regulations in the financial markets leaves them wide open to abuse by crime groups. While exchange booths in Russia keep records of all transactions, those exchanging money have to provide limited documentation or identification for the transaction. Registration of banks in Russia has been enhanced to guard against infiltration by organized crime groups, but the law enforcement investigators do not have access to the bank records which they need to conduct appropriate investigations.[80]

Inspection of the banking sector in major Ukrainian cities by the office of the Attorney General disclosed numerous violations in the credit sphere and in the work of the banking officials. Even more disturbing was the absence of the necessary response by the Ukraine National Bank.[81]

Banks in Russia and Ukraine are an important source of information for criminal groups on the profitability and assets of certain businesses. Because of the porousness of information in the banking sector, individuals are afraid to keep large sums of money in financial institutions. Employees of banks will sell or provide information to organized crime groups who will then use this information to extort money from businesses. Information concerning clients' bank accounts can also be sold by the criminals to the tax police who then use this information to their advantage. Crime groups use their ties with tax authorities to extort money from businesses who find it more advantageous to pay the crime groups rather than the exorbitant tax rates. Tax officials, paid off by crime figures, also share information they have with crime groups. These groups then extort money from businesses.

The problems in the banking sector exacerbate the problems of capital flight. They not only facilitate the departure of illicit capital but the lack of security of the banking industry means that major institutions and investors do not choose to keep their money in domestic financial institutions.

In Russia, the capital flight, at least partially explained by the political-criminal nexus is estimated at between $50 and $150 billion since 1991.[82] In Ukraine, capital flight attributable in part to the growth of corruption and organized crime, is estimated by one top Ukrainian specialist to be $15 to $20 billion since 1992.[83] Although the Ukrainian figure is substantially below that for Russia, it represents a similar share of the national exports on a proportional basis.[84] As in Russia, much of the capital flight is attributable to the political-criminal nexus exploiting the licensing process for the export of raw materials.

Foreign Investment

The political-criminal nexus is affecting foreign investment. Publicly traded companies in the United States have an obligation to disclose notable problems with their partners, particularly when they have a role in management.

Corruption and insider privatization have contributed to the departure of major multinational corporations from Ukraine. In spring 1997, American companies planning to invest nearly $1 billion in Ukraine withdrew, asserting that they could not function in the corrupted environment. This situation is jeopardizing extensive American aid to Ukraine. Ukraine, presently the third largest U.S. aid recipient, needs both financial investment and aid to be a viable country.

Western companies trying to enter the Ukrainian market are discovering that they must often turn to local partners with close ties to the government whose own histories are often sullied. A recent example of this is the alliance between Ronald Lauder, a former United States ambassador, and Vadim Rabinovitch, who was imprisoned for economic crime for nine years during the Soviet period. The deal concerns Ambassador Lauder's Central European Media Enterprises which used Mr. Rabinovitch to establish ties with a Ukrainian studio. A license was issued for the deal despite the interest of other companies in bidding and an existing moratorium issued by Parliament.[85]

Motorola recently announced its plans to withdraw from Ukraine, canceling a planned investment of $500 million. The Motorola announcement followed the Ukrainian government decision to award a license for mobile phones to Kyiv Star whose owners include an adviser to President Kuchma, a cabinet minister and a Ukrainian with links to organized crime.[86]

Hearings before the American Congress in April 1997 revealed that these were not isolated incidences. As one foreign investor in the telecommunications commented, "Some of us have reason to be very concerned about our safety in Ukraine. As a result of Ukraine's treatment of foreign investors, the nation's total foreign investment after nearly six years of independence is a paltry $1.4 billion—in a country with 52 million citizens that is the largest country in Europe after Russia."[87]

In Russia, the political-criminal nexus is also a deterrent to investment. American investors such as the Subway sandwich shop have had to pull out when their partners appropriated their investment. The Americans withdrew only after threats of force. But the government in St. Petersburg refused to act. While this is one of the most visible cases, it is hardly unique. The problems of defending foreigners' financial interests in court is made more difficult because there are links between crime groups and high-level governmental officials in law enforcement bodies.[88]

The political-criminal nexus impedes the investment of honest foreign capital but encourages the entry of capital of dubious origins. One of the most noted cases of this in Russia is that of the "Aluminum Mafia" linked to former First Vice Premier Oleg Soskovets. Soskovets, in partnership with the Cherny brothers, Russian emigres with links to organized crime, promised foreign currency to keep the financially pressed Aluminum industry solvent. Instead of the much needed capital, a subsequent Ministry of Interior investigation revealed, "billions in 'wooden notes' of dubious origin flowed into the accounts of the plants. And the main thing is that a significant part of the payments was performed by falsified telegraph bank payment authorizations."[89]

Divergence in Russian and Ukraine Political-Criminal Nexus

Although many manifestations of the political-criminal nexus were similar in the two societies there was gradual differentiation in the two countries. The legal and economic consequences of the political-criminal nexus are not as devastating in Russia as in Ukraine.

Large-scale foreign investors have withdrawn from Ukraine and others have hesitated to invest following the destructive experience of their predecessors. The standard of living in Russia, despite the presence of the political-criminal nexus and the August 1998 bank collapse, is still higher than in Ukraine. Citizens in both countries believe that crime and corruption are out of control and undermining the political and economic transformation. There is possibly an even greater sense of hopelessness in Ukraine than in Russia.

The factors accounting for the differentiation can be explained by (1) the pace and extent of privatization, (2) the institutional capacity to address the problem, (3) the extent of civil society and citizen mobilization, and (4) the extent of foreign pressure. Institutional factors have more explanatory value than personal characteristics of individual politicians.

Pace and Extent of Privatization

Russia privatized more rapidly. Ukraine has still not privatized much of its propert, but in the absence of formal privatization there has been an unofficial privatization by officials of valuable state resources that has occurred with much violence perpetrated by crime groups. Licenses have been awarded to favorites in both societies permitting a drain on the economy. In Ukraine, foreign competitors seeking licenses have been threatened with violence and have subsequently withdrawn.

Institutional Capacity

The institutional capacity to address the political-criminal nexus in Ukraine is limited. Russia inherited the organized crime specialists and the specialized bodies to address the problem from the Soviet state. A literature exists to train practitioners, necessary legislation has been adopted, and more international contacts exist for those engaged in law enforcement in Russia.

In contrast, Ukraine became an independent state with almost no expertise in this area and is only now slowly building the capacity to address the problem. Conflicts within the legislature and systemic corruption have impeded the development of the legal framework needed to address the most serious threat to the state. In Russia, the legal framework needed to fight the crimes of a market economy is now in place, whereas in Ukraine, the legislature has not been able to adopt any of the necessary laws in either the criminal area or in the commercial area needed to protect emergent property rights.

Neither society, however, lacks adequate law enforcement nor a sufficiently independent judiciary to deter the influence of organized crime. Russia, however, has a much larger and better financed system of training for its police and prosecutors than Ukraine which has limited institutional capacity to improve the qualifications of existing personnel. With even more limited financial resources than Russia, it can do little to prepare its personnel for new requirements or to prevent the pervasive corruption that results from the severe underpayment of personnel.

Civil Society

Civil society is still in its incipient stages in Russia, but there are hundreds of groups throughout the country that are functioning. Many of these, according to the vice-chair of the Moscow Helsinki Group, are beginning to report issues of corruption and are raising challenges in court.[90] In Ukraine, civil society is much less developed. Furthermore, the population's much more limited resources and the years of repression of Ukrainian society and culture have made it very hard for nongovernmental organizations to take root in society. Although it is hard to say that civil society has mobilized in either country, Russians have much more possibility to organize on a particular issue than their counterparts in Ukraine. The possibilities that they may try and confront the political-criminal nexus are higher because Russia's nongovernmental organizations are better financed, its citizens more highly mobilized and they have access to a more developed media.

Ukrainians still need to build the state and nonstate institutions that would give them the capacity to mobilize. Although significant foreign assistance is now being offered to develop civil society in Ukraine, the years of repression during the Soviet period have made it harder for citizens to assert their rights. The even more precarious situation of the citizenry makes it difficult for them to donate the time needed to develop the institutions of civil society.

Foreign Pressure

Intense pressure is presently being applied by the United States on Ukraine to address the political-criminal nexus. The United States is not making such direct statements to the Russian government. The differential political status of the two countries is certainly affecting the tactics taken by the American government. Likewise foreign investors in Ukraine are more ready to challenge the political-criminal nexus in Ukraine where they hesitate to do this in Russia because they want to be in such a potentially lucrative market for the long haul. The possible long-term benefits of access to Russian markets make them accept a situation that is intolerable in the less financially advantageous Ukrainian environment.

While the political pressure might force the Ukrainians to take decisive action, Ukrainians lack the institutional capacity to respond positively. The assistance programs that have been provided focus on economic development rather than the legal safeguards needed to protect the process or to create institutional and civil capacity to address the nexus. Assistance in the organized crime area has been slow in coming and is not coordinated by the United States and with other donor countries. The net result of this external pressure is that organized crime is a very delicate political issue in Ukraine yet few tangible steps have been taken to address the problem.

The divergence in the political-criminal nexus in Russia and Ukraine is already apparent. The coming years will see even more of a differentiation as state development proceeds along different lines in the two countries. Russian authorities, while still short in concrete measures, have gone far in comprehending the costs of the political-criminal nexus. That level of awareness has not yet been achieved in Ukraine. This different consciousness may prove decisive in the coming years.

Vulnerabilities of Political-Criminal Nexus

The political-criminal nexi which exist in the major successor states such as Russia and Ukraine show little vulnerability at the present time. The corruption runs to the top of the political leadership. There is very little incentive to change the existing system for the long-term benefit of the state The idea that individuals' interests should be subordinated to the long-term interests of the state is a concept that is alien to most citizens and leaders of Russia and Ukraine.

Despite this pessimistic assessment, the political-criminal nexus is presently more vulnerable than it was in the Soviet period because the political system is more open. While there are not open and fair elections, the control over the electoral process is not as complete as when the Communist Party was in complete control. Therefore, there are more possibilities for changes in political leadership at the national, regional and local levels. The strong showing of Lebed in the Russian elections who campaigned against the corruption and organized crime is evidence that many are ready to vote for individuals who challenge the political-criminal nexus.

An even more powerful illustration of the impact of the democratic process on the abilities of the political-criminal nexus to operate occurred with the Yeltsin reelection campaign. A new Criminal Code could not be adopted for years in Russia because elements of the political-criminal nexus fought the adoption of a law that would criminalize the economic activities so central to the political-criminal nexus. Russia remained for years without the criminal laws needed to protect a market economy from criminal activity. Only in the final weeks before the election, President Yeltsin announced on national television that he was signing the Criminal Code. This decision, opposed by many corrupt legislators and presidential advisors, reveals the recognition that political realities limit the ability to steal from the state. Since its adoption, the new Criminal Code has provided a limited check on the political-criminal nexus. The absence of a new Criminal Code in Ukraine has contributed to the even more serious situation in Ukraine.

The political-criminal nexus may become more vulnerable in the future if greater financial transparency is incorporated into the financial system. The World Bank and the International Monetary Fund are placing intense pressure on the financial systems of Russia and Ukraine to open up their banks, financial institutions, and emerging markets to more domestic and external scrutiny. While much of this pressure has been successfully resisted, the costs of this resistance have been clear in the delay of financial payments by international institutions and the failure to receive foreign investment.

Integration into the international financial community requires a greater openness in the financial system. The costs of the absence of this transparency has been made apparent with the Asian financial crisis of 1997. While the world tolerated economic corruption and crony capitalism in countries with high economic growth rates, there is much less tolerance in countries with limited growth and an inability to deliver on their contracts with foreign partners. The scrutiny provided to financial partners with criminal pasts as was the case with Central European Media Enterprises in Ukraine, mentioned earlier, reflects the impact that outside financial monitors can have on the political-criminal nexus.

Part of the Russian press is outspoken and ready to expose problems of the political-criminal nexus. The acquisition of the mass media by the oligarches and the controls placed on the regional press by the local political officials means that the press cannot be as vigilant in exposing corruption as it was in the Gorbachev era. Often journalists are hired by one political-criminal nexus to expose another. While this does not root out the total problem, it ensures that the political-criminal nexus is not entirely invulnerable to exposure.

The process of cultural change and a demand for good government will take a long time to develop. While foreign assistance is pouring millions into the development of civil society, this is still a rather superficial phenomenon in Russian society and a very undeveloped force in Ukraine. As civil society develops there can also be a demand for greater accountability by government officials. Some of this is already being seen in some regions of Russia; it is not yet apparent on any scale in Ukraine.

Government and Private Sector Techniques in Identifying Vulnerabilities

With international financial and political support for the Russian and Ukrainian governments, there is the possibility of placing high-level pressure on the politicians to disrupt the political-criminal nexus identified by intelligence and through reports of the international business community. There is little at the moment domestically to make the political-criminal nexus vulnerable in either of these countries.

The political-criminal nexus may be disrupted by attacking the core of the problem, the Russian and Ukrainian banking communities. This is particularly problematic in Russia where the banking oligarchies have achieved control over large sectors of Russia's natural resources and have branched into many other parts of the economy. While criticism came from the powerful Minister of Interior Kulikov, who also served as deputy prime minister, his capacity to address these structures was limited as have been those of the attorney general The legal system is still subordinate to the president and there is no independent rule of law operating within Russia.

Pressure on the banking community can be provided by the international community, but there has been a tendency to exclude the Russians rather to demand certain performance standards. The Ukrainians that lack the resources to expand internationally in the international financial community are exclusively subjected to pressures domestically. Precious little has been done to address either the criminalization of banking or privatization increasing the invulnerability of the political-criminal nexus.

The domestic legal system may be used to point out the financial and human costs of the political-criminal nexus. Yet the court systems in both Russia and Ukraine are still at a weak state and limited resources are available for those to defend their financial interests. Cases of abuse by the political-criminal nexus in Russia referred to the attorney general have been largely left unprosecuted. In the Ukraine, the powers of the Accounting Chamber have been so limited that their ability to probe the political-criminal nexus is limited.[91] Nongovernmental organizations in Russia have taken a few cases to court to contest illegal privatization as a consequence of the political-criminal nexus, but these are isolated and have not had a wider impact on the society. The possibilities of recourse in Ukraine are even more limited because of the absence of civil society.

Research centers that expand understanding of the political-criminal nexus may help facilitate the development of strategies to address the problem. While this research may expand the capacity to assess the problem, the connections of the participants in the nexus on the local, regional, and national levels makes them invulnerable. This information may, however, be useful as the political-criminal nexus expands internationally.

The political-criminal nexus is most vulnerable overseas. The coordination of international law enforcement working groups and intelligence information sharing on participants in the political-criminal nexus operating outside of Russian and Ukraine may allow some action to be taken. Such measures are essential because so much of the assets of these networks are now located in offshore havens and major banking centers.

Conclusion

The political-criminal nexus that emerged in the post-Soviet period represents a transformation of the relationships that existed in the Soviet period. The division of the property of the Soviet state gave ample possibilities for the political-criminal nexus to obtain significant political assets. They were able to transform their power from one that was rooted in the managerial apparatus of the Soviet state and the consumer economy into one with international dimensions and control of very large shares of the domestic economy.

The rise of the political-criminal nexus, while hardly surprising in light of the structure of power relations in the final decades of the Soviet period, precludes full democratization or the rise of a real market economy. In the initial years of the transformation process from a socialist to a post-socialist economy, insufficient attention was paid to the containment of the political-criminal nexus in both Russia and Ukraine. Most Western politicians and international organizations focused on the collapse of communism rather than the rise of these pernicious alternative power relationships.

The prognosis for the containment of the political-criminal nexus in either country is rather limited at the moment. Ukraine, however, is at a comparative disadvantage because it has failed to sufficiently acknowledge the high costs of organized crime and its political links. This has been done at the highest levels of Russian government although precious little has been done to address the problem.

The Ukraine situation is more difficult because its institutional resources are much more limited than those of Russia: the latter inherited a disproportionate share of the Soviet Union's financial and institutional resources. With limited civil society and the economic precariousness of much of the population, little can be done to control the problem at its roots.

The political-criminal nexus in Russia and Ukraine will remain a serious problem in coming decades. It cannot be ignored in appraising the development of the domestic political situation in either country or determining foreign policy in relation to these two newly independent states.

Appendix

A research study presently under way by the Irkutsk Organized Crime Study Center reveals that this more open era also permits scholars to investigate the political-criminal nexus in creative ways. Outside of Irkutsk is a 500-person labor camp, used to punish former law enforcement officials sentenced for bribe taking and abuse of their positions. Because the sentences for such crimes are generally short, there are few inmates now incarcerated who were tried during the Soviet era. The former deputy minister of interior, Brezhnev's son-in-law, was freed from this camp in the early 1990s.

One of the objectives of the research is to determine why these individuals in particular were caught when many others managed to evade prosecution for their criminal links. Inmates are now being surveyed on their contacts with the criminal population. The lengthy questionnaire asks how these contacts were established, how did they change over time and what led to them being disrupted. Individual interview sessions with inmates will follow if this initial phase produces results. This will help determine the biases of the sample and why these individuals became vulnerable to prosecution.

The other organized crime study centers are eager to pursue similar research in the other two such camps in Russia if Irkutsk's pilot study is successful. This will give a fuller picture of the regional differences in the phenomenon. A previous study on the psychological motivations of the imprisoned former law enforcement personnel in the same camp netted valuable results and the researchers are guardedly optimistic that this study will also yield information not available in other ways.

Notes

1. Matt Bivens and Jonas Bernstein, "Corruption and Its Cost in Russia and Ukraine," *Demokratizatsiya* 6, no. 4 (fall 1998): 613-647.
2. Daniel Rosenblum, "'They Pretend to Pay Us...':The Wage Arrears Crisis in Post-Soviet States," *Demokratizatsiya* 5, no. 2 (spring 1997): 298-311.
3. European Union Conference on "The Mutual Impact of and Measures aimed at Combating Organized Crime Within the European Union and the Russian Federation," Helsinki, 4-5 December 1996.
4. Joseph R. Blasi, Maya Kroumova, and Douglas Kruse, *Kremlin Capitalism: Privatizing the Russian Economy* (Ithaca, NY: Cornell University Press, 1997), 13-49.

5. Janine Wedel, "Clique-Run Organizations and U.S. Economic Aid: An Institutional Analysis," *Demokratizatsiya* 4, no. 4 (fall 1996): 571-602; J. Michael Waller, "'Delay, Postpone, Obfuscate, Derail': A Case Study of U.S. Government Response to Criticism of Assistance Programs in Russia," *Demokratizatsiya* 5, no. 1 (winter 1997): 102-104; "Author's Rebuttal to the Department of State," *Demokratizatsiya* 5, no. 1 (winter 1997): 115-142.
6. David Hoffman, "Powerful Few Rule Russian Mass Media," *Washington Post*, 31 March 1997, sec. 1A, pp. 1,18.
7. Donald D. Barry, ed., *Toward the Rule of Law in Russia? Political and Legal Reform in the Transition Period* (Armonk, NY: M. E. Sharpe, 1992).
8. Harold J. Berman, "The Rule of Law and Law-Based State (Rechtsstaat),with Special Reference to the Soviet Union" in *Toward the Rule of Law in Russia? Political and Legal Reform in the Transition Period*, ed. Donald D. Barry (Armonk, NY: M. E. Sharpe, 1992), 43-60.
9. Robert Putnam, *Making Democracy Work: Civil Traditions in Modern Italy* (Princeton, NJ: Princeton University Press, 1995). He identifies northern Italy as a region with a highly developed civil society and the south, where all organized crime groups have developed, as a region with a low level of civil society and citizen participation.
10. Yuri Feofanov and Donald D. Barry, *Politics and Justice in Russia: Major Trials of the Post-Stalin Era* (Armonk, NY: M. E. Sharpe, 1996), 3-14.
11. Louise I. Shelley, *Lawyers in Soviet Work Life* (New Brunswick, NJ: Rutgers University Press, 1984), 142-150.
12. Robert Sharlet, "The Communist Party and the Administration of Justice in the USSR," in *Soviet Law after Stalin*, Part 3, ed. Donald B. Barry, F. J. M. Feldbrugge, George Ginsburgs, and Peter B. Maggs, (Alphen aan den Rijn, Netherlands: Sijthoff and Noordhoff, 1979), 321-392.
13. The arbitrariness of the process is reflected in the trials discussed by Feofanov and Barry.
14. See, for example, F. J. M. Feldbrugge, "Government and Shadow Economy in the Soviet Union," *Soviet Studies* 36 (October 1984): 528-43; Gregory Grossman, "The 'Second Economy' of the USSR," *Problems of Communism* 26 (September-October 1977): 25-40 and Aron Katsenelinboigen, "Coloured Markets in the Soviet Union," *Soviet Studies* 29 (January 1977): 62-85.
15. Konstantin Simis, *The Corrupt Society* (New York: Simon and Schuster, 1982), 55.
16. Maria Los, ed., *The Second Economy in Socialist Countries* (London: Macmillan, 1990).
17. Maria Los, "'Virtual Property' and Post-Communist Globalization" *Demokratizatsiya* 6, no. 1 (winter 1998), 83.
18. Maria Los, "From Underground to Legitimacy: The Normative Dilemmas of Post-Communist Marketization," in *Privatization and Entrepreneurship in Post-Socialist Countries: Economy, Law and Society*, ed. Bruno Dallago and Bruno Grancelli (London: St. Martin's Press, 1992), 120.
19. Ibid., 121-2.
20. Arkady Vaksberg, *Soviet Mafia* (New York: St. Martin's Press, 1991), 66-7, 124-33.
21. See Aleksandr Grant, *Protsess Iaponchika* (Moscow, Act, 1996), 326-490 for a discussion of his trial.
22. Comment by a member of the law enforcement delegation at a conference at Moscow State University in fall 1996.

23. "Mafia's Growing Power Detailed by Sociologist," *Current Digest of the Post-Soviet Press*, XLVII (18 October 1995): 1.
24. Ol'ga Kryshtanovskaia, "Illegal Structures in Russia," *Sociological Review* (July/August 1996): 60-80.
25. Virginie Coulloudon, "Elite Groups," *Demokratizatsiya* 6, no. 3 (summer 1998), 535-49.
26. Aleksandr Solzhenitsyn, *The Gulag Archipelago* vol. 1 (London: Collins Harvill, 1974).
27. V. I. Seliverstov, "Nekotorye voprosy preduprezhdeniia prestupnoi deiatel'nosti v mestakh lisheniia svobody," in *Aktual'nye problemy teorii i praktiki bor'by s organizovannoi pretupnost'iu v rossii* (Moscow: Moscow Institute MVD, 1994), 41-46.
28. See Dennis O'Hearn, "The Second Economy in Consumer Goods and Services in the USSR," National Council for Soviet and East European Research, Washington, DC, 1986, and Gregory Grossman, "Notes on the Illegal Private Economy and Corruption," in *Soviet Economy in a Time of Change* Vol. 1 (Washington, DC: U.S. Government Printing Office, 1979), 834-55.
29. V. Stashis and V. Tatsii, "Otvetsvennost' za chastno-predprinimatel'skuiu deiatel'nost," *Sovetskaia Iustitsiia* 20 (1978):19.
30. For a discussion of the roots of the phenomenon see V. V. Luneev, "Kriminologicheskaia kharakteristika organizovannoi prestupnosti v Rossii," in *Izuchenie organizovannoi prestupnosti: rossiisko-amerikanskii dialog*, ed. N. F. Kuznetsova, L. Shelley, and Iu. G. Kozlov (Moscow: Olimp, 1997), 33-48.
31. Maria Los, *Communist Ideology, Law and Crime A Comparative View of the USSR and Poland* (London: Macmillan, 1988), 180-204, discusses the crimes of managers and entrepreneurs.
32. Stanislaw Pomorski and George Ginsburgs, "Enforcement of Law and the Second Economy in the USSR," working paper of National Council for Soviet and East European Research, Washington, DC, 1986.
33. Valery Savitsky, "What Kind of Court and Procuracy," in *Toward the "Rule of Law" in Russia?: Political and Legal Reform in the Transition Period*, ed. Donald D. Barry (Armonk, NY: M. E. Sharpe, 1992), 377-84.
34. "Party or Mafia: The Plundered Republic," *USSR Report Political and Sociological Affairs Foreign Broadcast Information Service*, 4 April 1983.
35. Evgeniia Evel'son, *Sudebnye protsessy po ekonomicheskom delam v SSSR* (London: Overseas Publication Exchange, 1986).
36. Los, *Communist Ideology, Law and Crime*, 111.
37. Valery Chalidze, *Criminal Russia: Crime in the Soviet Union* (New York: Random House, 1977).
38. Louise I. Shelley, *Policing Soviet Society: The Evolution of State Control* (London and New York: Routledge, 1996), 50-53.
39. See Vaksberg, *Soviet Mafia*, 1-73.
40. Paul Khlebnikov, "Joe Stalin's Heirs," *Forbes*, 27 September, 1993, 124.
41. Yegor Gaidar, "How Nomenklatura Privatized Its Power," *Russian Politics and Law* 34 (January-February 1996): 35.
42. S. Ovchinskii, *Strategiia bor'by s mafiei* (Moscow: Sims, 1993), 79.
43. Svetlana Glinkina, "Privatizatsiya and Kriminalizatsiya," *Demokratizatsiya* 2, no. 3 (summer 1994): 386.
44. Anthony Jones and William Moskoff, *Ko-ops: The Rebirth of Entrepreneurship in the Soviet Union* (Bloomington: Indiana University Press, 1991).

45. See, for example, Glinkina, "Privatizatsiya and Kriminalizatsiya," 385-39; N. F. Kuznetsova, "Ob elitno-vlastnoi prestupnosti," in _Prestupnost':Strategiia bor'by_ ed. A. I. Dolgova (Moscow: Kriminologicheskaia Assotsiatsiia, 1997),164-69; Stephen Handelman, _Comrade Criminal: Russia's New Mafiya_ (New Haven, CT: Yale University Press, 1995), 101-114; J. Michael Waller and Victor J. Yasmann, "Russia's Great Criminal Revolution: The Role of the Security Services," _Journal of Contemporary Criminal Justice_ 11 (December 1995): 276-297.

46. Yuri Voronin, "The Emerging Criminal State: Economic and Political Aspects of Organized Crime in Russia," in _Russian Organized Crime: The New Threat?_, ed. Phil Williams (London: Frank Cass, 1997), 53-62.

47. Frederico Varese, "Is Sicily the Future of Russia? Private Protection and the Rise of the Russian Mafia," _Archives Europeenne de Sociologie_ 35 (1994): 224-258.

48.   Louise I. Shelley, "Stealing the Russian State," _Demokratizatsiya_ 5, no. 4 (fall 1997): 482-91.

49. Lynn D. Nelson and Irina U. Kuzes, "Interest Representation in Sverdlovsk and the Ascendancy of Regional Corporatism," _Demokratizatsiya_ 5, no. 2 (spring 1997): 222-239.

50. V. S. Ovchinskii, ed. _"Griaznye" den'gi i zakon_ (Moscow: Infra-M, 1994), 7-10.

51. Vaksberg, _Soviet Mafia,_ 67-70.

52. V. V. Luneev, _Prestupnost' XX veka_ (Moscow: Norma, 1997), 277-78.

53. "Kravchuk Interviewed on Combating Crime," _FBIS Daily Report_, 25 January 1993, 47-48.

54. Ukraine National Integrity Survey, _Citizens' Experiences of Public Service Quality, Integrity, and Corruption_ Washington, DC: World Bank, 1997, mimeographed, 2.

55. Ibid., 13.

56. Raymond Bonner, "Ukraine Staggers on Path to the Free Market," _New York Times_ 9 April 1997: sec. 1A, p. 3.

57. Charles Clover, "Swiss Investigate the Profits from Unaccountable Gas Trading," _Financial Times_, 9 December 1998: 2; Elizabeth Olson, "Ex-Soviets are Focus of Inquiry by the Swiss," _New York Times_, 20 December 1998: sec. 1A, p. 19.

58. For an allusion to this, see House Committee on International Relations, _The Threat from Russian Organized Crime_, 104th Congress, Second Session, 30 April 1996, 19.

59. "Mafia's Growing Power Detailed by Sociologist," _Current Digest of the Soviet Press_ XLVII, No. 38 (1995): 1 reports on Olga Kryshtanovskaya's research.

60. Igor Pankov, "Ministru Kovalevu prikhoditsiia otmyvat'siia," _Komsomolskaya Pravda_ 24 June 1997: p.2 and Elena Loriia and Elizaveta Maetnaia, "Ministr Kulikov gonit prostitutok s Tverskoi a ministr Kovalev vstrechaet ikh v bane," _Komsomolskaya Pravda_ 27 June 1997: 19.

61. "Mafia's Growing Power Detailed by Sociologist."

62. Their abuses are revealed in the book of Yeltsin's former bodyguard, Aleksandr Korzhakov, _Boris El'tsin: Ot rassveta do zakata_ (Moscow: Interbuk, 1997).

63. "Russia: National Sports Fund Intrigues Viewed," _FBIS Daily Report_, 1 October 1996, 60-68.

64. "Ukraine: Security Chief Warns of Local Mafia's Political Ambitions," _FBIS Daily Report_, 8 November 1996.

65. Graham Turbiville, "Organized Crime and the Russian Armed Forces," _Transnational Organized Crime_ 4 (winter 1995): 60, 94.

66. See Penny Morvant, "Criminals to Enter Parliament?" _OMRI Daily Digest_, 65, Part I, 5 April 1995; _OMRI Daily Digest_, 195, Part 1, 6 October 1995.

67. Konstantin Kanterev, "Presidential Representative Says Criminals Competing for Seats in Novosibirsk Legislature," article from *Novaia Sibir* reprinted in Institute for East West Studies (IEWS) Russian Regional Report Vol. 2, 40, 20 November 1997.

68. Oleg Varfolomeyev, "Businessman's Murder Impacts Ukrainian Politics," *Open Media Research Institute Analytical Briefs*, 462, vol. 1, 14 November 1996.

69. Blasi, Kroumova and Kruse, *Kremlin Capitalism*, p.145.

70. Boris Reznik, "Kriminal'nyi shleif sakhalinskogo shel'fa," *Izvestiia*, 14 May 1997: 5.

71. Massimo Lugli, "In trappola il padrino russo," *La Repubblica*, 18 March 1997: 10.

72. Statement of Dr. Giovanni De Gennaro before the House Committee on International Relations, *The Threat from International Organized Crime and Global Terrorism*," 105th Congress, First Session, 1 October 1997, p.16.

73. Menachem Amir, "Organized Crime in Israel," *Transnational Organized Crime* 2, no. 4 (winter 1996): 33-4.

74. Anatoly Kulikov, "Criminal Revolution or the Crime's Evolution," *Rossiskie Vesti,* 13 January 1998: 1-2.

75. "Ukraine: Interior Minister on Crime Situation," *FBIS Daily Report* 7 December 1995; Presentations at Organized Crime Conference sponsored by Rule of Law program, Kyiv, Ukraine, 17-18 March 1996.

76. Louise I. Shelley, "Privatization and Crime," *Journal of Contemporary Criminal Justice* 11 (1995): 244-56.

77. "Ukraine Prosecutor Views "Tense" Crime Situation, Activities," *FBIS Daily Report*, 13 November 1996.

78. Varfolomeyev, "Businessman's Murder Impacts Ukrainian Politics."

79. St. Petersburg Gangsters Push for Economic Power," *Current Digest of the Soviet Press*, XLV (1994): 14.

80. V. I. Popov, *Ob''ektno-strukturnyi analiz organizovannoi prestupnoi deiatel'nosti v sfere chastnykh investitsii* (Moscow: Moscow Institut MVD Rossii, 1997).

81. "Ukraine: Prosecutor Views 'Tense' Crime Situation, Activities."

82. See Louise I. Shelley, "The Price Tag of Russia's Organized Crime," *Transition* 8 (February 1997): 7-8.

83. Taras Kuzio, "Crime Still Ukraine's Greatest Enemy," Jane's Intelligence Review, 9 (January 1997): 10-13.

84. Central Intelligence Agency, *The Handbook of International Economic Statistics 1996,* Washington, DC, 1997.

85. Douglas Frantz and Raymond Bonner, "A Cosmetics Heir's Joint Venture is Tainted by Ukrainian's Past," *New York Times*, 5 April 1997: sec. 1A, p. 4.

86. Raymond Bonner, "Ukraine Staggers on Path to the Free Market," *The New York Times*, 9 April 1997: sec. 1A, p. 3.

87. Joseph Lemire, "Statement before the US House Committee on Appropriations, Subcommittee on Foreign Operations, Exporting Financing and Related Programs, Washington, DC, April, 24, 1997," reprinted in *Trends in Organized Crime* 3, no. 1 (fall 1997): 19-20.

88. See, for example, Igor' Korol'kov, "Razval," *Izvestiia* No. 97, 1997: 4.

89. "Russia: Soskovets: Aluminum Business Mafia Linked," *FBIS Daily Report*, 6 September 1997: 34.

90. Interview with Lev Ponomarev conducted in July 1997.

91. Clover, "Swiss Investigate the Profits from Unaccountable Ukrainian Gas Trading."

8

Minimizing Crime and Corruption in Hong Kong

T. Wing Lo

Hong Kong was a British Colony between 1842 and 1997. It was governed by a British-appointed governor and the Executive and Legislative Councils, two advisory bodies comprising official and appointed unofficial members for the majority of the time. The Executive Council was the cabinet of the governor while the Legislative Council's role resembled that of a parliament. The government was led by the governor, the chief secretary, the financial secretary, the attorney general and a group of secretaries in charge of various functions and tasks, such as economy, education, transport, security, health, and social welfare (see Figure 8.1.). The Judiciary, led by the chief justice, was independent from the central administration and legislature.

For the purposes of examining the political-criminal nexus here, distinctions are made among levels of office and of political influence. Some appointed officials, including appointed Executive Council members, and appointed or elected Legislative Council members, are treated as high-level politicians. Certain members of the Urban Council, Regional Council and District Boards may have been involved in organized crime. For instance, a report released by the Security Branch in 1993 suggested that more than 10 percent of candidates in the 1985 District Board elections had connections with Triad societies.[1] In the 1994 District Board election, a candidate involved in the "vote planting" scheme in Tai Po was discovered to have received help from Triad elements in the area.[2] However, since the influence of this group is limited to district and regional affairs, they are regarded as ower-level politicians, and thus excluded from our discussion.

Figure 8.1
A Simplified Structure of the Hong Kong government
(as at 30 June 1997)

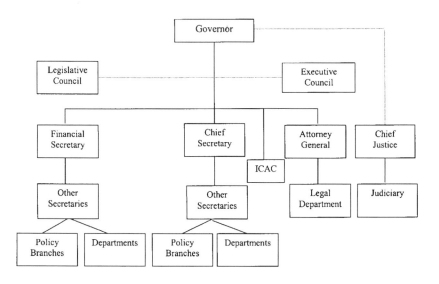

It is common practice in Hong Kong to define those civil servants employed at the master pay scale point forty-five or above as "senior government officials." The same would be true of officers with equivalent pay in the disciplinary forces. These officials are also entitled to the senior staff quarters provided by the government. They include:

Top Government Officials: The governor (chief executive of the Hong Kong Special Administrative Region after 30 June 1997), chief secretary, financial secretary, attorney general (secretary for Justice after 30 June 1997), and all other secretaries.

Judiciary: Chief justice, judges, and magistrates.

Policy Branches: All deputy secretaries, principal assistant secretaries, and assistant secretaries.

Government Departments: All directors, deputy directors, assistant directors, principal/chief officers, and staff of equivalent grades in the disciplinary forces.

In defining organized crime, discussion is not restricted to the crimes committed by Triad societies; other non-Triad-related organized crimes are also examined, if appropriate. Both forms of crime, however, share some of the following core elements: continual and self-perpetuating criminal conspiracy, goal of large financial gain, multiple criminal enterprises, involvement in legitimate businesses, violence, corruption, discipline, and limited vulnerability to prosecution.[3] Discussion here is based on crimes actually committed, and trials that have already taken place. Allegations that a crime has been committed do not meet the criteria of our samples.

Facilitating Factors for the Establishment of PCN

For the purposes of discussing the political-criminal nexus (PCN) in Hong Kong, there are two distinct phases in the historical development of the Colony. They are from the 1950s to early 1970s, and from the mid-1970s to the 1990s. The establishment of the Independent Commission Against Corruption in 1974 was a watershed. The political dynamics and social conditions differ significantly between these two stages, and the factors that facilitate or inhibit the development of PCN are quite unique also.

Phase 1 (1950s to early 1970s)

Autocratic Colonial Administration

In the postwar decades, the political structure of Hong Kong was that of an old-fashioned colonial autocracy, dominated by a small ruling minority. British nationals occupied virtually all the top official posts although they represented only 1 percent of the population. In 1947, there were only seven appointed unofficial members in the Legislative Council, and less than half of them were Chinese residents of Hong Kong. Calls for an enlarged legislature comprising elected Chinese members were turned down by the British in 1952. Thus, a small number of English-speaking people held complete power over a few million Chinese, 10 percent of whom could not even understand their rulers' language. Despite the unrepresentative political structure, the Colony still observed the British rule of law and maintained the kind of freedoms enjoyed in Britain.

The colonial government's primary concern was not social development, but economic growth. However, maintaining social stability was important to attract the capital and entrepreneurs necessary to compete with other Asian countries economically. Economic policy was based on the laissez-faire principle, and the government's role remained "one of providing a suitable framework within which commerce and industry can function efficiently and effectively with a minimum of interference."[4] Hong Kong was developed for the sole purpose of serving business interests, especially the interests of leading British companies, the *hongs*. It was said that the Colony was governed by the Jockey Club, Jardine and Matheson, the Hong Kong and Shanghai Bank, and the governor—in that order of importance,[5] since all the *taipans* (chief administrators) of the *hongs* residing in Hong Kong were either members of the Executive and Legislative Councils or Stewards of the Jockey Club.[6] The large number of British merchants and handful of rich Chinese appointed to the two Councils ensured that the interests of this dominant economic class were well represented in all political decisions. They could simply change or make laws to fulfill their own interests; it was unnecessary for them to violate the laws to meet their ends. At this stage high-level PCN was absent and unnecessary.

The business orientation, the undemocratic political structure, the language barrier, and cultural differences kept the British rulers out of touch with the majority of the Chinese people. Chinese civil servants of middle and lower ranks were entrusted with actually carrying out daily activities according to their policies. For instance, in 1961, the Colony was patrolled by an eight-thousand-strong police force. Ninety percent were Chinese and almost all the top fifty officers were British. The Colony relied heavily on this force to maintain law and order and to preserve stability and prosperity, both of which remain essential to Hong Kong's very survival. Similar situations existed in other government departments. This extreme centralization provided vast opportunities for Chinese civil servants to take advantage of their positions, including working with Triad members and other criminals for their own benefit.

A Refugee Population

Since 1945, thousands of refugees have fled to the Colony to escape civil war and communist rule on the mainland. In 1962, it was estimated that about one-third of the population of three and a half million were refugees who arrived in Hong Kong after the communist takeover in China.[7] Except for a very small number of merchants and industrialists, the majority of them arrived in the Colony with nothing but hope, and took almost any job they were offered. Unable to afford what an ordinary Briton would consider even minimum comforts, nonetheless they had to send food packets or money back to China every month to save their relatives from starvation. Even an old-fashioned colonial autocracy offered them more security, relative freedom, and a better material standard of living than their clan members in communist China. By comparison, Hong Kong was a paradise.[8]

After years of war and turmoil in China, the bulk of the population had lost all confidence in government. After escaping from communist rule, even those with money did not want to gamble with their lives in Hong Kong, itself a "borrowed place on borrowed time."[9] Most had no loyalty, no sense of belonging or responsibility to the community. Their ambition was to make money, enjoy life, and emigrate. On the other hand, the working class was exploited by both capitalists and public servants. Their upbringing in China where democracy and social justice remained strange political concepts had taught them not to criticize authority. This was reinforced by their negative experiences on the mainland: they had learned to stay out of trouble. The majority therefore had no stake in the system and no knowledge of their rights. Public servants on the other hand regarded their offices as businesses, and sought to maximize their incomes through illegitimate means.

Corruption: A Long-Standing Cultural Practice

In the postwar decades, corruption was commonplace. Bribery happened all the time among officials in China, and the people of Hong Kong had already become accustomed to it.[10] Although they had migrated to the Colony, they still accepted passively that all officials were corrupt. With little capital, they were unable to live up to Western standards of sanitation, hygiene, or construction regulations, and thus were subjected to extortion by public servants. Bribery became a form of taxation that they had to pay to survive.[11] As for the rich businessmen, they were only too happy to cut corners and speed things up to increase profits. Other corrupt practices, such as kickbacks and commissions, had been customary in business circles for decades. All parties involved were satisfied. Corruption became entrenched as an acceptable social norm in the community, paving the way for the development of the PCN.

Inhibiting Factors for the Development of PCN: Phase 2 (mid-1970s to 1990s)

The Rise of a New Generation and the Era of Reform

By the 1970s, Hong Kong's younger generation differed markedly in mentality and culture from their antecedents. Unlike their parents, these young people had none of their parents' negative experiences of China or governing authorities. They were born and brought up in the Colony with Westernizing influences from films, newspapers, youth subculture, and English education. To them, Hong Kong was no longer a haven of refugees, but their home. They had been molded into a generation whose liberal social values differed significantly from their parents' conservative attitudes. They had hope, ideals, and social consciousness, and most importantly, they wanted to have a stake in the system. Thus, they were more vulnerable to frustrations and more eager to speak out about injustice and inequality. This alone is a significant factor inhibiting the development of PCN.

In addition, the developments in Mainland China in the 1970s sparked off a social movement in the Colony. In the early stage of the Cultural Revolution, the leftists organized students to march through the streets of Hong

Kong shouting slogans. There were riots in 1967. Later, students participated actively in local affairs and organized community projects. A student movement under the title "recognizing our motherland, caring for our community" developed. It expanded in line with the encouraging events in China, such as the explosion of the first H-bomb, admission to the United Nations, and visits by U.S. President Nixon and Japanese Prime Minister Tanaka. The rising power of China in international politics awoke thousands of young people to their Chinese identity. They became fixated with the communist doctrines of self-reliance, impartiality, and incorruptibility, and thus began to accept the supremacy of socialism over colonialism.

The 1967 riots were followed by frequent challenges and counterchallenges between pro-government institutions and left-wing supporters centering around capitalist and communist ideologies. To demonstrate the supremacy of colonialism over socialism, the British administration was compelled to make changes. To capture popular support, the autocratic colonial rule had to be replaced by a liberal one. The government did not take public opinion seriously before 1967, but the riots brought home the importance of opening up more channels of communication. In 1974, Chinese was accepted as the second official language, and in 1975, the term "Colony" was replaced with "territory" in all official documents. The introduction of the City District Office scheme also served as a bridge between the rulers and the ruled.

As England observes, "never, in all Hong Kong's history, has there been such a rush of reforming legislation as followed the 1967 riots."[12] Social reforms were launched to accommodate people's needs. These included mass public housing projects, expansion of social welfare, compulsory education, community development programs, labor legislation, and anti-corruption and anti-crime campaigns.[13] The government also organized "Fight Crime Committees" at various districts to give advice or assist the police to combat Triad and other crime problems. The community of Hong Kong was united in its efforts to root out criminal elements.

The Formation of the ICAC and the Amnesty

In 1973, a scandal broke that was to have profound consequences. Peter Godber, a police chief superintendent, was discovered to have assets equal to six times his annual salary. Before he could be charged, he fled to Britain. He was the most senior government official to be investigated for corruption up to that point, and his flight caused an enormous public outcry. Young people marched on the streets to demand his extradition. The Anti-Corruption Bureau, then administered by the police force, lost public confidence. It was widely believed that the bureau could not work independently to investigate its own in such a corrupt force. This eventually led to the establishment of the Independent Commission Against Corruption (ICAC) in 1974.

In 1975, the ICAC took aim at corruption syndicates in the police force. Godber was extradited and found guilty. So were other expatriate officers. Chinese officers, too, had been targets of the ICAC investigation. This attention intensified discontent within police ranks and led to a demonstration by two thousand police officers in 1977. The ICAC headquarters was attacked and five officers were injured. The police rank and file was not satisfied with a reply from the commissioner of police to their petition, and threatened industrial action. A police strike would have left the city wide open to criminals and endangered social stability. The governor, Sir Murray MacLehose, was forced to grant amnesty: "In future the ICAC would not normally act on complaints or evidence relating to offenses committed before 1st January 1977, except in relation to persons who had already been interviewed (and allegations of an offense put to them), persons against whom warrants had been issued, and persons outside of Hong Kong on 5th November."[14] The phrase "not normally act" suggests that only offenses considered as heinous would be investigated, but that such cases would be rare.

As a result, the ICAC had to terminate eighty-three investigations.[15] Inevitably, this cast a shadow over the Colony's ability to control corruption. Not only did corrupt police officers escape punishment, but a large number of dishonest civil servants were protected from prosecution too. With the benefit of hindsight, this was not all bad. Although the corrupt had escaped punishment, the ICAC was freed from the burden of investigating past offenses and was able to concentrate their limited resources on monitoring the current situation. Its high profile campaign against corruption syndicates in the police force had created an atmosphere that discouraged further development of PCN. After the amnesty, corruption would no longer be a low-risk crime in the Colony.

The Rise of People's Power

The police corruption cases illustrate the power of the people, which had in fact been rising since the 1970s. The government had had to respond to public demands by forming an independent graft-fighting agency, having rejected similar proposals throughout the 1960s. This trend continued in the 1980s, and can be best illustrated by the defective housing scandal. It began in early 1980 when serious leaks were found in housing blocks at Kwai Fong Estate, built between 1971 and 1973, posing the possibility of substandard construction and corruption. Some residents were asked to move out so that maintenance programs could be carried out. They expressed their discontent at press conferences and meetings with the Housing Department. In 1984, some youth organizations and pressure groups discovered similar problems in seven other housing estates.[16]

The resulting publicity led to the formation of the Coalition on the Concern for Structural Safety of Public Housing. The Coalition organized open forums and petitions to the Housing Department and the Legislative Council. The mass media became involved. The Housing Department was charged with being bureaucratic, protecting the construction companies responsible, and causing severe distress and hardship to residents. The latter demanded reasonable compensation, re-housing, and an investigation into the scandal.

This activity eventually attracted the attention of some Legislative Council members. The Housing Department, after examining 940 housing complexes throughout the Colony, admitted that about half were defective and in need of substantial maintenance. The cost of repairs would be over HK$400 million.

There were allegations that bribes had been paid to allow substandard materials and inferior concrete to be used in the construction. The case was referred to the attorney general, but because the alleged offenses would have been committed fifteen years earlier, it was difficult to collect substantial evidence. At that time, the scandal aroused widespread public outrage. By April 1985, forty organizations, including religious and political groups, had already joined the Coalition to force the government to take action.[17] Finally, the attorney general announced that the amnesty notwithstanding, legal action would be taken against the construction companies concerned. This case illustrates how Hong Kong's citizens became more active, organized, and militant in articulating their rights, and thus exerted tremendous pressures on the government.

Development of Representative Government

For 143 years, Hong Kong had no elected politicians in its legislature. Before 1985, its members were either official or appointed members. This undemocratic political structure preserved a government led by the executive, with a legislature often regarded as a rubber-stamp. Power remained concentrated in the hands of the governor advised by a handpicked Executive Council, and assisted by a group of senior officials. During 1985 and 1988, in preparation for Hong Kong's return to China, indirect elections through various electoral colleges and functional constituencies, representing the legal, economic, and social sectors, were introduced to the Legislative Council. In 1991, direct elections in geographical constituencies were also held. Since then, the legislature has had an elected majority; among its sixty members in 1991 were three *ex-officio*, eighteen appointed, and thirty-nine elected members. In 1995, democratization was further enhanced, and there were no more official and appointed members in the Legislative Council.

Despite this democratization process, however, the governor could still command a majority through manipulation of the appointed unofficial members or other conservative members elected through functional constituencies or electoral colleges. This maneuver was important in view of the increasing number of liberal, directly elected members. It ensured that the laws drafted, budgets prepared, and other decisions made by the government would be passed. Thus, the executive-led government continued to function effectively in the last decade of colonial rule. Since real power was concentrated among senior officials, any attempt to influence government policies through bribes to politicians or funding their election campaigns in order to advance the interests of a specific syndicate might not necessarily succeed. However, the senior officials were under the surveillance of the ICAC.

Despite their lack of real power, the politicians have undertaken the scrutiny and control of the acts of the executive effectively. They also served as watchdogs over officials' conduct. In particular, directly elected members have been very critical of official misdeeds, often taking their case to the media. This vote-winning strategy constitutes a change in political dynamics and increases the checks and balances in the government. When the conduct of senior officials is subject to public scrutiny, their involvement in PCN becomes much less likely.

How Does the PCN Come into Existence and How is It Maintained?

To illustrate how the PCN develops and is maintained, a few important cases will be discussed, involving a chief police superintendent, an acting director of Building Development, a principal government building surveyor, a deputy director of Public Prosecution, a senior assistant director of the ICAC, and the head of the Prosecution, Intelligence and Investigation Bureau of the Customs and Excise Department. The criminals involved with these officials were Triad members, businessmen, and professionals.

The Police-Triad PCN

The Triad societies date back to the seventeenth century. Under the name of Hung Mun, their patriotic purpose was to overthrow the Ching Dynasty and to restore the Ming Dynasty in China. During the Japanese occupation of Hong Kong in the Second World War, Triads acted as Peace Aid Corps to assist the Japanese army to maintain law and order in the territory, and to locate anti-Japanese elements in Hong Kong.[18] In exchange, the Japanese allowed them to run vice, opium, and gambling dens.

After the Second World War, the conflict in mainland China between the Nationalist Government and the Communist Party intensified. In 1945, the Nationalist decided that "as large a proportion as possible of the population should now be drafted into the [Triad] Society to bind them, by oath and blood brotherhood, in defense of the Chinese (Nationalist) Government against foreign (Communist) invaders."[19] In 1949, the Communist Party won the civil war and the Nationalist Government fled to Taiwan. Many Nationalist supporters, including Triad members, escaped to Hong Kong to avoid persecution. Since then, Triad societies in the Colony have been reorganized, and the majority of them have become involved in crimes. In October 1956, a serious outbreak of crimes throughout the Colony alerted the colonial government to the need to eradicate Triad activities. About 600 Triad office bearers were deported to Taiwan or Mainland China and over 10,000 suspected members were detained.[20]

In 1960, there were about 200 Triads in Hong Kong, and the commissioner of police estimated that one-sixth of the Colony's 3 million population were Triad members.[21] It was alleged that many police officers in postwar Hong Kong were involved in the protection of prostitution, gambling, and bars, and that they worked hand-in-glove with gangsters and shared protection money.[22] Elliott, the noted "crusader for justice" suggested that the government permitted Triad racketeers to continue because it was "the easiest way to establish control in the Colony....To disturb the gangsters would upset the Police too and cause insecurity."[23] The Colony had long relied on the upholding of law and order to enhance its prosperity, stability, and capitalist mode of production. Any significant collapse of police morale would run the risk of surrendering the streets to opportunists and criminals and of jeopardizing business interests.

Elliott once commented: "British justice, of which we once imagined we were so proud, seems here to operate in reverse: very often its application is only a matter of...the extent of your worldly wealth."[24] Her statement was echoed by the notorious drug syndicate boss, Ng Sik-ho. In the trial of Lui Lok, one of the four most powerful detective staff sergeants, Ng confessed: "law did exist: police enforcing it did not...my money did."[25] With the assistance of intermediaries known as "rent collectors," Lui received money regularly from Ng's syndicate to protect his illegal business. Ng paid Lui HK$1,200 and HK$450 a day for his drug store and gambling business, respectively. In return, he received advance information about intended raids so that his followers could avoid being arrested, or if necessary, arrange for "opera actors" to be hired and arrested in their stead. Three other major syndicates that operated in different areas of Hong Kong also offered bribes to Lui. At one point, Lui insisted upon their combining their operations. He also received from Ng and other syndicates large sums of money approximately every other month after drug shipments arrived. Ng gave evidence that Lui "exercised considerable control over the operation of all these syndicates."[26]

A salient feature of police corruption in those days was the existence of an informal hierarchy in which middle-ranking Chinese officers, usually with a detective staff sergeant as the leader, were responsible for negotiations with criminal syndicates. Their direct supervisors, mostly expatriate officers, were paid modest sums each month for their acquiescence. Working within such a corrupt culture where the whole unit or even the whole station was "on the take," it was difficult for an expatriate officer to impose discipline. In the heyday of corruption, even a divisional superintendent, normally an expatriate, could be transferred if he was not sufficiently "cooperative."[27] This observation is confirmed in the trial of Peter Godber. After receiving a bribe from a Chinese officer, Cheng Hon-kuen, Godber used his influence to secure Cheng the post of divisional superintendent, Wanchai, where widespread vice and illegal activities generated a lucrative income. An expatriate officer, who had been promised the Wanchai post by his superior, "was surprised and chagrined when Cheng got it instead."[28] Thus, using their cultural advantages, operational roles, and direct access to the general public, the middle-ranking Chinese officers, not the senior expatriates, were able to organize the syndicates.

The Land/Housing Officials-Property Developers/Contractors PCN

Postwar growth in the Colony provided plenty of opportunity for corruption in the Public Works Department (PWD). The PCN that developed between property developers and corrupt officials in government departments was maintained through different forms of "give and take" relationships. In exchange for extravagant entertainment, free overseas trips, and bribes, the corrupt officials disclosed confidential information about land use, showed special favors to particular developers, and even turned a blind eye to faulty construction. The property developers and contractors not only got insider information, but bribery enabled them to get away with cheap or substandard materials. Work on job sites went ahead without interruption. This avoided cost overruns and increased their profit. In fact, the bribes were incorporated into their bids, usually as entertainment fees, and were added to the cost. As the defective housing scandal illustrates, their criminal behavior was especially heinous because of the negative impact on the thousands of residents affected.

Corruption payments to PWD officials were very common in the 1960s and 1970s. The ICAC noted that there was "an unhealthy degree of socializing between senior PWD staff and property developers and their representatives, during which the government servants were the recipients of lavish entertainment."[29] In the early 1980s, the ICAC was able to prosecute a number of middle-level officers and others for corruption. Two expatriate officers were convicted of soliciting free trips to Macau; an architect was convicted for providing a government official with paid trips to Las Vegas; and an expatriate senior geotechnical engineer in the PWD was found guilty of accepting a bribe in return for supplying documents about future government contracts to a commercial firm. The anti-corruption drive reached its climax when two senior officials (directorate grades) were convicted. In 1981, E. T. Kennard, a principal government building surveyor pleaded guilty to a Section 10 (Prevention of Bribery Ordinance) offence, "being in control of money or property disproportionate to his official compensation and allowances." In 1985, an acting director of the Building Development Department, Mok Wei-tak, was also found guilty of an offense under Section 10. The most senior government official ever to be convicted for corruption, Mok was found to have spent about HK$730,000 above his official compensation and allowances between November 1981 and November 1982.

The use of Section 10, under which the prosecution is not required to prove a corrupt act, suggests that while crimes and bribery at the middle-level of the hierarchy were comparatively easy to detect, they were far more difficult to uncover at the directorate level. However, the PCN involving housing officials and developers did exist in the top echelons of the government. Operating under strict secrecy, which provided a basis for security, mutual shielding, and protection, as well as solidarity against interference, the PCN had limited vulnerability to prosecution. Ultimately, that was not enough.

The Prosecutor-Lawyers-Businessmen PCN

In late 1989, a number of senior prosecutors in the Legal Department were under investigation for alleged corruption in connection with highly publicized commercial crimes. Eventually, Warwick Reid, a deputy director of Public Prosecution in charge of the Commercial Crime Unit, was charged with corruption. He surrendered his passport before being released on bail, but absconded two months later. In March 1990, Reid was arrested in Manila and pleaded guilty to a Section 10 offense. His total assets in March 1989 amounted to about HK$16 million, or about three and a half times his official compensation and allowances over fourteen years of service. The chief justice sentenced Reid to eight years in prison, adding that the chief executive of Hong Kong after 30 June 1997 might consider a sentence reduction of three years if Reid testified at trials against other syndicate members.

The investigation of other lawyers involved in the scandal continued. Kevin Egan, former senior assistant prosecutor, fought allegations that he gave his Australian passport and a gun to help Reid escape. In addition, Jim Chandler, a deputy Crown prosecutor, was forced out after failing to report that he had seen Reid in Manila after Reid had absconded. Similarly, Peter Cahill, a senior assistant prosecutor, faced a disciplinary hearing for not reporting a telephone request from Reid about the use of his passport while Reid was on the run. Cahill had refused. Outside the Legal Department, a solicitor, Alick Au, was charged with assisting Reid to escape with a fake passport. Two other lawyers in private practice, solicitor Oscar Lai and barrister Eddie Soh, were imprisoned for bribing Reid to fix seven cases involving well-known business figures. The initial set-up of the PCN took place when Reid and Soh, formerly a Crown Counsel, discussed how to profit from the stock market by buying the shares in a company that was under criminal investigation. Later the discussion evolved into a criminal conspiracy in which Reid agreed to accept money and use his position to influence prosecutions involving rich and prominent businessmen.

Reid's corrupt actions were diverse and profitable. In one case, he made a recommendation to the attorney general against prosecution of one of solicitor Oscar Lai's clients, Chuang, in exchange for a bribe of HK$3 million paid to Reid in three installments. After each payment, Lai met with Reid and told him how appreciative Chuang was. In another case, Reid persuaded the attorney general to drop one of the two charges of Lai's client, Lee. On the second charge, Lee was acquitted because the judge held that some of the evidence upon which the Crown prosecution was relying was inadmissible. This time the bribe was HK$6 million paid in two installments, one of which Reid collected from a building society owned by Lee in Singapore. Lai discussed representing another client, Low, who was told that Lee's case had been fixed in advance because the two lawyers had access to Crown papers and were close to the Crown.

Reid was offered HK$1 million by two lawyers to ensure that no charges would be brought against their client, Kwok. The case involved a police investigation into the financial affairs of a group of companies. Kwok paid the bribe money in the guise of legal fees to Lai's firm. Lai gave Soh the appropriate amount as a barrister's fee from which Reid was then paid. Acting in concert in another case, Lai and Soh suggested to a businessman, Chu, the need for "personal assistance" in his appeal against conviction. They asked for a fee of HK$800,000. Unknown to Chu, the Legal Department had already come to the conclusion that his conviction would be impossible to sustain. The two lawyers nonetheless duped Chu into paying the money to obtain a result that they knew, from Reid, was a foregone conclusion. The transaction was completed under the guise of legal fees.[30]

This PCN lasted for three years, from 1986 to 1989, when the ICAC cracked down. Collecting direct evidence against Reid sufficient to convict would have been difficult. However, the ICAC used the powerful Section 10 of the Prevention of Bribery Ordinance to prosecute him. Moreover, he agreed to testify as a tainted witness in other trials against his former PCN colleagues in return for a reduced sentence. All were eventually convicted.

The Connection between ICAC Officials and the Smuggling Syndicate

The ICAC itself has not proved immune to corruption. Legislative Council hearings on the firing of senior assistant director of ICAC, Alex Tsui, revealed the development of corrupt relationships over several years. Tsui had maintained a close association with some undesirable elements, such as Tin Sau-kwong, who ran the biggest cigarette smuggling ring in Hong Kong. Tin and Tsui had first worked together in the Customs and Excise Department in the early 1970s before Tsui joined the ICAC in 1974. A connection between the two came to light in 1986 with the discovery of a false loan application, which Tsui had made on Tin's behalf in 1978. During the inquiry that followed, Tsui told the ICAC that his friendship with Tin had already ended and his involvement was an "error of judgment." In 1988, Tsui was promoted to assistant director of operations.

In 1990, Tsui sought permission to reopen contact with Tin to obtain intelligence information. His request was granted, but he was required to open an informant's file in which their contacts would be recorded. Only four contacts were recorded, and none were documented after March 1991. In an interview with the director of Operations later, Tsui described Tin as a friend and not an informant, and he claimed that Tin had always been honest. The inquiry also revealed a connection between Tsui and another syndicate member, Hung Wing-wah. Immediately after Tsui opened an informant's file on Tin, another informant of Tsui disclosed that Hung and Tin were involved in cigarette smuggling. However, in a memo to the director of Operations, Tsui commended Hung's company and referred another two companies as suspects, thus diverting investigation away from Hung's company.[31]

Tsui was a boxing enthusiast and chairman of the Hong Kong Boxing Association in 1992. With his help, Tin became vice president, under an assumed name, Tin Hon-fai. Hung was made president. Hung paid HK$500,000 to sponsor a boxing event in 1992 through his company. Tsui failed to mention in the informant's file that Tin sponsored a boxing event in 1992, paying HK$160,000, nor did he record their visits to Macau and Singapore. In fact, Tsui and Tin traveled to Macau together hours after Tin had been interviewed by the ICAC about his association with a Triad-related shooting event. Tsui said that the trip was about boxing matters and denied that Tin had mentioned the interview. Since sponsorship of boxing events was neither corrupt nor criminal, no prosecution could be taken against Tsui due to insufficient evidence of criminality. However, he forfeited the confidence of the commissioner of the ICAC because of his prolonged association with members of the smuggling syndicate under conditions of secrecy and despite acknowledging the risks involved. Tsui was said to have taken advantage of his legal role to advance the relationship, using an informant relationship as cover but concealing the details.

After Tsui was dismissed, legal action was taken against the syndicate, which had offered bribes to customs officers as well as a senior staff member of British American Tobacco (HK) Ltd. Five ring members, including Tin, were charged. A former ring member and an ICAC tainted witness, Chui To-yan, who was also a vice president of the Boxing Association, was murdered. The ICAC suspected that the murder was ordered by Tin and carried out by five Wo On Lok Triad members. Tin was charged with conspiracy to murder Chui, cigarette smuggling, bribery, defrauding the government, and perverting the course of justice. He later pleaded guilty to a lesser charge of having conspired with the five Triad members to pervert the course of justice by interfering with Chui, and was sentenced to jail. Furthermore, one ring member was acquitted while another committed suicide prior to the trial. Other accomplices were convicted or were awaiting trial in 1998.[32]

Customs Official-Video Pirates PCN

Since the 1990s, pirated copies of compact discs have been flooding the Hong Kong and Mainland Chinese markets. This has proved very difficult to stop. In April 1998, in an operation against one of the largest criminal syndicates, the ICAC raided five factories with forty-one production lines capable of manufacturing about 1.2 million copies a day, and seized a few million pirated discs, a range of master discs, and production equipment worth about HK$650 million. It was the largest seizure to date in Hong Kong. The syndicate was running an illegal trade alongside a legal one under the name Science Technology Research Ltd. The charges included defrauding copyright owners; unlawfully copying sound recordings, films, electronic video games, and computer software; forging the trademarks of various films and computer software; and possessing video compact discs and CD-ROMs with forged trademarks for sale.

The involvement of the ICAC in this investigation was triggered by allegations that customs officers had accepted bribes and offered protection to the syndicate. Immediately before the ICAC operation, the head of the Prosecution, Intelligence and Investigation Bureau of the Customs and Excise Department, Superintendent Wong Pui-sum, was arrested. Wong was the most senior customs officer ever to be charged with corruption. The Customs and Excise Department had received information about criminal activities of the syndicate. After it was passed to the ICAC and the police, Wong was suspected of warning the syndicate of the impending raid, and was charged with perverting the course of justice. Wong was said to have developed his friendship with the syndicate leader during the course of his official duties, to have received a loan of HK$50,000 from him. After the failed raid, he attempted to delay repayment of the loan or to have it discharged. It was suspected that he had warned the syndicate about previous raids.[33]

Strategies for Preventing and Breaking the PCN

Strong Political Will

China always believed that Hong Kong was ceded to Britain under an unequal treaty, and the Colony faced the risk of takeover by the Maoists during the Cultural Revolution. Had that happened, the economic loss would have been enormous. The British *hongs* would have been deprived of the privileges of controlling the Executive and Legislative Councils, as well as the opportunities to make economic policies favorable to their own interests. The loss of Hong Kong's huge gold and foreign exchange reserves would also have hit the British economy hard. Between 1941 and 1974, Hong Kong was obliged to keep the reserves in sterling. In 1973, they represented a quarter of the total reserves held by the Bank of England, amounting to £736 million sterling.[34] Also, the loss of Hong Kong Airport, the last British owned airport in the region, would have adversely affected Britain's valuable air traffic negotiating powers with other nations.

The British also recognized that to maintain their economic interests, the younger generation would need to be co-opted into a disciplined labor force. The government had seen their potential to disrupt in the youth riots of 1967. That watershed had sensitized the British rulers and made them more responsive to social needs and more attentive to social problems. Eradicating bureaucratic corruption was part of the strategy. Since the Godber crisis there has been strong political determination to keep corruption under control, which, of course, would obstruct the development of PCN.

Powerful Anticorruption Ordinance

The government's political determination to combat graft is also manifested in powerful anti-corruption legislation. The infamous Section 10 of the Prevention of Bribery Ordinance prohibits public servants from having pecuniary resources, assets or property disproportionate to their present and past official compensation and allowances. Senior government officials such as Kennard, Mok, and Reid were prosecuted and convicted of Section 10 offenses. Once the director of prosecutions is able to prove that the value of suspect assets is disproportionate, defendants will be convicted unless they can prove the contrary. Most importantly, the assets of a suspect's close relatives are also assumed to have been under his/her control, which makes hiding of monetary gain even more difficult.

Because the ordinance places the burden of proof on the accused, it has been criticized as somewhat heavy-handed.[35] That is not the whole story. In the mid-1990s, Section 10 was challenged in the court as a violation of the Bill of Rights, but survived the challenge. The director of prosecution has to prove that the accused has maintained a standard of living beyond the means at their disposal. Only after this proof has been presented is the accused required to explain other sources of income to the court. Moreover, to safe-guard the rights of the suspects, they will first be informed of possible pros-ecution so that they can make representations in writing. Since corrupt practices normally involve two satisfied parties, this section has resolved the problems of identifying witnesses in relation to prosecutions.

The ICAC

Another inhibiting factor of PCN is the establishment of the ICAC in 1974. It has a staff establishment of over 1,200, making it one of the largest anti-corruption forces in the world. Supported by a powerful anti-corruption ordi-nance, the ICAC has enjoyed absolute independence, draconian powers of investigation, and has often made use of tainted witnesses to assist their prosecutions. The "three-pronged attack" is also a unique feature of its anti-graft approach.

Absolute Independence

The independence of ICAC is ensured by the fact that its commissioner is formally and directly responsible to the governor (the chief executive after 30 June 1997). Although the ICAC is fully financed by the government, the staff is not subject to the purview of the Public Services Commission. How-ever, its work comes under the close scrutiny of independent advisory com-mittees comprising prominent social figures from different segments of the community. Such independence is absolutely essential and necessary since it guarantees that any investigation of corruption in the government would not be interrupted or influenced by other bureaucratic or political forces.

Draconian Powers of Investigation

Before 1994, the ICAC enjoyed draconian powers of investigation which were criticized as infringing upon individual human rights.[36] These included the powers to search premises without a warrant, to seize any documents from passports to bank accounts, to forbid the mass media to disclose the identities of suspects, to disclose a suspect's identity before prosecution, and to detain anyone for up to three hours. After the dismissal of Alex Tsui, the governor appointed a Review Committee to examine the powers and accountability of the ICAC. The Committee recommended that some of the ICAC's former pow-ers be transferred to the courts and exercised by them on request by the ICAC. Since then, its power has been curbed.

Effective Use of Tainted Witnesses

Since all the parties involved in PCN should have benefited from it, it is difficult, in most cases, to find an eyewitness to prove the allegations of crime. The use of tainted witnesses thus becomes useful, as the trials of Godber and Reid's associates demonstrated. In these cases, the tainted witnesses were usually the members of the PCN ring who were granted immunity from prosecution or reduced sentences in exchange for their testimony.

Three-Pronged Attack

The ICAC uses a three-pronged attack strategy in its fight against corruption. There are three functional departments: Operations, Corruption Prevention, and Community Relations. The Operations Department, the largest of the three, is responsible for investigations. The Corruption Prevention Department examines the practices and procedures of government departments and public bodies to identify opportunities for corruption, and provides advice on how to eliminate them. Private organizations may also seek their advice. The Community Relations Department undertakes measures to enlist public support, educate the public about the effects of corruption, and monitors public attitudes towards corruption as well as community responses to the ICAC.

High Remuneration to Maintain Integrity

Senior officials are well paid for their work. As listed in April 1997, staff at directorate grades one to eight or equivalent received an annual salary of HK$1.1 million to HK$2.2 million plus other benefits such as children's educational allowance, free medical service, and government subsidized housing. Top colonial officials such as the chief secretary, financial secretary, chief justice and attorney general received even higher salaries. The British governor, who ruled a tiny city of some 6 million, was paid double the salary of the British prime minister, about HK$3 million per annum. Such high levels of reward are designed to increase resistance to the temptations that may be offered by organized criminal groups.

Declaration of Investment

In the 1990s, senior members of the directorate in the government and members of the Executive and Legislative Councils have been required to disclose their investments, including company directorship and real estate holdings. This information is made known to the public through the mass media, and is therefore subject to public scrutiny. These disclosures help ensure that politicians and senior officials do not use public office for personal gain. Any conflict between individual interest and public interest, if known, can be avoided. Such transparency would reveal financial connections with criminal gangs, if any; and if not, at least facilitate the "integrity checking" of senior officials conducted by the government. All this serves as a deterrent to the formation of PCN.

Integrity Checks

The government also undertakes integrity checks on senior officials. This was previously conducted by three bodies: "the ICAC has been assisting in the vetting process by checking candidates being considered for appointment or promotion to certain posts against its own records. The Police are responsible for criminal record checks and Special Branch [of the Government Secretariat] previously conducted the extended form of checking."[37] After the Special Branch was disbanded, the police began extended integrity checking. According to the secretary for Civil Service, these checks are conducted on senior civil servants at regular intervals, although not annually. Such reports will be sent to the Civil Service Branch as reference materials in the course of management, but the staff in question will not be informed of the findings.[38] Thus, with such double-checking mechanisms, the integrity of senior officials is assured.

In the hearings on Alex Tsui's dismissal, Tsui disclosed that he had been asked by the ICAC to pursue political scrutiny on senior government officials and pro-China political figures: "Investigations would be made to collect information including their secret and private personal activities and habits. The [target] list would eventually be extended to include political figures."[39] The ICAC was to gather information on the target about activities such as insider trading in the stock market, personal proclivities, and corruption.[40] Tsui's statement suggests an additional intelligence role of the ICAC, but the ICAC commissioner denied Tsui's allegations about political vetting. Whether or not the ICAC did political vetting of politicians, it does play an important role in the integrity checks on senior officials.

Immediate Dismissal of Unreliable Officials

The chief secretary, Mrs. Anson Chan, once declared that the conduct of senior officials should be exemplary because they are responsible for a range of essential policies that affect Hong Kong. "The Government demanded a high standard of personal integrity, absolute honesty and accountable behavior from senior civil servants."[41] Her statement is quite absolute; in fact, the government will not tolerate dishonest behavior from senior officials as the following cases have demonstrated.

In the mid-1990s, two senior officials were dismissed or forced to resign from their posts. As already discussed, the senior assistant director of ICAC, Alex Tsui, was dismissed after the commissioner lost confidence in him because of his association with smugglers. The director of Immigration, Lawrence Leung, was forced to tender his resignation after an ICAC investigation cast doubt on his integrity and credibility. Leung had connections with businessmen in several transactions, but he failed to declare some of them. This called into question his suitability to remain in a senior post. These two cases underline the strict standards maintained by the government for its senior officials. Those found to be dishonest are removed immediately. This inhibits the development of PCN at the top levels of government.

Scrutiny by the Mass Media

The 1990s has been an era of keen competition in the mass media; price wars have closed several newspapers. To survive journalists are paying far more attention to the private lives of public figures. As a result, government officials live something of a "fishbowl" existence. The case of Andrew Leung, director of Social Welfare, illustrates the media's role.

As welfare chief, Leung had pronounced payments of HK$12,000 per month for a family of four to be high. During the economic crisis of 1998, he had tried to push forward a cut in welfare payments to poor families. However, it was disclosed by the press that in the midst of the crisis, he had flown first-class to Tel Aviv via London for a welfare conference. The cost, HK$70,000, was about twice that of a direct flight to Israel. The misuse of public money, particularly his two-day stopover in England, aroused public anger. While Leung refused to comment on whether he had visited his sons there, he came under criticism by the media for abusing his position and power while being unsympathetic to the least privileged citizens of Hong Kong.

Under the civil service guidelines, senior directors are entitled to first-class travel for official trips of more than six hours. The secretary for Civil Service pointed out that as Leung did not start work immediately after leaving Hong Kong, he was not entitled to travel first-class, but since this was not clearly set out in the guidelines, Leung should be given "the benefit of the doubt." In his defense, Leung said that he had no "evil intention." Nevertheless, public discontent continued to mount. Media reports noted that it only took four hours to fly from England to Israel, thus Leung was not even entitled to travel first-class on his second journey. Under pressure, Leung eventually "volunteered" to pay back the difference between first class and business class, some HK$15,459, to pacify public discontent. [42] The incident indicates how the power of the mass media helps to maintain the transparency of the civil service, in particular the integrity of civil servants, in a territory without an elected governor (or chief executive after 30 June 1997) and legislature.

Table 8.1
Comparison of PCN

	1950s-Early 1970s	Mid 1970s-1990s
State Condition	Autocratic Colony; business-led government; weak citizenry	Open Colony; executive-led government; strong citizenry
Examples of PCN	Police - Triad PCN; Housing Officials-Property Developers PCN	Housing Officials - Property Developers PCN; Prosecutor - Lawyers - Businessmen PCN; ICAC official - Smuggling Ring connection; Customs official - Video pirates PCN
Seriousness of Problem	Overwhelming and widespread	Isolated Incidents
Organization	PCN with corruption syndicates in govern-ment; highly organized; close cooperation	PCN with corruption of individual officials in government; close linkage
Connection	Overt; face-to-face; use of intermediaries	Covert, personal frienship involved
Combat of PCN	Half-hearted	Very determined
Exchange	Money versus protection and administrative efficiency	Money versus protection, immunity, and administrative efficiency

In the postwar decades, Hong Kong was an autocratic colonial state in which a small elite of British businessmen and a few rich Chinese dominated. Their control of the Executive and Legislative Councils afforded them an advantageous position to make decisions to suit their own interests. As rulers, they were distant from the people, made up largely of newly arrived refugees from the Chinese mainland. In the absence of a democratic government, the elite ruled absolutely in the face of the people's submissiveness, ignorance, and indifference. In this unrepresentative political structure, civil servants were not accountable to the public. They had the power to manipulate their positions for private gain, whereas criminals used money in exchange for protection and administrative fixes. Organized crime and corruption were widespread. Groups were highly organized, and members of the PCN met face-to-face; their operations were assisted by intermediaries. Cooperation between criminals and officials was close and their connections overt. The police, many of whom were corrupt, were half-hearted in their investigations into these activities, whereas the people, accustomed to corruption in China, acquiesced in their own exploitation (see Table 8.1).

This changed in the 1970s, when a new generation began to push for a greater voice in affairs, at about the same time as the upheavals on the Mainland. The British administration was more responsive to social problems and launched a series of social reform. Since the 1980s, the development of representative government has made officials more accountable. Backed up by draconian powers and a heavy-handed anti-graft ordinance, the ICAC has been very determined and fairly successful in the fight against corruption associated with organized crime. The amnesty announced in 1977 allowed the ICAC to refocus its limited resources on investigating current offenses, making corruption a high-risk crime. The ICAC's absolute independence assures that government departments will not interfere with its investigation of corruption. The activities of corruption syndicates have also been kept under control, and those connections between corrupt officials and criminals that do exist have been driven underground.

Since the 1980s, Hong Kong has maintained an effective executive-led government. Power continues to reside with senior government officials rather than elected politicians. However, the government has been emphasizing its openness. A number of strategies have been employed to maintain the integrity of civil servants. The declaration of investments by politicians and senior officials increases the transparency of the government and avoids potential conflict of interest situations. Generous pay scales and benefits seem to have helped sustain the integrity of senior officials. The extended integrity checks and immediate dismissals of dishonest officials serve to maintain a clean government with a group of credible civil servants. Scrutiny by a competitive mass media reinforces all of the above. In these conditions, and with a zero tolerance policy by the government, a political-criminal nexus cannot be sustained in Hong Kong.

Notes

1. *ICAC Daily Press Review,* 26 and 27 June 1994, 1.
2. ICAC, *ICAC Operations Department Review 1996-97* (Hong Kong: Government Printer, 1997), 44.
3. Fight Crime Committee, *A Discussion Document on Options for Changes in the Law and in the Administration of the Law to Counter the Triad Problem* (Hong Kong: Government Printer, 1986), 6-7.
4. Hong Kong Government, *Hong Kong Yearbook 1975* (Hong Kong: Government Printer, 1975), 12.
5. Richard Hughes, *Hong Kong: Borrowed Place, Borrowed Time* (London: Deutsch, 1976).
6. C. N. Crisswell, *The Taipans: Hong Kong's Merchant Princes* (Hong Kong: Oxford University Press, 1981).
7. G. B. Endacott, *Government and People in Hong Kong 1841-1962* (Hong Kong: Hong Kong University Press, 1964).
8. Norman J. Miners, *The Government and Politics of Hong Kong* (Hong Kong: Oxford University Press, 1977).
9. Richard Hughes, *Hong Kong: Borrowed Place, Borrowed Time.*
10. See, for example, Henry J. Lethbridge, *Hong Kong: Stability and Change* (Hong Kong: Oxford University Press, 1978); and Rance P. L .Lee (ed.) *Corruption and Its Control in Hong Kong.* (Hong Kong: Chinese University Press, 1981).
11. Sir Alastair Blair-Kerr, *A Second Report of the Commission of Inquiry under Sir Alastair Blair-Kerr* (Hong Kong: Government Printer, 1973).
12. J. England, *Hong Kong: Britain's Responsibility* (London: Fabian Society, 1976), 29.
13. Hsin-chi Kuan, "Political Stability and Change in Hong Kong," in *Hong Kong: Economic, Social and Political Studies in Development,* ed. Lin, T. B., Lee, R. P .L., and Simons, U. E. (New York: M. E. Sharpe, 1979), 145-66.
14. *ICAC, Annual Report of the Independent Commission Against Corruption* (Hong Kong: Government Printer, 1977), 9.
15. Ibid.
16. SoCO, *Report on Structural Safety Issues in Public Housing and Kwai Fong Estate* (Hong Kong: Society for Community Organization, 1985).
17. Ibid.
18. W. P. Morgan, *Triad Societies in Hong Kong* (Hong Kong: Government Press, 1960), 72.
19. Ibid., 80.
20. Royal Hong Kong Police, "Triad Societies, General Briefing Paper," *Trends in Organized Crime,* Vol. 2, No. 2, (winter 1996): 29-32.
21. W. P. Morgan, *Triad Societies in Hong Kong,* ix.
22. G. Gleason, *Hong Kong* (London: Robert Hale, 1963).
23. Peter N. S. Lee, "The Causes and Effects of Police Corruption: A Case in Political Modernization," in *Corruption and Its Control in Hong Kong,* ed. Rance P. L. Lee (Hong Kong: Chinese University Press, 1981), 176.
24. Elsie Elliott, *The Avarice, Bureaucracy and Corruption in Hong Kong* (Hong Kong: Friends Commercial Printing, 1971), 2.
25. Hong Kong Law Reports Editorial Board, *Hong Kong Law Reports* (Hong Kong: Government Printer, 1984), 282.
26. Ibid., 282-3.

27. Tak-sing Cheung and Chong-chor Lau, "A Profile of Syndicate Corruption in the Police Force," in *Corruption and Its Control in Hong Kong*, ed. Rance P. L. Lee (Hong Kong: Chinese University Press, 1981), 199-221.

28. Hong Kong Law Reports Editorial Board, *Hong Kong Law Reports* (Hong Kong: Government Printer, 1975), 349.

29. *ICAC, Annual Report of the Independent Commission Against Corruption* (Hong Kong: Government Printer, 1980), 27.

30. See *R v Oscar Lai Ka-to & Lee Hoi-kwong* CA No.229 of 1992.

31. Legislative Council, *Enquiry into the Circumstances Surrounding the Termination of the Employment of Mr. Alex Tsui Ka-kit, former Senior Assistant Director of the ICAC, Volume I: Report* (Hong Kong: Government Printer, 1994).

32. ICAC, *ICAC Operations Department Review 1996-97* (Hong Kong: Government Printer, 1997).

33. At the end of 1998, Wong was still awaiting trial. For those interested, please refer to all major newspapers of Hong Kong on 28 April 1998 and 27 October 1998.

34. Norman J. Miners, The Government and Politics of Hong Kong (Hong Kong: Oxford University Press, 1995), 20.

35. Bernard Downey, "Combating corruption: The Hong Kong Solution," *Hong Kong Law Journal* (1976) 6(1), 27-66.

36. ICAC Review Committee, *Report of the ICAC Review Committee* (Hong Kong: Government Printer, 1994).

37. Ibid., 117.

38. Legislative Council, *Report of the Select Committee to Inquire into the Circumstances Surrounding the Departure of Mr. Leung Ming-yin from the Government and Related Issues, Volume I: Report and Minutes of Proceedings* (Hong Kong: Government Printer, 1997). Legislative Council, *Report of the Select Committee to Inquire into the Circumstances Surrounding the Departure of Mr. Leung Ming-yin from the Government and Related Issues, Volume II: Minutes of Evidence* (Hong Kong: Government Printer, 1997).

39. Legislative Council, *Enquiry into the Circumstances Surrounding the Termination of the Employment of Mr. Alex Tsui Ka-kit, former Senior Assistant Director of the ICAC, Volume I: Report* (Hong Kong: Government Printer, 1994), 12.

40. Legislative Council, *Enquiry into the Circumstances Surrounding the Termination of the Employment of Mr. Alex Tsui Ka-kit, former Senior Assistant Director of the ICAC, Volume II: Evidence and Verbatim Transcripts* (Hong Kong: Government Printer, 1994).

41. Legislative Council, *Report of the Select Committee to Inquire into the Circumstances Surrounding the Departure of Mr. LEUNG Ming-yin from the Government and Related Issues, Volume I: Report and Minutes of Proceedings* (Hong Kong: Government Printer, 1997), 14.

42. All major newspapers in Hong Kong reported Andrew Leung's case. See, for example, *South China Morning Post*, 25 November 1998.

References

Blair-Kerr, Alastair. *Second Report of the Commission of Inquiry under Sir Alastair Blair-Kerr.* Hong Kong: Government Printer, 1973.

Cheung, Tak-sing, and Lau, Chong-chor. "A Profile of Syndicate Corruption in the Police Force," in *Corruption and Its Control in Hong Kong*, ed. Rance P. L. Lee. Hong Kong: Chinese University Press, 1981.

Crisswell, C. N. *The Taipans: Hong Kong's Merchant Princes.* Hong Kong: Oxford University Press, 1981.

Downey, Bernard. "Combating Corruption: The Hong Kong Solution." *Hong Kong Law Journal* 6(1), (1976): 27-66.

Elliott, Elsie. *The Avarice, Bureaucracy and Corruption in Hong Kong.* Hong Kong: Friends Commercial Printing, 1971.

Endacott, G. B. *Government and People in Hong Kong 1841-1962.* Hong Kong: Hong Kong University Press, 1964.

England, J. *Hong Kong: Britain's Responsibility.* London: Fabian Society, 1976.

Fight Crime Committee. *A Discussion Document on Options for Changes in the Law and in the Administration of the Law to Counter the Triad Problem.* Hong Kong: Government Printer, 1986.

Gleason, G. *Hong Kong.* London: Robert Hale, 1963.

Hong Kong Government. *Hong Kong Yearbook 1975.* Hong Kong: Government Printer, 1975.

Hong Kong Law Reports Editorial Board. *Hong Kong Law Reports.* Hong Kong: Government Printer, 1975, 1984.

Hughes, R. *Hong Kong: Borrowed Place, Borrowed Time.* London: Deutsch, 1976.

ICAC. *Annual Report of the Independent Commission Against Corruption.* Hong Kong: Government Printer, 1977, 1980.

____. *ICAC Operations Department Review 1996-97.* Hong Kong: Government Printer, 1997.

ICAC Review Committee. *Report of the ICAC Review Committee.* Hong Kong: Government Printer, 1994.

Kuan, Hsin-chi. "Political Stability and Change in Hong Kong," in *Hong Kong: Economic, Social and Political Studies in Development,* ed. Lin T. B., Lee, R. P. L., and Simons, U. E. New York: M. E. Sharpe, 1979.

Lau, Chong-chor, and Lee, Rance P. L. "Bureaucratic Corruption and Political Instability in Nineteenth-Century China," in *Corruption and Its Control in Hong Kong,* ed. Rance P. L. Lee. Hong Kong: Chinese University Press, 1981.

Lee, Peter N. S. "The Causes and Effects of Police Corruption: A Case in Political Modernization," in *Corruption and Its Control in Hong Kong,* ed. Rance P. L. Lee. Hong Kong: Chinese University Press, 1981.

Lee, Rance P. L. (ed.). *Corruption and Its Control in Hong Kong.* Hong Kong: Chinese University Press, 1981.

Legislative Council. *Enquiry into the Circumstances Surrounding the Termination of the Employment of Mr. Alex TSUI Ka-kit, former Senior Assistant Director of the ICAC, Volume I: Report.* Hong Kong: Government Printer, 1994.

____. *Enquiry into the Circumstances Surrounding the Termination of the Employment of Mr. Alex TSUI Ka-kit, former Senior Assistant Director of the ICAC, Volume II: Evidence and Verbatim Transcripts.* Hong Kong: Government Printer, 1994.

____. *Report of the Select Committee to Inquire into the Circumstances Surrounding the Departure of Mr. LEUNG Ming-yin from the Government and Related Issues, Volume I: Report and Minutes of Proceedings.* Hong Kong: Government Printer, 1997.

____. *Report of the Select Committee to Inquire into the Circumstances Surrounding the Departure of Mr. LEUNG Ming-yin from the Government and Related Issues, Volume II: Minutes of Evidence.* Hong Kong: Government Printer, 1997.

Lethbridge, Henry J. *Hong Kong: Stability and Change.* Hong Kong: Oxford University Press, 1978.

Miners, Norman J. *The Government and Politics of Hong Kong*. Hong Kong: Oxford University Press, 1977, 1986, and 1995.

Morgan, W. P. *Triad Societies in Hong Kong*. Hong Kong: Government Press, 1960.

Royal Hong Kong Police. "Triad Societies, General Briefing Paper." *Trends in Organized Crime,* Vol. 2, No. 2 (Winter 1996): 29-32.

SoCO. *Report on Structural Safety Issues in Public Housing and Kwai Fong Estate*. Hong Kong: Society for Community Organization, 1985.

9

Black Gold Politics: Organized Crime, Business, and Politics in Taiwan

Ko-lin Chin

Over the past two decades (1980-2000), the political and economic status of Taiwan (Republic of China [ROC]) has changed dramatically. When the United States ended formal diplomatic ties in 1979, Taiwan appeared to be on the verge of collapse. For almost thirty years, America was Taiwan's most important ally in her struggle against the Communist Chinese in mainland China (the People's Republic of China [PRC]). In time, the ruling Kuomintang Party (KMT) and the people of Taiwan showed their tenacity and resilience by gradually developing Taiwan's economy into one of the strongest in the world.[1] Chiang Kai-shek's son Chiang Ching-kuo, who was then president of Taiwan and chairman of the KMT, was credited with launching most of the energetic and successful economic programs (Scalapino 1996).[2] The world was so impressed with the economic vigor of a tiny, mountainous island with few natural resources, that it dubbed this period of economic expansion the "Taiwan Miracle" or "Taiwan Experience" (Gold 1986).

After Chiang Ching-kuo led Taiwan to its prominence among leading developing nations, he continued to push for political reform. Before 1985, Taiwan was basically governed by an authoritarian regime (Tien and Chu 1994). In 1985, Chiang announced that none of his sons would "run" for the presidency, thus effectively removing the Chiang family from the governing process after his death. He also lifted martial law in 1986, which had been in effect since the KMT moved to Taiwan in 1949, enabling citizens to enjoy greater freedom in their lives. Many draconian social control apparatuses such as curfews, censorship, and bans on public demonstrations were either abolished or removed from military control (Rigger 1999). In 1987, Chiang lifted the ban on travel to mainland China. Then, as former mainlanders returned to China to visit families and friends whom they had not seen since 1949, not only did tensions ease between the KMT and the Communist Chinese, but also hopes were raised for an increase in cross-strait trade and investment (Leng 1996).[3]

After the People's Republic of China replaced Taiwan in the United Nations in 1971 and the United States established formal relations with the PRC in 1979, the KMT, or Nationalists, could no longer claim to represent all Chinese people. As a result, it had to fall back on the claim that it represented all the people of Taiwan, including mainlanders and Taiwanese (Scalapino 1996). However, as a political party established in China by mainland Chinese and later transplanted to Taiwan, the legitimacy of the KMT was also challenged by the indigenous Taiwanese who constituted almost 85 percent of the population on the island and who had lived there for centuries (Chen Ming-tong 1995). To strengthen its hold, the Nationalists had no choice but to bring more native-born Taiwanese politicians into their party. In the early 1980s, they began to hold more local, grass-roots elections. Eventually, all local as well as national officeholders were elected by popular vote. Taiwan's first major opposition party—the Democratic Progressive Party (DPP)—came into existence in September 1986. In January 1988, Chiang Ching-kuo died after serving as president for ten years (Tien 1996). The then-vice president, Lee Teng-hui, a Taiwanese with a Ph.D. from Cornell University, succeeded him, although many KMT leaders were reluctant to allow a Taiwanese to head the country and the party. More years of political reform followed and brought about the peaceful, national election of 1996 and Lee Teng-hui as the first popularly elected president in Chinese history (Rigger 1999).

For the last twenty years, a thriving economy and maturing democracy have enabled the people of Taiwan to enjoy a level of prosperity and freedom unprecedented in the long history of the Chinese people. Not only did real estate and stock values skyrocket, but the government itself also had one of the world's largest reserves of foreign hard currency. In the meantime, the press, the electronic media, and a variety of social, cultural, legal, and economic institutions were allowed to operate without much intervention. As Taiwan's relationship with China continued to improve after the ban on travel was lifted in 1987, there was growing confidence that the country's future could only become brighter.

Unfortunately, however, as the world marveled at the evolving economic and political miracles in Taiwan, the embryo of a monster that would later came to be known as "black gold politics" was taking form. In Taiwan, "black" means the underworld; "gold" means money or business. "Black gold politics" was the penetration into politics of violent underworld figures and greedy business tycoons and the inevitable subsequent social ills such as vote-buying, political violence, insider trading, bid rigging and official (and unofficial) corruption (Tsai Shi-yuan 1998).

This chapter analyzes why and how "black gold politics" developed into a major problem during the last fifteen years and what role it may have played in ending the KMT's rule in Taiwan after more than fifty years as the preeminent political party. Specifically, it is an attempt to show that, besides the political-criminal nexus, we also need to examine the political-business nexus and the business-criminal nexus. Further, this chapter examines how a nexus between politicians and gangsters could, under certain circumstances, transform itself into a much more formidable threat to the integrity and stability of a democratic society.

Gang Crime in Taiwan

Gangs and other crime groups have been an obvious fact of life in Taiwan since 1945, when China recovered the island from Japan after World War II. To protect themselves against native Taiwanese, the children of mainland Chinese, formed street gangs in urban centers. Later they became involved in street fights and a variety of petty crimes. Native Taiwanese juvenile delinquents and adult criminals in the countryside usually belonged to local groups called *jiaotou*. These groups were most likely to be involved in extorting money from businessmen within their turfs and operating illegal gambling operations (Pai Jai 1983).[4]

Serious clashes among gangs and jiaotou groups in the 1960s led authorities to launch several nationwide crackdowns on the underworld, an effort known as "saohei" or "sweeping away black societies" (Sheu Chuen-jim 1993). Leaders of the two largest mainlander gangs, the Bamboo United and the Four Seas, were arrested and sent to prison. A large number of gangs and jiaotou groups were ordered to disband. Nevertheless, the number of gangs and jiaotou groups continued to grow. Their penetration into the legitimate business sector in the early 1980s alarmed the public as well as the authorities (Chi Chiung-shien 1985).

On 15 October 1984, three Bamboo United leaders, under orders from the head of the Intelligence Bureau of the Ministry of National Defense (IBMND), arrived in the United States to kill Henry Liu. Liu, a Chinese-American writer in Daly City, California, had written a defamatory biography of Chiang Ching-kuo. After the three gang leaders returned to Taiwan, Taiwanese officials launched a major assault on crime groups throughout the country, code-named "Operation Cleansweep" or Yi-ching Program (Kaplan 1992). Thousands were arrested, and many were sentenced to three years in various prisons in southern Taiwan (Sheu Chuen-jim 1993).

In 1986, authorities abolished marital law, which had been in effect since the KMT moved to Taiwan in 1949. Although this action was hailed as perhaps the most important step in Taiwan's political reform movement, the damaging impact on law and order in the country proved to be enormous. A former chief of police of a southern city observed:

Before the abolition of martial law, the crime problem in Taiwan was a minor one. At that time, our main concern was the existence of gambling dens and commercial sex establishments. Even so, these businesses did not really pose major problems for us. After martial law was lifted in 1986, however, patrols of the coast became almost nonexistent, and as a result, it was easy to smuggle guns and drugs into Taiwan. That completely changed the crime scene here.[5]

Gang violence escalated. Instead of fighting with knives or swords, most self-respecting gangsters carried firearms and did not hesitate to use them. Gun battles among crime figures led to a dramatic increase in homicide rates in the late 1980s (Hsu Fu-sen 1999). The availability of handguns thus enabled many desperate and daring young underworld figures to achieve their goal of making money in a society where wealth is so highly prized.

In 1987, Taiwanese authorities began to release major crime figures that had been arrested during Operation Cleansweep (Chen Ji-fang 1988a). After these underworld leaders regained their freedom, they began to fight to regain command of the gangs they had relinquished to younger leaders. At the same time, some of them transformed themselves into businessmen and politicians. Instead of being called a "big brother," a gang leader-turned-businessman might call himself "dongshizhang" (chairman of the board) and a gang leader-turned-politician, "mindai" (elected representative) (Jin Si 1989; Ker Su-len 1989).[6] The release of these seasoned gangsters no doubt disrupted the fragile order that had been established by the younger leaders in the aftermath of Operation Cleansweep. The emergence of the Celestial Alliance—an underworld alliance formed in prisons by Taiwanese crime bosses who were arrested during Operation Cleansweep—also resulted in a number of bloody conflicts between the gang and its rivals (Chen Ji-fang 1988c; Yang Ji 1989).

In 1990, Taiwanese authorities came to the conclusion that another crackdown was needed in order to smash the rapidly expanding Celestial Alliance. Operation Thunderbolt or Shiun-lay Program was launched, and thousands of crime figures were arrested. Many other gang leaders fled the island. However, a large number of them were not targeted for reasons unknown (Chao Mu-sung 1990).

In the early 1990s, as Taiwan became more democratic and various political parties emerged, many gangsters became convinced that the best way to protect themselves from future crackdowns was to transform themselves into popularly elected deputies. Gangsters of mainland descent who did not have close ties to indigenous people were more likely to become board chairmen and general managers of business firms. Thus, in the early 1990s, a large number of gangsters had penetrated in either the political or economic arenas of Taiwan, or both.

The involvement of gangsters in politics and business forced government authorities to carry out a third major gang sweep in 1996. Operation Chih-ping targeted gangsters who were local politicians (Ministry of Justice 1998). Even though only a small number of politicians were actually arrested, the dramatic process—arresting key crime figures and immediately transporting them by helicopter to a prison on a remote island—gave the public the impression that the authorities were determined this time to wipe out the gangsters in both politics and business (Lin Hsin 1996).

Unfortunately, while Operation Chih-ping was underway, three extremely brutal, but apparently unrelated attacks against powerful public figures occurred. First, Liu Pang-yo, the commissioner of Taoyuan County was shot dead inside his mansion on 21 November 1996, along with two county councilors, five colleagues, and Liu's bodyguards (Yang Ji-jin 1999). On the night of 30 November 1996 a high-ranking female DPP member, Perng Wan-lu, was murdered in Kaohsiung, the second largest city in Taiwan, after she had attended a DPP meeting and stepped into a taxi. Then, on 14 April 1997, the teenage daughter of Pai Ping Ping, one of Taiwan's most popular and well-connected female entertainers, was kidnapped, tortured, raped, and murdered (Lo Sung-fan 1998). The entire island was shocked.

In the aftermath of these highly publicized incidents, tens of thousands of people gathered in protest in front of the office of the president in Taipei, and demanded that President Lee Teng-hui take responsibility for the murders. Since then, people in Taiwan have continued to be outraged by the deterioration of law and order in their society. Statistics show that the crime rate in Taiwan almost tripled between 1961 and 1997 (Hsu Fu-sen 1999). Neither Perng Wan-lu nor Pai Ping Ping's daughter were murdered by gang or jiaotou members. Although the murderers of Liu Pang-yo are still at large, most people assume that Taiwan's underworld was responsible for these bloody events. For the people of Taiwan, the problem of crime is basically a problem of organized crime, be it mainland gangsters or Taiwanese jiaotous, or both. It is widely believed in Taiwan that, if gangsters and jiaotou figures were removed, law and order could be dramatically improved.

Heidao: The Underworld of Taiwan

The Chinese often use the generic term "heidao" (the black way) to denote the underworld and "baidao" (the white way) to denote the upperworld. Gangsters are often labeled as *heidaorenwu* (gang figures), *daoshangde* (people of the way), and *youheidide* (people with shady background). Those who view themselves as heidao figures usually try to differentiate themselves from common criminals who victimize ordinary people. People who belong to both heidao and baidao or who could not be easily identified one way or the other are called *huidaorenwu* (gray way figures). Besides heidao figures, there are also ten of thousands of secret society members who belong to one of the two legendary organizations: the Hung and the Qing (Chi Chung-shien

1984). Members of the Hung and Qing societies do not view themselves as heidao figures, nor are they labeled as such by society, even though some members may belong to various crime groups.[7]

Deciding whether a person is a heidao figure or not has always been a challenge for the media, the public, and the law enforcement community, not only because it is an all-purpose term, but because the word is morally and politically charged. There are other terms that officials and journalists apply to a group of people who presumably do not belong to law-abiding, main-stream society. These terms refer to categories of persons that include:

1. *Hoodlums or Hooligans*: According to the Statute for Punishment of Hood-lums (the Anti-hoodlum Law), a hoodlum is anyone who is involved in one of the following activities: (i) participating in a gang, (ii) weapons possession, production, transportation, and selling, (iii) extortion, (iv) gambling, prostitution, and debt-collection, and (v) habitual loitering. The main difference between hooliganism and ordinary criminality is the level of damage to the social order. The former is considered to have significantly more impact on social order because hooligan activities are considered to be (i) not victim-specific (victims are randomly picked by offenders), (ii) predatory, and (iii) chronic. Any criminal act that meets one of the above three criteria is defined as hooliganism (Judicial Yuan 1992).

2. *Gang figures*: People who belong to criminal gangs, especially the ones dominated by mainlanders, are considered gang figures.

3. *Jiaotou figures*: Leaders and members of territorial groups established by Taiwanese are called jiaotou figures. At any given time, there are about one thousand large and small jiaotou groups in Taiwan.

4. *Brothers*: Many gang and jiaotou figures prefer to call themselves *xiongdi* or brothers. From their viewpoint, brothers are members of an unconven-tional subculture who may be involved in illegal activities but who also strictly adhere to a set of norms and values on which loyalty and righ-teousness are important. These norms and values also prohibit them from victimizing the poor and weak. Leaders are called big brothers, and fol-lowers are little brothers.

5. *Petty criminals*: People who are involved in opportunistic crimes such as theft, fraud, embezzlement, and robbery are viewed as petty criminals. They often commit those acts individually or in small groups and are considered to lack rules or values.

It is not always easy to differentiate these five types of individuals who are considered to be part of a criminal subculture. For example, according to the Judicial Yuan[8] of Taiwan: "Robbers and thieves are not hooligans; hooligans are mostly heidao members but not all heidao people are hooligans" (Judicial Yuan 1998: 6-7). At any rate, before the implementation of the Organized Crime Prevention Law in 1996, the only way the authorities could arrest and punish a career criminal was to accuse him as a hoodlum according to the Anti-hoodlum Law. As a result, most chronic offenders, including gang members, jiaotou figures, and brothers are often processed as hoodlums in the criminal justice system. Petty criminals are normally charged according to the Criminal Law.

In Taiwan, not only do government officials categorize criminal individuals, but criminal organizations are also classified as one of three types:

1. *Organized*: These groups are bigger and better organized than the other two types of groups. Members are predominantly offspring of mainland Chinese who followed Chiang Kai-shek to Taiwan in 1949. Some of the most powerful organized gangs in Taiwan are the Bamboo United, the Four Seas, the Celestial Alliance (the only Taiwanese organized gang), the Pine Union, and the Pei Lien. Although these groups may have hundreds, even thousands of members, they normally do not have their own territories, even though these gangs have many branches across Taiwan and overseas.
2. *Jiaotou*: These groups are territorial in nature and members are mainly Taiwanese. The groups are relatively small, ranging from twenty to fifty members. There are generally only two types of positions within a jiaotou group: laoda (big boss) and xioadi (little brother).
3. *Loosely knit*: These groups are even smaller than the jiaotou groups, ranging from only a few members to twenty or more. Like the jiaotou groups, they are made up of mostly Taiwanese, but they do not have their own turf.

According to the National Police Administration (NPA) of Taiwan, there were 1,274 gangs, jiaotous, and loosely knit groups in Taiwan in 1998, with a total of more than 10,000 members (Su Nang-heng 1998). Of the more than 1,000 criminal groups, 41 percent are loosely knit groups, 47 percent are jiaotou groups, and 12 percent are organized gangs (Su Nang-heng 1997).

Can these three groups be considered as organized crime groups? According to the Judicial Yuan (1998: 9):

> Organized gangs are organized crime groups; most jiaotous and loosely knit groups are not well organized, so we need to examine them case by case to determine whether they are organized crime groups or not. There are also criminal organizations (like drug trafficking groups) that do not belong to any of the above definitions and they could be considered as organized crime groups.

If a group is considered an organized crime group, the prosecutors can charge the group under the Organized Crime Prevention Law. However, since it was first implemented in 1996, few organized gangs, or jiaotou and loosely knit groups have been indicted as organized crime groups.

Problems in Defining Heidao

Chinese people often use the word *hei* (black) to denote things that are bad or evil (Nan Fang Sor 1996). For example, *heishehui* (black society) means organized crime groups, *heixinkan* (black heart) means evil intention, *heitou* (black head) means bandits, *heitu* (black earth) means opium, *heihuo* (black commodity) means stolen items, *heiguan* (black officials) means corrupt officials. Thus, if a person is considered to be hei, he or she will be thought to possess the negative traits; a heidao figure means, basically, a bad person.

My subjects who have been labeled as heidao figures by the Taiwan authorities often question what heidao actually means. A deputy speaker of a town council whom a local KMT official sarcastically described as someone who "did not have to serve in the army" (meaning he did not serve because of his criminal record), had this to say when I asked him about his alleged heidao background:

> What do you mean by the word "heidao"? OK, now that you bring this up, you've got my attention. This is the kind of stuff I have a lot to say about. The whole idea of heidao is nothing but a generalization. It's like the word *huanchang* (entertainment places), which includes a variety of special businesses such as nightclubs, massage parlors, karaoke clubs, hostess bars, and dance halls.[9] When we say heidao, it may include petty thief, robber, etc. The word heidao can't pinpoint a particular type of person or criminal. The word heidao is nothing but a generalization. We need to differentiate all the people we consider as heidao figures. Just as we can't say all the things beneath the water are fish, and therefore can be eaten. There are fish that can be eaten (good things) and fish that can't be eaten (bad things).

Some subjects argued that their position as a laoda (big boss) means nothing, and that it is unfair to accuse a person of being a laoda. According to a Bamboo United leader:

One of the accusations against me was this: Someone overheard that someone else had called me a laoda. In fact, [then] President Lee [Teng-hui] happened to have said that he's the laoda of Lien Chan [then-vice-president and now the chairman of the KMT]. So what?

A former member of the underworld told me a heidao person could not be all bad: "What do you mean by heidao? How would you define *xiongdi* [brother]? It's very difficult to define these terms. I don't deny that I am a heidao or a xiongdi, but I know my heart is red [good]."

Others pointed out that the heidao are the guardians against crime. A jiaotou from Kaohsiung told me: "Heidao has its own contribution to society. In the past, heidao helped the police maintain social order on the local level. Heidao can stop a crime before it occurs."

A leader of the Bamboo United insisted that brothers are not heidao figures:

We brothers are not involved in reckless activities. Those who commit robbery and rape are not brothers; they are heidao people. The media labels all of us as heidao and the police and government officials as baidao. In fact, police officers are the real heidao because they are greedy and will do anything to make money. They not only demand that little brothers take the blame for crimes they have never committed (for the sake of police's own reputation), they are also continually involved in shake-downs and intimidation.

One of the most influential Bamboo United leaders, Chang An-lo (nick-named White Wolf), said that he is a brother but not a heidao person: "I admit I am a brother but I don't think a brother is equivalent to a heidao person" (Teng Chi-jer 1996a: 52).

Even Lo Fu-chu, the alleged top boss of the powerful Celestial Alliance and a two-term legislator, often talked about the definition of heidao (Teng Chi-jer 1996b: 51-52):

Many people use my past to define my current status, but I have to ask them a question: What is heidao? What does it really mean? The word is very abstract and unclear. Does it mean a kind of color? Our society rarely shows any support to those who have committed minor crimes. You know what causes lawlessness in our society? It's because we all are just concerned for ourselves. In order to make our performance look good, we create the ten most wanted criminals list. Some of these people are involved in only minor crimes but we force them to go to the extreme, and that's created many serious crimes in our society. The same is true with bid rigging. The problem lies in the lack of a good system. If baidao people [government officials and legitimate businessmen] are not involved in bid rigging, then there is no room for heidao people to get involved.

A Four Seas leader also questioned the fairness in categorizing people into heidao and baidao: "Our society has changed. How do you define what is black and what is white? Many baidao people do things that are worse than what heidao people do, and not all heidao people are bad people" (*China Times Weekly* 8 January 1995: 42).

The word "heidao" then is often used by the upperworld to characterize the underworld, but most underworld figures are reluctant to see themselves as heidao figures and instead prefer to view themselves as brothers or xiongdi. For them, brothers do belong to an unconventional subculture but they are not involved in reckless crime against members of society at large. Even those subjects who have no objections to describing themselves as heidao figures insisted that they were not petty criminals.

Gangsters, Tycoons, and Politicians

Over the past decade, people in Taiwan have considered black gold poli-tics to be their number one concern. Black gold politics refers to the penetra-tion of violent racketeers and self-serving businessmen into politics, which has a corrosive effect on its legitimacy and honesty. Black gold politics is more serious and threatening to society than predatory street crime. Corrupting government officials undermines the trust and integrity of public institutions that constitute the very foundation of society. A 1999 poll conducted by *Commonwealth Magazine* showed that 22.9 percent of more than 1,000 respondents believed black gold politics made life in Taiwan "ignoble." Also, black gold politics tops the list as the most urgent issue to address in improving the country's future prosperity. [10]

When a high-ranking police officer was questioned about the seriousness of the problem of organized crime in Taiwan, he replied:

> It's extremely serious. If we don't do anything about it now, our country will be finished. Why? Because organized crime members are well connected to business people, law enforcement authorities, public officials, legislators, and local faction leaders.[11] These gangsters are involved in all kinds of legitimate and illegitimate activities. They are also deeply involved in elections. In the past, they helped certain political candidates get elected; these days, they run for public office themselves. After they become elected representatives, they make sure they become members of the Law and Order Committee, which is in charge of police budgets and personnel. Once they achieve that, they can humiliate police chiefs in the city or county assemblies by not allowing police chiefs to sit down while acting like they are interrogating the police chiefs during interpellation.

Before 1996, there was little real understanding of the extent of black gold politics in the country. But on 16 November 1996, in a speech at a meeting with leaders of the business community, Minister of Justice Liao Cheng-hao declared that out of the 858 city and county councilors across Taiwan, 286 had a heidao background.[12] Liao warned that, if the problem was not dealt with immediately, Taiwan could become another Sicily. The acknowledgement by Taiwan's highest law enforcement official that one-third of the locally elected deputies were either gangsters or criminals caught the island by surprise. Liao also indicated that 25 percent of the provincial assembly members and 5 percent of the legislators and national assembly deputies had questionable backgrounds. Moreover, about 200 town representatives were thought to be underworld figures (*United Daily News* 17 November 1996). Since Liao's 1996 revelations, other estimates have been publicized in the media. (See Table 9.1. The table also includes three little-known estimates that were made before Liao's highly publicized announcement.)

Even without these breath-taking figures, which become headline news whenever they are made public, people in Taiwan are aware of the seriousness of black gold politics. Many have intimate knowledge of how rampant vote-buying is during local and national elections; how violent it can become when there is fierce competition among rival candidates; how often business tycoons can buy a seat in the legislature and national assembly;[13] and how

Table 9.1
Estimates of the Extent of Heidao Involvement in Politics

Source	Year	Percentage
1. MJIB Director Wu Tung-ming	1994	62 councilors with heidao background
2. NPA's Hoodlum Division	1994	Out of 883 city and county councilors, 28 were hooligans, 29 were gangsters, and 150 with heidao affiliation
3. Intelligence reports	1995	Among town representatives, 37.8% with heidao background; among county and city councilors, about 26.5%, and among national representatives, about 3%
4. Minister of Justice Liao Cheng-hao	1996	Out of 858 city and county councilors, 286 with heidao background
5. NPA Commissioner	1997	Almost all chairs and members of the Law and Order Committees of the elected bodies were heidao affiliated
6. President of Academia Sinica Lee Yuan-tse	1999	Half of the elected deputies are affiliated with heidao

Source: Reports in the news media.

often government officials, elected deputies, and gangsters work together to benefit themselves in collusive bidding. Residents of Taiwan also see on TV physical assaults on the floor of the legislature, in the national assembly, and among local elected bodies. Hardly a day goes by without news reports about politicians, businessmen, and gangsters being involved in financial scandal, big rigging, corruption, vote-buying, violent confrontation, or fraud.

More often than not, the KMT is blamed for the development of black gold politics. The assumption is that, in order to maintain its power as a ruling party and to defeat the emerging opposition parties such as the Democratic Progressive Party (DPP), the Nationalists deliberately established a close relationship with anyone who was powerful and influential enough to assure that KMT candidates win elections. Many gang and jiaotou members are well connected to grassroots politics, and they become ideal campaign managers or so-called "pillars" or vote captains. After these heidao figures became familiar with the election process, they eventually decided to run for public offices themselves. When the KMT realized that these gangsters and jiaotou figures would be elected with or without their blessing and support, the party decided to embrace them, to make sure that the KMT remained the majority party in both local and national elected bodies.

Even though most people in Taiwan believe that the KMT is the only party to be closely associated with criminals, some insist that all political parties in Taiwan have ties to organized crime. A Bamboo United leader said:

Every political party in Taiwan is associated with heidao. Among them, the New Party (NP) is the least connected with heidao because it emphasizes good public image. The truth is, although the DPP criticizes the KMT for its relationship with heidao, many DPP members at the local level are themselves closely linked to heidao people. Moreover, when the DPP orchestrated those demonstrations in the past, it also relied on heidao people to achieve its goals.

Regardless of who is responsible for the development of black gold politics, alarming headlines have become a fact of life for people in Taiwan: "Mob Rule," "Just Like Sicily," "Fugitive Councilor Turns Himself In," "Judicial Yuan Sheds Light on the Darker Side of Politicians," "Former Chiayi Speaker Indicted," "Legislator Assaulted by Colleagues," "War Declared on Black Gold," "Raid on Legislator's Quarters Prompts Debate," "Legislator Claims Innocence over Land Deal," "Prosecutors Detain Township Chief for Quake Supply Theft," "Tainan Mayor Indicted over Bribe Cover-Up," "Suspected Gangster Elected to Judicial Committee [of the legislature]," and "KMT Legislator Gets 12 Years for Embezzling."

Research Methods

This study employs multiple research strategies, including in-depth interviews with key informants in Taipei; numerous research trips to southern Taiwan to interview subjects and observe the electoral process; four research trips to China, Cambodia, Thailand, and Vietnam to interview and spend time with fugitives from Taiwan; and a systematic collection and analysis of official and media reports. I interviewed 117 subjects altogether. Table 9.2 shows how many subjects from each of the five types of respondents were interviewed.

Table 9.2
Sample Study

Subjects	N
Government and law enforcement officials	29
Local officials and elected deputies	19
National elected deputies	12
Heidao figures	32
Other key informants	25
Total	117

The Nexus among Gangsters, Businessmen, and Politicians

In Taiwan, the convergence of interests among gangsters, businessmen, and politicians constitutes one of the main reasons for the development of black gold politics. Members from each group have their own reasons for mixing with members from the other two groups (see Figure 9.1). Most politicians are willing to be affiliated with businessmen because the latter can provide them with campaign funds. Politicians are also interested in befriending gangsters because gang members are good vote captains. As a jiaotou figure in Kaohsiung suggested: "Every elected deputy, even if he himself is not a heidao figure, is supported by a group of heidao figures." Another underworld figure told a reporter that, under pressure to win an election by all means, politicians are willing to mix with heidao figures: "If not because of the elections, I can't imagine what other resources heidao people have that attract baidao people [politicians]" (*China Times Weekly* 1995: 41-42). For political figures, votes are their main concern: anyone who can help them get votes is appreciated. In short, money from businessmen can help politicians buy votes and intimidation by the gangs can ensure the efficiency of vote buying.

Businessmen at all levels like to associate with politicians because the latter can help them in many ways. For example, enterprises that maintain a close relationship with powerful politicians are more likely to secure government contracts, less likely to be targeted by law enforcement authorities for irregular business practices, and more likely to receive government aid when they are in financial distress. These entrepreneurs also welcome the affiliation with gangsters because, in Taiwan, many business disputes, a result of fierce and unfair competition, are most efficiently settled in private. Many businesspeople have little confidence in the justice system, and they also think that, to protect themselves against gang victimization, the best thing to

Figure 9.1
The Nexus between Gangsters, Businessmen, and Politicians

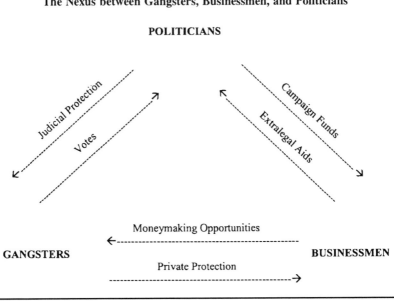

do is to have some underworld friends of their own. Many entrepreneurs who run for public offices might also be interested in having heidao figures to help them with their campaigns, as Hwang Kwang-kuo, a professor at National Taiwan University, has written (1984: 23):

> Heidao became more powerful in the mid-1970s when golden oxen [business tycoons] decided to run for public offices. Without any political ideology, they were only interested in getting elected and that's why they were actively involved in vote-buying and hiring heidao figures to campaign for them. After being elected, these golden oxen were only interested in earning money through involvement in illegal operations. That also led to their connections with heidao and law enforcement authorities.

Gang leaders and jiaotou bosses are eager to be connected with politicians because the latter can protect them from law enforcement authorities. In Taiwan, elected deputies often show up in police stations to express their "concern" whenever a person is arrested, and they see this as one of their many "services" to their constituents, regardless of why the person is being arrested. Many people also view the presence of elected deputies in the police stations as the most effective way to obtain a quick release. Gang members also need the support of politicians if they wish to avoid harassment and raids on their vice businesses. One of the main reasons for the dramatic increase in the number of gangsters in politics has to do with their disillusionment with politicians' willingness to protect them in time of crises. For example, many major crime figures were arrested during Operation Cleansweep, one of the three major crackdowns in the history of Taiwan. When these arrested gangsters were released from prisons, they realized that the best way to protect themselves from law enforcement authorities was for them to become elected deputies themselves.

Gangsters are also eager to be associated with businessmen because the latter not only can provide them with many money-generating opportunities but they also become the gangsters' major preys. When gangsters need money, they can always rely on businessmen to patronize their gambling operations; the gangsters know full well that the businessmen are going to lose all their money before they leave the gambling joints.

The symbiosis among gangsters, businessmen, and politicians can be more closely examined by looking at the various relationships within it: the political-business nexus, the political-criminal nexus, and the business-criminal nexus.

Political-Business Nexus

Due to the lack of campaign finance laws and the need for huge sums of money to run for office, many individuals within the business community can easily establish close relationships with politicians by contributing funds to their election campaigns. And politicians are willing to work with those businessmen in financial deals that could be mutually beneficial. The nexus between politicians and businessmen took hold during the early 1990s when the KMT was desperate for campaign funds. According to Chen Tung-sen (1995: 44):

> After martial law was lifted and authoritarianism had collapsed, economic groups continued to protect and expand their interests through various avenues. Eventually, economic groups and local factions penetrated into the core of the national political arena. What was once a political system dominated by authoritarian figures at the top has now been transformed into a complex web of relationships that includes central authorities, local factions, and economic interest groups. The political arena has now become a place where money buys influence and power, a situation that has created serious problems of social and economic inequality.

According to a survey by the *Journalist*, many wealthy people—with no political experience but plenty of experience in financial wheeling-and-dealing—ran in the 1992 legislature race (Tang Su-jan 1992; *Journalist* 1992a, 1992b). An assistant to a city councilor confirmed that business conglomerates mostly supported KMT deputies. A contractor also told me: "Many KMT legislators are still extremely close to big-time businessmen; the well-being of the businessmen is the legislators' utmost concern, not the welfare of the general public."

Chen Chi-li of the Bamboo United also commented: "There is a symbiotic relationship between government officials and businessmen in Taiwan, especially when the two parties work together to benefit themselves in the construction industry. Anybody who has ever been a city or county mayor has benefited."

Lee Teng-hui, the president of Taiwan between 1988 and 2000, is considered to be the one who promoted the close relationship between politicians and businessmen. He publicly declared that it is the responsibility of a government to help capitalists make money (Wang Jenn-hwan 1993). According to Ji Yen-ling et al. (1990: 20):

> For the past forty years or more, Taiwanese businessmen never had a better time. In the past, when they interacted with politicians, they had to do it secretly, just like a date in a garden for a young couple who are afraid of being seen together. Nowadays, businessmen and politicians can embrace one another in public; there is no need to be concerned how the public will react to their close relationship.

With the lifting of the martial law in 1987, the KMT could not use force to win elections, but had to use relationships, especially in local elections. These personal ties were crucial for the procurement of vote brokers, and these relationships always were based on money. Only through a personal relationship would the person who received the money help with getting votes. That was why Lee Teng-hui used money relationships to control personal relationships; that was how he got power for himself. He was very eager to be on good terms with various business-conglomerates (he always had many banquet dinners with businessmen wherever he went); as a result, his administrators were also very close to businessmen.

Political-Criminal Nexus

As mentioned earlier, many heidao members ran for office themselves if they had the money to do so; and if they did not, they would try to establish close relationships with politicians so that they would have protection against the authorities. Most politicians were willing to have close relationships with heidao figures because the latter could help them get votes. According to a Bamboo United leader:

> Why did the political-criminal nexus in Taiwan develop as it did? It is mainly because of the interchangeable roles of pillars and heidao. Heidao are pillars, and pillars are heidao. Politicians in Taiwan must have the support of heidao because heidao represent the public, and they have the ability to express the public's feelings and attitudes and to mobilize people's power. Without the support of heidao, a politician could

easily end up being alone at the top of the heap, isolated from other people. He or she really won't have any future in politics.

As a result, almost every major gang figure in Taiwan has been approached by all three political parties for support during elections. Chu Kao-jen, a former legislator, was candid about it when asked how close politicians are to heidao members. He said: "How could it be possible that a locally elected representative was not acquainted with heidao?" (Lee Jiao-nan 1996: 51). Thus, as an independent legislator, Lin Lwei-to, said: "In Taiwan, because of its small size, most political candidates could not help but be associated with heidao figures. Besides, you don't want to lose the votes controlled by heidao people." However, as Jin Si (1989: 39) commented, the nexus between politicians and heidao figures could not be viewed as normal because it had its down side:

Making friends is a personal choice, but if friendship extends to a partnership involving the councilmen's political power and the heidao's threatening ways of doing things, that could lead to a dangerous combination of forces. These two groups of people can then operate underground ballrooms, bars, nightclubs, and gambling dens to make money. Or the councilmen can hold shares in or act as advisors to the commercial sex business or illegal gambling industry. These are all lucrative businesses, and the councilmen's involvement in these businesses is a detriment to law and order in our society.

Business-Criminal Nexus

According to a businessman in Kaohsiung City, those who cannot be affiliated with powerful politicians are willing to be affiliated with gangsters, if these gangsters agree to support them. This way, these small-time businessmen can compete with their peers who are supported by politicians. Underworld figures want to be affiliated with businessmen for economic opportunities and financial support. For example, Tsai Kwan-lun, a leader of the Four Seas gang, was extremely close to Chiang Chu-ping, a businessman who was considered to be the "money man" of the gang because of his investment in the gang's financial ventures. Both Tsai and Chiang were arrested during Operation Chih-ping for their use of strong-arm tactics and threats made in a business deal. On the other hand, gangsters who are interested in bid rigging also need the help of legitimate contractors. At the very least, gang members need wealthy businessmen to frequent their sex and gambling establishments.

One way to get a glimpse of the symbiosis of gangsters, businessmen, and politicians in Taiwan is when a big brother or one of his immediate family members passes away. When a "big boss" dies, his followers take the opportunity to showcase their strengths by inviting rich and powerful dignitaries to attend the funeral. The latter are usually more than happy to come and pay tribute and show their connections to a powerful gang. Other big brothers will also attend, not only because it is socially desirable to show their respect for another gang, but also to showoff their group's strengths by coming with dozens of imported luxury cars or horses with their gang's flags prominently displayed. For example, the 1988 funeral of a godfather (Chen Ji-fang 1988b), the 1992 funeral of a Nyo Pu leader's mother (Teng Chi-jer 1992), and the 1996 funeral of a Four Seas leader (*United Daily News* 12 February 1996) were attended by some of Taiwan's most powerful figures from the business, political, and underworld communities.[14]

The Transformation of the Nexus

Certainly, the triangular relationship between organized crime, entrepreneurs, and corrupt politicians is neither new nor unique to Taiwan. In Italy, Russia, Colombia, Mexico, Nigeria and many other locales where mafia and organized crime groups flourish, the nexuses between gangsters, businessmen, and politicians that had developed (Stille 1995; Thoumi 1995; Shelley 1997). Della Porta and Vannucci (1999) have provided a detailed analysis of the triangular relationship among mafia, tycoons, and politicians in southern Italy, where these three groups are heavily engaged in what the authors call "corrupt exchanges."

As the nexus between the upperworld and the underworld is fortified, members of the underworld may attempt to transform their criminal identities into images of legitimate businessmen whenever their societies experience major changes in the institutional structures of the political economy. For them, crafting an additional identity of legitimacy as businessmen is just as effective as the practice of intimidation. The mafia in Italy in the 1970s became entrepreneurial after they gave up their role as mediators and devoted themselves to capital accumulation (Arlacchi 1987). The Italian-American crime families in the United States have been penetrating the legitimate business sector since the early twentieth century (Reuter 1985; Anderson 1995; Jacobs 1999; Kelly 1999). The transformation of mobsters into businessmen was also observed in Japan (Kaplan and Dubro 1986), Russia (Handelman 1995), China (Martin 1996), Hong Kong (Chu, 2000), and Colombia (Thoumi 1995).

To protect themselves from judicial intervention, gangsters naturally have a strong desire to establish close relationships with politicians and law enforcement authorities (Hess 1998). The collaboration of the political establishment with the criminal underworld, the political-criminal nexus, had been documented and analyzed by scholars such as Landesco (1968 [1929]), Dorman (1972), Alexander (1985), Small (1995),

Stille (1995), Martin (1996), and Godson (2001). When mobsters are under the protection of the political establishment, their ability to commit crimes with impunity and to corrupt the political establishment elevates the level of harm they pose to society.

Regardless of how criminals in some areas of the world have successfully and deeply penetrated the economic and political sectors of their respective societies, they still remain essentially gangsters who need to hide in darkness, even though they may be extremely rich and powerful. Their ties to business firms and powerful politicians cannot be publicly flaunted, because that could result in disentangling the connections. Thus, even though there is a link between the upperworld and the underworld, the two worlds remain separate. Members of the two worlds may conspire to commit crimes together or engage in corrupt exchanges, but they still belong to their respective worlds and they cannot pretend to be members of the other.

Black gold politics in Taiwan is qualitatively different from the problem of criminal penetration into business and politics in other parts of the world. It has evolved from a nexus or a relationship between the upperworld and the underworld into an integration of the two worlds and the development of public figures that are at the same time gangsters, entrepreneurs, and politicians in the fullest sense. An influential legislator who is the convener of the judicial committee of the legislature could also be one of the richest entrepreneurs in the country. He could also have proclaimed himself "spiritual leader" of a powerful gang and be listed as a hoodlum by the authorities. A county magistrate who was imprisoned as a hoodlum could also be the owner of a major construction company and other big businesses, and be considered by his constituents to be the best county executive in Taiwan. The integration of the upperworld and the underworld in Taiwan resulted in the development of a morally confusing society where politicians are talking and acting like gangsters and gangsters are talking and acting like politicians.

Certain influential figures in Taiwan are called huidao figures. They belong to both the upperworld and the underworld. It is not always clear what they really are. Consequently, the line between legitimacy and illegitimacy is blurred and many people move back and forth across that line.

Because of the development of black gold politics, there is now a symbiosis among gangsters, businessmen, and politicians in Taiwan. Worse, many influential figures occupy all three roles and shift from one role to another, whichever is most expedient in a given circumstance. Those who are not "clever" enough to occupy all three roles with credibility will assume one role and try to have as many friends as possible from the other two worlds. These people are "complete" in the sense that they have money, power, and muscle, all of which are considered indispensable in Taiwan's extremely competitive society. That is why so many wealthy businessmen have entered politics. They want to ensure that the local or national assemblies will pass only government policies that benefit them. Many heidao figures enter politics to avoid unwanted arrest and punishment by the police.

Conclusion

The problem of heidao penetration into business and politics is often reported in the media. It is also raised by DPP members whenever they criticize the KMT, and debated by the general public. Many people believe that gangsters are responsible for almost all social ills in Taiwan, including vote buying, campaign and street violence, bid-rigging, and poor quality public construction projects. They assume that once gangsters are removed from the legitimate business and political arenas, all these problems will disappear. However, there are also quite a few people who believe that corrupt government officials (baidao) and controversial figures (huidao, neither black nor white but gray) do more harm to society than businessmen and politicians with heidao backgrounds. Many observers feel that baidao and huidao play a more significant role than heidao figures in the development and penetration of black gold politics into important sectors of the society. According to a NP legislator who is close to black gold figures in the legislature:

> Black gold politics in Taiwan is not as serious as people think it is. Heidao groups in Taiwan are not well organized and they are not as powerful as the media and the DPP suggest. There is no doubt that some gangsters are active in local politics, but nobody really knows how many local deputies are gangsters. Very often, we read in the newspapers about the percentage of local deputies with a gang background, but I don't know how reliable these estimates are. Besides, I don't know how they define heidao. People say there are big brother legislators or heidao legislators, but they are not the worst people in the legislature. Instead, other legislators, take Tseng Jen-nung [a KMT legislator] for example, are considered the most despicable. You can say Tseng is a hooligan legislator, or that he is worse than a hooligan. In fact, the very people that are ruining Taiwan are not heidao figures. Rather, they are the corrupt officials, the greedy business figures, and people like Lee Teng-hui. These people's involvement in illegal activities deserves our utmost concern.

Chien Shih-cheih, the DPP legislator who was assaulted by Lo Fu-chu, agreed with the NP lawmaker:

> It is not easy to say exactly how many heidao legislators are in the Legislative Yuan. However, I want to stress the point that the existence of heidao legislators is only part of the problem of black gold politics. There are many non-heidao legislators who are affiliated with gangsters and are being supported by local factions. They are only concerned for themselves or the interest groups they represent. In my opinion, they are the real problem. The problem became especially serious after the abolition of the provincial government and the arrival in the Legislative Yuan of large numbers of former provincial assemblymen. These newly elected legislators continued to act as rudely and shamelessly as they did when they were in the provincial assembly. Since their arrival, the Legislative Yuan has never been the same.

Lee Yuan-tseh, the president of Academia Sinica and one of the most influential figures in Taiwan, also suggested "organized crime is terrible, but corrupt officials are a lot worse" (Liu 2000: 5). According to Lee, the attempt to dissect black gold politics must focus more on baidao and huidao than on heidao. In other words, corrupt and incompetent central government officials, county commissioners, town mayors, local administrators, and greedy and unethical businessmen are more detrimental to the development of Taiwan than heidao elected deputies.

Some believe that heidao people penetrated business and politics at the invitation of businessmen and politicians. Without the assistance and encouragement of the latter, the heidao would never have stood a chance of making an impact on the business and political worlds. However, when someone has to be blamed for campaign violence and bid rigging, those who initially welcomed the heidao now simply point their fingers at them and blame them for all the problems. According to Tung Nian-tai, an unofficial "spokesman" of the underworld:

> What disgusted me the most is that many baidao people use heidao figures and eventually turn against them. The baidao rely on the heidao in settling financial disputes, running political campaigns, and doing all sorts of dirty work. But when baidao people need a scapegoat for the crime problem, the first thing they do is to blame heidao people. I don't think it is fair to be harsh with the heidao and to be lenient with the baidao.

However, it is not easy to differentiate between a heidao figure and a baidao figure. So many baidao people are affiliated with the heidao and are actively involved in the kind of activities only heidao figures are supposed to be involved in. Similarly, many heidao people are associated with the baidao and often play a key role in the conventional business and political arenas. In time, the criminalization of the baidao and the "bleaching" of the heidao resulted in the emergence of a large number of huidao figures, people who are neither heidao nor baidao but who are sufficiently rich and powerful to pull all the strings behind-the-scenes. They stand to gain the most.

Black gold politics is basically a collusion of money, brute force, and political influence. To obtain political influence, one needs money to buy votes and brute force to assure that vote buying is effective. Gangsters provide strong-arm tactics and business entrepreneurs offer monetary support. In return, a politician, after being elected, needs to pay back the gangsters and the businessmen who have helped him to gain, and usually maintain, political power. Later on, gangsters and businessmen came to realize that they did not need to be merely supporting players. Some gangsters had enough money and some businessmen had enough connections with gangsters to run for office themselves. Consequently, the underworld, the business community, and the political arena in Taiwan became so entangled that it is almost impossible to differentiate among gangsters, businessmen and politicians.

Case study material of Taiwanese crime and political corruption suggests a leitmotiv of gangsters cunningly cultivating with money and promises of power ambitions, and avaricious political actors and politicians luring heidao/pillars into politics. However, these linkages cannot realistically be construed as a lopsided game of politician/victim and racketeer/victimizer; politics and organized crime appear to be more symbiotically interlocked so that the term "partnership" seems more apt as a description of such relationships. This study is an effort to illuminate how corrupt incentives and opportunities arise and how a system of illicit privileges and obligations preempts and excludes legitimate businesspeople and ordinary citizens from economic and political participation.

Through the infusions of illegal wealth and the utilization of criminogenic assets (violence and extortion, in particular), political entrepreneurs are able to exploit their political environments and interfere with vital community functions such that the processes of governability are jeopardized.

Factors that contribute to the development of a political-criminal nexus include types of communities that are economically depressed or under-politicized. In such cases public officials may exercise unbridled power over the distribution of public benefits and resources. In communities where political processes are contorted and constricted through a lack of collective political awareness or because of poor articulation of the linkages between community groups and government institutions, patterns of community insulation result. This leads to diminished leverage on governmental agencies. Predictably, constituent power over political actors and public officials is weakened and the way is opened for clientelist politics where power becomes increasingly discretionary and where political resources are likely to be disproportionately allocated and distributed to favored groups and individuals.

Industrial and commercial activities are another setting in which corruption is the principal means through which organized criminals manage to insinuate themselves. Further complicating the picture is the fact that criminals have developed strategies that exploit conditions of vulnerability in industry. Industry is burdened with a maze of codes, laws and statutes, many of which are outdated, create administrative sclerosis, discourage competition and investment, significantly increase building costs, and reduce the quality of public and private work products. Such conditions provide many opportunities for organized criminals.

As noted above, gangsters function as "rationalizing agents" in these work environments, facilitating through extra-legal means the completion of projects mainly by insuring the reliability of labor inputs, and through interventions into the construction process in other ways– primarily by stabilizing the flow of supplies and building materials for a nominal economic rent—or pay off.

In this case, a "crust" of regulatory protocols and mechanisms apparently engineer informal methods, which are less constrained by laws, unclog the system, get things done. Not only are laws circumvented and the components of the industry compromised but builders themselves become enveloped in the nexus through racketeer-dominated associations of builders that are nothing less than construction firm cartels.

This brings us to the issue of counter-strategies of control and containment, ways in which linkages among political authorities, gangsters and businesspeople can be broken and the criminal grip on industries relaxed. In a business where criminal influence is demonstrably rampant, one reform approach involves broadening the pool of competitors for public construction contracts. Another important option entails sweeping changes in the regulatory statutes that shape the bidding processes in order to make them more transparent. In the past, a lack of openness in industry appears to have been a major factor precipitating widespread collusion among builders. A third device constitutes an entry barrier or gatekeeping tool that screens industry participants. It requires state authorities to examine the backgrounds and performance-related histories of bidders so that, presumably, criminally tainted firms and individuals can be prevented from obtaining public works contracts.

Perhaps the most common and widely known type of public susceptibility to corruption is the financing of electoral campaigns. It would seem especially difficult to generate substantive, legitimate funding in a climate of voter complacency, and desperation in communities that are impoverished. Electoral campaigns oblige politicians to turn to the private sector for support and resources and this is conducive to alliances and networks of criminals and political actors.

Another aspect of the political-criminal nexus that needs to be explored in both its historic contexts and contemporary settings is how the scope of governmental control policies, which have expanded over the past two decades may actually contribute to the growth of political/criminal connections. As governmental regulatory activity increases, the candidates for corruption may grow more numerous as more officials and authorities function in environments where criminal corruption is present.

Notes

1.   The Republic of China on Taiwan officially uses the Wade-Giles system to transliterate names from Chinese, and the People's Republic uses the pinyin system. Therefore, this chapter uses Wade-Giles for names from or associated with Taiwan, and the pinyin system for names from or associated with the PRC. Because

the pinyin system is more widely used than the Wade-Giles system, names that are not from or associated with Taiwan will also use the pinyin system.

2. In this chapter, if the source is in English, I indicate only the last name of the author(s). If the source is in Chinese, I indicate the full name of the author(s) (last name first and followed by first name).

3. People on Taiwan categorize each other according to their place of origin: Taiwan or the mainland. The term *Mainlander* refers to Chinese on Taiwan who either came from the mainland in the late 1940s or early 1950s or are the Taiwan-born offspring of those people. Taiwanese refers to only those Han Chinese who already lived on Taiwan prior to the wave of migration that occurred at the end of the 1940s and the offspring of those people (Wachman 1994).

4. "Jiao" means corner, "tou" means leader, and "jiaotou" means a street corner leader or influential local figure. Besides individuals, the word is also used to denote a variety of both criminal and non-criminal local groups. "Jiaotou" was originally meant to describe those individuals or groups that were instrumental in managing and operating local temples and organizing religious ceremonies. Even nowadays, a jiaotou plays an important role in local religious activities (Ho Hoa 1993).

5. Throughout this chapter, I will often quote the 117 subjects I personally interviewed. To avoid redundancy, whenever I quote one of my subjects, I will not repeat that he or she is my respondent. If someone quoted is not one of my subjects, I will cite the source.

6. In Taiwan, elected representatives can be categorized into two political levels: national and local. Nationally elected representatives include legislators, provincial assembly members, and national assembly members. Both the provincial and the national assemblies were dissolved in the late 1990s for political and economic reasons. Locally elected representatives include city/county councilors and town/township councilors.

7. Chinese secret societies were formed during the Ming era (1368-1644) by patriotic Chinese for political purposes. These societies, especially the Hung societies and the Qing societies, played a pivotal role in the overthrow of the Qing dynasty (1644-1911) and the establishment of the Republic of China. Secret societies continued to be very active in the political arena thereafter, but some societies or members also increasingly engaged in criminal activities. After the Communists took over China in 1949, some branches were reestablished in Hong Kong and Taiwan. Although the societies have maintained a low profile in the past forty years, they are now making a comeback in Taiwan, publicly recruiting new members and vowing to become more active in politics.

8. The five branches of government are the Executive Yuan, the Legislative Yuan, the Judicial Yuan, the Examination Yuan, and the Control Yuan. The Judicial Yuan functions much like the judicial branches of government in other nations.

9. In Taiwan, most sex and entertainment businesses are lumped together and called "special businesses."

10. When the respondents were asked, "What makes you feel most ashamed to be Taiwanese?" 22.9 percent answered "black gold politics," 15.6 percent said the "lack of a law-abiding spirit," 15.1 percent mentioned the "decline in social order," and 11.3 percent indicated "low diplomatic status" (*Taipei Times*, 12 December 1999).

11. Local factions are interest groups formed by local elites with the support of the KMT. These groups can be found all over the island and, with the blessing of the Nationalists, they dominate the economic, political, and cultural arenas of local

communities. In turn, these groups support the KMT as the ruling party and actively participate in local elections to support KMT candidates (Chen 1996).

12. There are 21 cities and counties (excluding Taipei and Kaohsiung) in Taiwan and each had its own local government and elected body. The elected body is called a council, and it has approximately 20 to 50 councilors, depending on the size of the city or county. Each council has a speaker and a vice speaker, selected among councilors by the councilors themselves.

13. Business tycoons can get themselves nominated as "legislators at large"—rather than having to win an election—by funding the election campaigns of a few party favorites.

14. If politicians do not want to be identified with heidao, especially when it is considered undesirable under certain circumstances, they will find excuses such as: "As a political figure, you need to participate in many banquets, and you know that there are many heidao sharing the same table with you and you can't really do anything about it," or "You can't really conclude that certain politicians are affiliated with heidao by observing the politicians' participation in the heidao or their relatives' funeral. On most occasions, the politicians have no idea to whom flowers are sent under his or her name."

References

In English

Alexander, Herbert. "Organized Crime and Politics," in *The Politics and Economics of Organized Crime*, ed. Herbert Alexander and Gerald Caiden. Lexington, MA: Lexington Books, 1985.

Anderson, Annelise. "Organized Crime, Mafias and Governments," in *The Economics of Organized Crime*, ed. Gianluca Fiorentini and Sam Peltzman. Cambridge: Cambridge University Press, 1995.

Arlacchi, Pino. *Mafia Business: The Mafia Ethic and the Spirit of Capitalism*. London: Verso, 1987.

Chen, Ming-tong. "Local Factions and Elections in Taiwan's Democratization," in *Taiwan's Electoral Politics and Democratic Transition: Riding the Third Wave*, ed. Hung-mao Tien. Armonk, NY: M. E. Sharpe, 1996.

Chu, Yiu-kong. *Triads as Business*. London: Routledge, 2000.

della Porta, Donatella, and Alberto Vannucci. *Corrupt Exchanges: Actors, Resources, and Mechanisms of Political Corruption*. New York: Aldine De Gruyer, 1999.

Dorman, Michael. *Payoff: The Role of Organized Crime in American Politics*. New York: David McKay, 1972.

Godson, Roy. "The Political-Criminal Nexus and Global Security." Paper presented at the Joint Meeting of the U.S. and Chinese Working Groups, Beijing, China, 10-11 December 2001.

Gold, Thomas. *State and Society in the Taiwan Miracle*. Armonk, NY: M. E. Sharpe, 1986.

Handelman, Stephen. *Comrade Criminal*. New Haven, CT: Yale University Press, 1995.

Hess, Henner. *Mafia and Mafiosi*. New York: New York University Press, 1998.

Jacobs, James. *Gotham Unbound: How New York City was Liberated from the Grip of Organized Crime*. New York: New York University Press, 1999.

Kaplan, David. *Fires of the Dragon: Politics, Murder, and the Kuomintang*. New York: Atheneum, 1992.

Kaplan, David, and Alec Dubro. *Yakuza*. New York: Collier Books, 1987.

Kelly, Robert. *The Upperworld and the Underworld: Case Studies of Racketeering and Business Infiltrations in the United States*. New York: Kluwer Academic/Plenum Publishers, 1999.

Landesco, John. *Organized Crime in Chicago*. Chicago: University of Chicago Press [1929], 1968.

Leng, Tse-kang. *The Taiwan-China Connection*. Boulder, CO: Westview Press, 1996.

Liu, Shih-chung. "Dissecting the 'Black Gold' Phenomenon." *Taipei Times*, 13 January 2000: 5.

Martin, Brian. *The Shanghai Green Gang*. Berkeley: University of California Press, 1996.

Reuter, Peter. "Racketeers as Cartel Organizers," in *The Politics and Economics of Organized Crime*, ed. Herbert Alexander and Gerald Caiden. Lexington, MA: Lexington Books, 1985.

Rigger, Shelley. *Politics in Taiwan: Voting for Democracy*. London: Routledge, 1999.

Scalapino, Robert. "Foreword," in *Taiwan's Electoral Politics and Democratic Transition*, ed. Hung-mao Tien. Armonk, NY: M. E. Sharpe, 1996.

Shelley, Louise. *Policing Soviet Society*. London: Routledge, 1997.

Small, Geoff. *Ruthless: The Global Rise of the Yardies*. London: Warner Books, 1995.

Stille, Alexander. *Excellent Cadavers*. New York: Vintage Books, 1995.

Taipei Times. "'Black Gold' Tops List of Taiwan's Worst Social Ills," 12 December, 1999: 4.

Thoumi, Franceso. *Political Economy and Illegal Drugs in Colombia*. Boulder, CO: Lynne Riener, 1995.

Tien, Hung-mao. "Elections and Taiwan's Democratic Development," in *Taiwan's Electoral Politics and Democratic Transition: Riding the Third Wave*, ed. Hung-mao Tien. Armonk, NY: M. E. Sharpe, 1996.

Tien, Hung-mao, and Yun-han Chu. "Taiwan's Domestic Political Reforms, Institutional Change and Power Realignment," in *Taiwan in the Asia-Pacific in the 1990s*, ed. Gary Klintworth. St. Leonards, Australia: Allen & Unwin, 1994.

Wachman, Alan. *Taiwan: National Identity and Democratization*. Armonk, NY: M. E. Sharpe, 1994.

In Chinese

Chao, Mu-sung. "Heidao Figures Returning to Their Villages." *China Times Weekly* 652, 26 August 1990: 44-47.

Chen, Ji-fang. "Where's the Wind That Swirls Jianghu Comes From?" *China Times Weekly* 531, 1 May 1988a: 42-43.

_____. "Cheng Ker 'on the Road,' Ju Lien 'on the Horse.'" *China Times Weekly* 536, 5 June 1988b: 19-25.

_____. "The Structure of the Celestial Alliance." *China Times Weekly* 564, 18 December 1988c: 36-40.

Chen, Ming-tong. *Factional Politics and Taiwan's Political Evolution*. Taipei: Yuedan Publishing Company, 1995.

Chen, Tung-sen. *City of Money and Power: A Sociological Analysis of Local factions, Conglomerates, and Urban Development in Taipei*. Taipei: Chiu Liu Books, 1995.

Chi, Chung-shien. "Hung Mun in Taiwan." *United Monthly* 38, September 1984: 56-67.

_____. *Gangs, Election, and Violence*. Taipei: Jiao Dian Publishing Co., 1985.

China Times Weekly. "Speakers of the Councils Have Jiao and Tou," 880, 8 January 1995: 35-46.

Ho, Hoa. *The Legend of Gangs in Taiwan*. Taipei: Wan Shan Books, 1993.

Hwang, Kwang-kuo. "The Link among Elected Representatives, Law Enforcement Authorities, and Heidao Must Be Cut Off." *United Monthly*, 41, December 1984: 23.

Hsu, Fu-sen. "A Study on Current Crime Control Strategies in Taiwan." A paper presented at the Conference on Social Problems in Taiwan, Institute of Sociology, Academia Sinica, Taipei, 29-30 December 1999.

Ji, Yen-ling, Lin Po-wen, Chen Jer-ming, Tung Ching-fung, and Su Tze-ching. "Presidents and Businessmen." *The Journalist* 195, 3 December 1990: 19-41.

Jin, Si. "Brother, Which Party Are You Campaigning For?" *China Times Weekly* 608, 22 October 1989: 30-39.

The Journalist. "Ten Business Tycoons Entered the Race for the Legislature and This Year's Votes are Going to be Worth a Lot," 298, 21 November 1992a: 18-41.

_____. "The Revelation of Candidates' Court Cases" 301, 13 December 1992b: 18-40.

Judicial Yuan. *Judicial Research Annual Report* 12 (2). Taipei: Judicial Weekly Press, 1992.

_____. *Topics in Criminal Law Research* 12. Taipei: Judicial Weekly Press, 1998.

Ker, Su-len. "Brothers Who Used to Carry the Sedan Now Want to Sit on It." *China Times Weekly* 617, 24 December 1989: 30-41.

Lee, Jiao-nan. "Shi Tai-sen, Chou Per-lun, and Chu Kao-jen: The Three "Brothers" of the Three Political Parties." *Scoop Weekly* 423, 15 September 1996: 50-53.

Lin, Hsin. "Sweep, No Matter Mainlander or Local Gangster; Arrest, No Matter a Small Fly or a Big Shot." *China Times Weekly* 967, 8 September 1996: 46-56.

Lo, Sung-fan. *The Regret of Formosa*. Taipei: Ping An Publications, 1998.

Ministry of Justice. *The White Papers of Gang Sweep*. Taipei: Ministry of Justice Prosecutors' Division, 1998.

Nan, Fang Sor. "Heidao, Heihuo, and Heiqian." *The Journalist* 501, 13 October 1996: 101-102.

Pai, Jai. "Underground Gangs in Taiwan." *United Monthly* 21 April 1983: 17-29.

Sheu, Chuen-jim. *A Cross-Cultural Comparative Study on Combating Criminal Gangs*. Taipei: National Police Administration, 1993.

Su, Nang-heng. *The Practice of Organized Crime Prevention Law*. Taipei: Yung Lan Publications, 1997.

_____. "An Embarrassment to be a Laoda," in *Mobilizing Gang Sweep*, ed. Lee Yung-lan. Taipei: Law and You Magazine Press, 1998.

Tang, Su-jan. "Competing for Votes among Business Tycoons Running for the Legislature." *The Journalist* 282, 2 August 1992: 32-34.

Teng, Chi-jer. "Sister Ah Yu Died; Heidao and Paidao Influential Figures Attended the Funeral." *China Times Weekly* 735, 29 March 1992: 40-41.

_____. "Chang An-lo: Brothers Do Not Equal Heidao." *China Times Weekly* 946, 14 April 1996a: 52-53.

_____. "Lo Fu-chu: What is Heidao?" *China Times Weekly* 946, 14 April 1996b: 46-52.

Tsai, Shi-yuan. *Complete File of Black Gold*. Taipei: Tsai Shi-yuan Research Office in the Legislature, 1998.

United Daily News. "A Large Number of Politicians, Businessmen, and Gangsters Paid Their Last Tribute to Chen Yung-ho," 12 February 1996: 5.

_____. "Liao Cheng-hao's Warning: If We Don't Crackdown on Gangs, Taiwan Will Become Another Sicily," 17 November 1996: 3.

Wang, Jenn-hwan. *Who Governs Taiwan?* Taipei: Chiu Liu Books, 1996.

Yang, Ji. "Would Lo Fu-chu Be Able to Tolerate Such Act?" *China Times Weekly* 600, 27 August 1989: 48-50.

Yang, Ji-jin. *Words of Respect: A Memoir of Yang Ji-Jin's Criminal Investigation*. Taipei: Lien Ching Publishers, 1999.

About the Contributors

Ko-lin Chin is professor, School of Criminal Justice, Rutgers University. He received his Ph.D. from the University of Pennsylvania, Department of Sociology. He has been a Fulbright scholar, and is a leading expert on Chinese organized crime, both in the United States and in Asia. He has written extensively including: *Smuggled Chinese: Clandestine Immigration to the United States*, and *Chinatown Gangs: Extortion, Enterprise and Ethnicity*.

Obi N. I. Ebbe is currently department head, sociology, anthropology and geography at the University of Tennessee at Chattanooga. He specializes in political criminology, quantitative methods, statistics, and comparative and international criminal justice systems. He is the Coordinator of the International Police Executive Symposium (IPES). He received his Ph. D. in sociology from Southern Illinois University at Carbondale. His most recent book is *Comparative and International Criminal Justice Systems: Policing, Judiciary, and Corrections*, 2nd edition.

Roy Godson is professor of government at Georgetown University in Washington, DC. His current work focuses on identifying nontraditional security challenges and developing strategies to combat them. His most recent books include *Dirty Tricks or Trump Cards: U.S. Covert Action and Counterintelligence*; and (with John Bailey) *Organized Crime and Democratic Governability: Mexico and the US-Mexican Borderlands*. He was editor of the quarterly journal *Trends in Organized Crime* from1995-2001. In 1999 and 2000 he was Guggenheim Fellow.

Robert J. Kelly was formerly Broeklundian Professor of Social Sciences at Brooklyn College and professor of criminal justice and sociology at the Graduate School, City University of New York. He is a former president of the International Association for the Study of Organized Crime. Among his many books on organized crime are *The Upperworld and the Underworld: Case Studies of Racketeering and Business Infiltrations in the United States*, and most recently *Encyclopedia of Organized Crime in the United States: From Capone's Chicago to the New Urban Underworld*.

Rensselaer W. Lee III is president of Global Advisory Services, a research firm in McLean, VA, specializing in international security and political issues. He also is an associate scholar at the Foreign Policy Research Institute (FRPI) in Philadelphia, and has extensive research experience in the fields of international organized crime, international drug trafficking, and smuggling of nuclear materials. His books include *Smuggling Armageddon: the Nuclear Black Market in the Former Soviet Union* and *The White Labyrinth: Cocaine and Political Power.* His works have been funded by the National Council for Soviet and East European Research, the U.S. Institute of Peace and the Heinz Endowment.

T. Wing Lo is associate professor in the Department of Applied Social Studies of the City University of Hong Kong where he also directs Youth Studies Net, and is coordinator of the Social Data Research Unit. He has written extensively about Hong Kong's anti-corruption programs. He specializes in juvenile justice issues and has tracked the efficacy of education against crime and corruption among young people. He has contributed to several major government reports. His most recent articles are "AntiCorruption Strategies and Housing Scandals in Hong Kong," and "Curbing Draconian Powers: The Effects of Hong Kong's Graft-Fighter" in *International Journal of Human Rights.*

Letizia Paoli is a senior research fellow in the Department of Criminology at the Max Planck Institute for Foreign and International Law in Germany. She obtained her doctorate in political and social sciences at the European University Institute in Florence. She has been a consultant to the Italian Ministry of the Interior, the Direzione Investigativa Antimafia, the UN Office for Drug Control and Crime Prevention in Vienna, and the UN Interregional Crime and Justice Research Institute in Rome. She is the author of *Fratelli di Mafia: Cosa Nostra e 'Ndrangheta.*

Stanley Pimentel was a senior career FBI official who worked in Latin and Central America for many years, and served two tours as legal attaché in Mexico before retiring in the late 1990s.

Louise I. Shelley is a professor in the Department of Justice, Law and Society and the School of International Service at American University. She is director of the Transnational Crime and Corruption Center (TraCCC), a center devoted to teaching, research and training and public outreach on these issues. She holds an M.A. in criminology from the University of Pennsylvania and a Ph.D. in sociology. She is also the recipient of Guggenheim, NEH, Kennan Institute grants, and received a MacArthur grant to establish the Russian Organized Crime Study Centers. Her publications include *Policing Soviet Society.* She serves on the editorial boards of *Transnational Organized*

Crime, Demokratizatsiya (the journal of post-Soviet organized crime), and *The International Annals of Criminology.*

Francisco E. Thoumi received his Ph.D. in economics from the University of Minnesota in 1972. He has been a professor at the Universidad de Los Andes, in Bogotá, and the Universidad Nacional de Colombia, as well as at several universities in the U.S., most recently Florida International University. His current research involves the socioeconomics of the illegal drug trade. He has worked for the United Nations in the Office of Drug Control and Crime Prevention as research coordinator for the Global Programme Against Money Laundering. Among his many publications are *Illegal Drugs, Economy and Society in the Andes; Political Economy and Illegal Drugs in Colombia.*

Index

.